Christ in His Mysteries

BLESSED COLUMBA MARMION

CHRIST

IN HIS

MYSTERIES

Translated by

Alan Bancroft

ZACCHEUS PRESS

Bethesda

Nihil Obstat: Rt. Rev. D. Hugh Gilbert, O.S.B.,
          Abbot of Pluscarden.
          August 27, 2008

Imprimatur: Monsignor Canon Mark Davies,
          Vicar General,
          Diocese of Salford.
          September 1, 2008

ZACCHEUS PRESS and the colophon are trademarks of Zaccheus Press. The Zaccheus Press colophon was designed by Michelle Dick. The text is set in Arno.

Library of Congress Cataloging-in-Publication Data

Marmion, Columba, Abbot, 1858-1923.
  [Christ dans ses mystères. English]
  Christ in his mysteries / Blessed Columba Marmion ; translated by Alan Bancroft.
-- [New ed.].
      p. cm.
  ISBN 978-0-9725981-9-4 (pbk. : alk. paper)
  1. Jesus Christ--Meditations. I. Title.
  BX2183.M33 2008
  232--dc22

                                                                    2008035528

10 9 8 7 6 5 4 3 2 1

To learn more about Blessed Columba Marmion, please visit our webpage:

Contents

BOOK TWO
The Mysteries of Christ (Cont.)

FOREWORD

by

Father Benedict J. Groeschel, C.F.R.

In my Foreword to *Christ, the Life of the Soul* I pointed out the many great blessings of this new set of translations of the writings of Blessed Columba Marmion. All I said of that new edition I now reiterate about *Christ in His Mysteries*. This new translation with the abundant scriptural quotations rendered in English make this classic of Christian spirituality available to the average reader. In fact, it can easily serve as an excellent introduction to the monumental library of Abbot Columba Marmion for the great number of young men and women discovering the riches of their faith at this time.

In *Christ in His Mysteries*, Blessed Columba, with beautiful faith and enthusiasm, opens up for us the theology of Christ according to Saint Paul; so it is especially fitting that such a book be published during the year commemorating this great Apostle. It is said that Marmion knew the whole New Testament by heart and this fact seems indicated by this classic work itself. If you want to know Saint Paul and what is called his gospel—that is, his teaching about Christ—Marmion will present to you the entire panorama of the Apostle's teaching. There is a very important reason for reading Marmion's work at this time, especially *Christ in His Mysteries*. As Pope Benedict pointed out so well in the Foreword to his own superb book *Jesus of Nazareth* (Doubleday, 2007) the result of a purely "historical-critical" approach to the Gospels has left many with the impression that we have "very little certain knowledge of Jesus" and that "only at a later stage did faith in his divinity shape the image we have of him." According to the Pope, the result of this is that "intimate friendship with Jesus on which everything depends is in danger of clutching at thin air."

Christ in His Mysteries in this splendid new edition and all of Marmion's work are powerful remedies to the superficiality and skepticism observable at the moment in many popular theological and scriptural enterprises. The present JPII generation as they are aptly called, are looking for some relief from the spiritually anemic fare that they've been fed in religious education and in supposedly Catholic institutions of higher learning. My advice to the members of this generation is to run to the library for Guardini, Sheen, Benedict XVI, and Marmion before you succumb to malnutrition. Read *Christ in His Mysteries* as soon as possible and you will get some idea of what you have been missing and where to find it.

It is observable in the present religious scene that the emphasis is moving off scriptural criticism to biblical theology which was one of the riches of the Church during Marmion's time. Sooner or later a genuine synthesis will be made of exegesis and biblical theology. To get yourself ready for the emergence of this synthesis it would be very wise to have a grasp of Christian biblical theology, which in terms of the mystery of Christ is eminently well represented by the writings of Blessed Columbia Marmion.

Introduction

by

Aidan Nichols, O.P.

Christ in His Mysteries is the central work in Blessed Columba Marmion's trilogy—a trio of books which are at one and the same time theology and spirituality, the product of thought and the fruit of prayer.

The trilogy opens with *Christ, the Life of the Soul. Christ, the Life of the Soul* is Marmion's description of all the main elements which go into the marvelous mix that is the Christian life. Marmion shows how the inner coherence of that life is to be found by reference to the mystery of Jesus Christ, the God-man, as the title of this first book makes plain. In that way, *Christ, the Life of the Soul*—of which Alan Bancroft, the translator of the present work, gave us a supremely natural and fluent translation in 2005—has the task of setting the scene for *Christ in His Mysteries*, though, to be sure, the latter can perfectly well be read and appreciated on its own.

Christ in His Mysteries will take us through the principal events of the human life of the eternal Word, beginning from His pre-existence "in the bosom of the Father," as St. John puts it in the Prologue to his Gospel. That is a phrase which Bancroft translates here as in the Father's "heart's-embrace," one of the many felicitous renderings which will attract to this new version the readership it deserves. In *Christ in His Mysteries*, Marmion's insight, as simple as it was brilliant, is that practicing Catholics will draw maximum profit from their meditation on the life of Christ if they contemplate its chief happenings through the lens provided by the Church's liturgical year. In that year those happenings are celebrated in feasts and seasons. The Liturgy is the way the Church as Bride gazes lovingly—and therefore penetratingly—at her Bridegroom, laying out her understanding of His heart: His purposes, the grand design of the Father which He carried out for our sake. What we experience in the texts and chants of the Liturgy at Mass and the other Offices dovetails beautifully with what we read of the life of Christ in the Gospels.

If I may be allowed the pun, the Gospels and the Liturgy "dovetail" because in different senses both are inspired by the same Holy Spirit, whom Scripture and Tradition present under the image of a dove, since He is the Peace of the Father and the Son. Once we have been to school with *Christ in His Mysteries*, the lessons we learn about the virtues to be developed on the basis of the call of the Father, the work of Christ and the communication of their Holy Spirit can then be put into practice by us in ascetical effort and the fruitful reception of mystical graces.

That pointed Marmion to the third and final book of his trilogy, *Christ, the Ideal of the Monk* which in an obvious sense was written specifically for his Benedictine brethren. In another, if less obvious, sense *Christ, the Ideal of the Monk* has application to all Christians, since the life of the monk is the life of the Christian when stripped down to its bare essentials and lived out in relation to others (for the monk, that means a community) and a spiritual father or guide (for the monk, that will be an abbot).

Were one to draw out one distinguishing feature of *Christ in His Mysteries* which gives it its excellence as a contribution to Catholic theology and spirituality it would be, I think, its *wonderfully unified and organic character*. This derives from the absolute consistency with which Marmion holds to his central doctrine.

What is that doctrine? He sums it up in a simple maxim, "The mysteries of Christ are our mysteries." When the Word incarnate presented Himself to us in the mysteries of His historic life He did so in order that those amazing events might in a threefold way be "ours."

First, they were carried out for our salvation, for the sake of the overflow to us of all supernatural good, for we are united with Him in the humanity He took in the womb of our Lady. We are His kin, and therefore we are the appropriate recipients of His bounty. Secondly, while those mysteries are quite inimitable in that they were the actions of One who was God, they are highly imitable inasmuch as they found expression in human virtues. In His mysteries He is our exemplar, our moral model—the well-known theme of the "imitation of Christ." Thirdly (and this is the dimension we are most likely to overlook), the mysteries are "ours" in the sense that we are invited to participate intimately, by contemplation and desire, in the states and conditions of the Word incarnate. While these states and conditions succeeded one another in time (He was an infant on the lap of the Virgin before He was the transfigured Jesus of Tabor, He was the Victim of Calvary before He was the mighty ascending Lord), in their cumulative sequence they made Him comprehensively and permanently the Savior of the human race and so have an everlasting aspect or reality. All His mysteries co-inhere in Him as He now exists at the Father's right, always interceding for us as the Mediator between God and man. When we seek union with Him in these mysteries we allow Him to communicate to us the grace His mysteries embody and signify: individually or severally, and not just altogether. That is what the Church invites us to do as we follow the sacred course of her year, where each great feast and season has its own gift to make us *precisely because of its reference to one or more of the mysteries of Christ.* Incidentally, that explains why Marmion does not end *Christ in His Mysteries* with Pentecost, which is the closing feast of the Christological cycle so far as the Gospels are concerned. Instead, he goes on for three further chapters to present to us the Christ of Corpus Christi, the Christ of the Solemnity of the Sacred Heart, and the Christ of All Saints'. The last of these is especially notable as I shall explain in the closing sentence of this Introduction.

Readers of *Christ in His Mysteries* have opened to them in this work the theological and spiritual treasures of Latin Catholicism at its best. If Marmion makes constant reference to the Scriptures, he also invokes the Roman Liturgy, the Latin Fathers and great mystics from, especially, the Benedictine, Cistercian, Dominican and Carmelite traditions. If he does not make so much overt reference to St. Thomas Aquinas as in *Christ, the Life of the Soul*, his theology of grace in *Christ in His Mysteries* is still thoroughly Thomistic. But it is amplified and made more Christocentric by covert appeal to the "French school" of the seventeenth century, to whom he owed his key concepts of the "states and conditions of the Word incarnate." And the whole enterprise is palpably animated by pastoral care. He wants his hearers (and now his readers), like his monks, not just to learn about spirituality. He wants them to become saints.

FOREWORD
to the original edition
by
Abbot Marmion

In allowing publication of the talks entitled *Christ, the Life of the Soul,* the author had the sole aim of expounding the basic characteristics of the Christian life in accordance with the Gospels, the Epistles of St. Paul and the conclusions of theological teaching. The Christian life is essentially supernatural, and we can draw it forth only in Christ, unique model of perfection, infinite treasury of our graces and efficacious cause of all holiness.

The talks that make up the present volume follow logically from those of the preceding one.

The life of Christ, the divine but at the same time accessible Exemplar of the Christian life, was manifested to our sight by the states and the mysteries, the virtues and the actions, of the sacred humanity. Human in its outward expression, the life of the Incarnate Word is wholly divine in its origin.

And so the mysteries of the God-man are not only models that we ought to ponder; they also contain within themselves treasures of merit and of grace. By His almighty power Christ Jesus, ever living, produces the interior and supernatural perfection of His states in those who are moved by a sincere desire to imitate Him, and who put themselves in contact with Him through faith and love.

It is in the light of these truths that the author has expounded the principal mysteries of Jesus.

The plan is simple.

Two preliminary talks show how much Christ's mysteries are ours also, and how, in a general way, we can assimilate their fruits.

We shall not really understand the transcendent value of these mysteries, their wonderful splendor, their logical sequence, and the deep unity that links them together, unless we first consider Him who lived them for us. That is why in the First Part an attempt has been made to sketch the essential features of *the Person* of Jesus: the Eternal Word—made flesh—who came here below to redeem the world through His Sacrifice.

The Second Part is devoted to a contemplation of *the mysteries* of the God-man. Taking as his basis the Gospel and the words of the liturgy, the author has sought to show the reality of the mysteries—human and divine, both together; to draw attention to their significance and to indicate their applications to the faithful soul. As to the choice of mysteries, it was thought best to dwell on those which the Church puts before us in her liturgical cycle. Who better than she, indeed, knows her Spouses's secrets and possesses the art of spreading the Gospel? Who better than she is able to lead us to the Savior?

The extremely kind welcome which the public, especially the laity, have been good enough to give to the preceding volume, *Christ, the Life of the Soul,* has not only been a precious encouragement to the author; it is also a most comforting sign in the midst of the sorrows and anxieties of our particularly troubled time. It shows that under pressure of events there are many recollected souls, docile to the voice of God. Starved of safety, peace and light, they have turned towards the One who alone is the infallible Way, the Truth that enlightens every man here below, the Life that saves from death.

It is "in Him," as St. Paul says, that all things must be restored: *Omnia instaurare in Christo*. For, according to the thought of the same apostle, outside this divine foundation nothing is stable, nothing is lasting. The author's whole ambition in letting these talks be published is that he on his small part may contribute to the great work of Christian restoration.

May Christ deign to bless these pages! Written for Him, they speak only of Him. May they reveal to souls more of the secret of the love of one who is God, appeared among us! May this book make them quench their thirst more often at those founts of living water which, for our salvation and our joy, flow out from the pierced heart of Jesus: "Draw waters with joy out of the Savior's fountains."

Feast of the Annunciation
25 March 1919

Our minds remain finite, and so can never wholly contain the Infinite. This is the fact about us whch accounts for the existence of what we call Mysteries in religion... But a Mystery is not something that we can know nothing about: it is only something that the mind cannot *wholly* know. It is not to be thought of as a high wall that we can neither see over nor get around: it is to be thought of rather as a gallery into which we can progress deeper and deeper, though we can never reach the end—yet every step of our progress is immeasurably satisfying.

—Frank Sheed

Some Observations by the Translator

Like Newman, and the "Gerontius" of his dramatic poem, Marmion believed firmly and truly.

> Firmly I believe and truly
> God is Three and God is One.
> And I next acknowledge duly
> Manhood taken by the Son.

Marmion—Blessed Columba Marmion (1858-1923), beatified in 2000—steeped himself in Scripture, not as a mere "historical-critical" exercise of the sort of which Fr Groeschel appositely speaks, but in order to perceive more fully the wonder Scripture contains for the dimension of our life on earth, and that of eternity to which our life here is but a short, though crucially important, prelude.

Christ in His Mysteries is the second volume of his great trilogy (the written record of spiritual talks he gave). And it is extraordinary, is it not, that the words of this Dubliner, who became the abbot of a Benedictine community in Belgium and spoke and wrote in French, have to be translated back into his native language (or one of them, alongside his Irish). But there it is.

Extension of our usual concepts

As I wrote in my Translator's Introductory Note in *Christ, the Life of the Soul*: "We creatures, who each had a beginning, find it hard to grasp the concept of the Son's taking His being from the Father and yet taking it thus *eternally*, having existed always as the Father has always existed. But that is how it is in fact (except that the past tense—'having existed'—strictly has no application to the Father, the Son and the Holy Spirit)."

Marmion loves and adores the Triune God—Father, Son and Holy Spirit. The reader will see this. But one facet of Marmion's terminology may need explanation if he is not to be misunderstood. In very many cases, when he says "God" (that word used on its own) he means God *the Father*. He speaks of "God" and "God's Son" who at the Incarnation took flesh. Does that mean (to borrow his own question-and-answer style) that Marmion doesn't regard the Son as being God in the full sense that the Father is God? Oh, most certainly that is not what he means! Look at what he in fact says. "Christ, being His Son, is likewise God" (p. 8). "He is God's own Son, equal to His Father" (p. 14). "God [eternally] begets God [the Son] and gives Him His [the Father's] own nature" (p. 46). The Son is "equal to the Father but distinct from Him, and a Divine Person as the Father is" (Ibid.) "Christ is the Son of God, and consequently is Himself God" (p. 67). One could go on with such quotations.

That Marmion so frequently uses "God" on its own to mean God the Father is precisely because, like the New Testament itself, he all the time has in mind the Eternal Fatherhood of the First Person of the Trinity; that is to say, that the Son, the Word, "proceeds from"—is eternally "begotten by"—the Father (though, as St. Gregory Nazianzen wrote and as Marmion would reiterate, we know the *fact* of this "begetting" but "the mode of it we cannot admit that even angels understand").

What Marmion calls "the property of being Father" is from all eternity the Father's, and "the property of being the Son" is from all eternity the Son's. All three Persons of the Trinity, Marmion writes, "have the same eternity, the same infinity of perfection, the same wisdom, the same power, the same holiness—because the divine nature is but one for the three Persons. But each Person possesses exclusive properties—those of 'being Father,' 'being Son,' 'proceeding from the Father and the Son'—which establish the ineffable relations between themselves and distinguish them from each other. *There is an order of [eternal] origin, without there being any priority of time, or any hierarchical superiority, or any relation of dependence*" (pp. 45-46; see also pp. 374-376).

Christ, God and man

Then we come to the Incarnation—not something eternal (except in its being eternally planned and intended), but an event in *time*. Is Jesus Christ God? Yes, he is "true God and true man." He became man when He took flesh in the womb of the Virgin Mary. He has two natures, the nature of God and the nature of man. (Marmion speaks of His "divinity" and His "humanity," His divine nature and His human nature.) But it is one only *Person*— Christ, the Eternal Son of God, incarnate—who has those two natures.

People puzzle about how two particular sayings of Christ fit in with each other. Marmion has interesting words to say on this (p. 90): "From the instant of the Word [the Son] becoming incarnate, He unites in Himself two natures: the divine nature, by which He was able to say: 'I and the Father are one,' one in the unity of the Godhead, the Trinity, one in equality of perfections; the other, the human nature, which made Him say: 'The Father is greater than I.'" That surely is illuminating; I find it so at least.

We should not "make God in our own image"

Something else I haltingly said in my Introductory Note in the previous volume is perhaps worth repeating: "We shall be utterly wide of the mark if in reading this book we (so to say) make God in our own image: ourselves in a bigger, even an immensely bigger, size. As one example: the Eternal Father and the Eternal Son, and the Third Person of the Trinity whose eternal origin is the mutual love of the Father and the Son, are *spirit*—not spirit and body (it was only at the Incarnation that the Son took to Himself a human body and soul, which he retains, glorious in heaven). And God—the Trinity of Persons—is Infinite Love *transcending all our perceptions and analogies.* 'God is a spirit, and those who worship Him must worship Him in spirit and in truth' (John 4:24)."

If we make God in our own image we immeasurably diminish and misrepresent what one might call God's "Is-ness."

"...in His Mysteries"

I have always liked the Frank Sheed passage quoted on page xviii. Marmionesque in this, it is so balanced. That we created beings cannot know everything about God does not mean we can know nothing about God—especially, above all, now that the Light has shone on this earth, *Lumen Christi.* I hope no reader of this book will be like those of whom Newman said that they were "determined to know nothing unless they know everything." That would be a mistake, just as "making God in our own image" would.

While we are still *ici-bas* ("here below" in the lovely French phrase), we cannot "know everything" about the glorious eternal destiny offered to us. For "eye has not seen nor ear heard, neither has it entered into the heart of man to know" what wonders God has prepared... But they will indeed be wondrous.

Scriptural versions in English

I repeat, in abridged form, what I said in the Translator's Introductory Note in *Christ, the Life of the Soul.*

The vernacular scriptural version with which Marmion would have been familiar during his Irish education is the Douai-Rheims (Douai, Old Testament; Rheims, New Testament). In this translation, whenever I give a direct (in inverted commas) quotation from the New Testament *without further attribution,* and without the word "See" in the relevant footnote, the quotation is from: "A revision of the Challenor-Rheims version, edited by Catholic scholars under the patronage of the Episcopal Committee of the Confraternity of Christian Doctrine" (St. Anthony Guild Press, Paterson, New Jersey, 1941)—the "Confraternity version," for short. One can think of it as a revised and, to some extent, modernized Rheims. I am very grateful to Dom Placid Murray, OSB, of Glenstal Abbey, Co. Limerick, for his suggestion of the use of this version.

Whenever I give a direct quotation from the Old Testament without further attribution, the quotation is from the Douai. (More precisely, it is from an early nineteenth century edition I have of the Douai-Rheims.)

In a relatively small number of instances I have used other versions where this assists the onward flow, as also where I deem them particularly familiar or felicitous or, more important, helpfully close either to Marmion's own words or the (French) wording of his quotations.

Those other versions are: *For the New Testament*: The old Rheims version, unrevised (indicated in the footnotes by "Rheims").

For the Old Testament: The Holy Bible, St. Paul Edition, translated by members of the Catholic Biblical Association of America, 1959 (indicated by "St P").

For both New and Old Testaments: The Jerusalem Bible (Darton, Longman & Todd, London, 1966); The Holy Bible, Knox version (Burns & Oates, London, 1955); and The Holy Bible, Revised Standard Version, Catholic Edition (Ignatius Press, San Francisco, 1966)—indicated respectively by "Jerus.," "Knox" and "RSV, Cath."

I have confined myself to the versions stated above.

Where, in a footnote, I give a scriptural reference preceded by "See," this signals that the direct quotation in the text to which the note refers is not a *precisely* verbatim quotation from any of the versions mentioned above, though this does *not* of itself imply any substantial difference. It may be a translation of the words

Marmion actually uses. Unless, conceivably, taken from some particular French translation he had in mind, a number of the quotations in Marmion's talks are from the many that were "in his ear," so to speak, rather than from a book open before him or consulted. Whilst being clear and accurate on their substantial meaning, he may have misremembered the precise wording of some of the texts he quoted, and sometimes it might be truer to say that he *paraphrases*—his paraphrases being illuminating or at least interesting.

In giving the scriptural quotations I again have changed "*he*," "*him*," "*his*" to "*He*," "*Him*," "*His*," where they refer to Christ or to the Father or the Holy Spirit. Seeking readability to the modern eye and ear, I have in the scriptural quotations allowed myself the liberty of changing (without the signal of a "See") "thou" and "thee" to "you," "thy" to "your," "thine" to "yours"; as also intrusive forms like "hath," "hast," "do thou," etc., to their present-day equivalents.

It remains to add that Marmion often gave scriptural quotations in the Latin of the Vulgate, as well as or instead of French. I have here used English versions throughout.

Christ in His Mysteries was first published in 1919. This translation is from the edition of 1926 and is the first full translation into English since that of the "Nun of Tyburn" in 1924.

Acknowledgments

I have many people to thank. Dom Mark Tierney, OSB, never fails to provide advice and support for which I am very grateful. Special thanks are due to the kind and perceptive Dom Hugh Gilbert, OSB, Abbot of Pluscarden, for he not only read the book for Nihil Obstat purposes but also, beyond the call of that duty, helped and enlightened me wonderfully on matters of content and style.

Within the Diocese of Salford my gratitude goes to the Vicar General, Monsignor Mark Davies, for his encouragement and kind co-operation. I want also to mention Father Brendan Curley who gave me the hospitality of his computer and presbytery when, at a late and crucial stage, my own computer failed.

My good friend Peter R. Dunne generously helped me again on matters of Latin translation. Father Aidan Nichols, OP, amongst his other kindnesses, put me wise on the best English translation of the repeated phrase *l'Homme-Dieu* (pointing out that it was euphony that made Marmion put it that way round in French); and I am grateful to Sister Marian Teresa Murphy, OCD, of the Liverpool Carmel, for mentioning to me the brilliantly apposite Hopkins poem *As Kingfishers Catch Fire* (p. 404).

Finally, I thank the publisher, John O'Leary of Zaccheus Press, with whom it has been a pleasure to work. His patience with me knows no bounds, and my gratitude to him is in proportion, both on that account and because of his high and imaginative standards for the printed page.

All remaining inadequacies are mine, as they say: and never were those words more true.

Alan Bancroft
Manchester, England

List of Abbreviations

Acts	The Acts of the Apostles
The Apoc.	Apocalypse (Revelation)
Col.	St. Paul's Epistle to the Colossians
1 Cor.	St. Paul's First Epistle to the Corinthians
2 Cor.	St. Paul's Second Epistle to the Corinthians
Deut.	Deuteronomy
Douai	The Douai version of the Old Testament
Enarr. in Ps.	Commentaries [by St. Augustine] on the Psalms
Eph.	St. Paul's Epistle to the Ephesians
Exod.	Exodus
ff.	and what follows the numerical reference given
Gal.	St. Paul's Epistle to the Galatians
Gen.	Genesis
Hebr.	St. Paul's Epistle to the Hebrews
Ibid.	Ibidem, the same place
Isa.	Isaiah (Isaias)
James	The Epistle of St. James
Jerus.	The Jerusalem Bible
John	The Gospel of St. John
1 John	St. John's First Epistle
2 Kings	Second Book of Kings (otherwise known as Second Book of Samuel)
3 Kings	Third Book of Kings (otherwise known as First Book of Kings)
Knox	The Holy Bible, Knox version
Levit.	Leviticus
Luke	The Gospel of St. Luke
Mark	Gospel of St. Mark
Matt.	Gospel of St. Matthew
Num.	Numbers

1 Peter	St. Peter's First Epistle
2 Peter	St. Peter's Second Epistle
Phil.	St. Paul's Epistle to the Philippians
pp.	pages
Prov.	Proverbs
Ps.	The Psalms
Rheims	The Rheims version of the New Testament
Rom.	St. Paul's First Epistle to the Romans
RSV, Cath.	The Holy Bible, Revised Standard Version, Catholic edition
St P	The Holy Bible, St. Paul Edition, translated by members of the Catholic Biblical Association of America
1 Thess.	St. Paul's First Epistle to the Thessalonians
2 Thess.	St. Paul's Second Epistle to the Thessalonians
St. Thomas	St. Thomas Aquinas (*Summa Theologica*, unless otherwise stated)
1 Tim.	St. Paul's First Epistle to Timothy
Titus	St. Paul's Epistle to Titus
Tract. in Johann.	*Tractatus in evangelium Johannis*, Treatise [by St. Augustine] on St. John's Gospel
Vatican II	The Second Vatican Council
vv.	verses

He who was God has been made man, by taking to Himself what He was not, but without losing what He was. It is in this way that God has become man. You have there something for your weakness, and you have there something for your perfection. May Christ raise you up, through His being *man*. May He lead you, through His being the *God-man*. May He take you all the way to what *God* is.

St. Augustine, *Tract. in Johann.*, XXIII, 6.

PRELIMINARY TALKS

Chapter One: *The Mysteries of Christ Are Our Mysteries*

Chapter Two: *How We Assimilate the Fruit of
the Mysteries of Jesus*

CHAPTER ONE

The Mysteries of Christ
Are Our Mysteries

Introduction.

When you read the epistles of St. Paul attentively and try to get right down to the unity of teaching and work of the great apostle, you have no difficulty in seeing that everything for him is summed up in a knowledge—put into action—of the mystery of Christ.

He writes to the Ephesians: "By reading what I have written, you can recognize the understanding I have of the mystery of Christ.... For to me—I who am less than the least of all the saints—this grace was given: both to announce to the Gentiles the unfathomable riches of Christ, and to enlighten all men about the dispensation of the mystery which has been hidden in God before all time began."[1]

It is about this mystery,[2] ineffable though it is, that I am counting by the grace of God on speaking to you. I shall in a little while be telling you about the degree of God's intimacy with us. This first talk is precisely on that subject.

But before entering upon an account of this truth which is of such capital importance and so beneficial, it will be useful for us

[1] See Eph. 3, vv. 4, 8-9. [*Translator's note*: The meaning of "See" before some of the scriptural references is explained on pp. xx-xxii, as is the source of other references where the version is not identified.]

[2] [*Translator's note*: See note 48 on p. 12.]

to consider for a few moments how St. Paul has spoken of it, seeing that he was established as its herald by Christ in person. And from whom better than from St. Paul could we learn the extent to which a knowledge of this mystery is both fruitful and life-giving for our souls?

1. How St. Paul puts into high relief the mystery of Christ.

As you know, it was straight after his conversion that St. Paul received the mission of making known the name of Jesus. From that moment nothing was dearer to his heart than fulfilling this mandate. If he undertook numerous journeys full of perils;[3] if he preached unremittingly in the synagogues, in the Areopagus, before the Jews, before the learned men of Athens, the Roman procurators; if, even in prison, He wrote long letters to his faithful; if he suffered a thousand persecutions[4]—it was so that he could carry Christ's name "among nations and kings and the children of Israel."[5]

It is especially in his preaching to the pagan nations to whom he was constituted the apostle, that we grasp, from real life, how deeply St. Paul lived by this mystery. He went to the pagan world in order to regenerate it, renew it, save it. And what did he bring to this corrupt society, the deep depravity of which he himself described in frightening terms?[6] Did he bring the advantages of birth? the wisdom of philosophers? the knowledge of the learned? the strength of conquerors?

The Apostle possessed nothing of all that. He declared that he was no more than "one untimely born"—an undersized child;[7] he wrote to the Corinthians that it was "in weakness and in fear and in much trembling" that he came among them;[8] he recalled to the Galatians that he was overwhelmed with infirmity the first time he preached the Gospel to them.[9] Thus, he brought neither

---

[3] 2 Cor. 1:5 ff.   [4] 2 Cor. 11:26.   [5] Acts 9:15.   [6] Rom. 1:24-32.
[7] 1 Cor. 15:8 (Jerus.)   [8] 1 Cor. 2:3.   [9] Gal. 4:13.

attractiveness of person, nor prestige of learning, nor the authority of natural wisdom, nor the sparkle of eloquence, nor the charm of human oratory. He disdained all that. "I ... did not come with high-flown speech or wisdom ... my speech and my preaching were not in the persuasive words of human wisdom ... not in the wisdom of men."[10]

What did he bring, then? Nothing but Christ, and Christ crucified.[11] All his preaching comes down to this knowledge; he contains all his knowledge within this mystery.

So penetrated with it is he, that he makes it the very object of his prayer for his disciples: "For this reason I bend my knees before the Father of our Lord Jesus Christ ... that He may grant you strength in abundance from His Spirit so as to form the interior man within you; in such wise that ... you may be able to comprehend with all the saints what is the breadth and length and height and depth [of the mystery of His Son]. I ask Him even that you may come to an awareness of Christ's love which surpasses all knowledge, so that you may be filled [by Christ] with the very plenitude of God."[12]

What a prayer! How one feels, between these lines, the inner conviction of the Apostle and the ardor of his soul to make others share the same conviction!

And besides, that prayer is unceasing. "That is why we have been praying for you unceasingly ... asking that you may have the fullest knowledge of His will, in all wisdom and spiritual understanding."[13]

Why, then, does St. Paul constantly return to this subject, to the point of making it the one doctrinal theme of his preaching? Why does he every moment raise up to God for his Christians these continual supplications? Why does he burn with a desire to see the mystery of Christ not only known but experienced by all the Christians? For notice that he addresses his letters, not to a few

---

[10] See 1 Cor. 2, vv. 1, 4-5.   [11] 1 Cor. 2:2.   [12] See Eph. 3, vv. 14, 16, 18-19 (words in square brackets are Marmion's interpolations).   [13] See Col. 1:9.

initiates but to all the faithful of the churches he has founded; his lines are intended to be read publicly in the Christian assemblies. What, then, is the deep motive for his doing things in that way?

The Apostle himself gives us the answer in his letter to the Colossians: "I wish you to know how great is my concern for you, how much I desire that your hearts ... be enriched with full conviction in what has regard to knowledge of God the Father and of Christ Jesus, because in Him [within Christ] are hidden all the treasures of wisdom and knowledge."[14]

This last phrase reveals to us the reason for the whole of St. Paul's conduct. He is convinced that in Christ one finds everything—"How can He (the Father) fail to grant us all things in Him (Christ)?";[15] that in Christ nothing is lacking for us— "Christ has been made so firm in you that you lack no grace";[16] this Jesus Christ "who was yesterday, who is today, and who remains for ever and ever."[17]

To renew the pagan society, to lift up the fallen world, St. Paul brings to it one means only: Christ, and Christ crucified. It is true that this mystery is "a stumbling-block for the Jews and a foolishness for the learned men of Greece";[18] but it contains the power of the Holy Spirit of God[19]—the Spirit who alone can "renew the face of the earth."[20]

In Christ Himself is found all the "wisdom, and justice, and sanctification, and redemption"[21] of which souls of every time have need. And that is why St. Paul brings the whole formation of the interior man down to a knowledge, put into action, of the mystery of Jesus.[22]

---

[14] See Col. 2:1-3 (words in square brackets Marmion's interpolations again).
[15] See Rom. 8:32.   [16] 1 Cor. 1:6-7.   [17] See Hebr. 13:8.
[18] See 1 Cor. 1:23.   [19] 1 Cor. 2, vv. 4, 12.   [20] Ps. 103 (104):30.
[21] 1 Cor. 1:30.   [22] Cf. Eph. 3:16-18 and Col. 1:27-28. Cardinal Mercier wrote: "How often do we waste our time in sterile speculations, in laborious detours, when we have available to us in Christ so simple a means by which we can go straight to God and live in habitual union with Him! ...And when the authorized spokesmen of the Eternal Word, instead of giving Christ 'the

2. How greatly God desires that this mystery be known.

In this, moreover, the Apostle, having been instructed for a while[23] by Christ Himself, is but the faithful echo of his Divine Master.

In that ineffable prayer after the Last Supper[24] in which our Blessed Savior allowed the intimate feelings of His sacred soul to overflow in the presence of His enraptured disciples, during the final moments of His earthly existence, we hear these words: "Father ... this is everlasting life, that they may know you, the only true God, and Him whom you have sent, Jesus Christ."[25]

So we learn from the very lips of Jesus Christ Himself, from Infallible Truth, that the whole of the Christian life—of which life eternal is but the due flowering and the natural completion—comes down to a knowledge, put into action, of God and His Son.

You will immediately say to me that we do not see God: "No-one has ever seen God."[26] That is true. We shall only know God perfectly when we see Him face-to-face in eternal bliss.[27]

---

resurrection and the life' to souls, take away their taste for God by giving them as food and drink the insipid dilutions of mere human thought or of writings lacking in solid body, one cannot refrain from asking oneself with the Apostle St. Paul: Where are the faithful transmitters of the Gospel?—'Now here it is required...that a man be found trustworthy'" (Cardinal D.J. Mercier, *Devotion to Christ and His Holy Mother*, quoting 1 Cor. 4:2).   [23] Gal. 1:15-17.

[24] John 17:1-26.   [25] John 17, vv. 1, 3.   [26] John 1:18 (Jerus.)

[27] [*Translator's note*: "face-to-face." Christ, the Son-made-man, has for ever in heaven a glorified body and a face. But how are we to "see" the Father and the Holy Spirit in heaven, when both these Persons of the Trinity are pure spirits? We shall indeed see God, the Three Persons, *clearly* (1 Cor. 13:12). It is the Beatific Vision. But, emphasizes Marmion, the manner of it—the "how"—is unknown to us here below: *What it is in itself, this 'seeing,' we cannot know now. But the soul will be given strength by 'the light of glory,' which is nothing else than grace itself reaching its full resplendence in heaven*" (*Christ, the Life of the Soul*, Book II, Ch. 13.1). Cf. J.P. Arendzen, *What becomes of the Dead?*, section on Heaven: "We shall, by a wonder of God's omnipotence, directly and without intermediary [of the senses] see God ... we shall dispense with any sense-data whatever. How this is possible we cannot understand, but it shall be so."]

But, here below, God reveals Himself to our faith through His Son Jesus. Christ, the Word Incarnate, is the great Revelation of God to the world: He "has shone in our hearts ... in the face of Christ Jesus."[28] Christ is God appeared among men, talking with them beneath the skies of Judea, and showing them through His human life how One who is God lives among men, so that men may know how they themselves ought to live if they are to be pleasing to God.

It is therefore upon Christ that all our gaze ought to be concentrated. Open the Gospels indeed, and you will see there that the voice of the Eternal Father has been made heard by the world but three times.[29] And what does this Divine Voice say? Each time, the Heavenly Father tells us to contemplate His Son, to hear Him that He may be glorified. "This is my beloved Son, in whom I am well pleased; hear Him."[30] Everything the Father asks of us comes down to this point: Contemplate and hear His Son Jesus, so as to love and imitate Jesus, because Jesus, being His Son, is likewise God.

And we ought to contemplate Him in His Person, in all the actions of His life and of His death, in the states of His glory.[31] Our Lord being God, the least circumstances of His life, the smallest features of His mysteries, are worthy of attention. Nothing is "small" in the life of Jesus. The Eternal Father regards the least action of Christ with more pleasure than He regards the entire universe. Before Christ's coming, God makes everything converge upon Christ. After the Ascension He makes everything relate to Christ. Everything about Christ has been foreseen and

[28] 2 Cor. 4:6 (Rheims).

[29] [*Translator's note*: At the Baptism in the Jordan and at the Transfiguration; the third occasion referred to by Marmion being that recorded in John 12:28.]

[30] Matt. 17:5; 3:17; Mark 9:6; 1:11; Luke 9:35; 3:22; 2 Peter 1:17. [*Translator's note*: The words "hear Him," following "This is my beloved Son," appear in the accounts of the Transfiguration.]

[31] [*Translator's note*: For "states" see p. 20, note 84.]

foretold. All the important particularities of His existence, all the details of His death, have been appointed by Eternal Wisdom and announced by the prophets a long time before they actually happened.

Why is it, then, that God was careful to prepare so long in advance the coming of His Son to the earth? Why did Christ leave us so many divine teachings? Why did the Holy Spirit inspire the sacred writers to note down so many details, sometimes seemingly insignificant ones? Why did the Apostles write to their Christians such long and such pressing epistles?

So that those teachings might remain buried in the depths of the sacred books, like a dead letter? Not at all. It was so that (as St. Paul desires) we might scrutinize the mystery of Christ, contemplate His Person, study His actions: those actions of His reveal to us His virtues and His will. We ought to contemplate Him, not through a purely intellectual study—such a study is often dry and sterile—but "in all wisdom, and spiritual understanding,"[32] in a spirit full of heavenly wisdom that will make us seek in the divine gift the truth that enlightens our life. We ought to contemplate Him so as to conform our own lives to this model who makes God accessible to us, so as to draw on Him for divine life, in order that our thirst be fully quenched.

3. This knowledge is the real basis of our piety and a source of joy.

This knowledge acquired by faith, in prayer, under the inspiration of the Holy Spirit, is the true source of the living water that wells forth unto eternal life: "a fountain of water, springing up into life everlasting."[33] For—and this is a truth of first importance that will become clear in the course of these talks—the Eternal Father has placed within Christ Jesus for us all the graces,

[32] Col. 1:9 (Rheims).   [33] John 4:14.

all the gifts of sanctification, that He destines for souls. "No-one can come to the Father except through me."[34] Without Christ we have nothing, but with Him we have everything, we "can do all things,"[35] because "in Him dwells all the fullness of the Godhead bodily."[36] Whoever has understood the mystery of Christ, so as to live by it, has found that "pearl of great price" of which the Gospel speaks,[37] the pearl which, on its own, is worth all treasures put together: for what is gained along with it is life everlasting.[38]

The more we know Christ, the more deeply we fathom the mysteries of His Person and of His life, the more we prayerfully study the circumstances and details that Revelation has confided to us—the more also will our piety[39] be true and our holiness have solidity.

Our piety should be based on faith and on the knowledge which God has given us of super-natural[40] and divine things. A piety that is founded only on sentiment is as fragile and as ephemeral as the sentiment which serves as its base; it is a house built on sand, one which falls down at the first tremor that comes. When, on the other hand, our piety is founded on faith, is based on convictions that themselves result from a deep knowledge of the mysteries of Jesus who alone is true God with His Father and the Spirit common to Father and Son, then that piety is an edifice which is built upon rock—which is to say, unshakeable. It is "founded on rock."[41]

· · ·

[34] John 14:6 (Jerus.)   [35] Phil. 4:13.   [36] Col. 4:9.   [37] Matt. 13:46.

[38] "Keep the life of the Lord Jesus, day and night, like a precious pearl hidden in the cupboard of your breast. Carry it round with you everywhere; look at it lovingly with the eyes of your soul, whether you go forth or are at rest, as a gift of God which He Himself will have worked into your heart": Louis de Blois (Blosius), *Canon vitae spiritualis*, c. 19.

[39] [*Translator's note*: "piety," meaning a reverent and loving devotion. That is the meaning of "piety" and "pious" throughout the book.]

[40] [*Translator's note*: This word, thus hyphenated in the present translation, is used throughout as meaning "above the merely natural."]   [41] Matt. 7:25.

Furthermore, this knowledge is for us an unfailing source of joy.

Joy is the feeling arising in a soul conscious of possessing something that is good. The good of our intellect is truth, and the more abundant and luminous this truth is, the deeper is the mind's joy.

Christ brings us truth; He is Truth itself,[42] Truth full of sweetness who shows us the munificence of our Heavenly Father.[43] From the heart's-embrace of the Father,[44] where He ever lives, Christ reveals to us the divine secrets[45] that we possess by faith. What a feast, how satisfying and joyful it is, for the faithful soul to contemplate God, Infinite and ineffable Being, in the Person of Christ Jesus; to listen to God in the words spoken by Jesus; to discover (if I can express it thus) the feelings of God in the feelings of the heart of Jesus; to look at the divine actions, to enter into their mystery in order to drink, as at a spring there, the very life of God: *"in order that you may be filled unto all the fullness of God."*[46]

O Christ Jesus, our God and our Redeemer, Revelation of the Father, our elder brother and our friend, make us know you! Purify the eyes of our heart, so that we may contemplate you with joy. Silence the noise of created things, so that we may follow you with no obstacle in our path. Reveal yourself to our souls as you did to the disciples at Emmaus when you explained to them the pages of Sacred Scripture which spoke of your mysteries, and we shall then feel *"our hearts burn within us"*[47] to love you and attach ourselves to you!

---

[42] John 14:6.   [43] John 1:18.

[44] [*Translator's note*: For this translation of *"In sinu Patris,"* *"au sein du Père,"* see note in Book I, Ch. 1.1, of my translation of *Christ, the Life of the Soul.*]

[45] John 1:18: "He has revealed Him."   [46] Eph. 3:19.   [47] Luke 24:32 (Jerus.)

4. Threefold reason why the mysteries of Jesus are ours: Christ lived them for us; in them Jesus reveals Himself as our Exemplar; and in them He unites us with Himself.

In the talks that follow, we shall have the joy of pausing to consider each of the principal mysteries[48] of Jesus, of contemplating His actions, of recalling His words. We shall see what is inexpressibly divine, and what is profoundly human, in everything that was done by the Incarnate Word. We shall see that each one of His mysteries contains its own teaching, brings its special light; is for our souls the source of a particular grace, the object of which is to "form Jesus in us."[49]

What I would like to show you in this first talk is that the mysteries of Jesus have this characteristic: *that they are ours as much as they are His.*

There we have a fundamental truth on which we cannot meditate enough at the start of these talks, a truth of which we ought never to lose sight in all that will follow; for it is singularly fruitful for our super-natural life.

---

[48] [*Translator's note:* In a later passage Marmion defines this word "mysteries" as "human and visible signs of a divine and hidden reality" (p. 32). Christ being God as well as man, and God's depths being unfathomable, both "mystery," singular ("the mystery of Christ") and "mysteries," plural ("the mysteries of Christ") have a connotation of that which is *beyond* what we know and know with clarity. Sheed likened this to "a gallery into which we can progress deeper and deeper, though we can never reach the end." It seems to me that when Marmion uses the phrase "the mystery of Christ," that connotation is primary, uppermost. But when He uses "mysteries," plural ("the mysteries of Christ") his primary reference is to *the events or circumstances* of Christ's life on earth: "The mysteries of Jesus are states of His sacred humanity" (p. 29); on earth "Christ has passed through diverse states..." (p. 41). It is the same meaning as in "the fifteen mysteries of the rosary," the medieval "York Mystery Plays"—the use of the word "mysteries," rather than simply "events" or "circumstances," indicating that by reason of Christ's divinity *all* the events and circumstances of His life here below, no matter how small, have a divine significance and dimension. That God became man is certain and we can understand that that is so, but our minds cannot fully sound the depths of so tremendous a fact.]   [49] See Gal. 4:19.

Indeed, to know oneself to have been intimately united by Jesus Himself to each of His mysteries is for the devout soul an unfailing source of confidence. That truth gives rise to acts of gratitude and love that deliver the soul up, whole and entire, to Him who with such generosity has wished to give Himself, to unite Himself, to the soul.

But that truth—isn't it a dream, a figment of fancy? Is it indeed a reality? Yes, it is a reality, a divine reality; but it is only faith that receives it—just as it is only Love that has given it to us: "... we have believed in the love God has for us."[50]

Why is it that Christ's mysteries are *our* mysteries?

First because *Christ lived them for us.*

Undoubtedly it was love for His Father that was the deep motivation of all the actions of the life of the Word Incarnate. At the time of His completing His work on earth, Christ declares to the apostles that it is for love of His Father that He is about to deliver Himself up: "that the world may know that I love the Father."[51] In the wonderful prayer which He addresses to His Father at that time, Jesus says that He has accomplished His mission, which was that of glorifying His Father on earth: "I have glorified you on earth; I have accomplished the work that you have given me to do."[52] At each moment of His life, indeed, He has been able to say in all truth that He has sought only the good pleasure of His Father: "I do always the things that are pleasing to Him."[53]

But love for the Father is not the only love with which the heart of Christ beats: He loves us also, and in an infinite way. It was truly for our sakes that He came down from heaven, to redeem us, buy us back, to save us from death: "For us men and for our salvation..."[54] It was so as to give us life: "I am come, so that they may have life, and may have it more abundantly."[55] For Himself,

---

[50] See 1 John 4:16.   [51] John 14:31.   [52] John 1:4.
[53] John 8:29.   [54] Nicene Creed.   [55] John 10:10 (Rheims).

He had no need of satisfying and of meriting, as He is God's own Son, equal to His Father, at whose right hand He is seated in highest heaven; but it was for us that He bore everything. He became incarnate, He was born at Bethlehem, He lived in the obscurity of a life of labor, He preached and worked miracles, He died and rose again, He ascended into heaven, He sent the Holy Spirit—*and all this was for us, for love of us.* "Christ," says St. Paul, "loved the Church"—that is to say, the kingdom that was to be formed of the elect[56]—"and delivered Himself up for her, that He might purify her, sanctify her, making of her a conquest without spot or wrinkle or any such thing."[57]

So then, all the mysteries were lived by Jesus for us, in order to grant us to be, some day, with Him where He is by right—in the glory of His Father. Yes, each of us can say with St. Paul: Christ "loved me and gave Himself up *for me.*"[58] And His immolation on the cross was not only the crowning point of the mysteries of His earthly life. It was for me, because He loved me, that He accomplished everything.

Let thanks be rendered to you, O my God, for this gift that is beyond all words—this gift you have given us in the person of your Son, our salvation and our redemption: "Thanks be to God for His inexpressible gift!"[59]

Another reason why the mysteries of Jesus belong to us is that *in them all, Christ reveals Himself to us as our Exemplar.*

He came on earth to be our model. It was not only to announce salvation to us, and to effect (in principle) our redemption, that the Word was made flesh; He came in order to be the ideal of our

---

[56] [*Translator's note:* Marmion by no means implies that the members of the Church on earth are identical with "the elect." The Church here below has a mission to sanctify her members through God's grace, given that they cooperate with grace by the exercise of their free will. For each person the decisive factor is that of being in God's holy friendship at the moment of death.]

[57] Eph. 5:27.   [58] Gal. 2:20.   [59] 2 Cor. 9:15 (Jerus.)

souls as well. Christ Jesus was God living in our midst; God who had appeared to us, God made visible, tangible, brought within our reach, and showing us the way of holiness, by His life as much as by His words. We have no need to search beyond Him for the model of our perfection. Each one of His mysteries is a revelation of His virtues. The humility of the manger, the toil and self-effacement of the hidden life, the zeal of the public life, the abasement of His immolation on the cross, the glory of His triumph—these are virtues we ought to imitate, feelings we ought to share, or states in which we ought to participate. At the Last Supper, after having washed the feet of the apostles and having thus—He, their Master and Lord—given them an example of humility, Our Lord said to them: "I have given you an example, *that as I have done to you, so you also should do.*"[60] He could have said that about everything He did.

He said on another occasion: "I am the way...";[61] but He is only the way so as to precede us on it: "He who follows me does not walk in the darkness"[62] but arrives at eternal life. Jesus, by His mysteries, has (so to say) marked out all the stages that we ought to follow—follow after Him and with Him—in our super-natural life; or rather, He Himself draws the faithful soul forward along the course that He runs like a giant: "He ... has rejoiced as a giant to run the way."[63] "I created you all in my image and likeness," said Our Lord to St. Catherine of Siena; "and, what is more, by taking your nature I made myself resemble you. In consequence, I never stop working to make you resemble me, so far as you are capable of this; and I strive to renew in your souls as they go forward towards heaven everything that took place in my body."[64]

---

[60] John 13:15.   [61] John 14:6.   [62] John 8:12.   [63] Ps. 19 (18):6(5).

[64] *Life of St. Catherine* by Blessed Raymond of Capua, Part I, Ch. 11. It was to St. Catherine also that the Eternal Father deigned to say: "Know well, my daughter, that all the mysteries, all the actions which my Truth performed in this world, with the disciples or without the disciples, were representative of what takes place in the intimacy of soul of my servants and of all men. You can

That is why contemplation of the mysteries of Christ is so fruitful for the soul. The life, the death, the glory of Jesus are the example for our life, our death, our glory. Never forget this truth: we are only acceptable to the Eternal Father to the extent that we imitate His Son, to the extent that He sees in us a resemblance to His Son. Why is that? Because this very resemblance is what, from all eternity, we have been destined for.[65] There is for us no other form of holiness than that which Christ has shown us; the measure of our perfection is fixed by the degree of our imitation of Jesus.

Finally, there is a third reason—one more intimate and more deep—which makes the mysteries of Jesus ours. Not only has Jesus lived them for us, not only are they models for us but, as

---

draw forth from all those deeds a lesson and a rule of life. Let them be meditated upon in the light of reason, and the most uncultured minds as well as the most subtle, the commonest intellects as well as the highest ones, are able to draw profit from them. Each can take his share, if he wishes to": *Dialogue*, Hurtaud, II, 213-214. [*Translator's note*: A remarkable expression: the Eternal Father calls His Son His "Truth."]

[65] Rom. 8:29. [*Translator's note*: Marmion's word is *prédestinés*, "predestined," but it is important to keep in mind throughout the book that this word, and "predestination" as Marmion uses it, does not in any way involve a denial of our wills being free to win heaven; not the slightest suggestion that God offers the eternal inheritance to some and not all. Marmion, indeed, insists that it is *offered* to all without exception. But he emphasizes, also, that the achieving of it is not automatic; hell exists no less than does heaven. In the individual case, the achieving of the destiny depends upon a person's free response, in accordance with his or her lights, and crucially upon the person's soul-state at the moment of death. The inheritance of eternal joy in heaven is not unlike a human inheritance planned and desired by the testator, but subject to the fulfilment of some condition or conditions on the part of the planned beneficiary. See Marmion, p. 123 (paragraph beginning: "It is this grace..."), and also p. 92 (italicized words). The *"pré"* in *prédestinés* connotes destinies desired and planned by God from all eternity, but dependent for their fulfillment on the exercise of free will by individuals, aided by grace. That God, being outside time, knows which individuals will in the event achieve the eternal destiny planned for them does not mean that it is otherwise than truly within the reach of each individual.]

well as this, *in His mysteries Christ is but one with us.* There is no truth that St. Paul could have insisted on more than that, and my liveliest desire is that you understand the full depth of it.

Christ and we are but one, *in the mind of God.*

It is in Him (Christ) that God the Father has chosen us: "He chose us *in Him*"—not outside of Him—"before the foundation of the world."[66] God does not separate us from His Son Jesus; He destines us to resemble His Son in order that His Son be the firstborn of a multitude of brethren; wishes us "to become conformed to the image of His Son, *that* He should be the firstborn among many brethren."[67]

This union that God wishes to bring about between His Son Jesus and the elect is so intimate that St. Paul compares it to that which exists between the members and the head of one and the same body. The Church, says the great apostle, is the body of Christ, and Christ is its head; united they form what St. Augustine calls "the whole Christ": "The whole Christ is the head and the body; the head is the only-begotten Son of God and the body is His Church."[68] There we have it, the divine plan: "All things He made subject under His feet, and Him He gave as head over all the Church."[69] Christ is the head of this mystical body which He and the Church constitute, because He is its Lord and Master, and because He is for all His members the source of life. The Church and Christ—this is one and the same being, so to say: "we are members of His body, made from His flesh and from His bones."[70] God the Father unites the elect to His Divine Son in such a way that all the mysteries that Christ lived were lived by Christ *as head of the Church.*

See how explicit St. Paul is on this point. "God, who is rich in mercy," said St. Paul, "by reason of the great love with which He loved us, even when we were dead to eternal life because of our sins, brought us to life *with* Christ; raised us up with Him, seated

---

[66] Eph. 1:4. [67] Rom. 8:29. [68] *De unitate Ecclesiae,* 4.
[69] Eph. 1:22. [70] Eph. 5:30.

us in heaven *in* Jesus Christ that He might show in the ages to come the infinite riches of His grace through the goodness He manifests to us in Jesus Christ."[71] This thought returns more than once in the writings of the Apostle: "For we were buried *with Him*—Christ—by means of Baptism into death"[72]—*CONsepulti enim sumus CUM ILLO*; and God wants us to be one with Christ in His Resurrection, in His Ascension.

Nothing is more assured than this union of Christ with His elect in the mind of God. What makes the mysteries of Jesus ours is, above all, that the Eternal Father saw us when seeing His Son in each one of the mysteries Jesus lived, and that Christ accomplished them as head of the Church. Because of that, I will even say that the mysteries of Christ are more our mysteries than they are His. Christ, inasmuch as He is the Son of God, would not have had to submit to the humiliations of the Incarnation, the suffering and pains of the Passion; He would have had no need of the triumph of the resurrection that followed the ignominy of His death. He went through all that as head of the Church; He took upon Himself *our* miseries and *our* weaknesses: "He has borne *our* infirmities."[73] He willed to tread the road that we have to tread ourselves, and He merited for us, as our head, the grace to walk where He walked in each one of His mysteries.[74]

Christ Jesus, indeed, does not separate us from Himself in anything He does. He declares that He is the Vine and we are the

---

[71] See Eph. 2:4-7.   [72] Rom. 6:4.   [73] Isa. 53:4.

[74] For a development of these ideas, we permit ourselves to refer the reader to the talk *The Church, Mystical Body of Christ* in our preceding work, *Christ, the Life of the Soul*. St. Leo the Great wrote: "Granted that individuals each have their proper place among those who have been called, and that all the sons and daughters of the Church are spread out across the succession of the ages, still, in the same way that the whole community of the faithful, arisen from the baptismal font, have been crucified with Christ in His Passion, raised up with Him in the Resurrection, and at the Ascension placed along with Him at the right hand of the Father, so also have they been born with Him in this Nativity": *Sermo XXVI, On the Lord's Nativity*, VI, 2.

branches.[75] What closer union is there than that, since it is the same sap, the same life, that circulates in the root and in the vine-shoots? In such a way does Christ unite us to Him, that everything one does to a soul who believes in Him[76] (no matter who this soul is) is done to Christ Himself: "When you did it to one of the least of my brethren here, you did it to me."[77] He wills that the union which, by grace, binds Him to His disciples be the same as that union which, by nature, identifies Him with His Father: "that all may be one, even as you, Father, in me and I in you."[78] There it is, the sublime goal to which He wills to lead us by His mysteries.

Moreover, all the graces that He has merited by each of His mysteries are graces He has merited so as to distribute them to us. He received from His Father grace in its fullness: "We saw His glory ... full of grace"; but He did not receive that grace for Himself alone, for St. John adds immediately that it is from this same fullness that we all have to draw: "Of His fullness we have all received."[79] It is from Him that we receive grace, because He is our head and because His Father has subjected all things to Him: "All things He made subject under His feet, and Him he gave as head over all the Church."[80]

And this in such a way that His wisdom, His justice, His holiness, His strength, have become *our* wisdom, *our* justice, *our* holiness, *our* strength; Christ "has become *for us* God-given wisdom, and justice, and sanctification, and redemption."[81] Everything that

---

[75] [*Translator's note*: These four words of Marmion's own, "who believes in Him," derive from Christ's reference to His "brethren." Believers, in whom, as living vine-shoots, the sap of super-natural life flows from the Vine are indubitably Christ's "brethren" in the full sense: charitable acts done to them are as though done to Christ. But I am sure Marmion cannot by those four words be taken as implying that charitable acts done to unbelievers are not as though done to Christ. It is this same Marmion who is constantly emphasizing that the whole human race has been redeemed in principle, *en principe*, and that every individual is at least a potential recipient of Christ's super-natural life.]

[76] John 15:5.   [77] Matt. 25: 40 (Knox).   [78] John 17:21.
[79] John 1:14-16.   [80] Eph. 1:22.   [81] 1 Cor. 1:30.

belongs to Him belongs to us, is ours; we are rich with His riches, holy with His holiness. "O man," wrote the Venerable Louis de Blois, "if you truly desire to love God, behold yourself rich in Christ, however poor and destitute you may be on your own. For you can humbly appropriate to yourself that which Christ has done and suffered for you."[82]

Christ truly belongs to us, for we are His mystical body. His satisfactions,[83] His merits, His joys, His glories, are ours. Oh, ineffable condition of the Christian—the Christian associated so intimately with Jesus and His states![84] Oh, astonishing greatness of the soul to whom nothing is lacking of the grace merited by Christ in His mysteries: "you lack no grace"![85]

5. The power of His mysteries is ever present.

It is true that in their historical, material duration the mysteries of Christ's life on earth are now past; but *their power remains*, and the grace that allows us to share in them operates always.

Christ, in His glorious state, no longer merits; He was only able to merit during His mortal life, up to the time when He breathed His last upon the cross. But the merits that He won on earth—He does not stop making those merits ours. "Christ is the same, yesterday and today, yes, and forever."[86] Let us not forget that Christ Jesus *wills* the holiness of His mystical body: all His mysteries come down to the firm establishment of that holiness: Christ "loved the Church, and delivered Himself up for her, *that* He might sanctify her."[87] But what is this Church? That minimal portion of beings who had

---

[82] Louis de Blois (Blosius), *Canon vitae spritualis*, c. 37.

[83] [*Translator's note:* "satisfactions," meaning the satisfactions He has made to Divine Justice.]   [84] [*Translator's note:* "states" (*états*): In the broad picture, His state as God the Son from all eternity; His state on earth, incarnate and susceptible of suffering; His glorified state in heaven after the resurrection and ascension. Frequently, however, a context indicates that Marmion's "*états*" signifies particular circumstances of Christ's life on earth: see pp. 41 and 405 ("In the same way...") for specific examples of the earthly "states" of Christ.]

[85] 1 Cor. 1:7.   [86] Hebr. 13:8.   [87] Eph. 5:25.

the privilege of seeing the God-man living on earth? Assuredly not. Our Lord did not come solely for those inhabitants of Palestine who were living in His time, but for all men throughout all ages: "Christ died for all."[88] The gaze of Jesus, being a divine gaze, was cast upon every soul; His love extended to each one of us; His sanctifying will remains in itself as sovereign, as efficacious, as on the day when He shed His blood for the salvation of the world.

Though the time for meriting has ceased for Him, the time for communicating the fruit of His merits endures and continues up to the salvation of the last of the elect; Christ is ever living: "He lives always to make intercession for us."[89]

Let us lift us our thoughts to heaven, up to the sanctuary to which Christ ascended forty days after His resurrection, and there let us see Our Lord taking His place for ever before the face of His Father; He entered heaven "to appear *now* before the face of God on our behalf."[90] Why does Christ remain constantly before the face of His Father?

Because He is His Son, the only Son of God. There is for Him no unjust pretension in proclaiming Himself the equal of God[91]— because He *is* the true Son of God. The Eternal Father looks on Him and says to Him: "You are my Son; I have begotten you this day."[92] At this moment, as I am now speaking to you, Christ is there before His Father, and says to Him: "You are my Father,[93] I am truly your Son." And as Son of God, He has the right to look His Father in the

---

[88] 2 Cor. 5:15.   [89] See Hebr. 7:25.   [90] Hebr. 9:24.   [91] See Phil. 2:6. [Translator's note: Marmion takes the interpretation found in the Rheims: that Christ "thought it not robbery to be equal to God"—not a pretension, He in fact *being* God, as His Father is. Other translations, e.g. the Confraternity version, have the interpretation: "He did not consider being equal to God a thing to be clung to," in that He "emptied Himself" by becoming incarnate. That He did proclaim Himself "equal to God," that He is indeed equal to God the Father, is common to both interpretations, however. See also John 5:18.]

[92] Ps. 2:7 (Knox). [Translator's note: "this day": see p. 276 as to Marmion's exegesis of this phrase: "that is, '*in an eternal present*.'" This, then, so to say, is the language of eternity, not time. But the beginning of Marmion's very next sentence ("At this moment, as I am now speaking to you") has proceeded seamlessly to the language of time, viewed from our perspective here below.]   [93] Ps. 88 (89):27.

face, to treat with Him as equal to equal, just as He has the right of reigning with Him for ever and ever.

St. Paul adds that it is *for us* that He makes use of this right; it is "on our behalf" that He takes His place before His Father. What is the meaning of that, unless that Christ takes His place before the face of His Father not only by right of being God's Son, the object of God's delight, but also in His capacity as Mediator? He is called "Jesus," that is to say "Savior"; this name is divine, because it comes from God, because it was given Him by God.[94] Christ Jesus is in heaven, at the right hand of His Father, as our representative, our High Priest, our Mediator. It was in that capacity that, here below, He carried out the will of His Father, to the last iota and in all its details; that He willed to live all His mysteries. It is in that capacity, too, that He lives now at the right hand of God, to present to Him His merits and ceaselessly to communicate the fruit of His mysteries to our souls in order to sanctify them: "He lives always to make intercession for us."

Oh, what a powerful cause for confidence it is to know that Christ, of whose life we read in the Gospels, whose mysteries we celebrate, is ever living, ever interceding for us; that the might of His divinity is ever active; that the power possessed by His sacred humanity (as instrument united to the Word) to cure the sick, to console the afflicted, to give life to souls, is the same always. As in days of old, Christ is still the infallible Way that leads to God, is the Truth to enlighten everyone who comes into this world, is the Life that saves from spiritual death: "Christ is the same, yesterday and *today*, yes, and forever."

I believe in you, Lord Jesus, but increase my faith! I have full confidence in the reality and the plenitude of your merits, but strengthen this confidence! I love you, O you who showed us your love in all your mysteries, love *in finem*, "to the end";[95] but make my love of you a larger one!

---

[94] Matt. 1:21: "and you must name Him Jesus" (Jerus.)   [95] John 13:1.

CHAPTER TWO

How We Assimilate the Fruit
of the Mysteries of Jesus

The mysteries that Christ Jesus, the Word Incarnate, lived here below were lived for us. In them he shows us Himself as our model; but above all He wills to be one with our souls as leader of one single mystical body, of which He is the head and we are the members.

These mysteries have a power that is always active and efficacious. From heaven, where He is seated at the right hand of God His Father, Christ continues to communicate to souls the fruit of His states, so as to effect in those souls their divine resemblance to Him.

Participation in the mysteries of Jesus requires the co-operation of the soul.

If God reveals to us the secrets of His love for us, it is so that we may accept them, so that we may enter into the way He sees things, into His thoughts, so that we may adapt ourselves to the eternal plan, outside of which neither holiness nor salvation is possible. If Christ opens to us the immeasurable treasures of His states and of His mysteries, it is so that we may draw upon them and make them bear fruit, on pain of being, at the Last Day, cast out of the kingdom like the negligent servant in the Gospel,[1] into darkness unending.

But one cannot seek after what one doesn't know about. The will does not attach itself to good things that the intellect does not repre-

------

[1] Matt. 25:30.

sent to it: *Ignoti nulla cupido*, those who do not know of something have no desire for it.

How, then, now that Christ has deprived us of His presence perceivable by the senses, are we to know about His mysteries, their beauty, their harmony, their virtue, their power? How, above all, shall we put ourselves into life-giving contact with them, so as to draw from them those fruits that, little by little, will transform our souls and effect in us that union with Christ which is an indispensable condition for being numbered among His disciples?

This is what now remains for us to see, in completion of the exposition of this very fruitful truth, that the mysteries of Jesus are ours as much as they are His.

1. **We associate ourselves with the mysteries of Christ by meditating on the Gospels, and especially by uniting ourselves with the Church, the spouse of Jesus, in her liturgy.**

Knowledge of Jesus and of His states is drawn first of all from the Gospels.

Those sacred pages, inspired by the Holy Spirit, contain a description, and the teachings, of the life of Jesus on earth. To see and understand Christ Himself, it is enough for us to read those pages, so simple and sublime, but to read them with faith. The devout soul who, in praying, goes frequently through this unique book, the Gospels, arrives little by little at a knowledge of Jesus and His mysteries, comes to penetrate the secrets of His sacred heart, to understand that magnificent Revelation of God to the world—the Revelation that is Jesus: "He who sees me sees also the Father."[2] For this book is inspired; a light and a strength come from it, to illuminate and fortify hearts that are true and sincere. Happy the soul who opens that book every day! That soul drinks from the very source of living waters.

[2] John 14:9.

Another way of knowing the mysteries of Jesus is to associate oneself with the Church in her liturgy.

Before ascending to heaven, Christ said to His apostles on whom He founded His Church: "All power in heaven and earth has been given to me."[3] "As the Father has sent me, I also send you."[4] "He who hears you, hears me."[5] And that is why the Church is like a prolongation, throughout the ages, of the Incarnation. She stands before us representing Jesus. From Him, her heavenly Spouse, she has inherited the divine tenderness. Along with the power to sanctify souls, she has received from Him as a dowry the riches of grace won by Him on the cross on the day of their mystic wedding.

Always preserving due proportion, one can therefore say of the Church what Christ, her Spouse, said of Himself: that she is for us the way, the truth and the life. The *way*, because we can only reach God through Christ Jesus, and we can only be united to Christ through being incorporated (in fact or desire) into the Church through baptism.[6] The *truth*, because with all the authority of her Founder she guards as a deposit, and proposes for our belief, the truths that Revelation has brought to us. Finally, the *life*, because through the public worship that she alone has the right to organize, through the sacraments which are hers alone to administer, she distributes the life of grace to souls and maintains it within them.

You see at once that we sanctify ourselves in the measure that we let ourselves be instructed and directed by the Church. For as Jesus said to the Church, His spouse: "He who hears you, hears me"; and to hear Jesus—is not that to go to the Father?

---

[3] Matt. 28:18.   [4] John 20:21.   [5] Luke 10:16.

[6] [*Translator's note*: See the notes, "Salvation and those outside the Church" and "Those not baptized by water," in Book I, Chs. 5.1 and 1.4 respectively of the present translator's translation of *Christ, the Life of the Soul*. Quoting from recent documents of the Church, those two notes expand (and in a sense qualify) Marmion's words in this sentence, while holding to their essential truth.]

As you know, it is especially through the liturgy that the Church educates, brings to maturity, the souls of her children so as to make them resemble Jesus and thus to perfect in them that copy or "image" of Christ which is the very shape of our planned destiny.[7]

Guided by the Holy Spirit, who is the Spirit of Jesus Himself, the Church each year unfolds before the eyes of her children the complete cycle of the mysteries of Christ, from Christmas to the Ascension, sometimes much abbreviated, sometimes in their exact chronological order as during Holy Week and Easter. In this manner she makes each of the mysteries of her Divine Spouse be re-lived—not just anyhow, but in an animated and living way. She makes us go over every one of the stages of His life. If we allow ourselves to be led by her, we shall infallibly arrive at a knowledge of the mysteries of Jesus, and enter especially into the feelings of His divine heart. Why is that?

The Church, who knows the secrets of her Spouse, chooses from the Gospels the pages that best make each of His mysteries stand out. Then, with perfect art, she illustrates them by passages from the Psalms, from the prophecies, from the letters of St. Paul and the other apostles, by quotations from the early Fathers of the Church. In this way she throws a fuller and more vivid light upon the teachings of her Divine Master, the details of His life, the basis of His mysteries.

At the same time, through the choice of quotations from the sacred books and from holy authors, through the aspirations she suggests to us, through her symbolism and her rites, she generates in our hearts the dispositions necessary for a full and generous assimilation of the spiritual fruit of each mystery.

[7] Rom. 8:29.

2. Variety and fruitfulness of the grace of the mysteries represented in the liturgy.

For, though it be always the same Savior, the same Jesus, laboring at the same work of our sanctification, each mystery nevertheless constitutes for our souls a new manifestation of Christ; each has its special beauty, its particular splendor, as also its own grace. The grace that flows down for us from the Nativity has not the same character as that brought to us by the celebration of the Passion. At Christmas we cannot but rejoice; but when we contemplate the unspeakable pains by which Christ expiated our sins, we are saddened by those transgressions of ours. In the same way, the interior joy which floods our souls at Easter wells forth from another source and possesses another splendor than that which thrills us when we sing of the coming of the Savior upon earth.

The early Fathers of the Church quite often speak of what they call the "*vis mysterii*"—the power, the strength, of the mystery celebrated, the significance proper to it. In relation to each of Christ's mysteries we can apply to Christians what St. Gregory Nazianzen says of the faithful on the occasion of the Easter Feast: "It is impossible to present to God a more acceptable gift than that of offering ourselves with a right understanding of the mystery."[8]

There are some minds who see nothing else in the celebration of the mysteries of Christ than the perfection of the ceremonies, the beauty of the singing, the splendor of the vestments, the harmony of the rituals. All that may be there; all that is encountered indeed: all that is excellent.

In the first place because, the Church having herself settled all the details of the worship of her Spouse (this Church who is the spouse of Christ), the perfect observation of those details honors God and His Son Jesus. "It is an established law for all

---

[8] St. Gregory Nazianzen, *Orat.* I, *in sanct. Pascha* IV.

the mysteries of Christianity that, to reach our understanding, they must first be presented to the senses: and this had to be so in order to honor Him who, being invisible by nature, willed to appear, for love of us, under a form that was perceptible."[9]

Further, it is a psychological law of our nature—our nature being matter and spirit—that we go from the visible to the invisible. The exterior elements of the celebration of the mysteries are to serve for our souls like the rungs of a ladder, so as to raise us to the contemplation and love of realities that are heavenly and supernatural. This, furthermore, is the plan of the Incarnation itself, as we sing at Christmas: "... so that while we recognize God in visible form, we may *through this* be seized with a love of things invisible."[10]

These exterior elements, therefore, have their use, but we ought not to rest upon them exclusively; they are but the fringe of Christ's garment. The glory, the splendor, the power of the mysteries of Jesus are chiefly *interior*, and are what we should be seeking above all. More than once, the Church asks God to give us, as a fruit of holy communion itself, an understanding of the power special to each mystery, in order that we may enter deeply into it and live it: "... that what we celebrate in solemn office, we may attain through the discernment of a purified mind."[11] This is knowledge of Christ as St. Paul wishes it: "in all wisdom and spiritual understanding."[12]

[9] Bossuet, *Sermon sur la parole de Dieu, œuvres oratoires*, ed. Lebarcq, III, 581.

[10] The holy Council of Trent expressly teaches this about the rites of the Mass, about the primordial action of the liturgy: "As the nature of men is such that they are not easily able to meditate on divine things without the support of exterior aids, our holy Mother the Church has on that account instituted ... certain rites and brought in ceremonies by which the minds of the faithful are stirred up by these visible signs of religion and piety ... to the contemplation of higher things" (Sess. XXII, c.5). This teaching can perfectly be applied to the whole of the liturgy.   [11] Postcommunion of the Epiphany and of the Transfiguration. See also the postcommunion for the Octave day of the Epiphany: "... that we may behold with pure eyes, and also feel with a worthy disposition, the mystery in which thou hast been pleased to let us share."   [12] Col. 1:9.

It is indeed the case that the mysteries of Christ are not only models, subjects for contemplation: they are also sources of graces.

It is said of Jesus that when He was here on earth there went forth from His Person a power that healed the sick: "power went forth from Him and healed all."[13] Christ Jesus is always the same: if we contemplate His mysteries with faith, be it in the Gospels or in the liturgy presented to us by the Church, it produces in us the grace that He merited for us when He lived those mysteries. In such contemplation we see how Jesus our Exemplar practiced the virtues, we enter into a sharing of the particular feelings that animated His divine heart in each of those sets of circumstances; but above all we draw from Him the special graces He merited for us then.

The mysteries of Jesus are states of His sacred humanity; all the graces He had, He received from His divinity in order that they might be communicated to His humanity and, through His humanity, to each of the members of His mystical body "according to the measure of Christ's bestowal."[14] The Word, by taking on a human nature from our race, has, so to speak, married to Himself the whole of humanity, and each soul (in a measure known to God and proportioned, in what has regard to ourselves, to the degree of our faith) partakes of the grace that inundates the sacred soul of Christ.

In this way each mystery of Christ, representing one set of circumstances of the sacred humanity, brings us a special sharing in His divinity. For example, at Christmas we celebrate the birth of Jesus on earth; we sing of that "wonderful exchange"[15] between divinity and humanity that took place in Him—from us He took to Himself humanity in order to give His divinity to us—and each Christmas celebrated in a holy way becomes for the soul, by a more abundant communication of grace, like a new birth to

---

[13] Luke 6:19.   [14] Eph. 4:7.

[15] Antiphon of the Office of the Feast of the Circumcision.

divine life. Upon Calvary, we die to sin with Christ. Jesus gives us the grace to detest more deeply everything that wounds Him. At Eastertime we share in that liberty of soul, in that more intense life for God, of which He is the model in His Resurrection. On Ascension Day, through faith and holy desires we are lifted up with Him to heaven so as to be, as He is, in the presence of the Heavenly Father, in the heart's-embrace of the Father, in the depths of the divine sanctuary.

By following Christ Jesus in all His mysteries in that kind of way, by uniting ourselves with Christ, we share little by little, but surely, in His divinity, in His divine life; and each time in greater measure and with a deeper intensity.[16] According to the beautiful words of St. Augustine, that which was confirmed long ago in a divine reality is renewed spiritually in devout souls through repeated celebration of the mysteries: "What truth indicates to have happened once in history the solemnity renews so as to be celebrated again and again in pious hearts."[17]

It is therefore true to say that when we contemplate in their successive order the different mysteries of Christ, we do so not only for the purpose of recalling to our minds the events accomplished for our salvation and of glorifying God for them by our praises and thanksgiving; not only so that we may see how Jesus lived and seek to imitate Him, but as well as this, with the object that our souls may participate in a special set of circumstances of the sacred humanity and may draw forth, from each of those circumstances, the specific grace it has pleased the Divine Master to attach to it by meriting that grace as head of the Church, for His mystical body.

That is why the Sovereign Pontiff Pius X, of glorious memory, was able to write that "active participation of the faithful in the sacred mysteries and in the public and solemn prayer of the

---

[16] We have expounded these ideas at greater length in the chapter *The Voice of the Spouse* in our preceding volume *Christ, the Life of the Soul.*

[17] *Sermo* CCXX, on the Easter Vigil, II.

Church is *the first and indispensable source of the Christian spirit.*"[18]

Indeed, on this subject there is a truth of great importance that is too often forgotten, or even sometimes not known.

A man can imitate the Exemplar who is Christ in two ways. He can strive to do so by a wholly natural labor as when one imagines oneself reproducing the human ideal presented by a hero or an individual one likes or admires. There are some souls who think that is the way in which one should imitate Our Lord and reproduce in us the features of His adorable person. The "imitation" of Christ that such a path leads to is an imitation conceived according to our human ideas.

That is to lose sight of the fact that Christ is a *divine* model. His beauty and His human virtues have their roots in His divinity, and draw all their splendor from His divinity. Aided by grace, we can and assuredly ought to bring all our efforts to understanding Christ and to modeling our virtues and our actions on His; but only the Holy Spirit, "Finger of God's right hand," is capable of reproducing in us the true image of the Son—because our imitation has to be an imitation of a super-natural order.

Well now, this work of the Divine Artist is above all effected in prayer which is founded upon faith and set afire by love. During the time when we contemplate the mysteries of Christ with the eyes of faith and a love desirous of self-giving, the Holy Spirit (who is the Spirit of Christ) acts in the depths of the soul and, by His sovereignly efficacious touches, fashions the soul in such a way as to reproduce there, as if by a sacramental power, the features of the Divine Model.

---

[18] Here is how the Vicar of Christ expresses it: "Our most lively desire being that the *true* Christian spirit may flourish anew in every way and be maintained by all the faithful, it is *necessary* to provide, *above all*, for the holiness and dignity of the temple where the faithful come together *precisely* to find there that spirit at its *first and indispensable source*, namely: *active* participation in the sacred mysteries and in the public and solemn prayer of the Church": St. Pius X, *Motu proprio* of November 23, 1903. [Marmion's italics]

That is why this contemplation of the mysteries of Jesus is in itself so fruitful; that is why the essentially super-natural contact with the circumstances of the life of her Spouse that the Church, guided in this by the Holy Spirit, causes us to have in the liturgy is so vital for us. There is no surer way, no more infallible means, of causing us to resemble Christ.[19]

3. **The dispositions we ought to bring to the contemplation, in order to draw down all the fruits of it, are: faith, adoration and love.**

This contemplation of the mysteries of Jesus will not produce fruits so great in us, however, unless we bring certain *dispositions* to it. We can reduce them to three in number: *faith, reverence and love.*

Faith is the primordial disposition for putting us into vital contact with Christ.

These are *mysteries* we celebrate—that is to say, human and visible signs of a divine and hidden reality. To understand, to touch this reality, faith is needed. Christ is at the same time God and man; in Him the human is always alongside the *divine.*

In each of these mysteries we see appearing before us one who is both man and God. Often even—as in the Nativity, as in the Passion—the divinity is more than ordinarily hidden. To lay hold of it, to pierce the veil and reach it; to see God in looking at the child in the stable, at the "cursed one"[20] hanging on the gibbet of Calvary; to see God under the outward appearances of the Eucharist—all this needs faith: "Let faith supply what the senses lack."[21]

Without faith we shall never penetrate to the depth of the mysteries of Jesus; but with it we have no cause to envy the

---

[19] See, at the end of this talk, a quotation, too long to be given here, from one of the masters of the spiritual life.   [20] See Gal. 3:13.

[21] "*Praestet fides supplementum sensuum defectui*" (Hymn, *Pange lingua*).

contemporaries of Christ. We do not see Our Lord as He was seen by those who lived in Palestine with Him, but faith grants us to gaze on and to dwell with Him, united to Him in a way which is no less efficacious than for those who were His contemporaries. We sometimes say: "Oh, if only I had lived at His time, if I had been able to follow Him with the crowd, with the disciples; if I could have waited on Him like Martha, have listened at His knees like Mary Magdalene!" But He has said: "*Blessed* are they who have not seen, and yet have believed"[22]—blessed are those who have not seen me but have believed in me. Why "blessed"? Because contact with Christ in faith is no less fruitful for our souls: and especially is it no less glorious for Jesus, to whom we render this homage of believing in Him without having seen Him. There is no cause for us to envy the disciples who lived by His side. If we have faith, we too will dwell as united to Jesus as those could be who saw Him with their eyes and touched Him with their hands.

I will even add this: that, so far as we are concerned, the measure of this faith is what determines the degree of our participation in the grace of Jesus contained in His mysteries. Look at what happened during His life on earth: those who lived at His side, who had material contact with Him, like the shepherds and the wise men in the stable, like the apostles and the Jews during the years of His public life, like St. John and Mary Magdalene at the foot of the cross, like the disciples who saw Him risen and saw Him ascend to heaven—all these souls who sought Him received grace according to the degree of their faith. It is always to faith that He grants the miracles asked of Him; all the pages of the Gospels show us that He makes faith in Him an indispensable condition for receiving His grace.

Now in our case there is no contact of the eyes with Jesus; He has ascended to heaven. But faith takes the place of sight; and

[22] John 20:29.

the degree of this faith (as it was, moreover, for the contemporaries of Christ) is what, along with love, determines the degree of our union with Him. Let us never forget this important truth: Christ Jesus, without whom we can do nothing and from whose plenitude we have to receive everything, will only grant us a share of His grace in the measure of our faith. St. Augustine says that we approach the Savior not by going towards Him but through our ardent faith: "For we do not run to Christ on our feet, but by believing."[23]

The more, then, that this faith in Jesus the Word Incarnate, the Son of God, is a living and deep one, the more intimately shall we approach Christ.

Besides this, faith makes two other sentiments arise in us—ones that are needed to complete the attitude of our soul in the presence of Christ. These are respect and love.

We should approach Christ with unspeakable *reverence*. For Christ Jesus is God—that is to say, the Almighty; the Infinite Being who possesses all wisdom, all justice, all the perfections; the Sovereign Master of all things; the Creator of everything there is and the Last End of all that exists; the Source of all bliss. Wherever He is, Jesus remains God. Even when He gives Himself with the greatest kindness and liberality, He is still always He before whom the highest angels veil their face: "The Dominations adore, the Powers tremble."[24] In the stable at Bethlehem, He allows Himself to be held by hands; the Gospel tells us that the crowd pressed upon Him from every side;[25] at the time of His Passion He lets Himself be slapped, struck, insulted—but He is always God. Even when He is scourged, when His face is covered with spittle, when He expires upon the cross, He is always He who has created heaven and earth by His power and has governed them by His wisdom. And that is why, whatever page of

---

[23] *Tract. in Johann.*, XXVI, 3.

[24] "*Adorant Dominationes, tremunt Potestates*": Preface in the Mass.

[25] Mark 5:31.

the Gospels we read, whatever mystery of Jesus we celebrate, we ought to adore Him.

When faith is a lively faith, that reverence is so profound that it makes us prostrate ourselves before this God-man to adore Him: "You are the Christ, the Son of the living God."[26] "And falling down, he adored Him."[27]

Adoration is the first impulse of a soul that is led by faith to Christ; and the second is *love*.

I said to you just now that love underlies all the mysteries of Christ. The humility of the manger, the obscurity of the hidden life, the hardships of the public life, the torments of the Passion, the glory of the Resurrection—all these are due to love: "Jesus ... having loved His own who were in the world, loved them to the end."[28] It is love above all that reveals itself and shines out in the mysteries of Jesus. And it is above all through love that we understand them: "We know and believe the love God has for us."[29]

If we wish to contemplate the mysteries of Jesus fruitfully, we must do it with faith, with reverence, but above all with love, with the love that seeks to give *oneself*, to yield oneself up to God's good pleasure so as to carry out and accomplish it.

It is then that contemplation of the mysteries of Jesus becomes fruitful. "He who loves me ... I will love him and manifest myself to him," said Our Lord.[30] What is He saying there? That if someone loves me in faith, He says, contemplates me in my humanity, in the events of my incarnation, I will disclose to that person the secrets of my divinity.

Happy, thrice happy, is the soul in whom so magnificent a promise is fulfilled! To that person Christ Jesus will reveal "the gift of God."[31] Through His Spirit who "searches ... the deep things of God,"[32] He will make that soul enter into the sanctuary

---

[26] Matt. 16:16.   [27] John 9:38 (Rheims).   [28] John 13:1.
[29] 1 John 4:16 (RSV, Cath.)   [30] John 14:21.   [31] John 4:10.   [32] 1 Cor.2:10.

of that "mystery which has been hidden from eternity in God";[33] He will open to that person those "wine-cellars of the king" of which the Song of Songs speaks,[34] where the soul quenches its thirst for truth and joy. Doubtless, this inward manifestation of Jesus to the soul will not, here below, go as far as the Beatific Vision. That remains the privilege of the blessed in heaven. But it will fill the soul with divine lights which will strengthen it in its ascent to God: "to know Christ's love which surpasses knowledge, *in order that you may be filled unto all the fullness of God.*"[35]

There is truly "the fount of living water, springing up into life eternal,"[36] for is it not eternal life "... to know you, the only true God, and know your Divine Son,"[37] to proclaim with our lips and our life that Jesus is your beloved Son, the Son you love tenderly, the Son in whom you have placed all your delight, and in whom you wish us to find everything?

NOTES BY MARMION

I. **Extract from the Catechism of Christian Doctrine promulgated by order of His Holiness Pope Pius X (1913).**

The Feasts of the Church have been instituted so as to render God, in common in the holy temples, the supreme worship of adoration, praise, thanksgiving and reparation. In them everything has been so well disposed and adapted to circumstances— the ceremonies, the words, the singing, the outward ordering in all its details—that *they can make the mysteries, truths or acts which we celebrate penetrate deeply into the mind and bring us to corresponding feelings and actions. If the faithful were well instructed in this* matter and *celebrated the feasts in the spirit desired by the Church* when she instituted them, *a renewal and a notable increase of faith,*

---

[33] Eph. 3:9.   [34] See Song of Songs 1:3.   [35] Eph. 3:19.
[36] See John 4, vv. 11 and 14.   [37] See John 17:3.

of piety, of religious instruction would be obtained, and, in conse-
quence, the interior life of Christians would be found to be reanimated
and improved.

Let every good Christian, aided by sermons or by some appropriate book, study to *understand* and *make his or her own the spirit*
of each feast, directing the mind to the object and special aim of
the feast, meditating the truth, the virtue, the wonder, the benefit, that is found particularly commemorated by it, seeking in
every way to derive a personal improvement therefrom. The
Christian will thus better know and will with more fervor love
God, our Lord Jesus Christ, the Blessed Virgin and the Saints; will
have a fondness for the sacred liturgy, for sermons, for the Church,
and will even try to make others have an attachment to them.
From then on, every feast-day will be for that person a Lord's Day,
a true feast that will rejoice that person's soul, restore it, reinvigorate
it, fill it with a new strength for bearing sufferings and daily struggles
during the week.

II. Quotation from Msgr. Gay.[38]

The great secret for leading this Christian life, a life that is free,
pure and already almost superhuman [of which Jesus's earthly life
at His coming forth from the tomb is the real type and is the life
which baptism obliges us to imitate] is not so much to consider the
vanity of the world, the fragility and baseness of the present life,
and those of its miseries that are special to oneself, and its passions,
and everything that, without grace, one would be capable of by
nature, and its failures and its sins—which however one should
detest and deplore (all of that is useful, all of that is something like
indispensable; every wise soul brings all this to mind and thinks
of it at certain times, but it is not always the time for thinking
about it, and in any case doing so is not the most efficacious

[38] Msgr. Gay, *Élévations sur la vie et la doctrine de Notre Seigneur Jésus-Christ,*
91st elevation; the words in square brackets and the italics are Marmion's.

thing for us.) *The most efficacious thing, in this as in every matter, the most decisive and most triumphant thing, is to look, as far as one can and habitually, on high. It is to consider God and Jesus;* the perfections of God, His rights, His attributes, His calls to us, His challenges; His patient waiting; His plans, His promises; *the mysteries of Jesus and the wholly divine graces that flow down from what He says, from what He does, from what He commands, from what He suffers. It is to remember always that He personally is the starting-point and the leader of the Christian life; and that the great virtue of baptism is to incorporate us in Him, to give us His life, to make us be of His race, and to pour out His Spirit within us*—which means a light and strength by which we are enabled, and called on, not merely to sin no longer, as St. John says expressly, but as well as this to weigh up all things, to discern our way and to follow it and, ascending from splendor to splendor, from liberty to liberty, to come to the interior state of him who said "For me, life means Christ."[39]

---

[39] Phil. 1:21 (Knox).

BOOK ONE

THE PERSON OF CHRIST

CHAPTER THREE[1]

"In Sinu Patris"—In the Heart's-Embrace of the Father

Introduction: Christ is, above all else, the Son of God.

The mysteries of Christ are ours; the union that Jesus Christ wishes to contract with us is one in which everything He has becomes ours. With a divine liberality, He wants us to share in the inexhaustible graces of salvation and sanctification that He has merited for us by each of His mysteries, so as to communicate to us the spirit of His states and thus to bring about in each of us a resemblance to Him—the infallible pledge of our destiny planned from eternity.

Christ has passed through diverse states; He has been a child, an adolescent, a teacher of the truth, a victim on the cross, glorious in His resurrection and ascension. By thus going through all the successive stages of His earthly existence, He has sanctified the whole of human life.

But there is an essential state that He never leaves: He is always the only Son of God, living in the heart's-embrace of the Father: *"Unigenitus Filius qui est"*—who IS—*"in sinu Patris."*

[1] [*Translator's note:* This chapter-numbering has been adopted to accord with that of the French original. Whereas in *Christ, the Life of the Soul* Book One started with a chapter numbered 1, and Book Two started afresh with a chapter similarly numbered, the numbering in the French of *Christ in His Mysteries* is consecutive throughout (Chapters 1 and 2 being the "preliminary" chapters before the *Première Partie*—here Book One—opens).]

Christ is the Son of God, incarnate—is the Word made flesh. Before becoming man, Christ was God. In becoming man, He did not cease to be God: "*Quod fuit, permansit,*" "What He was, He remained."[2] Whether you consider Him as a little child in the crib, or laboring in the workshop at Nazareth, or preaching in Judea, or dying on Calvary, or manifesting His triumphant glory to the apostles, or ascending to heaven He is, always and above all, the only Son of God.

It is, then, His divinity that we should first contemplate, before speaking of the mysteries that flow from the Incarnation itself. All the mysteries of Jesus are founded on His divinity; it is from His divinity that all their splendor is derived; from it that all their fruitfulness is drawn.

There is a big difference, as regards the way they start, between St. John's Gospel and those of others of the sacred writers. The latter begin their account by drawing up the human genealogy of Jesus, in order to show how He is descended from the royal race of David. But St. John, he who is loath to walk upon the earth, rises up at the start, like an eagle, with a wonderful soaring of spirit, up to the highest heaven, so as to tell us what happens in the sanctuary of the Godhead.

Before he recounts the life of Jesus to us, this evangelist tells us who Christ was before He became incarnate. And how does St. John put it? "In the beginning[3] was the Word, and the Word was with God; and the Word was God..."[4] And so as to reassure us on the value of his testimony, John adds without more ado: "No-one has ever seen God"[5] but that "the only-begotten Son who is in the heart's-embrace of the Father, *He* has revealed Him."

For three years indeed, Jesus has made known to His disciples the hidden things of God. On the eve of His death, He recalled those hidden things to mind, by saying that they were a sign of His friendship which He had given only to them and to those

---

[2] Antiphon of the Office of the Circumcision.   [3] [*Translator's note:* that is, before anything at all was created.]   [4] John 1:1.   [5] John 1:18.

who, coming after them, would believe in His words: "I have called you friends, because all things I have heard from my Father I have made known to you."[6]

To understand who Jesus is, who He was, we have therefore only to listen to the disciple who is reporting His words to us: or rather, we have only to listen to Jesus Himself. But let us listen with faith, with love, with adoration: for He who makes Himself known to us is God's own Son.

The words He brings us are not words that can be understood only with the ears of the flesh; they are words which are altogether heavenly, words of eternal life: "The words that I have spoken to you are spirit and life."[7] Only the humble and faithful soul can hear them.

Let us no longer be surprised at what these words reveal to us of deep mysteries: Jesus Himself has willed it. It is He who, in order to bring about our union with Him, has made those words heard; He willed that they be set down by the sacred writers; He sends His Holy Spirit, who "searches the deep things of God,"[8] to "bring them to our minds,"[9] that we may taste, "in all spiritual wisdom and understanding,"[10] the mysteries of His inner life as God. And does not a sharing in this life constitute the very basis of Christianity and the substance of all holiness?

1. **Divine fecundity: the Church's teaching on the Fatherhood of God.**

Faith reveals to us this truly astonishing mystery—that the power to be fruitful, and the effecting of this, is found in its perfection in God.

God is the plenitude of Being, is the shoreless ocean of all perfection and of all life. The clumsy images that often serve us in depicting Him, the ideas we apply to Him by way of analogy in

---

[6] John 15:15. See also John 17:20 (those also "who through their word shall believe in me," Rheims).   [7] John 6:64.   [8] See 1 Cor. 2:10.

[9] See John 14:26.   [10] Col. 1:9.

speaking of that which is best in creatures—all these are powerless to represent Him. In order to rise to a notion that does not belie God's infinity, what is needed is, not to push further—even indefinitely—the limits created being has, but, in the most positive way, to deny any limits at all as applying to God. He is Being itself, necessary Being, subsisting of Himself, possessing in His plenitude all perfection.

And here is a marvel that Divine Revelation uncovers for us. God[11] is fruitful; there is in Him a Fatherhood that is wholly spiritual and ineffable; He is a Father, the Source[12] of all divine life in the Trinity.

Infinite Understanding, God comprehends Himself perfectly. In a single act, He sees all that He is, all that is in Him. In a single glance, so to say, He comprehends the plenitude of His perfections: and in one thought, one word that leaves no other word to say, He expresses to Himself this infinite knowledge. This thought, conceived by Eternal Understanding, this Utterance, by which God expresses all of Himself, is the Word. Faith tells us that this Word is God—"*And the Word was with God; and the Word was God*"[13]—because the Word has (or, better to say, is) with the Father one and the same divine nature.

And because the Father communicates to this Word a nature that is not only similar to but identical with His own nature, Holy Scripture tells us that He "begets" Him, and it calls the Word "*the Son.*" The inspired books convey to us the ineffable cry of God as He contemplates His Son and proclaims the beatitude

---

[11] [*Translator's note*: "God" at the start of this sentence means God the Father; but the sentence then extends the gaze: the Fatherhood, to which Marmion refers, connotes the Sonship in God and, further, the Trinitarian nature of God.]   [12] [*Translator's note*: Marmion's word, here translated as "Source," is *Principe*. The Son proceeds from the Father, is "begotten by" the Father; but, as Marmion makes clear five paragraphs further on: "There is an order of origin, without there being any priority of time, or any hierarchical superiority, or any relation of dependence." The Son, like the Father, exists from all eternity. His existence, like the Father's existence, is eternal, without any beginning.]   [13] John 1:1.

of His eternal Fatherhood: *"Before the day-star I begot you"*[14]—from the heart of Divinity, before ever creating light, I communicated Life to you. *"You are my beloved Son, in you I am well pleased."*[15]—you are my Son, my beloved Son, the object of all my delight. Because, indeed, this Son is perfect; He possesses with the Father all the divine perfections, save for the property of "being Father." So perfect is He, that He is the equal of His Father by unity of nature. A creature can only give to another creature a nature *like* his own—*"simile sibi."* But God begets God and gives Him His own nature. It is God's glory to beget the Infinite and to contemplate Himself in another "Himself" who is His equal—so equal that He is the only Son of the Father, for there is but one divine nature and this Son is the complete fullness of the eternal fecundity: "the only-begotten of the Father."[16] That is why He is one with His Father: "I and the Father are one."[17]

Finally, this beloved Son—equal to the Father yet distinct from Him, and a Divine Person as the Father is—does not leave the Father at all. The Word lives always within the Infinite Understanding who conceives Him; the Son lives always within the heart's-embrace of the Father who begets Him: *"Unigenitus Dei Filius qui est"*—who IS—*"in sinu Patris."*[18] The Son dwells there by virtue of the unity of nature [of the Father and the Son]. He dwells there, too, by virtue of the love they bear for each other, mutually—whence, as from one single Source, there proceeds the Holy Spirit, the substantial Love of the Father and the Son.

You see now what is the mysterious order of the ineffable communications of the inner life of God in the Trinity. The Father, the fullness of all life, begets a Son. From the Father and the Son, as from one Source only, proceeds the Spirit of Love. All three have the same eternity, the same infinity of perfection, the same wisdom, the same power, the same holiness—because the divine nature is one, only, for the three Persons.

---

[14] Ps. 109 (110):3.   [15] Mark 1:11; Luke 3:22.
[16] John 1:14; 1:18; 3:16; 3:18; 1 John 4:9.   [17] John 10:30.   [18] John 1:18.

But each Person possesses exclusive properties—those of "being Father," "being Son," "proceeding from the Father and the Son"—which establish the ineffable relations between themselves and distinguish them from each other. There is an order of origin, without there being any priority of time, or any hierarchical superiority, or any relation of dependence.

Such is the language of Divine Revelation; we would not have been able to arrive at a knowledge of these things if they had not been unveiled to us. But Christ Jesus has willed to make them known to us—for the exercise of our faith and the joy of our souls.[19] When, in eternity, we contemplate God, we shall see it as of the essence of infinite life, see that it is natural to the Divine Being to be One in Three Persons. The true God whom we must know in order to have everlasting life[20] is the God of whom we adore the Trinity of Persons in One-ness of nature.

Come, let us adore this marvelous fellowship in One-ness, this wonderful equality of perfection in the distinctness of Persons! O God, Father whose majesty is beyond measure, *Patrem immensae majestatis*, I adore you. I adore your Son, for He, like you, is worthy of all reverence, being your true and only Son, being God like you, *Venerandum tuum verum et unicum Filium*. O Father, O Son, I adore the Spirit common to you both, your eternal bond of love, *Sanctum quoque Paraclitum Spiritum*.[21] Blessed Trinity, I adore you!

---

[19] "Why plunge into these abysses? Why has Jesus Christ disclosed them to us? Why does He return to them so often? And can we not give serious attention to these truths, not forgetting the sublimity of the Christian doctrine? But we must give the attention *with trepidation*, we must give it in faith; we must, when hearing Jesus and His wholly divine words, believe that they come from One who is God; and at the same time believe also that this God from whom they come, Himself comes from God and that He is the Son; and at each word we hear we must rise upward to its very Source, must contemplate the Father in the Son and the Son in the Father": Bossuet, *Meditations on the Gospels*, The Last Supper, First Part, 86th day.   [20] "Now this is everlasting life, that they may know you, the only true God....": John 17:3.

[21] These Latin quotations of Marmion's are from the *Te Deum*.

2. **"Functions" of the Word in the Trinity.** He knows that everything comes to Him from the Father; He is the image of the Father; He relates Himself to the Father by love.

Let us now stay the eyes of our faith upon the Word, the Son, so as to know and be filled with wonder at some of the things concerning Him. It is the Son who, begotten eternally of the Father, was to be born of a virgin in the sphere of time so as to become the God-man and bring into being the mysteries of our salvation. How can we imitate Him, how can we stay united with Him, without first knowing Him?

In the Blessed Trinity, the Son is distinguished from the Father by His property of "being Son."

When we say of a man that he is someone's son, we establish two different things: his individual human nature and his position of being a son. It is not so within the Trinity. The Son is really and truly identified with the Divine nature (which He possesses in an indivisible way with the Father and the Holy Spirit). What distinguishes Him from the Person of the Father, what properly speaking constitutes His Personality, is not being God, but being Son. And, as a Divine Person, *He is nothing but the Son, entirely the Son, and that uniquely.* He is (if I may express it thus) a Living Sonship; He is "orientated" entirely towards the Father.

And in the same way that the Father proclaims His ineffable fecundity—"You are my Son; I have begotten you this day,"[22] the Son knows that He is Son, that the Father is His Fountainhead, His Source, and that everything comes from the Father. There (if one may put it like this) is the first "function" of the Word.

Open the Gospels, especially that of St. John, and you will see the Incarnate Word constantly drawing attention to this property so as to make it stand out in high relief. Christ loves to proclaim that, as the only Son, He holds all from His Father. "I live by the Father," He says to His apostles;[23] "My teaching is not my own, but

[22] Ps. 2:7 (Knox). [*Translator's note:* "This day" being the "eternal now" of eternity; see pp. 21 and 276.]   [23] John 6:58 (Rheims).

His who sent me";[24] "The Son can do nothing of Himself, but only what He sees the Father doing. For whatever He does, this the Son does also in like manner";[25] "I cannot of myself do any thing. As I hear, so I judge; and my judgment is just: because I seek not my own will, but the will of Him that sent me";[26] "I do nothing on my own authority but speak thus as the Father taught me."[27]

What does Our Lord want to make us understand by these mysterious words, if not that it is *as Son* that He holds all things from the Father, while being His equal? Everywhere, in all the remarkable circumstances of His life, as for example at the raising of Lazarus from the dead, Christ Jesus draws attention to the ineffable relationship that makes Him the only-begotten of the Eternal Father.

Read especially the discourse and prayer of Jesus at the Last Supper. There, as He comes to consummate His succession of mysteries by His sacrifice upon the cross, He lifts a corner of the veil that hides the divine life from our eyes, and you will see how insistently He comes back to the Eternal Sonship and the properties that are its privilege: "Father, the hour has come! Glorify your Son, that your Son may glorify you... Glorify me with yourself, with the glory that I had with you before the world existed..." The "men whom you have given me ... have learnt that whatever you have given me is from you"; they have truly "known that I came forth from you... and all things that are mine are yours, and yours are mine" ... Father, "keep in your name those whom you have given me, that they may be one even as we are ... I will that where I am, they also ... may be with me; in order that they may behold my glory, which you have given me, because you have loved me before the creation of the world."[28]

What a wonderful revelation these words confide to us, of the Father and the Son and of the incomprehensible relationship between them! Not indeed (to echo St. John at the beginning of

---

[24] John 7:16.   [25] John 5:19.   [26] John 5:30 (Rheims).
[27] John 8:28 (RSV, Cath.)   [28] John 17, vv. 1, 5, 6-8, 10-11, 24.

his Gospel) that we have ever seen God: but the only Son, who is in the heart's-embrace of the Father, has revealed something of the secrets of His life: "The only-begotten Son ... has revealed Him."[29] I believe, Lord Jesus, that you are the only-begotten Son of the Father, God as He is God. I believe this, but increase my faith!

The second "function" of the Word is to be, as St. Paul says, the image of the Father: "the image of the invisible God."[30]

Not just any image, but a perfect living image. The Word is the splendor of the Father's glory, the very image of His substance, the reflection of His eternal light: *the brightness of His glory and the image of His substance.*"[31] He is, as the Greek word indicates, the complete likeness—the stamp—of God the Father, like the impression a seal imprints upon the wax. The glory of a son is to be "the living image" of his father, and so it is with the Word. The Eternal Father, in beholding His Son, sees in Him the perfect reproduction of His own divine attributes. The Son reflects perfectly, as in "a spotless mirror,"[32] all that the Father gives Him.

And that is why the Father, in contemplating His Son, sees in Him all His own perfections; and, enraptured by the sight, declares to the world: "This is my beloved Son, in whom I am *well pleased*"[33]—that His Son is the object of all His delight.

Therefore the Word, when become incarnate, reveals the Father to us, manifests God to us. At the Last Supper, after He had spoken of His Father in terms that were so touching, He was asked by Philip: "Lord, show us the Father, and that will be enough for us"—we shall then be satisfied. And what does Christ Jesus reply? "Have I been with you all this time, and you still do not know me? Philip, *whoever sees me, sees my Father.*"[34] What a deep revelation those words are! It is enough for us to see Jesus, the Word Incarnate, in order to know the Father, of whom He is

---

[29] John 1:18.   [30] Col. 1:15.   [31] Hebr. 1:3.   [32] Wisdom 7:26 (RSV, Cath.)
[33] Matt. 3:17, 17:5; Mark 1:11; Luke 3:22; 2 Peter 1:17.   [34] See John 14: 8-9.

the image. Christ translates all the perfections of the Father into human actions, into language accessible to our poor minds. Let us always remember those words: "Whoever sees me, sees my Father."

We shall presently be running through the principal mysteries of Jesus. He whom we shall be contemplating *is God*. He is Infinite Being, Almighty and Sovereign. This child, lying in the manger and adored by the shepherds and wise men—is God. This adolescent who in a lowly workshop labors in manual work—is God. This man who heals the sick, who multiplies the loaves, who pardons sinners and saves souls—is God. He is God still, this prophet persecuted by His enemies; this man who, agonizing in Gethsemane, struggles against worry, fear and sadness; this condemned man who dies upon a cross. This Consecrated Host whom the tabernacle encloses, and whom I am about to receive at the Holy Table—this Host *consists of God*. "Whoever sees me, sees my Father."

And all the perfections which the states or mysteries of Jesus show forth: that incontrovertible wisdom; that power which astonishes or enraptures the crowds; that unprecedented mercy towards sinners; that passionate zeal for justice; that unalterable patience under insult; that love, self-giving and self-surrendering— these are the perfections of one who is God, our God: for whoever sees Jesus, sees the Father, contemplates God.

At the end of His priestly prayer, Christ said to His Father: "I have made you known to these my disciples, Father, and will continue to make you known, so that the love with which you have loved me may be in them..."[35] O Jesus, by your mysteries show us your Father, His perfections, His greatness, His rights, His will. Reveal to us what He is for you, what He is for us, so that we may love Him and He love us—and we shall then ask for nothing more: *"Show us the Father, and that will be enough for us!"*

· · ·

[35] See John 17:26.

The third "function" of the Word is to relate Himself to the Father by love.

Within the Blessed Trinity, the Son's love for the Father is infinite. The Word proclaims that He receives all from His Father, and likewise He relates that "all" to His Father, lovingly; and from this movement of tender love which meets that coming from the Father, proceeds the Third Person whom Divine Revelation calls by a mysterious name: *the Holy Spirit*, and who is the substantial Love of the Father and the Son.

Here below, Jesus's love for His Father shines forth in an ineffable way. All of the life of Christ, all His mysteries, are summed up in these words St. John reports to us: *"Diligo Patrem"*—"I love my Father." Our Lord has Himself indicated to His apostles the infallible criterion of love: *"If you keep my commandments,* you will abide in my love."[36] And immediately he gives Himself as example: "as I also have kept my Father's commandments, and abide in His love."[37] Jesus has abided constantly in the love of His Father, because He has always done His will. St. Paul expressly declares to us that the very first movement of heart of the Word-made-Flesh was a movement of love: "Behold, I come to do your will, O God."[38] In that first gaze of His life on earth, the soul of Jesus saw the whole succession of His mysteries—the abasements, the wearinesses and the sufferings of which they were formed, and, by one act of love, His soul agreed to carry out that program.

That movement of love towards His Father has never ceased. Our Lord was able to say: "I do always the things that are pleasing to Him."[39] He does everything the Father asks of Him, does it to the last iota. He accepts it—even as far as the bitter chalice of the agony: "Not my will but yours be done";[40] even as far as the ignominious death on a cross; *"that the world may know that I love the Father ... so do I."*[41] And when it is all completed, the last

---

[36] See John 14:31.   [37] John 15:10.   [38] Hebr. 10:5-7; Ps. 39(40): 7-9 (6-8).
[39] John 8:29.   [40] Luke 22:42.   [41] John 14:31 (Rheims).

beat of His heart, His last thought, are for His Father: "Father, into your hands I commend my spirit."[42]

The love of Jesus for His Father is the basis of all His states and explains all His mysteries.

3. We should imitate the Divine Word in His "states."

This Divine Word is our model, the very shape of our planned destiny. For, even after the Incarnation, He remains what He is: the Word co-eternal with the Father. That is why our imitation of Christ should extend not only to His human virtues, but also to His divine being.

Like Jesus and with Him, we should first recognize and declare that everything comes to Him from the Father.

When, at the Last Supper, Christ prays to His Father for His apostles, what grounds does He put forward for commending them to Him? "Father, the men you have entrusted to me know now that everything you have given me comes from you... They have truly recognized that I am come forth from you, and they have believed that it is you who have sent me. It is for them that I pray..."[43] The Word Incarnate insists that we recognize that He receives everything from His Father; so often has He repeated it to His disciples! *Our declaring it with Him is therefore pleasing to Him.*

Equally, our declaring it is pleasing to the Father. At that same Last Supper, Jesus said to His apostles: "The Father loves you." What words are sweeter, what words could make greater confidence arise in us, than those? Were they not spoken by Him who knows the secrets of the Father? "The Father loves you..." And what reason for that does Christ give? "Because you have loved me, and have believed that I am come forth from the Father."[44] Believing (with a faith put into practice, which delivers ourselves up to Him to serve Him), believing that Jesus, the Incarnate

---

[42] Luke 23:46.   [43] See John 17:6-9.   [44] See John 16:27.

Word, is come forth from the Father—this is the best way to please God.

Let us, therefore, with profound reverence, especially after holy communion, repeat the words of the *Credo*: "O Christ Jesus, you are the Word, eternally begotten of the Father; you are God from God, Light from Light, true God from true God, begotten not made, consubstantial with the Father. Through you all things were made. This is the song now on my lips; grant me grace to declare it through my works!"

We ought next to recognize that *we also* hold everything from the Father, and that by a twofold title: as created beings and as children of God.

As created beings. It is true to say that creation is the work of the entire Trinity. But, as you know, it is especially attributed to the Father.[45] Why is that? Because in the inner life of God, the Father is the eternal origin of the Son and, with the Son, the eternal origin of the Holy Spirit. That is why the outward works where the character of origin is especially revealed are attributed very particularly to the Father: "We believe in ... the Father, the Almighty, maker of heaven and earth."[46] The whole of creation came forth from the hands of the Father, not through an emanation of His nature, as the pantheists would have it, but because it was produced from nothing through the power of Divine Omnipotence.

It is very useful for us to recognize this dependence of ours, to rejoice at it. Certainly, God has no need our praise: but it is fitting for us to declare our condition as creatures, by giving thanks to Him who has given us being and life: O my God, it is you who have created me—"Your hands have made me, and fashioned me wholly round about."[47] Everything I have: body, soul, intellect, will, health—I hold it all from you, you who are my Creator: I

---

[45] We have explained at greater length this doctrine of *appropriation* in the talk on the Holy Spirit in our volume *Christ, the Life of the Soul.*

[46] Nicene Creed.   [47] Job 10:18.

adore you and thank you. In return I deliver myself up wholly and entirely to you, in order to carry out your will.

But the main reason for keeping alive such feelings within us is our status as children of God. The Divine Sonship of the Father's only-begotten is of the essence and eternal. But, in an infinitely free act of love, the Father has willed to add a sonship, a child-ship, of *grace*. He adopts us as His children, to the extent that one day we shall share in the beatitude of His own inner life. This is an inexplicable mystery; but faith tells us that when a soul receives sanctifying grace at baptism, that soul participates in the divine nature: "that you may become partakers of the divine nature";[48] the soul becomes truly a child of God: "You are gods, and all of you the sons of the Most High."[49] St. John speaks of a "divine birth": "born ... of God"[50]—not in the proper sense of the Word, by nature, not like the Word who is born in the heart's-embrace of the Father, but in some way that is analogous to that: "Of His own will He has begotten us by the word of truth."[51]

In a very real, a very true sense, we are divinely begotten by grace. With the Word, we can say: "O Father, I am your son, I have come forth from you." The Word says this necessarily, by right, He being of His essence God's only Son. But we—we can only say it through grace, in our capacity of adopted children. The Word says it from all eternity; but we say it in the sphere of time, though the decree of that destiny is eternal. For the Word, what He says indicates no more than a relation of *origin* with the Father. For us, there is added a relation of dependence. But for us, as for Him, it is a true childship; we are, by grace, God's children. The Father wills that, despite our unworthiness, we give Him the name of "Father": "Because you are sons, God has sent the Spirit of His Son into our hearts, crying 'Abba, Father.'"[52] He "sends the Spirit of His Son" for that. When we whisper "Father," our Father in heaven is pleased. This is something beyond words, but it is the truth.

[48] 2 Peter 1:4. [49] Ps. 81 (82):6; John 10:34. [50] John 1:13.
[51] James 1:18. [52] Gal. 4:6.

"Behold what manner of love *the Father* has bestowed upon us, that we should be called children of God; and *such we are.*"[53]

And, to give assurance of this decree of our adoption, to bring about this childship of love, God with magnificent largesse multiplies heavenly favors along our path: the Incarnation, the Church, the Sacraments (especially the Eucharist), the inspirations of His Spirit. And this, in such a way that "every good gift and every perfect gift is from above, coming down from the Father of Lights."[54]

This thought fills the soul with a great confidence, but also with deep humility. If I can put it this way, we need to make sure that everything we do begins from God. We should lay at His feet all our own thoughts, all our own judgment, all our own desires, so that we no longer think, judge, choose or act except as He wills. Didn't Jesus do precisely this? The Word Incarnate, He Himself, said that He "does only what He sees the Father doing."[55] That is how it should be with ourselves (due proportion being preserved between Him and us). We ought to make a sacrifice to God of what is disordered within us—the disorder of our feeling the need to be something of ourselves, to have only ourselves as support. And for this, before everything we do, let us implore the help of our Heavenly Father, as Jesus did.

That is the homage, a practical homage, by which we recognize our dependence on our Father who is also our God; and by which we declare, as Jesus declared that everything we have, is from the Father. The apostles, He said to His Father, have learned "that all you have given me comes indeed from you."[56]

We ought also to imitate the Word in that He is the image of the Father. Holy Scripture tells us that God has created us in His own image and likeness. As created beings, we bear within us traces of God's power, wisdom and goodness.

[53] 1 John 3:1. [54] James 1:17. [55] John 5:19. [56] John 17:7 (Jerus.)

But it is above all through sanctifying grace that we become like God. As St. Thomas says, this grace is "a shared similitude to the Divine nature."[57] To employ a theological term, grace is *deiform*, because it puts within us a likeness to God. When He contemplates His Word, the Father exclaims, on beholding the perfection of His Son who, begotten of Him, reflects so exactly His own perfection: "You are my beloved Son, in you I am well pleased."[58] Something analogous happens in regard to a soul adorned with grace; the Father takes delight in that soul. Jesus said: "If anyone love me ... my Father will love him, and we will come to him and make our abode with him."[59]

Sanctifying grace is the first and fundamental element of our assimilation to God, of the divine likeness within us. But we must also be the image of our Father by our virtues. Christ Jesus told us this Himself: "You, therefore, must be perfect, as your heavenly Father is perfect."[60] Imitate His goodness, His forbearance, His mercy: it is thus that you will reproduce His features in you. "Be you," repeats St. Paul after Jesus, "imitators of God," as is fitting for "very dear children."[61]

Doubtless this resemblance is not visible to the eyes of flesh, although it reveals itself externally by works of holiness. It is within the soul that it takes shape and is perfected. Here below, its brightness is hidden, its splendor is veiled. But the day will come when it will shine forth and be manifested to the eyes of all. When we see God "just as He is," we "shall be like to Him," because on that day we shall be pure mirrors where Divinity will come and be reflected: "We shall be like to Him, for we shall see Him just as He is."[62]

. . .

---

[57] St. Thomas Aquinas, *Summa Theologica*, III, q. LXII, a. 1.   [58] Mark 1:11; Luke 3:22; see also Matt. 3:17; 17:5; Mark 9:6; Luke 9:35; 2 Peter 1:17.
[59] John 14:23.   [60] Matt. 5:48 (RSV, Cath.)   [61] Eph. 5:1.   [62] 1 John 3:2.

Finally, like the Word, we should relate ourselves, in all of our being, to our Heavenly Father through love. Everything within us ought to come from God through grace; everything within us ought to return to our Father by a movement of love. God should be, not only the beginning but also the goal of all our works.

In order that our works be pleasing to our Father in heaven, they must be animated by love. In all things, whether what we do is big or little, illustrious or hidden from others, we ought to seek no other glory than that of our Father, to act with nothing in view except the glorifying of His name, the extending of His reign and the accomplishing of His will. There we have the whole secret of holiness.

4. How Christ is the means established by God for bringing into effect within us a sharing in the Sonship of His Word.

The marvels of the divine adoption are so great that human language can never sound their depths. It is a wonderful thing for God to adopt us as His children; but the means He has chosen for effecting and establishing that adoption within us is something more wonderful still. And what is this means? It is His own Son: "in His beloved Son."[63] I have already expounded this truth elsewhere,[64] but so vital is it, that I cannot refrain from going back to it here.

God creates us by His Word. After having said: "In the beginning [of creation] ... the Word was God," St. John adds: "All things were made by Him: and without Him was made nothing that was made."[65] What do these words signify? In the Blessed Trinity, the Word is the expression, not only of all the perfections of the Father, but also of all possible created beings. The

---

[63] Eph. 1:26.   [64] *Christ, the Life of the Soul*, section 4 ("Effecting of this decree...") of Book I, Ch. 1.   [65] John 1, vv. 1, 3 (Rheims).

latter have in the Divine Essence their prototype and their Exemplar. When God creates, He produces beings that realize, are the actualizations of, one of His thoughts. Further, He creates by the power of His word: "He spoke and they were made."[66] That is why Holy Scripture says that the Father creates all things by His Word.

You can already see what an intimate relation with the Word is established in us by creation. From the sole fact of our creation, we correspond to a divine idea, we are the fruit of an eternal thought contained in the Word. God knows His own essence perfectly; expressing this knowledge, He begets His Word; and He sees in His Word the Exemplar of every created being. Thus, each one of us represents a divine thought, and our individual holiness consists in bringing into effect this thought which God has conceived of us before our creation.

In one sense, therefore, we proceed from God through the Word; and we ought, like the Word, to be the pure, perfect expression of the thought of God concerning us. What stands in the way of this thought's becoming reality is the distortion that we bring to the work of God. For *distorting the divine*—such indeed is the work that is *our* sole prerogative within creation—"our sole prerogative" meaning that it belongs to us alone, God being excluded. So, all that comes from us and is in disharmony with the divine will: sin, infidelities, resistances to inspirations from on high, views which are purely human and natural—these are so many things by which we spoil the divine idea of ourselves.

But in the work of our adoption, this relation with the Word, the Son, is a much more profound one still.

The Apostle James tells us that "every good gift"—every grace—"is from above, coming down from the Father of Lights," and he adds: "Of His own will He has begotten us by the word of truth."[67] Divine adoption through grace which makes us children of God is brought into effect by the Son, by the Word.

[66] Ps. 148:5.   [67] James 1:17-18.

This truth is one of those to which St. Paul returns most often. Like St. James, he declares that all blessings spring from the Father and that all of them come down to is the decree of our adoption in Jesus Christ, His beloved Son. In the eternal plan, we only become children of God in Jesus Christ, the Word Incarnate: He has chosen us "in Him."[68] The Father will only recognize us as His children if we bear within us the features of His Son Jesus: He planned that we be "conformed to the image of His Son."[69] Thus, it is only in the capacity of co-heirs with Christ that we are one day to be "in the heart's-embrace of the Father."

That is the divine purpose. Let us now look at the bringing into effect, in the sphere of time, of this eternal decree; or rather, the way in which the divine plan (which the sin of Adam had cut across) has been restored.

The Eternal Word was made flesh. The Psalmist says that this Word ran forwards from the starting-line: "rejoiced as a giant to run the course."[70] It was from highest heaven, "*a summo coelo*," that He arose, like the sun: and it was to this sublime summit that He went up again—up to the highest heaven, "*ad summum ejus.*" This coming forth, like the sun from the heavens, is His eternal dawn in the heart's-embrace of the Father: "I came forth from the Father."[71] His return is His ascension to the Father: "I leave the world and go to the Father."[72]

But He does not go up unaccompanied. This giant was sent to seek lost humanity: He regains it; and, in an embrace of love, bears it away with Him along the course He runs, so as to place it near Him in the heart's-embrace of the Father: "I ascend to my Father, who is also your Father."[73] I go there to "prepare a place for you"—a place in "my Father's house."[74]

Such is the work of this divine giant: to bring back fallen humanity into the heart's-embrace of the Father, to the divine

---

[68] Eph. 1:3-4.   [69] Rom. 8:29.   [70] Ps. 18 (19):6.   [71] John 16:28.
[72] Ibid.   [73] See John 20:17.   [74] John 14:2.

source of all bliss, by giving it back the grace of adoption through His life and His sacrifice.

Oh, let us say, with the St. Paul: "Blessed be the Lord and Father of Our Lord Jesus Christ for having, through His Son and in His Son, filled us with every spiritual blessing";[75] for having enabled us to sit with the Father in those celestial splendors where, in the midst of eternal happiness, He begets[76] the Son of His delight: "He has seated us together in heaven in Christ Jesus."[77] Oh, blessed be the Father! Blessed also be the Divine Word, who was made flesh for us, and who, through the shedding of His blood, has restored our the eternal inheritance. O Jesus, beloved Son of the Father, to you be all praise and all glory!

5. Practical consequence of these doctrines: remaining united to the Incarnate Word through faith, works, and the Sacrament of Penance.

What are now for us the *practical consequences* of these doctrines?

As the Eternal Father has decreed that we be His children, but that we be this only *in His Son*, by being "adopted *through Jesus Christ*,"[78] as He has decided that we have part in the inheritance of His beatitude only through His Son, therefore we can only make the divine plan become actuality for us, and assure our salvation in consequence, by remaining united to the Son, to the Word. Let us never forget: there is for us no other way for us to go to the Father: "No-one comes to the Father but through me."[79] *No-one* can flatter himself that He can reach the Father otherwise than through the Son. And going to the Father—is not this the whole of salvation and the whole of sanctity?

---

[75] See Eph. 1:3.   [76] [*Translator's note:* Marmion, speaking the language of eternity, not time, uses the present tense here, "*engendre,*" "begets," not "begot." The eternal begetting of the Son, a "begetting" that has no beginning, has no ending either, for its context is the eternal but dynamic "now" of God's existence, a concept that, here below, is beyond our experience and understanding.]

[77] See Eph. 2:6.   [78] Eph. 1:5.   [79] John 14:6.

Well, how shall we remain united to the Word, to the Son?

In the first place, *by faith*. "In the beginning was the Word ... and the Word was God... All things were made by Him."[80] He came into this world made by Him, and "His own received Him not." But to "as many as received Him," He gave the power to become children of God—to those "that believe in His name" and therefore are "born ... of God."[81]

The whole of our perfection consists in our faithful imitation of the Son of God. Now, St. Paul tells us that all fatherhood comes down from the Father: "from whom all fatherhood in heaven and on earth receives its name."[82] One can say also of the Son: "From whom all sonship receives its name." It is He alone, the Son, who, through His Spirit, teaches us how we are to be sons: "Because you are sons, God has sent the Spirit of *His Son* into our hearts, crying 'Abba, Father.'"[83]

We ought to receive the Son Himself—to see in Him, whatever be the state in which we behold Him, the Word co-eternal with the Father. Next, we ought to receive His teachings, His doctrine. He is in the heart's-embrace of the Father; and by His words He reveals to us what He knows: "The only-begotten Son ... He has revealed Him."[84] Faith is the knowledge we have, through the Word, of divine mysteries. Whatever page of the Gospels we read or the Church presents to us in the course of the celebration of the mysteries of her Spouse, let us therefore say: "These are the words of the Word"—*Verba Verbi*; the words of Him who expresses the thoughts, the desires, the wishes of our Father in heaven: "This is my beloved Son: *Hear Him*."[85] Let us sing *Amen* to everything we hear from the Word, to every page which, in the liturgy, the Church picks out from the Gospels to propose it to our faith. Let us say to God: "O Father, I do not know you, since I have never seen you; but I accept everything your Divine Son, your Word, reveals to me about you." That is an excellent prayer; and often, when it is made with

---

[80] John 1, vv. 1, 3 (Rheims).   [81] John 1:10-13.   [82] Eph. 3:15.
[83] Gal. 4:6.   [84] John 1:18.   [85] Matt. 17:5; Mark 9:6; Luke 9:35.

faith and humility, a ray of light descends from above, from "the Father of Lights,"[86] illuminating those texts we read and making us penetrate their depths so that we find sources of life there.

For the Word is the expression not only of the perfections of His Father, but also of everything the Father wills. All that the Word commands us, prescribes for us in His Gospels or through His Church, is the expression of the adorable will and desires of our Heavenly Father. And if we carry out (above all, if we carry out through love) the commands Jesus gives us, we remain united to Him, and, through Him, to the Father: "If you keep my commandments you will *abide* in my love,"[87] and: "Anybody who loves me will be loved by my Father."[88]

There is the whole formula for sanctity: Adhere to the Word, to His doctrine, to His commands; and, through Him, to the Father who sent Him and gives Him the words we ought to receive.[89]

Finally, we remain united to the Word above all through the sacrament of union, the Eucharist. This is the Bread of Life, "the children's Bread."[90] Under the Eucharistic species is truly hidden the Word, He who is born eternally in the depths of the Godhead. What a mystery! He whom I receive in holy communion is the Son, begotten of the Father from all eternity, the beloved Son to whom the Father communicates His own Life, His Divine Life, the fullness of His Being and His infinite beatitude. How great a reason Our Lord had to say: "As I live because of the Father, so he who eats me, he also shall live because of me";[91] "He who eats my flesh ... abides in me and I in him."[92]

If we ask Our Lord what we can do that will be most pleasing to His sacred heart, it is certain that, above all things, He will tell us to be like Him, to be a child of God. If, therefore, we wish to please Him, let us receive Him every day in Eucharistic Com-

---

[86] James 1:17.   [87] John 15:10.   [88] John 14:21 (Jerus.)
[89] Cf. John 17:8: "...the words that you have given me I have given to them."
[90] Sequence, *Lauda Sion*, Feast of Corpus Christi.
[91] John 6:58.   [92] Ibid., v. 57.

munion, and say to Him: "O Jesus, you are the Son of God, the perfect image of your Father; you know the Father, you are wholly His, you behold His Face. Increase in me the grace of adoption that makes me a child of God; teach me to be, through your grace and my virtues, teach me to be, like you and in you, a worthy child of the Heavenly Father." It is certain that if we beg for this grace, the Word will give it to us.

He Himself has told us that He wills only what the Father wills: "I seek not my own will, but the will of Him who sent me."[93] It follows that the Son enters fully into how the Father sees things; and when He gives Himself it is for the purpose of establishing, preserving and increasing within us the grace of adoption. The whole of His personal divine Life consists of being *ad Patrem*, directed towards the Father. In giving Himself to us, he gives Himself as He is—entirely "orientated" towards His Father and His Father's glory. And that is why when we receive Him with faith, trust and love, He makes real in us our own orientation towards the Father. It is this that we ought constantly to be asking and seeking: that all our thoughts, all our aspirations, all our desires, all our activity may go, by the grace of childship and love, to our Heavenly Father in His Son Jesus: "Alive for God in Christ Jesus."[94]

6. These truths, sublime though they are, constitute the very foundation of Christianity and the substance of all holiness.

These, you will say to me, are very elevated truths; this state is a very sublime one. That is true; and yet have I done anything other than to repeat to you what the Word Himself has revealed to us, what St. John and St. Paul have restated to us after Jesus? No, these are not dreams, but realities—divine realities.

[93] John 5:30.   [94] Rom. 6:11 (Jerus.)

And these realities constitute the very substance of Christianity. We shall understand nothing—I do not say only of perfection, of holiness, but even of simple Christianity—if we do not grasp that its most essential foundation is constituted by the state of a child of God; participation, through sanctifying grace, in the eternal Sonship of the Word Incarnate. All the teachings of Christ and of the apostles come down to this truth; all the mysteries of Jesus aim at establishing in our souls this wonderful reality.

Let us, then, never forget it. The whole of the Christian life, like the whole of sanctity, amounts to *being by grace what Jesus is by nature: the Son of God.* This is what constitutes the sublimity of our religion. The source of all Jesus's greatness, of the value of all His states, of the fruitfulness of all His mysteries, is His divine begetting and the fact that He is the Son of God. Likewise, the highest saint in heaven is the one who here below was most perfectly a child of God, who made the super-natural adoption in Jesus Christ bear the greatest fruit.

That is why all our spiritual life should be tied to this fundamental truth; all the work of perfection should come down to safeguarding faithfully, and making blossom in largest possible measure, our participation in the Divine Sonship of Jesus.

And let us not say that such life is too elevated, that such a program is beyond achieving. Yes, for our nature left to itself, that life is beyond the exigencies, the laws, the strengths of our being—that is why we call it *super-natural,* above our nature.

But our Heavenly Father "knows what you need";[95] He calls us to Him, but He also gives us the means to reach Him. He gives us His Son, so that His Son may be our Way, may deliver Truth to us, and communicate Life to us. For us one day to share in His glory in the heart's-embrace of the Father, it is enough that we remain united to this Son through grace and our virtues.

[95] Matt. 6:8.

Look, what did Jesus say to Mary Magdalene after His resurrection? "I am ascending to my Father": and then He adds: "who is also your Father."[96] And what was He going to do? To prepare a place for us: "I go to prepare a place for you," for "in my Father's house there are many mansions."[97]

He has ascended into His Father's presence, but as a precursor: "Our forerunner Jesus has entered for us."[98] He has preceded us there, but so that we may follow Him there. For life here below is only a passing thing, a time of trial. "In this world you will have tribulations," said Jesus in the same discourse[99]—you will have obstacles within you to overcome; temptations by the prince of this world to bear; difficulties arising from things that will happen: for "the servant is not greater than his master."[100]

But, He added: "Do not let your heart be troubled," do not be discouraged; "Have faith and trust in God and in me"[101]—I who am equally God and who "am with you all days, even until the consummation of the world."[102] "You shall be sorrowful, but your sorrow will be turned into joy";[103] I truly "am coming again, and I will take you to myself; that where I am"—in the kingdom of my Father—"there you also may be."[104]

O Divine promise given by the Uncreated Utterance of God, by the Word in person, by Infallible Truth, a promise full of sweetness: "I myself am coming again"! We shall belong to Christ, and through Him to the Father, in the heart's-embrace of His beatitude. In that day, says Christ, you will know—not *in umbra fidei*, in the darkness of faith, but in the full radiance of eternal light, *in lumine gloriae*—will know "that I am in my Father, and you in me, and I in you."[105] You will see my glory—the glory "of the only-begotten of the Father"[106]—and this blest sight will be for you the everlasting wellspring of an imperishable joy.

---

[96] See John 20:17.   [97] John 14:2.   [98] Hebr. 6:20.   [99] See John 16:33.
[100] John 15:20 (Rheims).   [101] See John 14:1.   [102] Matt. 28:20.
[103] John 16:20.   [104] John 14:3. [*Translator's note*: This refers to the Second Coming of Christ on the Last Day, when the bodies of the departed will be resurrected and joined again to their immortal souls.]   [105] John 14:20.   [106] John 1:14.

CHAPTER FOUR

"And The Word Was Made Flesh"

Introduction: Christ is perfect God and perfect man.

"In the beginning was the Word ... and the Word was God... And the Word was made flesh, and dwelt among us."[1]

Christ is the Word Incarnate. Revelation teaches us that the Second Person of the Blessed Trinity, the Word, the Son, took to Himself a human nature, so as to unite Himself personally to it. That is the mystery of the Incarnation.

Let us pause a few moments to consider this dogma—as unprecedented as it is touching—of a *God-man*. It is the fundamental mystery on which all the mysteries of Jesus rest. Their beauty, their splendor, their power, their strength, their value, all derive from this ineffable union of the humanity to the divinity. We shall not understand them properly unless we have first considered the underlying mystery, both in itself and in the general consequences that flow from it. Jesus is God and man; if we want to know Jesus the Person, to participate in His states, we must endeavor to understand not only that He is the Word, but also that this Word has been *"made flesh."* If we want to honor Him worthily, it is just as necessary for us to recognize the reality of His human nature as it is to adore the divinity to which this nature is united.

[1] John 1, vv. 1, 14.

What are there in Christ, according to our faith?

Two natures—the human nature and the divine nature. Christ is perfect God and perfect man, both together. Further, these two natures are united in so close a way that there is only one single Person, that of the Divine Word in whom the humanity subsists. From this union results the infinite value of Jesus's actions, of His states, of His mysteries.

Let us contemplate these truths. From that contemplation, made with humility and love, will spring forth, quite naturally, the feelings which ought to animate us in the face of this mystery.

1. **Christ is perfect God and perfect man. Ineffable union of the divine and the human in the life of Our Lord.**

Christ is perfect God and perfect man.

When He presents Himself to us in the manger at Bethlehem, in the workshop at Nazareth, on the roads of Judea, seated in the synagogues teaching, nailed to the cross, or ascending glorious to heaven, He manifests Himself at one and the same time *as God and as man*.

He is perfect God. In taking to Himself our human nature, the Word remains what He is: "what He was, He remained"[2]—God, the Eternal Being, possessing all life, all perfection, all sovereignty, all power and all beatitude in their fullness.

Let us listen to the Incarnate Word Himself proclaim His divinity: "As the Father has life in Himself, even so Has He given to the Son also to have life in Himself"[3]—eternal life, divine life. "My Father and I are one."[4] "Whatever the Father does the Son does too."[5] Addressing the Father: "All I have is yours and all you have is mine."[6] Look at it: there is an identity of perfections, an equality of rights, because there is unity of nature.

Christ is the Son of God, and consequently is Himself God.

[2] Antiphon for the Feast of the Circumcision.   [3] John 5:26.
[4] John 10:30 (Knox).   [5] John 5:19 (Jerus.)   [6] John 17:10 (Jerus.)

The Pharisees recognize that only God can forgive sins. In their presence, so as to show that He is God, Jesus pardons the paralytic man and underlines the gracious gift of forgiveness by working a miracle.[7] He declares that He is the Bread of Life that has come down from heaven, the Bread that gives life eternal:[8] and likewise that He alone can, by His own power, ascend into heaven, because He alone has come down from heaven.[9] And thus He asks His Father that the humanity which He, the Word, has taken be glorified "with the glory that I had with you before the world existed"[10]—the eternal glory He possesses as the Word, as God. He treats as equal to equal with God, because He is the very Son of God.

Perfect God, Christ is also perfect man: "And the Word was made flesh."[11] He took to Himself a human nature from us, a human nature that He made His own by uniting Himself to it physically, substantially, personally, by ineffable bonds: "What He was *not*, He took to Himself."[12]

This Being, necessarily subsistent of Himself—Eternal God—is born in the sphere of time, "born of a woman."[13] Christ has, like us, a human nature—complete, entire in its constituent elements: "It was right that He should in all things be made like unto His brethren."[14] Like us, Christ has a created soul, endowed with faculties like ours; His body is a real body, formed from the most pure blood of His mother. There were in the early days of the Church those who asserted that the Word had taken only the *semblance* of a human body; but the Church condemned them as heretics. Christ is authentically one of us—one of our human race. He genuinely suffered hunger, thirst, fatigue, as the Gospels show. He shed tears, and sufferings weighed down His soul and His body

---

· [7] Mark 2:1-12.   [8] John 6:51-52.   [9] John 3:13.   [10] John 17:5.

[11] John 1:14.   [12] Antiphon cited above: *Quod fuit permansit; quod non erat assumpsit*, "What He was, He remained. What He was not, He took to Himself."

[13] Gal. 4:4.   [14] Hebr. 2:17.

as truly as they overwhelm ours. Even after His Resurrection, He retains this human nature; He was concerned to prove the reality of it to His incredulous disciples: "See my hands and my feet ... handle me and see; for a spirit has not flesh and bones as you see that I have."[15] And as they still remain skeptical, He said to them: "Have you anything here to eat?" They offered Him a piece of broiled fish and a honeycomb. He took these, and ate in their presence.

Everything that is ours, He has made His own—"*sin excepted.*"[16] Christ has known neither sin nor that which is the source or moral consequence of sin: concupiscence, error, ignorance. His flesh is susceptible of suffering because He comes to expiate sins by suffering; but sin itself has no hold on Him: "Which of you can convict me of sin?"[17] This challenge issued to the Jews remained unanswered; and, in order to condemn Christ to death, it was necessary to have recourse to false witnesses. He is a man, but a man of unstained purity, as befits the dignity of this God-man: "holy, innocent, undefiled, set apart from sinners."[18]

Christ, then, possesses a divine nature and a human nature; He is at one and the same time God and man, perfect God and perfect man.

Open the Gospels, and on each page you will see that in everything He does or accomplishes, the Word Incarnate shows Himself to be God and man.[19] The divinity and the humanity are everywhere manifested, each according to its nature and properties.

Christ is born of a woman; but He wills that His mother be and remain a virgin. In the manger, He is a baby who needs a little milk to sustain Him; but angels celebrate His coming as that of

---

[15] Luke 24:39 (RSV, Cath.)   [16] Hebr. 4:15.   [17] John 8:46.
[18] Hebr. 7:26.   [19] "Christ always did this, in His words and His deeds, so that He might be believed to be God and man; the God who made us, the man who sought us ... so that to be the Christ, made man, He should not desist from being God. Remaining God, He who made man, took man to Himself": St. Augustine, *Tract. in Johann.*, XXVIII.

the Savior of the world. He is put to bed upon straw in a stable; but a marvelous star leads the wise men from the East to His feet. Like every Jewish boy, He undergoes circumcision; but at the same time He receives a name that comes from heaven and that indicates a divine mission.[20] He "grows in age and wisdom";[21] but when twelve years old He throws the very doctors of the Law into admiration by His astonishing answers. He allows Himself to be baptized by John, His precursor, as though He stood in need of penance; but at that same time the heavens are opened, and the Eternal Father witnesses to His being "my beloved Son."[22] In the desert, He feels hungry; but angels come and minister to Him.[23] During His journeys through Palestine, He suffers weariness, thirst, destitution; but, at a word, by His own authority, He makes paralytics walk, He cures the lame,[24] He multiplies loaves of bread so that thousands who are gathered around Him eat and are filled.[25] On the Sea of Galilee, sleep closes His eyelids whilst His disciples struggle against a storm; but a moment after being roused from His slumber by the frightened apostles, He calms the furious waves by one gesture of His hand.[26] At Lazarus's tomb, He is moved, He sheds tears—real human tears; but by a word He raises to life His friend who had been dead for four days.[27] In the garden of Gethsemane, after an agony full of worry, sorrow and distress, He lets Himself be captured by His enemies:[28] but it is enough for Him to declare that He is Jesus of Nazareth, for them to draw back and fall to the ground.[29] On the cross, He dies like the most despised of men; but the whole of nature proclaims, by the upheaval it undergoes, that this one who dies on the cross is God.[30]

[20] "You must name Him 'Jesus'" (Savior): Luke 1:32 (Jerus.)   [21] See Luke 2:52.
[22] Matt. 3:17; Mark 1:11; Luke 3:22.   [23] Matt. 3, vv. 2, 11; Mark 1:13.
[24] Matt. 11:4-6; 15:30-31; 21:14; Luke 7:22.   [25] Matt. 14:19-21; Mark 6:39-44; Luke 9:14-17; John 6:7-13.   [26] Matt. 8:23-27; Mark 4:35-40.
[27] John 11:32-44.   [28] Matt. 26:36-50; Mark 14:32-46; Luke 22:39-54.
[29] John 18:6.   [30] Matt. 27:51-53.

So, to quote the beautiful words of St. Leo: "Majesty is united to lowliness, power to weakness, that which is mortal to that which is eternal ... an inviolable nature to a nature capable of suffering... True God is born into the nature—the whole and perfect nature— of a true man, entirely with what is His, entirely also with what is ours": *Totus in suis, totus in nostris.*[31]

Everywhere, from the very entrance of Jesus into this world, there is manifested in Him the union of divinity and humanity— a union which takes away nothing of the divine perfections and which leaves intact the reality of the human nature. The Incarnation is an ineffable union.[32]

O Eternal Wisdom, how deep your thoughts are, and how wonderful your works!

2. The mode of union: the two natures are united in one and the same Divine Person.

What puts the finishing touch to making this mystery astonishing is the manner in which the union of natures is effected.

The human nature and the divine nature are united in one sole Person, who is the eternal Person of the Word, of the Son.

In us, the soul and the body, united to each other, form a human person. In Christ, it is by no means the same as this. His human nature, which is entire, complete, both in its essence and its constituent elements, nevertheless only has existence through the Word, in the Divine Person of the Word. It is the Word who gives this human nature real existence—which in the circumstances is to say, its personal "subsistence." There is thus in Jesus but one single Person, that of the only Son of God.

---

[31] St. Leo the Great, *Epistola* (28) *dogmatica* to Bishop Flavian of Constantinople.   [32] "Recognize the Mediator between God and men, who from the beginning of His Nativity allies human things with divine, the lowliest with the highest": St. Bernard, *Sermo* I *de Circumcisione.*

Yet, you know, as intimately united as they be, the two natures keep their particular energies and their specific operations. Between the two natures there is no mixture or confusion: united inseparably in the one Person of the Word, each of them retains the authority proper to it.

Finally, the human nature is rooted in the divinity. It is a human activity which manifests itself in Jesus—an activity *really*, authentically human; but it has its ultimate mainspring in the divinity. The Divine Person of the Word is the source of all the perfections of Christ. In the Blessed Trinity, the Word expresses the perfections of the Father by an infinitely simple act. By uniting Himself to the humanity, the Word expresses the Father's perfections through that humanity, in many and varied acts conformed to the human nature. Thus does a ray of light, passing through a prism, emerge from it as a beam in which the light is separated into different shades of color. The virtues of the sacred humanity of Jesus: His patience, His gentleness, His goodness, His meekness, His kindness, His zeal, His love, are virtues which are put into action through the human nature but which, having their deep root in the divinity, at the same time show to the eyes of us on earth the perfections of the invisible God. Human in its outward expression, the life of Jesus is divine in its source and wellspring.

What is the consequence of that doctrine? You know the answer, but it is extremely useful to return to it.

It is that all the actions of Jesus are the actions of one who is God. The actions of the sacred humanity are finite actions, limited in time and space—just as the sacred humanity is a created one. But their moral value is divine. Why is that? Because every action, even though it be carried out through such or such a faculty of nature, is attributable to the *person*. In Christ, it is always God *who* acts, but sometimes *through* His divine nature, sometimes *through* His human nature. It is therefore true to say that it is *one who is God* who toiled, who wept, who suffered, who died—even though all these actions were carried out through the human nature. However minimal they be in their physical reality, all the actions of Christ Jesus have a divine value.[33]

And that is why Christ's whole life is so pleasing to His Father. The Father finds all His delight in Jesus, in His Person and in His actions, in the most humiliating of His states as in His most glorious mysteries, because always He sees the Person of His own and only-begotten Son. The Father, in gazing at Christ Jesus, sees Him as no created being has ever seen Him. If I can put it this way, He is the only one who appreciates the worth of everything His Son does. As Our Lord Himself said: "No-one knows the Son except the Father."[34] Try as we may to raise our souls high and to immerse ourselves deep in the mysteries and the states of Jesus, we shall never come to appreciate them as they deserve. Only one who is God *could* understand, could recognize properly, what one who is God does. But to the eyes of the Father, the smallest actions of the humanity of Jesus, the very least movements of His sacred heart, were a source of rapture and joy.

Another reason why the Eternal Father contemplates the soul of Jesus with delight is that it is a soul filled with every grace. After having proclaimed the divinity of the Word and the reality of His incarnation, St. John adds immediately: "And we saw His glory ... *full of grace and of truth.*"[35]

What is this fullness of grace that St. John admired in Jesus, and of which he said: "From His fullness have we all received, grace upon grace"?[36]

In Christ, there is first, as you know, the "grace of union," *gratia unionis*, by virtue of which a human nature is united substantially to a Divine Person. Through this grace the union that

---

[33] In theological terms, these actions are called *theandric*, from two Greek words, signifying: divine-human. [34] Matt. 11:27.

[35] John 1:14. [36] John 1:16 (RSV, Cath.)

constitutes the Incarnation is effected. It is a unique grace, the only one of its kind, and it was given to Christ Jesus alone.

In addition, Jesus's soul, created as our souls are, has been endowed with the fullness of sanctifying grace. Through the grace of union, the humanity in Jesus became the humanity of one who is God. Through sanctifying grace, the soul of Jesus was rendered worthy of being and acting in a way that was fitting for a soul united to God by a personal union. This sanctifying grace was given to Jesus in all its fullness. To us it is given in greater or lesser measure, according to the designs of God and our co-operation. To Jesus, it was conferred in its fullness, as much because of His personal position, that of Son of God, as because of His title of head of the mystical body to whose members He was to distribute that grace: "according to the measure of Christ's bestowal."[37]

Finally, the humanity of Jesus is holy because it possesses in an incomparable degree the virtues (those at least that are compatible with His dignity as God's only Son)—because that humanity is adorned to a unique extent[38] with the gifts of the Holy Spirit.

Nothing, then, is lacking to the humanity of Jesus for it to be worthy of the Word to whom it is united. In that humanity is indeed the fullness of every grace: we saw Him "full of grace and of truth." All the treasures of wisdom and knowledge,[39] without any limit to them, can be found gathered together in Jesus. He has "the first place," for "it has pleased God the Father that all His own fullness should dwell in Him," Christ[40] and should remain there for ever. This in such wise that St. Paul says: "In Him dwells *all the fullness* of the Godhead bodily, and in Him who is the *head* of every principality and power, you have received of that fullness."[41] In this, St. Paul echoes St. John's "From His fullness we have all received"—received because He is our head.

---

[37] Eph. 4:7.   [38] "He whom God has sent speaks the word of God, for not by measure does God give the Spirit": John 3:34.   [39] Col. 2:3.
[40] See Col. 1:18-19.   [41] Col. 2:9-10.

3. **Our duties towards the Word Incarnate: first of all,
to recognize Him as God, by faith, adoration and
submission.**

What should be the attitude of our soul in the presence of this
fundamental mystery of the God-man?

The first attitude we should have is that of faith. I have already said it to you, but this truth is one of capital importance,
which is why I am not afraid of coming back to it now.

At the beginning of his Gospel, after having sung the glory of
the Divine Word, St. John points out that the Word came into
this world, and that this world—that He had created, that was
His domain, that was "His own"—did not receive Him. But, St.
John adds, all those who "believe in His name" receive Him.[42] We
receive the Incarnate Word *through faith*. Through faith we accept
the divinity of Jesus: "You are the Christ, the Son of the living
God."[43]

This is the attitude the Eternal Father requires of us. "This is
His *commandment*, that we should believe in the name of His
Son Jesus Christ...," says St. John.[44] It is exactly what the Father
has said to us Himself: "This is my beloved Son; hear Him."[45]
These words, heard on Mount Tabor when the splendor of the divinity filled with its rays the sacred humanity of Jesus, are but
echoes, in the created world, of what the Eternal Father declares
in "the brightness of the saints,"[46] in the sanctuary of heaven:
"You are my Son, this day [in an eternal present] have I begotten
you."[47]

So we are very pleasing to our Heavenly Father when, accepting His testimony, we profess that Jesus is His own Son, who is
co-eternal with Him, and who shares with Him the divine glory:
"You alone are the Most High, Jesus Christ, with the Holy Spirit,
in the glory of God the Father."[48]

---

[42] John 1:10-12.   [43] Matt. 16:16; John 11:27.   [44] 1 John 2:23.
[45] Mark 9:6; Luke 9:35; Matt. 1:5.   [46] Ps. 109 (110):3.
[47] Ps. 2:7.   [48] *Sanctus* of the Mass.

It is what St. Paul says. The mystery of the self-abasement of the Word-made-flesh plunges the apostle into such depths of wonder that he does not have the words to proclaim the glory which, according to the mind of God Himself, is to accrue to Jesus as a result of it. Listen to what he says: "Christ Jesus, who though He was by nature God, did not consider being equal to God a thing to be clung to,[49] but emptied Himself, taking the nature of a slave and being made like unto men"—putting Himself into the condition of a created being. "And appearing in the form of man"—showing Himself to be a man in all things—"He humbled Himself, becoming obedient to death, even to death on a cross. *Therefore*"—that is why—"God also has exalted Him and has bestowed upon Him the name that is above every name, so that at the name of Jesus every knee should bend of those in heaven, on earth and under the earth, and every tongue should confess that the Lord Jesus Christ is in the glory of God the Father."[50]

We ought often to unite ourselves in spirit to this will the Eternal Father has, of glorifying His Son: "Now is the Son of Man glorified, and God is glorified in Him. If God is glorified in Him [in Christ His Son, the Son of Man], God will also glorify Him in Himself [will glorify Christ] and will glorify Him at once."[51] We ought never to open the Gospels or prepare to celebrate the mysteries of Jesus without first entering into the Father's mind about His Son Jesus, by our declaring, in an intense act of faith, that this Christ whom we are going to think about, pray to, be united with, is *God* like the Father and the Holy Spirit.

This attitude of soul is extremely fruitful because it lifts us up

[49] [*Translator's note*: Marmion's words, "*il n'a pas retenu avidement son égalité avec Dieu*" are in exact accordance with this (the Confraternity) version, rather than the slightly different Rheims translation.]   [50] Phil. 2:6-11.

[51] John 13:32. [*Translator's note*: These words of Christ at the Last Supper have been substituted here as apropos to Marmion's point, whereas Marmion's own reference to John 12:28 (doubtless made from memory) was indeed relevant but only indirectly so. See note 1 on p. 186 of the present translator's translation of *Christ, the Life of the Soul*.]

to the divine level and makes us pleasing to the Father: "The Father Himself loves you because you have loved me,"[52] said Christ. Faith, as St. Leo puts it so well, "the faith that justifies the impious in the sight of God and makes men holy, from being the sinners they were, is that which accepts that in the one and the same Jesus Christ Our Lord is truly both divinity and humanity— the divinity by virtue of which before all ages He is God, equal to His Father, having with His Father the same eternal nature; the humanity through which, in these latter days, He has united Himself to us by taking to Himself the form of a servant"—our condition as creatures.[53]

This act of faith in the divinity of Jesus should be the source of our adoration. Often, in the Gospels, we see an impulse of adoration accompany the act of faith. It is what the Magi did—"We have seen His star in the East and have come to worship Him";[54] it is what Peter did after the miraculous draught of fishes—"he fell down at Jesus's knees";[55] what the disciples did when they saw Jesus walk on the water—"they who were in the boat came and worshipped Him";[56] what the man blind from birth did after his cure—"'I believe, Lord.' And falling down, he adored Him."[57]

By this act of adoration the soul delivers itself up whole and entire to the Divine Word. When Our Savior is dwelling in our hearts, especially after holy communion, we should, as St. Francis de Sales advises,[58] bring all our faculties to His feet, in order that all of them may listen to Him, espouse His interests, share His feelings, obey His commandments and work for His glory.

---

[52] John 16:27.   [53] St. Leo the Great, on the Epiphany (*Sermo* 4).
[54] Matt. 2:2.   [55] Luke 5:8.   [56] Matt. 14:33.   [57] John 9:38 (Rheims).
[58] "On the day of your holy communion, be as devoted as you possibly can, longing ardently for Him to be present within you; and, seated or lying prostrate in your own heart as before a throne, gaze on Him with your inner eye incessantly, and ask Him to come to each of your senses, your powers, one after the other, in order that each obey His commandments. And promise to be faithful to Him": St. Francis de Sales, *Advice and resolutions for Holy Communion*.

To do that is to imitate the sacred humanity of Jesus, which belongs so closely to the Word, is delivered up to the Word so absolutely, that it has not any personality of its own. That is one of the essential aspects of the Incarnation.

All due proportion kept as between the two situations, that is the way it ought to be with us, for Christ Jesus is our model in all things. His humanity never acted otherwise than as being subject to the Word in whom that humanity subsisted, the Word who gave it existence. May there never be any movement in *us* that does not come from God, any desire not in accordance with the divine good pleasure, any action not aimed at serving as an instrument of His glory. A soul that is in such a dependence of love, of will and of action in regard to God, can say in all truth, as the sacred humanity said: "The Lord rules me," "*Dominus regit me.*"[59]

And the sacred writer adds: "and I shall want nothing"—from now on, there is nothing I shall want. Indeed, because that soul is wholly delivered up to the Word, the Word says to His Father: This soul is mine; He is therefore, O Father, yours too: "All I have is yours."[60] The Word gives that soul to the Father, in order that the Father—well-pleased in that soul, as He is well-pleased in His Son Jesus—shall send down upon it His most perfect gifts.

4. **Recognizing, by adoration and an absolute trust, the reality of His humanity united to the Word: "He was weary, by whom the weary are refreshed."**

Christ is God and man. Faithful souls are not contented with proclaiming the divinity of Jesus; they wish likewise to honor His sacred humanity. Our piety would by no means be perfect, complete, if while confessing Jesus's divinity we were to lose sight of His humanity.

There are some souls who believe that in their spiritual life they do better not to occupy themselves with Christ's humanity,

[59] Ps. 22 (23):1, in the Rheims version.   [60] John 17:10 (Jerus.)

but only to contemplate His divinity. That was the error of St. Teresa of Avila during a certain period. The great contemplative later recognized that it was an error. In what bitter terms she deplored it! In what a lively way she put her spiritual daughters (and through them every soul) on guard against this opinion, one she declares "erroneous" and on which she could never look back without being "seized with sorrow," for she had been "setting out on a detestable road," and it seemed to her that she had been "guilty before the Lord of the blackest treachery." In actual fact, it was no more than "ignorance."[61]

According to the Saint, such an illusion has for its cause "a little lack of humility, so disguised that one does not perceive it..." For we should count ourselves "very rich" to have the power to dwell in the presence of the humanity of Jesus in His mysteries. "It is a slight lack of humility ... not to be content with so excellent an object as the humanity of Jesus Christ." This "this little lack of humility ... appears to be nothing, yet it is a great hindrance to progress in contemplation."

The Saint brings out another disadvantage of the error. It is that the soul is left without support. "We are not angels," she says, "we have a body. In the midst of our concerns, in the midst of persecutions, trials, periods of dryness, He is an excellent friend, is Jesus Christ. We see Him, a man like us, we contemplate Him in His infirmity, His suffering... Being men ourselves, it is very advantageous to us, for as long as we are in this life, to consider God made man."[62] Indeed, is it not a very law of our nature that our way to the invisible is through things that are visible? Well, the Incarnation is the most divine application of that psychological law.

The bride in the Song of Songs said: "I sat down under the shadow of him I desired."[63] That "shadow" is the sacred humanity which permits our eyes to contemplate the divinity revealed to us under outward signs perceptible to our senses.

[61] St. Teresa of Avila, *Life, written by herself*, Chapter XXII. The whole of this admirable chapter should be read.   [62] Ibid.   [63] See Song of Songs, 2:3.

Also, concludes St. Teresa: "God is extremely pleased to see a soul humbly placing His Divine Son as intermediary between the soul and Him."

And what is the deep reason for that?

It is that the Incarnation is a *divine* mystery: it is the masterpiece of Divine Wisdom and Infinite Love. Why do we not enter into God's reach of view, God's designs? Why do we refuse to submit our wisdom—limited, bounded in reach, as it is—to Infinite Wisdom? Is the divine resourcefulness, then, so ineffective that we perhaps think we have to correct it by our human reckonings? If God has willed to bring about our salvation and our holiness by means of the humanity united to His Word, to His Son, why may we not reach out and take the offered means? The divine wisdom of those means is as much a matter of wonder as is the divine stooping-down to us. Do not, then, be afraid to contemplate the man in Christ when reading the Gospels, when celebrating Jesus's mysteries. That humanity is the humanity of one who is God. That man whom we see acting and living in the midst of men in order to draw them to Himself through marks of His love perceptible to the senses *is God*, our God.

Do not, especially, be afraid to render to this humanity itself all the homage that is its due.

Our adoration, first of all. It is true that this humanity is created, as ours is. We do not adore it on account of itself; yet we ought to adore it *in itself*, *on account of its union* with the Son of God. Our adoration goes to the humanity, but it ends up with the Divine Person to whom that humanity is substantially united.

Next, an absolute trust. God has willed to make the humanity of Christ the instrument of grace; it is through its intermediacy that grace flows down to us. It is not of the Word in the heart's-embrace of the Father, but expressly of the Word *Incarnate* that St. John has said that He was "full of grace and of truth" and that "of His fullness we have all received."[64]

[64] John 1, vv. 14, 16.

During His life on earth Our Lord, being God, would have been able to work all His miracles and give grace to men simply by an act of His divine will. Every time the sick were brought to Jesus to be cured, or the dead to be raised to life, He would have been able, by a single interior act of His eternal will, to work the miracle asked of Him. But He did not do this. Read the Gospels, and you will see that He wished to touch with His hand the eyes of the blind, the ears of the deaf, to put spittle on the tongue of the mute, to touch the bier of the son of the widow of Naim, to take by the hand Jairus's daughter, to give the Holy Spirit to His apostles by breathing upon them. It is therefore through the contact of His sacred humanity that Christ did His miracles and gave grace; the humanity served as instrument united to the Word. And this wonderful and moving law can be verified in all the mysteries of Jesus.

Well, that divine arrangement (willed as it is by God Himself) subsists always, because the union of the two natures in Christ remains indissoluble. When, therefore, we go through the pages of the Gospels, or when we follow the Church in her liturgy; when we unite ourselves to the sacred humanity of Jesus by an act of faith, and, above all, when we receive His Body in the Eucharist, then the sacred humanity of Christ, inseparable from the Divine Word, serves as instrument of grace for our souls.

"What is quite evident to me," writes St. Teresa, "is that in order to please God, in order to receive from Him great graces, it is necessary—and such is His will—that they pass through the hands of this sacred humanity in whom He has declared Himself well-pleased. I have had experience of this an endless number of times and Our Lord has told me of it. I have recognized clearly that this is the door through which we must enter if we want the Sovereign Majesty to disclose to us high secrets ... one walks with assurance upon that path."[65]

[65] St. Teresa of Avila, citation as above.

And if you really reflect on the above, you will note that all the divine disposing of the super-natural life itself is based on that truth. The Church, the Sacraments, the Holy Sacrifice of the Mass, preaching—all these are means perceptible to the senses whereby God brings us to Himself. It is like an extension of the Incarnation.[66]

You see how important and advantageous it is to remain united to the sacred humanity of Jesus. In that sacred humanity, says St. Paul, "dwells all the fullness of the Godhead bodily,"[67] and it is from the Word through the intermediacy of His humanity that we receive all grace: "And the Word was made flesh" and we saw Him "full of grace and truth," and "of His fullness we have all received." The humanity of Jesus is the divinely-established means for transmitting grace to souls.

The sacred humanity is also the means for souls to reach the divinity. This is a no less important truth, one we ought not to forget. We should not stop at the humanity of Jesus as at the final end of a road. You might say to me indeed: "For me, all my devotion consists in giving myself, in delivering myself up, to Christ Jesus." That is good, that is excellent; nothing is better than giving oneself to Christ. But what *is* giving oneself to Our Lord? It is to unite our will to His. Well then, it is Jesus's will to lead us to the Father. That is the whole of His work; the "end of the road" is the Father. "I am the Way," said Christ Himself, in speaking of His humanity. He is the one and only Way, it is true; but this *is* a Way. The supreme destination to which this Way leads us is the Eternal Father: "No-one comes *to the Father* but through me."[68] The humanity delivers us up to the Word, the Word to His Father.

That is what St. Paul said to the Christians of his day: "All things are yours"—all things are for you—"and you are Christ's, and Christ is God's."[69] The great Apostle indicated by these simple words the stages of the divine work on earth.

[66] See the development of this idea in the talk *The Church, Mystical Body of Christ* in Book I, Ch. 5 of our preceding work *Christ, the Life of the Soul.*

[67] Col. 2:9.   [68] John 14:6.   [69] 1 Cor. 3:22-23.

Through the humanity of Jesus we belong to the Word, to the Son. Through the Son, we go to the Father. It is thus that Christ takes us home, into the heart's-embrace of the Father, *in sinu Patris*. There it is, looked at from our side of things: the inner *raison d'être* of the ineffable mystery of the God-man.

St. John tells us that at the beginning of His public life our Divine Savior, passing through Samaria, came to a town called Sychar, near Jacob's Well. Among the details of the scene carefully noted by the Evangelist, there is one which particularly moves our hearts: "Jesus, tired from His journey, sat down on the coping-stone of the well"[70]—just that. What a touching revelation of the reality of the humanity of Jesus!

You ought to read the admirable commentary on these details given to us by St. Augustine with that opposition of ideas and of terms which was his special secret—above all when he is wanting to make the union, and the contrast, of the divine and the human in Jesus stand out in high relief. "He yields to tiredness," he says, "this very same one who restores the strength of those who are exhausted; this one whose absence lies heavy upon us and whose presence invigorates us. It was for you that Jesus became tired on the road. We find Jesus full of strength and of weakness. Why full of strength? Because He is the Eternal Word, and all things have been created by His wisdom and power. Why full of weakness? Because the Word was made flesh and dwelt among us. The divine strength of Jesus Christ has created you; His coming into the weakness of humanity has re-created you"[71]—has redeemed you.

And the Saint concludes: "Jesus is weak in His humanity. But you—*you* take care not to remain in your weakness. Come, instead, to draw divine strength in Him who, being Omnipotence by nature, willed to make Himself weak for love of you!"

[70] See John 4:6.   [71] *Tract. in Johann.*, XV.

CHAPTER FIVE

SAVIOR AND HIGH PRIEST

Introduction: Necessity of contemplating the work and the mission of the Word made flesh, for understanding His Person better. The names of the Word Incarnate declare His mission and characterize His work: "Jesus Christ" is the Son of God, He is the Supreme High Priest who by His Sacrifice saves humankind.

Christ Jesus is the Incarnate Word, who has appeared in the midst of us; God and man, both—true God and true man, perfect God and perfect man. In Him, two natures are inseparably united in the embrace of one single Person, the Person of the Word.

These features constitute the very being of Jesus. Our faith and our piety adore Him as their God, at the same time as they declare the touching reality of His humanity.

If we want to penetrate deeper into a knowledge of the Person of Jesus we must now, for a few moments, begin to contemplate His mission and His work. The Person of Jesus gives His mission and work their value; the mission and work of Jesus complete the revelation to us of His Person.

And what is more remarkable is that the names that designate the very Person of the Word are names which at the same time declare His mission and characterize His work. Those names, indeed, are not destitute of significance (as is too often the case with our own names). They come from heaven and are rich in meaning. What are these names? They are numerous, but the Church, inheritor of St. Paul in this, has especially kept hold of two of them: that of "Jesus" and that of "Christ."

As you know, "*Christ*" signifies one who is *anointed, dedicated solemnly, consecrated*. In days past, in the Old Testament, kings were quite often consecrated; prophets more rarely; the high priest always. The name "Christ," anointed one, like the mission of king, of prophet, of high priest that it designates, was given to several other personages of the Old Testament before being that of the Word Incarnate. But none of these was to make real the significance of the name in all its fullness, as He did. He is *the* "Christ," for He alone is the King of the ages; the Prophet par excellence; the one Supreme and Universal High Priest.

He is *King*. He is so by His Divinity: "King of kings and Lord of lords";[1] He rules over all creatures, whom, by His almighty power, He has drawn forth from nothing: "Come, let us adore, and fall down ... before the Lord";[2] "He made us, and not we ourselves."[3]

He still is that as the Word Incarnate. The scepter of the world has been foretold as Jesus's by His Father: "I am appointed King by Him over Sion, His holy mountain," says the Messiah.[4] "I will proclaim the decree of the Lord: The Lord said to me, 'You are my Son; this day I have begotten you. Ask of me and I will give you the nations for an inheritance and the ends of the earth for your possession.'"[5] The Word became incarnate in order to establish the "Kingdom of God." This expression is found again and again in the preaching of Jesus. In reading the Gospels you will have noticed that a whole group of parables—the pearl of great price,[6] the treasure hidden in a field,[7] the sower,[8] the mustard seed,[9] the murderous vine-dressers,[10] the guests invited to the wedding-feast,[11]

---

[1] Apoc. 19:16.   [2] Ps. 94 (95):6.   [3] Ps. 99 (100):3.   [4] Ps. 2:6; Marmion gives a translation as in the Rheims. Other translations give the declaration as coming from the Father.   [5] Ibid., vv.7-8 (St P)   [6] Matt. 13:45.   [7] Matt. 13:44.
[8] Matt. 13, vv.3-9, 18-23; Mark 4, vv. 1-9, 13-20; Luke 8, vv. 4-8, 11-15.
[9] Matt. 13:31-32; Mark 4:30-32; Luke 13:18-19.
[10] Matt. 21:33-41; Mark 12:1-11; Luke 20:9-16.   [11] Matt. 22:1-14.

the darnel in the wheat,[12] the servants awaiting their master,[13] the talents,[14] etc.—are intended to show the greatness of this kingdom, its origin, its development, its extension to the nations after the reprobation[15] of the Jews, its laws, its struggles, its triumphs. Christ oganizes this kingdom by the choosing of the apostles and the founding of the Church, the Church to which He entrusts His doctrine, His authority, His sacraments. A kingdom wholly spiritual, having nothing of the temporal or political such as the worldly minds of the majority of the Jews were then dreaming of; a kingdom that every soul of good will enters; a wonderful kingdom, its final splendor wholly heavenly and its beatitude eternal.

St. John celebrates the magnificence of this kingdom; he shows us the elect bowed down before their Divine Head, Christ Jesus, and proclaiming: "You have redeemed us with your blood"— *bought us back* for God—"out of every tribe and tongue and people and nation" and have made us "a kingdom," the kingdom in which in which the glory of His Father is to shine: "You have made them for our God a kingdom."[16]

The Christ has to be a *Prophet*. He is not just *a* prophet, but *the* Prophet—the Prophet par excellence, because He is the Divine Word, the *Word* in person, the "Light of the world,"[17] the only Light that can truly "enlighten every man who comes into the world."[18] "In times past," said St. Paul to the Hebrews, "God ... spoke to you by His prophets"—who were simply messengers— "but in these latter days He has taught you by His own Son."[19]

---

[12] Matt. 13, vv. 24-30, 36-43.   [13] Luke 12:35-48; Matt. 24:42-51; Mark 13:32-37.
[14] Matt. 25:14-30; Luke 19:11-28.   [15] [*Translator's note*: This is Marmion's term, but he used it without explanation and before the Church had spoken in the clear way she recently has. Yes, Christ's Church is "now the new people of God," but "the Jews should not be presented as rejected or accursed by God, as if this followed from the Holy Scriptures" (*Nostra Aetate*, 4; as to which see further p. 158 of this book). And note Marmion's own words in the present paragraph: "a kingdom that every soul of good will enters."]   [16] Apoc. 5:9-10.
[17] John 8:12.   [18] See John 1:9.   [19] See Hebr. 1:1-2.

His Son is not a prophet who proclaims God's still-hidden plans from afar, to a very small portion of humanity and under sometimes obscure symbols. This is He who, living always in the heart's-embrace of the Father, alone knows all the divine secrets and who brings to the whole human race the astonishing revelation: "He has made Him known."[20]

From the beginning of His public life, as you know, Our Lord applied to Himself the prophecy of Isaiah declaring: "The Spirit of the Lord is upon me." That is why He has been consecrated by the Lord's "anointing" to "bring good news to the poor, to announce to the captives release, and sight to the blind, to make known to all that the time of redemption has arrived."[21]

He is therefore par excellence God's Envoy, Legate—who by miracles worked on His own authority proves the divinity of His mission, His words and His Person. Thus do we hear the crowd, after the marvel of the multiplication of the loaves, cry out about Jesus: "This is indeed the prophet who was to come into the world."[22]

Above all, the Word Incarnate showed the meaning of His name "Christ" to be true in His capacity of *High Priest* and Mediator—Supreme High Priest and Universal Mediator.

But here we have to join to the name "Christ" that of "Jesus." The name "Jesus" signifies "Savior": "You must name Him Jesus," said the angel to Joseph, "because He is the one who is to save His people from their sins."[23] There we have His essential mission: "The Son of Man has come to save that which was lost."[24] Well now, it is in fact only by His Sacrifice, by His accomplishing His work as High Priest, that Jesus makes the significance of His divine name come fully true: "The Son of Man came ... to give His life as a ransom for many."[25] The two names, therefore, complete

[20] John 1:18 (RSV, Cath.)   [21] See Luke 4:18-19; Isa. 61:1.
[22] See John 6:14.   [23] Matt. 1:21 (Jerus.)
[24] Matt. 18:11 (Knox); cf. Luke 19:10.   [25] Matt. 20:28 (Jerus.); Mark 10:45.

each other and are henceforth inseparable. "Christ Jesus" is the Son of God, established as Supreme High Priest; and by His Sacrifice He *saves* the whole of humanity.

That is why it is in contemplating Christ's Priesthood and Sacrifice that we complete our understanding of the adorable Person of the Word Incarnate (in so far as such an understanding is possible).

As we are about to see, indeed, it was by His Incarnation itself that Jesus was consecrated High Priest, and He began His Sacrifice at His very entry into the world. All His life here bore a reflection of His mission as High Priest and was marked by features of His Sacrifice.

By seeing this we shall get a better grasp, equally of the greatness of Christ's mysteries as of the arrangement of them; we shall see what a profound unity binds all those mysteries together. Jesus's Sacrifice, because it is His essential work, is the culminating point towards which all the mysteries of His life on earth converge, and it is the source from which all the states of His life in glory draw their splendor. We shall also see of what abundant graces that Sacrifice is the wellspring for all those souls who are desirous to drink, in Him, of life and joy.

1. In becoming incarnate, Christ is established as High Priest.

It was above all in his letter to the Hebrews that St. Paul expounded in terms full of breadth and power the ineffable greatness of Christ as High Priest: "On this point we have much to say, and it is difficult to explain it."[26] We see indicated there Christ's mission of Mediator, the transcendence of His Sacrifice over the priesthood of Aaron and the sacrifices of the Old Testament: a unique Sacrifice, consummated on Calvary; a Sacrifice the offering of which continues with inexhaustible efficacy in the sanctuary of heaven.

[26] Hebr. 5:11.

St. Paul reveals to us this truth, that Christ Jesus possesses His Priesthood from the instant of the Incarnation.

What is a priest? He is, says the Apostle, a mediator between man and God. The priest offers to God the homage of the creature, gives God, "the Holy One," to men. Hence the name "*sacerdos,*" "priest."

"For every high priest taken from among men is appointed for men in the things pertaining to God."[27] In times past, this consecration was ordinarily carried out by a special "anointing" which signified that the Spirit of the Lord was upon the chosen one, thus marking him in a particular manner for his mission of high priest. In the human priesthood, this sacerdotal character is a quality that is added, so to speak, to the person of the man.

But in Christ, this character is altogether transcendent, as the mediation He undertook is unique. Jesus became High Priest from the time of His Incarnation and through His Incarnation.

In order to penetrate this profound mystery we must listen to faith alone, for the human intellect is confounded before such grandeurs. Let us transport ourselves to Nazareth so as to be present at that heavenly dialogue between the angel and the Virgin. God's messenger says to Mary, to explain to her the wonder that is to be accomplished within her: "The Holy Spirit shall come upon you and the power of the Most High shall overshadow you; and therefore the Holy One to be born of you shall be called the Son of God." The Virgin replies: "Behold the handmaid of the Lord; be it done to me according to your word."[28]

At that moment, the Word is made flesh; the Word unites Himself for ever, by an ineffable union, to a humanity, a human nature. By the Incarnation, the Word enters into our race, He becomes authentically one of us, like us in everything, sin excepted. He can therefore become High Priest, Mediator, since, being God and man, He can reunite man to God: a High Priest "taken from among men."

---

[27] Hebr. 5:1.   [28] See Luke 1, vv. 35, 38.

In the Blessed Trinity, the Second Person, the Word, is, indeed, the infinite glory of the Father, His essential glory: "the brightness of His glory and the image of His substance."[29] But, *as the Word*, before the Incarnation, He does not offer to His Father any sacrifice. Why is that? Because sacrifice supposes homage, adoration—that is to say, the recognition of our own abasement in the presence of Infinite Being. The Word, being equal in everything to His Father, being God with Him and like Him, cannot therefore offer Him sacrifice. The priesthood of Christ was only able to begin at the moment when the Word was made flesh. From the instant of the Word becoming incarnate, He unites in Himself two natures: the divine nature, by which He was able to say: "I and the Father are one,"[30] one in the unity of the Godhead, the Trinity, one in equality of perfections; the other, the human nature, which made Him say: "The Father is greater than I."[31] It is therefore inasmuch as He is God-man that Jesus is High Priest.

Learned authors derive the word "pontiff," high priest, from *pontem facere*, "to establish a bridge," to throw it as over a chasm. Whatever be the truth of that etymology, the idea as applied to Christ Jesus is exactly right. In the conversations that He deigned to have with St. Catherine of Siena, the Father explained to her how, through the union of the two natures, Christ has thrown a bridge across the abyss that was separating us from heaven: "I want you to look at the bridge I have built for you in my only Son, and to contemplate its greatness that goes from heaven to earth; seeing that the greatness of the Godhead is united to the earth of your humanity. That was necessary in order to restore the way that had been severed and to permit a crossing over the bitterness of the world so as to arrive at life (eternal)."[32]

. . .

---

[29] Hebr. 1:3.   [30] John 10:30.   [31] John 14:28.   [32] *Dialogue*, Part II, Ch. VI, Hurtaud translation, vol. I, pp. 76-77. This was an idea familiar to St. Catherine. One finds it again in many places in the *Dialogue*, and in her letters.

Moreover, it was through the same mystery of the Incarnation that the humanity of Jesus was "consecrated," "anointed."[33] Not by an exterior anointing, like that which happens for those who are simply creatures, but by a anointing wholly spiritual. Through the action of the Holy Spirit, whom the liturgy calls "Spiritual Annointing," "*Spiritualis Unctio*,"[34] Divinity is poured out upon the human nature of Jesus[35] like an "oil of gladness": "God, your God, has anointed you with the oil of gladness above your fellows."[36] This anointing is so penetrating; so much "consecrated to God" is this humanity, that no closer belonging is possible. For this human nature has become the very own humanity of One who is God, of the Son of God.

That is why at the moment of this Incarnation which consecrated the first priest of the New Covenant a cry resounds in heaven: "You are a priest for ever."[37] St. Paul, whose eyes pierced so many mysteries, reveals to us this one too: "No man," he says,[38] "attributes to himself this dignity of priesthood; he must have been called to it by God. No more did Christ: He did not arrogate to Himself the glory of being High Priest; He received it from Him who says to Him: 'You are my Son, this day I have begotten you,'[39] as He also says to Him elsewhere: 'You are a priest for ever.'"

So then, by the Apostle's testimony, it was from the Eternal Father Himself that Christ received the supreme High Priesthood; from this Father who says to Him: "You are my Son, this day have I begotten you." The Priesthood of Christ is a necessary and immediate consequence of His Incarnation.

Let us adore this holy, this stainless, High Priest, who is God's own Son; let us prostrate ourselves before this Mediator who, because He is at the same time God and man, was the only one

---

[33] St. Augustine, *De Trinitate*, XV, 27.   [34] Hymn, *Veni, Creator Spiritus*.
[35] [*Translator's note*: i.e. at the very moment of the Incarnation, when the human nature which the Eternal Son took to Himself came into being.]
[36] Ps. 44 (45):8.   [37] Ps. 109 (110):4.   [38] See Hebr. 5:4-6.   [39] Ps. 2:7.

who could fully carry out His mission of salvation and restore to us the gifts of God by the Sacrifice of His humanity. But also, let us trust fully in His divine power which, equally, was the only power mighty enough to reconcile us with the Father.

God, speaking of the earth, said to St. Catherine: "No-one could establish a bridge big enough to rejoin life eternal, seeing that the earth of human nature was incapable by itself of satisfying for sin and of destroying the stain of Adam's sin which corrupted and infected the whole human race. It was therefore necessary to join that human nature to the height of my nature, eternal Deity, so that it should be able to satisfy for the whole human race. It was necessary for human nature to suffer pain, and for the divine nature united to that human nature to accept the sacrifice my Son offered me, so as to destroy death and restore life to you. In that way Height went down as far as the very earth of your humanity. By uniting me to that humanity, it built a bridge and established a road. But for obtaining life, it is not enough that my Son has become the bridge *unless you yourselves cross over upon that bridge.*"

2. How Christ, by entering into the world, also inaugurated His Sacrifice.

The Sacrifice of this unique High Priest is on the same footing as His Priesthood: it was at the very moment of His Incarnation that Jesus inaugurated that Sacrifice.

In Christ, as you know, the soul, created like ours, was nevertheless not subject to the progressive development of the bodily organism for the exercise of its own faculties, intellect and will. From the first moment of its existence it had the perfection of its own life, as befitted a soul united to Divinity.

Well, St. Paul reveals to us the first movement of the soul of Jesus at the moment of His Incarnation.

In one glance, Jesus's soul embraced all the ages which had been before His coming. Along with the abyss in which the whole of humanity lay powerless to free itself, it beheld the multiplicity and the insufficiency of all the sacrifices of the Old Law (for creatures, however perfect, cannot worthily make reparation for the insult sin has perpetrated against the Creator). It saw the program of immolation God asked of it in order that salvation be brought about.

What a solemn moment for the soul of Jesus! What a moment also for the human race!

And what does this soul do? By a movement of intense love, it delivers itself up whole and entire to perfect the divine-human work which alone can give glory to the Father by saving humanity. "O Father, you want no more of these offerings, of these sacrifices, that are not sufficiently worthy of you. But you have formed for me a body. And why have you given it to me?—for, behold, I come to do your will, Father. You require that I offer it to you in sacrifice ... here I am. At the head of the book of my life it is written that I am to do your will, Father; so that is also my will, because it is pleasing to you."[40]

With His whole will, Christ accepted that sum of sorrows which began with the humility of the manger and was completed only by the ignominy of the cross. From His very entry here below, Christ offered Himself as a victim: the first action of His life was a priestly action.

What creature can measure the love with which that priestly action of Jesus was filled? Who can know its intensity and describe its splendor? The only thing that to a small extent can praise it is the silence of adoration.

Never did Christ Jesus retract that action, or withdraw anything from that gift. Rather, the whole of His life would be directed towards His Sacrifice upon the cross. Read the Gospels in that light, and you will see how in all Jesus's mysteries and states you find a portion of sacrifice that leads Him little by little to the

[40] See Hebr. 10:5-7; cf. Ps. 39(40):7-9 (6-8).

summit of Calvary, so much is the character of High Priest, of Mediator, of Savior, essential to His Person. We shall completely fail to grasp the true physiognomy of the Person of Jesus unless we constantly have in view His redeeming mission through the sacrifice and immolation of Himself. That is why, when St. Paul tells the Corinthians that he judged himself to know nothing among them except the mystery of Jesus Christ, he immediately adds: *"and Him crucified."*[41]

Consider the facts: Christ was born in the most absolute destitution; He had to flee into a foreign land to escape the fury of a tyrant; He knew hard and hidden labor in the workshop at Nazareth. During His public life, He had nowhere to lay His head; He was exposed to persecution by His mortal enemies, the Pharisees; He experienced hunger, thirst, fatigue. Furthermore, He burned to complete His Sacrifice: "I have a baptism to be baptized with, and how I am *constrained* until it is accomplished!"[42]

If one can put it this way, there was in Jesus something like a sort of enthusiasm for His Sacrifice. Look again at when, in the Gospels, our Divine Savior started to disclose to His apostles the mystery of His sufferings—little by little, out of compassion for their weakness. One day He told them that He must go to Jerusalem and suffer many things at the hands of His enemies, and be put to death. At which Peter immediately took Him aside and said: "God forbid, Lord! This shall not happen to you." But Jesus forthwith replied: "Get behind me, you are an obstacle in my path, for you do not know the things of God; your thoughts are only human ones."[43] In the midst of the splendors of His transfiguration on Tabor, what did the Savior talk about with Moses and Elijah? His approaching Passion.[44]

Christ thirsted to give His Father that glory which His Father would obtain from Christ's Sacrifice: "not one jot or tittle shall be lost from the law till all things shall have been accomplished."[45]

---

[41] 1 Cor. 2:2.   [42] Luke 12:50 (RSV, Cath.)
[43] See Matt. 16:21-23; Mark 8:31-33.   [44] Luke 9:31.   [45] Matt. 5:18.

He wished to accomplish all things, to the last iota—that is, to the final detail. When, in His agony, anguish and sorrows pile up in His soul, He feels them so deeply that "Father," He says, "if it is possible, let this cup pass away from me." However, He wishes to accomplish the will of His Father to the very end: "Yet not as I will, but as you will."[46] Finally, on Calvary, He completes His immolation and is able to say, before He yields up His last breath, that He has accomplished in its fullness the program His Father has given Him: "It is consummated!"[47] This final cry of the Divine Victim upon the cross corresponds to His "Here I am" at His incarnation in the womb of the Virgin.

3. Diversity of the acts of offering Christ Jesus makes.

The offering of Himself that Christ Jesus has made was a full, total, continuous one, but it included different acts.

Adoration, first of all.

In the Blessed Trinity, the Son belongs entirely to His Father; all His being is directed (so to speak) to the Father. From the time the Word "was made flesh," the humanity—the human nature—thus united to Him has been swept along in that ineffable current that bears the Son towards His Father. But because that humanity is *created*, inferior to the divinity, this movement to the Father, within the humanity, is expressed by adoration. And this adoration is intense, perfect. From the very moment when it was united to the Word, that humanity, in Jesus, was engulfed in a deep adoration, in an abasement of itself before the divine majesty of the Eternal Word,[48] whose infinite perfections it contemplated, through the Beatific Vision.

.   .   .

---

[46] Matt. 26:39; Mark 14:36; Luke 22:42.   [47] John 19:30.

[48] [*Translator's note*: These remarkable words are especially to be noted. The *human soul* of Jesus, God-made-man, is expressed by Marmion as being in adoration not only before the Eternal Father, but before Jesus as Divine and Eternal Son.]

There was also *thanksgiving*.

It is certain that of all the graces, of all the mercies, that God can grant, the greatest and highest is that given to the humanity of Jesus. God chose, predestined, that human nature above all human natures, "beyond its fellows"—"*prae consortibus tuis*,"[49] to be the human nature of His Son—to unite it, in an incomprehensible union, to His Word.[50] This is a unique grace so far as communication between the Godhead and creatures is concerned; it is beyond every possible dream of the human mind.

Therefore Jesus's soul—replete, through this union, with all the delights of Divinity itself—overflowed with thanksgiving. If we ourselves sometimes do not know how to express to our Heavenly Father the abundance of our gratitude, what must the thanks that rose up from the soul of Jesus not have been?—thanks for the ineffable grace given to it, thanks for all the incomparable privileges which were to flow down from its union with the Word, and not only in a personal capacity but as head of the mystical body?

And also there was *expiation*.

The race from which the Word took a human nature so as to unite Himself with it was a sinful, a fallen, race. The Word espoused a body of sin, He took on "the likeness of sinful flesh."[51]

To be sure, sin has never had contact with Him personally. In every respect He was "tempted as we are, *yet without sinning*."[52] He—the "Christ," that is to say, the High Priest par excellence—is such a High Priest, says St. Paul, that His offering is "fitting" to be acceptable to God: He is "holy, innocent, undefiled, set apart

---

[49] See Ps. 44; Hebr. 1:9.   [50] [*Translator's note*: Again, it is important to note that creation of Jesus's human soul took place (as Marmion has earlier made perfectly clear) *at the very instant of the Incarnation*. At that instant the human soul of Jesus was created and united to the eternal Divine Word. From the other direction (so to speak), the Son's divinity was *at that instant* united to the created soul of Jesus. There is here no question of a human person, pre-existing the Incarnation, to whose human soul the divinity was thereafter united.]   [51] Rom. 8:3.   [52] Hebr. 4:15 (RSV, Cath.); cf. Ibid., 2:17.

from sinners, and become higher than the heavens."[53] But His Father laid on His shoulders the sins of all men: "The Lord has laid on Him the iniquity of us all."[54] Jesus became, in the vigorous expression of the Apostle, "*sin*"[55] for our sakes, and, with that as motive, the offering of Himself which He made to His Father at the moment of the Incarnation embraced the poverty of the manger, the abasements of the hidden life, the wearinesses and struggles of the public life, the terrors of the Agony in the garden, the ignominies of the Passion and the torments of a death by shedding of His blood. "Christ Jesus ... though He was by nature God, did not consider being equal to God a thing to be clung to, but emptied Himself, taking the nature of a slave"—taking, through the Incarnation, the condition of a created nature—"and being made like unto men. And appearing in the form of man, He humbled Himself, becoming obedient to death, even to death on a cross."[56]

This death on Calvary was an expiation of infinite value because Christ is God, but also because His abasements reached the very limit of humiliation. The dying Christ on the cross had accepted to become for us like a piece of trash, something accursed: "the reproach of men and the outcast of the people."[57] And this unheard-of abasement to which He was to descend in order to expiate sin was something the soul of Jesus had willed from the time of His entry here below, with all the humiliations, ignominies and sufferings it entailed.

Finally, we find in this offering *impetration*—that is, supplication. The Gospels tell us nothing of Christ's prayer for us at the Incarnation, or even during His public life, though we are told that He would spend the whole night praying: "He continued all night in prayer to God"[58] But St. John has preserved for us the words of the prayer Jesus made, for His disciples and for us, at

[53] Hebr. 7:26.   [54] Isa. 53:6.   [55] 2 Cor. 5:21.   [56] Phil. 2:7-8.
[57] Ps. 21 (22):7.   [58] Luke 6:12.

the Last Supper—at the time when He was inaugurating His Passion and completing His Sacrifice. It is the sacerdotal prayer of Jesus. In the whole of the Gospels there is no more beautiful page than that. And can we doubt that this prayer would have been the resumé and final echo of all the prayers that Christ had addressed to His Father during His entire life on earth?

"Father, the hour has come! Glorify your Son, that your Son may glorify you, seeing that you have given Him authority over all mankind, in order that to all whom you have given Him He may communicate life eternal.... I have manifested your name to the men you have entrusted to me.... They now know that everything you have given me comes from you... It is for them that I pray ... because they are yours.... Holy Father, keep them in your name, that they may be one even as we are.... I make this prayer while I am in the world in order that they may have in them the fullness of my joy.... I do not ask you to take them out of the world, but that you keep them from evil.... I am going to offer myself in sacrifice in order that they may be truly sanctified.... I do not pray only for them [the apostles], but also for those who, through their word, are to believe in me, that they all may be one, even as you, Father, in me and I in you.... Father, I will that where I am, they also whom you have given me may be with me; in order that they may behold my glory, which you have given me, because you have loved me before the creation of the world."[59]

What a prayer! And springing forth from what a heart!—from the heart of Jesus, Supreme High Priest of the whole of humanity, our High Priest, at the time when He was about to make Himself our Victim! Oh why, then, do we so often doubt the power of Christ? Why do we get discouraged when Jesus, true God as well as true man, addressed such a prayer to His Father at the time of glorifying Him with an infinite glory by immolating Himself for our sins?

[59] See John 17:1-24.

O Christ Jesus, say once again that prayer for us: "Father, keep from evil those you have given me ... that they may have my joy ... that they may have that joy in its fullness... that they may joy in my glory ... that they may be one in us!"

4. Continuousness, in heaven, of the priesthood and oblation of Christ.

Jesus's prayer has been granted; the immolation which followed on it merited, for the whole human race, abundant graces of pardon, justification, union, life, joy, glory.

After saying that Christ has been established Supreme High Priest of the human race (as from the time of His Incarnation),[60] St. Paul added immediately: "Jesus, in the days of His earthly life, with loud cries and tears, offered up prayers and supplications to Him who was able to save Him from death; and He was heard because of His reverent and loving submission to His Father;[61] for, Son though He was, He learnt by His Sacrifice what it is to obey. And now, having achieved that fully, He saves for ever all those who walk in His footsteps."[62]

St. Paul, further, makes our sanctification go back to the oblation that was offered by Jesus at the time of His entry into this world;[63] for that offering has within it the seed of that final flowering which is the immolation of Calvary: "It is by virtue of that will that we are sanctified through the oblation that Jesus Christ made of His own body once and for all."[64]

So you see, every grace, whatever it is, flows down for us from the cross: there is not one grace that has not been paid for by the love and the blood of Jesus. Christ's priesthood makes Him our one and only Mediator, and one who is always heard. That is

---

[60] Hebr. 5:1-6.   [61] [*Translator's note*: Marmion's actual words are "because of His piety (*piété*) towards His Father."]   [62] See Hebr. 5:7-9.
[63] "Behold, I come to do your will, O God": Hebr. 10:9; Ps. 39(40):8 (7).
[64] See Hebr. 10:10.

why the Apostle Paul, in His lively conviction, cries out that in giving us His Son, God has given us everything: "He who ... gave up His Son for our sakes, how can He fail to grant us also all things in Him?"[65] See how rich we have become, Paul says later; so abundantly rich, that henceforth we lack no grace: "*nothing* is wanting to you in *any* grace."[66]

Oh, what absolute and unshakeable confidence this revelation begets in us! In Christ Jesus we find everything, we possess everything, and, if we will, in Him nothing is lacking to us. He is our salvation, the Source of all our perfection and of all our sanctification.

For so great is our High Priest, so wide His priesthood, that *at present* Christ fulfills His role of Mediator and continues His Sacrifice for our sanctification. How so?

First, in heaven.

In this, above all, is the mystery an ineffable one. The Eternal Priesthood of Christ Jesus contains hidden depths of which St. Paul and St. John afford us glimpses—St. Paul in his Epistle to the Hebrews, St. John in his Apocalypse.[67]

The Apostle has some magnificent expressions for extolling the Eternal Priesthood of Jesus. "Jesus ... sits at the right hand of the throne of God,"[68] in highest heaven. "In Jesus the Son of God we have the Supreme High Priest who has gone through to the highest heaven."[69] "Jesus has entered for us into the sanctuary of the heavens, as a forerunner, in the capacity of Supreme High Priest."[70] "Because He lives and continues for ever, He has an everlasting priesthood ... He is always living to intercede for us, raised high as He is above all the heavens."[71] "We therefore have a Supreme High Priest who is seated at the right hand of the throne of the Divine Majesty, as the one and only minister of that true sanctuary which the Lord, not the hand of man, has made"[72]

All these remarkable expressions show us that in heaven

---

[65] See Rom 8:32. [66] 1 Cor. 1:7 (Rheims). [67] Apoc. 5:6.
[68] Hebr. 12:2. [69] Hebr. 4:14 (Jerus.) [70] See Hebr. 6:20.
[71] See Hebr. 7:24-26. [72] See Hebr. 8:1-2; cf. Hebr. 9:24.

Christ Jesus remains eternally our High Priest and prolongs His oblation for us.

Undoubtedly St. Paul does not forget that there is only one Sacrifice, that of the cross: "For by *one* offering He has perfected for ever those who are sanctified."[73] There cannot be another Sacrifice: this Sacrifice is unique and definitive.

But, he says, in the same way that in the Old Testament every year the high priest, after having offered the sacrifice in the first tabernacle of the Temple, went through alone, taking with him the blood of the victims, into the second tabernacle, the Holy of holies, and thereby completed his work of high priest by presenting himself before the Lord—so also, continues St. Paul, Christ, after having offered His Sacrifice on earth, entered once and for all, through His own blood, not into a tabernacle built by the hand of man, but into the sanctuary of the Godhead: "not by virtue of blood of goats and calves, but by virtue of His own blood, into the Holy of holies."[74] He therefore completed in glory His divine role as Mediator: "now once at the end of ages, He has appeared ... by the sacrifice of Himself."[75]

What is it that Christ Jesus does in this sanctuary? What is His work?

He can no longer merit, it is true: the time of meriting ceased for Him at the moment when He rendered up His last breath upon the cross. But the time of applying His merits to us remains for ever.

And it is this that Our Lord does. He is henceforth present before the face of His Father to intercede for us; He "appears *now* before the face of God on our behalf."[76] There, "since He *lives always* to make intercession"[77] (for "death shall no more have dominion over Him"),[78] He ceaselessly offers to His Father for us His Sacrifice, already accomplished but subsisting in His Person. He shows His Father His five wounds, having willed to keep their scars—those wounds that are the solemn attestation and

---

[73] Hebr. 10:14.   [74] See Hebr. 9:12.   [75] Hebr. 9:26 (Rheims).
[76] See Hebr. 9:24.   [77] Hebr. 7:25.   [78] Rom. 6:9 (Rheims).

full token of His immolation on the cross. In the name of the Church, whose head He is, He unites to His oblation our adoration, our homage, our prayers and supplications, our thanksgivings. We are ceaselessly present in the thoughts of our compassionate High Priest; he puts to work ceaselessly, for our sanctification, His merits, His satisfactions, His Sacrifice.

So there is in heaven, and there will be till the end of time, a Sacrifice celebrated for us by Christ Jesus in a manner which is high and sublime, but in perpetual continuity with His one immolation on the cross.[79]

As we know, it was after having glimpsed its grandeurs and its power [on the road to Damascus] that St. Paul let us hear this pressing exhortation: "Since in Jesus, the Son of God, we have the Supreme High Priest who has gone through to the highest heaven, we must never let go of the faith that we have professed."[80] What faith? Faith in Jesus Christ the Supreme Mediator, faith in the infinite value of His Sacrifice and His merits, faith in the unlimited extent of His Father's trust in Him. *"Let us be confident, then, in approaching* the throne of grace, that we shall have mercy from Him and find grace when we are in need of help."[81]

What grace, indeed, *could* be refused us by this High Priest who knows how to have compassion on our weakness, our infirmities, our sufferings, since, in order to resemble us, He has experienced them all; this High Priest of such power, in that, being Son of God, He treats with His Father as equal to equal ("Father, I will"[82]—it is my will...); this High Priest who wills to be united with us, as in a body the head is united to the members? What graces of pardon, of perfection, of holiness, can a soul not hope for who sincerely seeks to remain united to Him through faith, trust and love? Is He not the "High Priest of the good things to come"?[83] Is He not "able to accomplish all things in a measure beyond"—infinitely beyond—"what we ask or conceive"?[84]

---

[79] See Hebr. 9:25-26. [80] Hebr. 4:14 (Jerus.) [81] Hebr. 4:16 (Jerus.)
[82] John 17:24. [83] Hebr. 9:11. [84] Eph. 3:20.

That is why, in the whole of her worship, the Church, who knows her Spouse better than anyone, addresses no prayer to the Heavenly Father, does not ask Him for any grace, without marking her request with the sign of the cross, without calling upon the name of Jesus Christ, our Savior and our High Priest: *"Through our Lord Jesus Christ, your Son..."* This formula, in the Church, is one used every day and at all times. It is an unceasing proclamation of the universal mediation of Christ, but it is also a most explicit and solemn confession of His divinity, for the Church immediately adds: "who lives and reigns with you and the Holy Spirit, one God, for ever and ever. Amen."

5. **How upon earth the Sacrifice of the cross is renewed. The Church does not celebrate any of Christ's mysteries without offering the Eucharistic Sacrifice.**

In expounding, after St. Paul, the work of Christ the High Priest in heaven, we have not exhausted the marvels of the Priesthood of Jesus.

Heaven has its oblation—high, ineffable, but continual and wholly glorious. The Word Incarnate did not will to leave the earth without leaving a Sacrifice to it also. It is the Holy Mass, which both recalls, and at one and the same time reproduces, the immolation of Golgotha. As I have told you, the historical Sacrifice of the cross is the unique Sacrifice; it suffices for everything. But Our Lord has willed that it be renewed so as to apply its fruits to souls. I shall expound this truth to you in detail when we come to contemplate the mystery of the Eucharist. Here, I simply want to tell you how our High Priest perpetuates *here below* His Sacrifice.

Christ chooses certain men to whom He gives a real participation in His Sacrifice. These are the priests whom the bishop consecrates on the day of their ordination. With hands extended over the head of the one who is going to be ordained, the bishop invokes the Holy Spirit, praying Him to descend upon that soul.

One could at that moment repeat to the ordinand the words of the angel to Mary: "The Holy Spirit shall come upon you."[85] The Holy Spirit overshadows him, so to say, and effects within him a resemblance to, and so close a union with, Christ Jesus that he is, as Christ is, a priest for eternity. Christian tradition has called the priest "another Christ," *Alter Christus*: he is chosen to be—in the name of Christ, and like Christ—a mediator between heaven and earth. This is a super-natural reality. See: when the priest offers the Sacrifice of the Mass, which reproduces the Sacrifice of Calvary, he identifies himself with Christ. He does not say: "This is the body of Christ, this is the blood of Christ."—if he said that, there would be no sacrifice at all. What he says is: "This is my body, this is my blood."

From that moment, the priest, consecrated to God by the Holy Spirit, becomes a high priest and mediator (as Christ is) between men and God. Or rather, it is the unique mediation of Christ that is prolonged here below, across the ages, through the ministry of priests. In the name of the faithful, the priest offers to God upon the altar the Eucharistic Sacrifice: and from the altar he brings to the people the Holy Victim, the Bread of Life, and, with that Holy Victim, all gifts and all graces.

The altar is, upon earth, the center of the religion of Jesus, exactly as Calvary is the summit of His life. As I have told you, all the mysteries of Jesus's existence on earth converge upon His immolation upon the cross; all the states of His glorified life derive their splendor from the cross.

That is why the Church never commemorates, never celebrates, any of the mysteries of Jesus without offering the Holy Sacrifice of the Mass. The whole of the public worship oganized by the Church gravitates around the altar; and all that ensemble of readings, prayers, praises, homage which is called the Divine Office, and in which the Church re-traces beneath the eyes of her children, and extols, the mysteries of her Heavenly Spouse, has

---

[85] Luke 1:35.

been settled on for no other purpose than to be a setting for the Eucharistic Sacrifice.

Whichever mystery of Jesus we celebrate, therefore, we cannot, after having contemplated it and meditated on it with the Church—we cannot participate in it more perfectly, nor better dispose ourselves to receive its fruits, than by being present with faith and love at the Sacrifice of the Mass and by uniting ourselves, through holy communion, with the Divine Victim immolated for us on the altar.

In the life of Blessed Marie d'Oignies it is recounted that Our Lord was accustomed, on the occasions of different feast-days, to show Himself to her in the Blessed Sacrament under a form analogous to the particular mystery the feast was commemorating.[86]

There is nothing we should envy in that favor given to her. Through holy communion, Christ Jesus does not only *show* Himself only to the soul; He comes within the soul, He communicates Himself, whole and entire, to the soul: with His human nature of compassionate High Priest who knows our weaknesses, with the power of His divinity that can raise us right up to where He is, at the right hand of His Father. He comes within us, not to manifest Himself to us, but to pray, in us and with us, to His Father; to offer divine homage to His Father, to unite our supplications with that homage; but above all, to effect, in the intimacy of our soul, through His Spirit, the fruit of each one of His mysteries.

You will have noticed that the prayer of thanksgiving that follows the holy oblation and the communion (the "postcommunion") takes diverse wordings from and according to the different mysteries. What does this indicate, if not that through holy communion Christ wishes there to arise in us the thoughts, the feelings, that He experienced in living the mystery that is being celebrated that day; and consequently wishes to apply to us the particular fruits and graces proper to that mystery? That is what

[86] F.W. Faber, *The Blessed Sacrament*, Book IV, Ch. 6.

the Church asks in the postcommunion of the Feast of the Holy Rosary, the feast in which she solemnly celebrates the union of the mother of the Incarnate Word with all the mysteries of her Son Jesus. What does the Church ask in the Prayer of that Mass? "O God, whose only-begotten Son, by His life, death and resurrection, has merited for us the rewards of eternal salvation, *grant, we beseech you, that, by commemorating these mysteries, we may imitate what they contain, and obtain what they promise.*" A thought of the same kind inspires the postcommunion of the feast: "We beseech you, Lord ... that we may perceive the power of your mysteries which we commemorate, and obtain the effect of the sacrament which we have received."

It is in this way that, little by little, our identification with Jesus is effected: "Have this mind in you which was also in Christ Jesus."[87] Is not that the very formula of the destiny eternally planned for us: "to be conformed to the image of His Son"?[88]

Such are the essential features of the Person and the work of Christ Jesus.

The Eternal Word—"made flesh" for us—becomes, through His mysteries and His Sacrifice, our High Priest and our Mediator. A Mediator who knows our needs, because He has been a man on earth like us; a Mediator who is omnipotent because He is, with the Father and the Holy Spirit, God; a Mediator whose mediation is unceasing—in heaven by His eternal oblation, on earth by the Eucharistic Sacrifice.

And that work—it is *for us* that Christ accomplishes it: *pro nobis.* It is for no other reason than to associate us with His glory that Christ saves us by His Sacrifice.

O Lord, who can ever recognize how ineffable the designs of your wisdom are? who sufficiently praise the greatness of the gift you have given us? who ever render you worthy thanks for it?

---

[87] Phil. 2:5. [88] Rom. 8:29.

BOOK TWO

THE MYSTERIES OF CHRIST

CHAPTER SIX

THE DIVINE PREPARATIONS
(*Advent*)[1]

Introduction: Why God willed to prolong for so many centuries the preparations for the Incarnation.

All the blessings of God upon us have their source in the election He has made of our souls from all eternity, to make them "holy and without blemish in His sight."[2] In this divine decree, so full of love, is included our destiny as adopted children of God, with the whole body of favors that attach to it.

Well, says St. Paul, it is through the grace of Jesus Christ, sent by God the Father in the fullness of time, that such adoption has been given to us: "When the fullness of time came, God sent His Son, born of a woman ... that we might receive the adoption of sons."[3]

This eternal intent of God, of sending His own Son on earth so as to redeem the human race, lost and blighted by sin, and to

---

[1] [*Translator's note*: The editor of some of the French editions has added these references to the liturgical seasons to which Marmion's chapters on the individual mysteries are especially appropriate. In the case of this chapter he also refers the reader to two chapters of Marmion's *Christ, the Life of the Soul*: Book I, Ch. 1, *The Divine Plan of Our Adoptive Predestination in Jesus Christ*, and Book I, Ch. 2, *Christ, the One and Only Model of All Perfection*.]

[2] Eph. 1:4.   [3] Gal. 4:4-5; see also Eph. 1:5-6.

restore to it His gift of all its rights of inheritance as children, and heavenly beatitude,[4] is the masterpiece of His wisdom and His love. God's ways of seeing things are not our ways; all His thoughts surpass our thoughts as heaven surpasses earth; but above all it is in the work of the Incarnation and Redemption that the sublimity and grandeur of the divine ways shine forth. This work is such a high one, is so closely united to the life of the Most Blessed Trinity itself, that it remained hidden in the depths of the divine secrets throughout the ages: "hidden from eternity in God."[5]

As you know, God willed to prepare humanity over some thousands of years for the revelation of this mystery. Why did God will to defer during so many centuries the coming of His Son among us? Why so long a period? Mere creatures that we are, we cannot penetrate the ultimate why and wherefore of the conditions in which He effects His works; He is infinitely sovereign and has no need of any counselor.[6] But as He is also Wisdom itself, who rules all things with measure and balance,[7] who "reaches from end to end mightily and orders all things sweetly,"[8] we can nevertheless, in humility, seek out some of the suitabilities He makes shine forth from His mysteries.

It was necessary that men, who had sinned through pride— "You shall be as gods"[9]—should be obliged, through an experience which was prolonged by their weakness and the extent of their misery, to recognize the absolute need they had of a Redeemer, and to yearn for his coming with every fiber of their nature.[10]

And, indeed, the whole religion of the Old Testament can be summed up in that ceaseless cry that burst forth from the hearts of the Patriarchs and of the just and faithful: "Drop down dew, ye heavens ... let the earth be opened, and bud forth a savior."[11] The idea of this future Redeemer was everywhere throughout

---

[4] Gal. 4:4-5.   [5] Eph. 3:9.   [6] Rom. 11:34; Isa. 40:13.   [7] Job 28:25.

[8] See Wisdom 8:1; cf. the Great Antiphon *O Sapientia*, of December 17.

[9] Gen. 3:5.   [10] Cf. St. Thomas, III, q.1, a.5.   [11] Isa. 45:8.

the Old Law; all the symbols, all the rites and sacrifices prefigure it: "All these things happened to them in figure";[12] all the wishes, all the desires, focus upon him. According to the beautiful expression of an author of the early centuries, the Old Testament was carrying Christ in its womb: "The Law was pregnant with Christ."[13] The religion of Israel was a waiting for the Messiah, the liberator.

Further, the greatness of the mystery of the Incarnation and the majesty of the Redeemer required that the revelation of Him to the human race should happen only in stages, bit by bit. In the immediate wake of his fall, man was neither worthy of receiving nor capable of welcoming the full manifestation of the God-man. That is why, by a divine disposing full of both wisdom and mercy, it was only little by little, through the mouths of the prophets, that God revealed this ineffable mystery. When humanity was sufficiently prepared, the Word, so many times foretold, so often promised, so long awaited, would Himself appear upon this earth to instruct us: "God, who at sundry times and in divers manners spoke in times past to the fathers by the prophets, last of all in these days has spoken to us by His Son."[14]

I will therefore indicate to you some features of the divine preparations for the Incarnation. We shall see thereby with what wisdom God has disposed humankind to receive salvation; and that will be an occasion for us to render fervent thanksgivings to "the Father of mercies"[15] for having made us live in "the fullness of time"[16]—for it still continues—when He grants to men the inestimable gift of His Son.

---

[12] 1 Cor. 10:11 (Rheims).   [13] Appendix to the works of St. Augustine, *Sermo* CXCVI.   [14] Hebr. 1:1-2.   [15] 2 Cor. 1:3.   [16] Gal. 4:4.

1. How Eternal Wisdom, by recalling the original promise of
    a Redeemer and making it more precise through the voice
    of the prophets, prepared the souls of the just of the Old
    Testament for the coming of the God-man upon earth.

As you know, it was immediately after the sin of our first parents, at the very cradle of the human race (a race rebellious already), that God began to reveal the mystery of the Incarnation.
Adam and Eve, prostrate before the Creator, in the shame and
despair of their fall, no longer dared to raise their eyes to heaven.
Yet, look—that is when, even before pronouncing the sentence
of their expulsion from the earthly paradise, God let them hear
the first words of pardon and of hope.

Instead of being accursed and expelled for ever from the presence of their God as the rebel angels had been, they would have a
Redeemer: He it was who would break the power the devil had
acquired over them. And as their fall had begun through a woman's betrayal of trust, it would be through the Son of a woman
that this redemption would be brought about: "I will put enmities
between you [the serpent] and the woman, and your seed and
her seed: she shall crush your head."[17]

This is what has been called the "Proto-gospel," the first word
of salvation. It is the first promise of redemption, the dawn of the
divine mercies towards the earth that had sinned, the first ray of
that light which was one day to give life to the world, the first
manifestation of the mystery hidden in God from all eternity.[18]

Since that promise, all the religion of the human race, and,
later, all the religion of the chosen people, is focused upon this
"offspring of the woman," this "seed of the woman," that was to
set men free.

As the years rolled on, as the centuries advanced, God made
His promise more precise; and the more it was repeated, the
more solemn it was. He assured the patriarchs Abraham, Isaac

---

[17] Gen. 3:15.   [18] Eph. 3:9.

and Jacob that it was from their race that the blessed Seed would come forth: "And in your seed shall all the nations of the earth be blessed."[19] To the dying Jacob He showed that from within the tribe of Judah would arise the one who was to come, the object of all the people's longings: "he that is to be sent, and he shall be the expectation of nations."[20]

See how the nations, forgetful of the first revelations, sank by imperceptible degrees into error. God then chose a people who would be the guardians of His promises. Across the centuries, God would remind that people of His promises, renew those promises, make them clearer and more abundant: that would be the era of the prophets.

If you go through the sacred oracles of the prophets of Israel, you will note that the features by which God delineates the person of the future Messiah and specifies the characteristics of His mission are sometimes so opposite to each other that they seem not to be capable of being encountered in the same person. Sometimes the prophets attribute to the Redeemer prerogatives that can only be appropriate to one who is God; sometimes they predict for this Messiah a sum of humiliations, of contradictions received by him, of infirmities and of sufferings, by which the vilest of men would scarcely deserve to be so weighed down.

You are constantly finding this striking contrast.

For example, look at David, the king dear to the heart of God. The Lord swears that He will establish his race for ever: the Messiah will be of the royal family of David. God shows the Messiah to David as both as David's son and as David's Lord[21]—son through His humanity which He would one day take to Himself from a virgin of David's family, Lord through His divinity. David contemplates Him in the holy splendors, eternally begotten before day-star ever arose; as Supreme High Priest according to the

---

[19] Gen. 22:18; cf. Gal. 3:16.   [20] Gen. 49:10.
[21] Ps. 109 (110):1; cf. Matt. 22:41-45.

pattern of Melchizedek,[22] consecrated to reign over us through His gentleness, His truth and His justice;[23] in a word as the Son of God Himself, the Son to whom all the nations would be given as inheritance.[24] St. Paul points out to the Hebrews that these are prerogatives in which only one who is God can glory.[25]

But David contemplates also His hands and feet pierced; His garments divided up, lots being cast for His clothes,[26] gall and vinegar offered to Him to drink.[27] And then, look, the divine attributes again: He will not undergo the corruption of the tomb— "you will not ... allow your holy one to see corruption"; He, the conqueror of death, will be seated "at the right hand" of God.[28]

This contrast is no less striking in Isaiah, the great Seer. So precise, so abundant is it, that one could call Isaiah the fifth Gospel-writer; one might almost say that he is recounting events which had taken place, rather than prophesying those that were to take place in the future.

The prophet, rapt to the heavens, proclaims as indescribable this Messiah's coming to be—"who shall declare his generation?";[29] he gives Him names that no man had ever borne before: "Wonderful, Counselor, God the Mighty, Father of the world to come, the Prince of Peace."[30] "Behold, a virgin shall conceive, and bear a son" who shall be called "*Emmanuel*," God-with-us.[31] Isaiah describes Him: one "come forth as brightness"—rising like the dawn; "lighted as a lamp"—radiant like a torch-flame;[32] he sees Him opening the eyes of the blind, unstopping the ears of the deaf, making the dumb speak, the lame to leap as though a hart.[33] He shows Him established as Leader and Master of the Gentiles[34]—

---

[22] Ps. 109 (110):3-4.   [23] Ps. 44 (45):5; Marmion follows the Rheims.
[24] Ps. 2:7: "The Lord said to me: You are my Son ... Ask of me, and I will give me the Gentiles for your inheritance, and the utmost parts of the earth for your possession."   [25] Hebr. 1:13.   [26] Ps. 21 (22):17-19.
[27] Ps. 68 (69):22.   [28] See Ps. 15 (16):10-11.   [29] Isa. 53:8.
[30] Isa. 9:6.   [31] Isa. 7:14.   [32] Isa. 62:1.
[33] Isa. 35:5-6.   [34] Isa. 55:4; 2:14ff.

the pagan nations; he sees the idols utterly destroyed before Him.[35] And he hears God's oath and promise: that before this Savior every knee should bend and every tongue confess His power.[36]

And, nevertheless, this Redeemer, whose glory the prophet thus extols, was going to be crushed by such sufferings, submerged in such humiliation, that He would be regarded as "the most abject of men," as though "a leper"; like "one struck by God,"[37] like one in the depths of disgrace; "led as a sheep to the slaughter," taken like a lamb to its shearers,[38] because "it was the will of the Lord to bruise Him."[39]

In the case of the majority of the prophets, you may be struck by that contrast in their descriptions between the greatness and the abasements, the power and the weakness, the sufferings and the glory, of the Messiah. You can see with what loving condescension and wisdom God prepared minds for the revelation of the ineffable mystery of a God-man, at one and the same time Supreme Lord the adored of all the nations and victim for the world's sins.

You know, the scheme of the Divine Mercy is based entirely upon faith; the latter is the "root and foundation"[40] of all justification. Without this faith, even the material presence of Christ Jesus would not be able to produce in souls the fullness of its effects.

Now then, faith is communicated to us by the Holy Spirit's interior action which accompanies the exposition of the divine

---

[35] Isa. 2:18.   [36] Isa. 45:23; Phil 2:5-11.   [37] Isa. 53:3-4.

[38] Ibid., v.7.   [39] Ibid., v.10 (RSV, Cath.) [*Translator's note*: Remark these other words of Isaiah in that passage: verse 8, "...for the wickedness of my people have I struck Him"; verse 5, "He was wounded for our iniquities, He was bruised for our sins ... and by His bruises we are healed"; verse 7, "He was offered because it was His own will"; verse 4, "Our weakness, and it was He who carried the weight of it." (Knox)]

[40] Council of Trent, *Decree on Justification*, c. 8.

truths given by the prophets and the preachers: *Fides ex auditu,* Faith, *from hearing.*[41]

By so often recalling His first promises, by revealing through the mouth of the prophets, little by little, the features of the Redeemer-to-come, God willed to produce in the hearts of the just of the Old Testament the dispositions needed for the coming of the Messiah to be salutary for them. And so the more the just of the Old Covenant were filled with faith and trust in the promises announced by their prophets, the more that they burned with a desire to see those promises come to pass—the better were they prepared to receive the abundance of the graces the Savior was to bring to the world. It was thus that the Virgin Mary, Zacharias and Elizabeth, Simeon, Anna, and the other faithful souls who lived at the time of Christ's coming, had recognized Him straight away and been inundated with His favors.

You see how God was pleased to prepare men for the coming of His Son on earth. St. Peter could truly say to the Jews that they were "the children of the prophets"[42] and St. Paul could write to the Hebrews that before God had spoken to them by His Son in person, He had spoken *"at sundry times and in diverse manners ...* to the fathers by the prophets."[43]

So the faithful Jews were constant in awaiting the Messiah. Their faith discerned in the person of this Redeemer a divine messenger, king, God; they awaited the one who was to put an end to their miseries, to deliver them from the burden of their sins. They had but one devout plea: "Send, Lord, the one who is to come." They had but one desire: to behold with their own eyes the face of the Savior of Israel. The promised Messiah was the objective on which all their sighs, all their wishes, all their worship, all the religion of the Old Covenant, converged. The whole of the

[41] Rom. 10:8 ("the word of faith, which we preach"); Gal. 3:2 ("Did you receive the Spirit in virtue of the works of the Law, or *in virtue of hearing and believing?*")   [42] Acts 3:25.   [43] Hebr. 1:1-2.

Old Testament is one prolonged Advent, the prayers of which are all summed up in this appeal of Isaiah's: "Send forth, O Lord, the lamb, the ruler of the earth...,"[44] "Drop down dew, you heavens, from above, and let the clouds rain the just: let the earth be opened and bud forth a savior."[45]

2. St. John the Baptist, forerunner of the Incarnate Word, sums up and surpasses all the prophets.

We have marveled at how profound were the ways of Divine Wisdom in the preparations for the mystery of the coming of the God-man. And yet this is not all.

While, through a succession of wonders, God's Wisdom was preserving intact the original promises to the Chosen People, and was ceaselessly confirming and developing those promises through the prophets, and was even making the successive captivities of the Jewish people (unfaithful as the latter had sometimes become) serve to spread a knowledge of those promises among the foreign nations as well—all this time Eternal Wisdom was likewise directing the destinies of those nations.

You know how, during that long period of centuries, God, who "holds the hearts of kings in His hand"[46] and whose power is equal to His wisdom, set up and broke the vaster empires, one after another. He made the empire of Babylon, reaching as far as Egypt, succeed that of Nineveh; then, as Isaiah had foretold, He called His servant Cyrus,[47] king of the Persians, and placed in his hands the scepter of Nebuchadnezzar. After Cyrus, it was Alexander whom He made master of the nations, waiting till He should finally transport the empire of the world to Rome, an empire the unity and peace of which would serve the mysterious plans for the spreading of the Gospel.

[44] Isa. 16:1.   [45] Isa. 45:8.   [46] Cf. Prov. 21:1.
[47] Isa. 45:1: "Thus says the Lord, to my anointed Cyrus..."

Now the "fullness of time"[48] had come. Sin and error were inundating the whole world; man was finally feeling the weakness in which his pride was holding him fast. All the peoples stretched out their arms towards this liberator, so often promised, so long awaited: "And the desired of all nations shall come."[49]

When this fullness of time had arrived, God crowned all His preparations by the sending of St. John the Baptist, the last of the prophets. But that He would make him greater than Abraham, greater than Moses, greater than all the rest, He Himself declared [through His Son]: "Among those born of women there has not arisen a greater than John the Baptist."[50] It is Jesus Christ who says this. And why did He say it?

Because God wished to make John the herald par excellence, His beloved Son's own forerunner—he "shall be called the prophet of the Most High"[51] In order to heighten further the glory of this Son whom at last He was to present to the world after having promised Him for so long, God was pleased to raise up the dignity of the forerunner who was to witness that the Light and Truth had finally appeared upon the earth: John the Baptist "was to bear witness to" the Light.[52]

God wished him to be great because his mission was to be great, because he had been chosen to precede, so closely, the One who was to come. For God, the greatness of the saints is measured by the comparison they bear to His Son Jesus.

See how He exalted this forerunner, so as to show once again, by the excellence of this last prophet, what the dignity of His Word is. He chose this forerunner from a particularly holy race; it was an angel who announced his birth, said what his name was to be, indicated the extent and greatness of his mission. God sanctified him in the womb of his mother; He made wonders burst forth around his cradle, to the point that the happy witnesses of

---

[48] Gal. 4:4.   [49] Haggai 2:8.   [50] Matt. 11:11; Luke 7:28.
[51] Luke 1:76.   [52] John 1:8.

these marvels asked themselves, completely astonished: "What then will this child be?"[53]

Later, John's holiness would appear so great that the Jews would come and ask him whether he was the awaited Christ. But he, preceded by those divine favors as he was, protested that he had only been sent to be the voice crying in the wilderness: "Prepare the way for the Lord, for He is coming."[54]

The other prophets have only seen the Messiah from a distant time, but he points with his finger to the Messiah and in terms so clear that all sincere hearts will understand what He is saying: "Behold, the Lamb of God"—behold Him who is the object of all the desires of the human race because He is to "take away the sins of the world";[55] you do not know Him yet, though He has stood in the midst of you;[56] He "takes rank before me, for He was when I was not";[57] so great is He, that I am not worthy to loose the strap of His sandal;[58] so great, that I have seen the Spirit descend from heaven like a dove and rest upon Him.[59] "And I have seen and have borne witness that this is the Son of God."[60]

What else did he say about Jesus? "He comes from above, from heaven; He is over all. And He bears witness to that which He has seen and heard."[61] "He whom God has sent speaks the word of God, for not by measure does God give the Spirit. The Father loves the Son, and has given all things into His hands. He who believes in the Son has everlasting life; he who is unbelieving towards the Son shall not see life, but the wrath of God rests upon him."[62]

There we have the last words of the forerunner. It is with those words that he completed his work of preparing souls to receive the Messiah. Indeed, when the Incarnate Word, who alone can speak words from on high because He is always *in sinu Patris*, in the heart's-embrace of the Father[63]—when the Incarnate Word began His public mission as Savior, John disappeared; He

---

[53] Luke 1:57-66.   [54] See John 1:23.   [55] John 1:29.   [56] Ibid., vv. 26-27.
[57] Ibid., v. 30 (Knox).   [58] Ibid., v. 27.   [59] Ibid., v. 32.   [60] Ibid., v. 34.
[61] See John 3:31-32.   [62] Ibid., vv. 34-36.   [63] John 1:18.

no longer bore testimony to the Truth, except by the shedding of his blood.

The Christ, whom he has presented, has finally come. He is the Light to whom John bore testimony, and all those who believe in this Light have life eternal. It is to Him alone that, from then on, one must say: "Lord, to whom shall we go? You have the words of eternal life."[64]

3. Living in "the fullness of time" though we are, the Holy Spirit wills that the Church brings to our minds each year the memory of these divine preparations. Threefold reason for that super-natural arrangement.

We ourselves have the good fortune to believe in this Light, the Light which from this time on would "enlighten everyone coming into this world";[65] and moreover we live in the blessed "fullness of time"; we have not been deprived, as the Patriarchs were, of seeing the reign of the Messiah. Though we are not amongst those who beheld Christ in person, who heard His words, who saw Him going about everywhere doing good, we have the signal good fortune of belonging to those nations of whom David sang that they would be the "inheritance" of Christ.[66]

And nevertheless the Holy Spirit, who directs the Church and is first author of our sanctification, wills that the Church each year dedicate a period of four weeks to a remembrance of the amazing length of the divine preparations, and to put it all to work in order to redispose our souls to have the inner dispositions in which faithful Jews lived when awaiting the coming of the Messiah.

You will perhaps say to me at once: "That preparation for the coming of Christ, those longings, that waiting—all that was excellent for the souls of the just who were living under the Old Testament; but now that Christ has come, why still cultivate that attitude which does not seem to correspond to the truth?"

[64] See John 6:69.   [65] See John 1:9.
[66] Ps. 27 (28):9; Ps. 32 (33):12; Ps. 93 (94):14; Ps. 105 (106):5.

There are several reasons for this.

First, God wishes to be praised and blessed in all His works.

All of them, indeed, are marked by His infinite wisdom: "In wisdom have you made them all."[67] All are admirable, as much in their preparation as in their effecting. That is especially true of those that have as their direct object the glory of His Son, for it is the Father's will that His Son be exalted for ever.[68] God wishes us to admire the works He performs, wishes us to render thanksgiving to Him for having thus prepared, with so much wisdom and power, the reign of His Son among us. We enter into the mind of God when we recollect the prophecies and promises of the Old Covenant.

Next, God wishes us to find in these preparations a confirmation of our faith.

That He gave so many signs, signs multifarious and precise, and so many and such clear prophecies, was in order that we might recognize as His Son Him who fulfilled them in person.

See how, in the Gospels, Our Lord invited His disciples to reflect on this. "Search the Scriptures," He said to them—the "Scriptures" of that time were the books of the Old Testament—search them, and you will see that they are full of my name;[69] for "all things must be fulfilled that are written in the ... prophets and the psalms concerning me."[70] Again, we hear Him soon after His resurrection explaining to the disciples on the road to Emmaus, in order to strengthen their faith and dispel their sadness, "the things referring to Himself" throughout the Scriptures, beginning with Moses and all the prophets.[71] When, therefore, we read the prophecies that the Church puts before us during Advent, let us in the fullness of our faith say, like the first disciples of Jesus: "We have found Him whom the prophets foretold."[72] Let us repeat it to Christ Jesus Himself: Yes, you are truly He

---

[67] Ps. 103 (104):24 (RSV, Cath.)   [68] John 12:28.   [69] See John 5:39-40.
[70] Luke 24:44.   [71] Luke 24:27.   [72] See John 1:45.

who was to come: we believe it and we adore you—you who, to save the world, deigned to become incarnate in the womb of a virgin: "Thou, in undertaking the freeing of man, didst not abhor the Virgin's womb."[73]

This profession of faith is extremely pleasing to God; let us never tire of repeating it. Our Lord will then be able to say to us, as He said to His apostles: "The Father Himself loves you, because you ... have believed that I came forth from God."[74]

Finally, there is a third reason, one more profound and more intimate. Christ did not come specially for the inhabitants of Judea, His contemporaries; He came for all of us, for all men and women, of all the nations and all the ages. Do we not sing in the *Credo*: "For *us* men and for *our* salvation, He came down from heaven"? The "fullness of time" has not come to a close yet: it will endure as long as there are chosen ones to save.

It is to the Church alone that, since His ascension, Christ has left the mission of bringing Him forth in souls. You are "my little children," said St. Paul the apostle of Christ Jesus among the nations; my little children with whom "I am in labor again, until Christ be formed in you."[75] The Church, guided in this by the Holy Spirit (who is the Spirit of Jesus) labors at this work by causing us each year to contemplate the mystery of her Divine Spouse. For, as I said to you at the beginning of these talks, every one of Christ's mysteries is a living mystery; it is not only an historical reality, the memory of which we bring to mind; it is also a solemn celebration that contains in itself its own grace, a special power, which should make us live with the very life of Christ—Christ, whose members we are—by making us share in all His states.

So then, the Church celebrates at Christmas the nativity of her Divine Spouse: "When the sun rises in the heavens you will see the King of kings ... like a bridegroom coming in splendor

---

[73] Hymn, *Te Deum*.   [74] John 16:27.   [75] Gal. 4:19 (Rheims).

from his wedding-chamber";[76] and she, the Church, wishes to prepare us, by the weeks of Advent, for the coming of Christ within us. It is a coming that is wholly interior, mysterious, taking place in faith, but full of fruitfulness.

Christ, it is true, is already within us by the sanctifying grace which gives us spiritual birth as children of God. But the Church wishes this grace to be renewed, wishes us to live with a new life, one that is set freer from sin, more disengaged from imperfections, more free of all attachment to ourselves and the merely created: "Grant ... that the new birth of your only-begotten Son in the flesh may set us free, who are held by the old bondage under the yoke of sin."[77] She wishes us above all to understand that Christ, in exchange for the humanity that He has taken to Himself from us, will give us a share in His divinity, and will work within us to take a more complete, more full, more perfect possession of us. It will be like the grace of a new divine birth within us: "... that, by thy bounteous grace, through this holy exchange, we may be found like unto Him in whom is our substance united with thee."[78]

It is this grace that the Word Incarnate has merited for us by His birth at Bethlehem. But if it is true to say that He was born, lived and died for us all—"Christ died for all"[79]—it is also true to add that the application of His merits, and the conferring of His graces, will only materialize for each soul in the measure of that soul's dispositions.

It is only in proportion to our dispositions that we shall share in the graces Christ's nativity should bring us, abundant as those graces are. The Church knows this perfectly, and that is why she neglects nothing for producing in our souls that interior attitude which Christ's coming within us demands. Not only does the Church say to us by the mouth of the Forerunner: "Prepare a way

[76] Prayer of Matins for Christmas; Ps. 18 (19):6. [77] Collect for the Third Mass of Christmas Day. [78] Prayer at the Christmas Mass of Midnight. [79] 2 Cor. 5:15.

for the Lord"[80] for "He is already close at hand";[81] but, like a wife attentive to the desires of her husband, like a mother thoughtful for her children's good, she herself suggests to us, and gives us the means of making real, this necessary preparation. She takes us back under the Old Testament, as it were, so that we may make our own, quite naturally, the feelings of those faithful and just persons who longed for the coming of the Messiah.

If we let ourselves be guided by her, our dispositions will be perfect, and the solemn feast of the birth of Jesus will produce within us all its fruits of grace, of light and of life.

4. **Dispositions we ought to bring so that the coming of Christ may produce the fullness of its fruits in our souls: purity of heart, humility, trust and holy desires. Uniting ourselves to the feelings of the Virgin Mary, mother of Jesus.**

What are these dispositions? Consider: who was the person best disposed to the coming of the Word upon earth? Without any doubt, the Virgin Mary. At the moment when the Word came into this world, He found the heart of this virgin perfectly prepared, and capable of receiving the generous gifts He wished to shower on her. And what were the dispositions of this soul?

Assuredly, she possessed them all, perfectly; but there is one of them that shines out with a wholly particular brilliancy. It is her virginal purity. Mary is a virgin; her virginity is so precious to her that she mentioned it to the angel when the latter proposed the mystery of the divine motherhood to her.

Not only is she a virgin, but her soul is without stain. The liturgy shows to us that God's own purpose in granting Mary the unique privilege of her being conceived with an unstained soul was to prepare a worthy dwelling for His Son: "O God, who by

---

[80] Luke 3:4 (Jerusalem); Isaiah 40:3.   [81] Invitatory of Matins for Third Sunday of Advent.

the immaculate conception of the Virgin *didst prepare a dwelling place* worthy of your Son..."[82] Mary was to be the Mother of God; and this eminent dignity demanded not only that she be a virgin, but that her purity surpass that of the angels and be a reflection of the holy splendors in which the Father begets His Son: "*In splendibus sanctorum,*" "in the brightness of the holy ones."[83] God is holy, thrice holy; the angels, the archangels, the seraphim hymn that infinite purity: "*Sanctus, sanctus, sanctus,*" "Holy, holy, holy."[84] The heart's-embrace of the Father, of immaculate splendor, is the natural dwelling of the only-begotten Son of God. The Word is always "*in sinu Patris,*" "in the heart's-embrace of the Father"; but in becoming incarnate, He wished, by an ineffable condescension, to be also "*in sinu Virginis Mariae,*" in the womb of the Virgin Mary. It was necessary that the tabernacle the Virgin offered Him should remind Him, through its incomparable purity, of the indefectible splendor of that eternal light where, as God, He ever dwells. "*Christi sinus erat...,*" "Christ's dwelling place was: in God the Father, Divinity; in Mary His mother, virginity."[85]

There we have the first disposition that attracts Christ: great purity. But we—we are sinners; we cannot offer to the Word, to Christ Jesus, that immaculate purity He loves so much. What is it that will take the place of it in us? It is humility.

God has in His heart's-embrace the Son of His delight; but He presses closely to Himself another son—the prodigal son. It is Our Lord Himself who tells us this. When, after his wrongdoings, the prodigal returns to his father, he prostrates himself in the dust, he recognizes he is a miserable and unworthy person; and straight away, without a word of reproach, his father receives him into the embrace of his mercy, "moved with compassion."[86]

---

[82] Collect of the Mass for the Feast of the Immaculate Conception.
[83] See Ps. 109 (110):3.   [84] Isa. 6:3.   [85] *Sermo* XII, appendix to the Works of St. Ambrose.   [86] Luke 15:20.

Let us not forget that the Word. the Son, only wishes what His Father wishes: that He became incarnate and appeared on earth so as to seek out sinners and bring them back to His Father: "I have not come to call the just, but sinners to repentance."[87] So true is that, that Our Lord would later have a predilection—to the great scandal of the Pharisees—for being in the company of sinners, of sitting at the same table with sinners. He would allow Magdalene to wash his feet and to water them with her tears.

We do not have the purity of the Virgin Mary, but let us at least ask for the humility of Magdalene, for a contrite and penitent love. O Christ Jesus, I am not worthy that you should enter and live within me: my heart will not be for you a habitation of purity; misery dwells there. But this misery I recognize, I avow. Come and empty me of it, O you who are mercy itself; come and deliver me, O you who are all-powerful! "Come to us and save us, Lord God almighty!"[88] A prayer of that kind, joined with the spirit of penitence, attracts Christ, because a humility which abases oneself in one's nothingness renders thereby, in itself, a homage to the goodness and the power of Jesus: "If anyone comes to me, I shall not cast that person out."[89]

The sight of our own infirmity ought not to discourage us, however—far from it. The more we think of our weakness, the more must we open our soul to *confidence*, because salvation comes from Christ alone.

"Faint-hearted ones, take courage and fear not: behold, our God"—God, *our* God—"will come and will save us."[90] See what confidence the Jews had in the Messiah. For them, the Messiah was everything; all the aspirations of Israel, all the desires of the people, all the hopes of their race, were summed up in Him. To contemplate the Messiah was to encompass the whole of their

---

[87] Luke 5:32; Matt. 9:13; Mark 2:17.   [88] Responsory for Vespers of Fridays in Advent; Ps. 79 (80):2.   [89] See John 6:37.
[90] Communion prayer for Third Sunday of Advent; Isa. 35:4.

ambition; to see the Messiah's reign established was to be the fulfillment of their every wish. So, how the desires of the Jews made them both confident and impatient! "Stir up your might, and come to save us"[91]—come, Lord, and do not delay. "Show us your face, and we shall be saved."[92]

How much more is that borne out for us who possess Christ Jesus, true God as well as true man. Oh! if we only understood, really understood, what the sacred humanity of Jesus is, we would have unshakeable confidence in it. In it resides all the treasures of knowledge and wisdom; in it dwells Divinity itself. This God-man, who comes to us, is Emmanuel, is "God-with-us," is our elder brother. The Word has espoused our nature, He has taken upon Himself our infirmities so as to experience what suffering is. He comes to us to give us a share of His divine life. All the graces we could hope for, He possesses in their fullness so as to grant them to us.

The promises which, through the prophets, God made to His people in order to stir up in them a wish for the Messiah are magnificent. But many of the Jews understood these promises in the material and worldly sense of a temporal and political reign. The good things promised to the just who awaited the Savior were only a figure of the super-natural riches we find in Christ. The majority of the Israelites lived by earthly *symbols*; we live by the divine reality—that is to say, by the grace of Jesus. The liturgy of Advent speaks to us unceasingly of mercy, of redemption, of salvation, of deliverance, of light, of abundance, of joy, of peace. "Behold the Savior comes; on the day of His birth the world shall be flooded with light."[93] "Exult then with joy, O Jerusalem, for your Savior shall appear."[94] "Peace shall fill our earth when He shows Himself."[95] All the blessings that can fill a soul to overflowing, Christ brings with Him: "... all things with Him."[96]

---

[91] Ps. 79 (80):3.   [92] Ibid., v. 8.   [93] Antiphon of Lauds for the First Sunday of Advent.   [94] Antiphon of Lauds for the Third Sunday of Advent.   [95] Responsory of Matins for the Third Sunday of Advent.   [96] Rom. 8:32.

Let us, therefore, allow our hearts to proceed to an absolute confidence in Him who is to come. It makes us very pleasing to the Father, our believing that His Son Jesus can do everything for the sanctification of our souls. We declare by this that Jesus is His equal, and that the Father "has given all things into His hand."[97] Such a certitude therefore can never be a mistaken one. In the Mass of the First Sunday in Advent, the Church goes to the lengths of giving us this firm assurance three times: "None of those who wait on you, O Lord, shall be confounded."[98]

This confidence will above all be expressed in *ardent desires* to see Christ within us so that He reign there more: "Thy Kingdom come!" These desires, the liturgy formulates for us. At the same time as she places before our eyes and makes us re-read the prophecies, especially those of Isaiah, the Church puts upon our lips the aspirations and the sighs of the just of ancient times. She wishes to see us prepared for the coming of Christ into our souls, in exactly the way that God wished the Jews to be prepared to receive His Son: "Send, Lord, Him whom you have promised."[99] "Come, Lord, come and forgive the sins of your people!"[100] "Lord, show your mercy and grant that the Author of our salvation may appear."[101] "Come and deliver us, Lord God Almighty!"[102] "Stir up your might, and come!"[103]

The Church makes us constantly repeat these aspirations; let us make them ours, let us appropriate them to ourselves with faith, and Christ Jesus will enrich us with His graces.

There is no doubt that God is master of His gifts, as you know; He is sovereignly free, and no-one can ask Him to account for His preferences. But, in the ordinary dispositions of His Providence, He is attentive to the supplications of the humble who lay their

---

[97] John 3:35.   [98] Ps. 24 (25):3.   [99] Cf. Gen. 49:10: "... till he come that is to be sent, and he shall be the expectation of nations."   [100] Alleluia for the Fourth Sunday of Advent.   [101] Offertory for the Second Sunday of Advent; Ps. 84 (85):8.   [102] Short Response for Lauds of Advent.
[103] Collect for the Fourth Sunday of Advent.

needs open before Him: "You listen to the wants of the humble."[104] Christ gives Himself in the measure of the desire we have to receive Him. And desires enlarge the capacity of the soul that expresses them: "Open your mouth wide, and I will fill it."[105]

If, then, we wish the celebration of the nativity of Christ to give great glory to the Holy Trinity, if we wish it to be a consolation of the heart of the Word Incarnate, and a source of abundant graces for the Church and for ourselves, let us seek to purify our hearts, let us preserve a humility that is full of trust, and, above all, let us enlarge our souls through the largeness and the vehemence of our desires.

Let us also ask the Virgin Mary to make us share the feelings that animated her during the blessed days that preceded the birth of Jesus.

The Church has willed—and what could be more appropriate?— that the liturgy of Advent be full of the thought of her. She, the Church, constantly causes us to sing of the divine fruitfulness of this virgin, a wonderful fruitfulness that throws all nature into astonishment: "Nature marveling, you became the mother of Him who made you; and before and after this are a virgin."[106]

The virginal womb of Mary was an immaculate sanctuary, from which rose up the most pure incense of her adoration and homage.

It is something truly ineffable, the interior life of the Virgin during those days. She lived in intimate union with the Child-God she was bearing in her womb. Jesus's soul, through the beatific vision, was immersed in the Light Divine, and this Light was shining upon His mother. To the sight of the angels Mary truly appeared as the "woman clothed with the sun,"[107] wholly irradiated with heavenly splendors, wholly shining with rays of light from her Son. How her feelings rose to the height of her faith! How well she summed up

---

[104] Ps. 9 (10):17 (Jerus.)   [105] Ps. 80 (81):11.

[106] Antiphon, *Alma Redemptoris Mater*.   [107] Apoc. 12:1: "A great sign appeared in heaven: a woman clothed with the sun..."

in herself all the aspirations, all the heart-soarings, all the hopes of humanity as it awaited its Savior and its God. Summed up? Her dispositions surpassed all these. By the purity and intensity of her emotions she conferred on them a value they had never before attained. What a holy ardor was in her desires! How unshakeable the assurance with which she trusted! What a fervor there was in her love!

She, this humble virgin, is queen of the patriarchs, because she is of their holy line, and because the Child she brought into the world is the Son who is the embodiment, in person, of all the magnificence of the ancient promises.

She is queen of the prophets also, because she brought to birth the Word by whom the prophets spoke; because her Son fulfilled every prophecy, and because He Himself proclaimed to all peoples the good news of redemption.[108]

Let us humbly ask her to help us enter into her dispositions. She will hear our prayer; we shall have the immense joy of seeing Christ born afresh in our hearts by the communication of a more abundant grace; and like the Virgin, albeit in lesser measure, we shall be able to taste for ourselves the truth of those words of St. John: "The Word was God... And the Word was made flesh, and dwelt among us. And we saw His glory ... full of grace and truth... And of His fullness we have all received, grace for grace."[109]

---

[108] Luke 4:18; Isa. 61:1.   [109] John 1, vv. 1, 14, 16.

CHAPTER SEVEN

O Wondrous Exchange!

(*Christmas*)

Introduction: What the mystery of the Incarnation comes down to is a wondrous exchange between Divinity and humanity.

The coming of the Son of God upon earth is so momentous an event that God wished to prepare it over long ages. Rites and sacrifices, figures and symbols—He made everything converge towards Christ; He foretold and proclaimed Him though the mouth of prophets who succeeded each other from generation to generation.

And look, now, at this present time—it is the very Son of God who comes to instruct us: "In the past ... in various different ways, God spoke to our ancestors through the prophets; but in our own time ... He has spoken to us through His Son."[1] For Christ was born not only for the Jews of Judea who lived when He was on earth; it was for all of us, for all men, that He came down from heaven: "For us men and for our salvation, He came down from heaven."[2] The grace that He merited by His nativity, He wishes to communicate to every soul.

That is why the Church, guided by the Holy Spirit, has taken to herself the sighs of the Patriarchs, the aspirations of the Just of ancient times, the longings of the Chosen People, so as to put

---

[1] Hebr. 1:1-2 (Jerus.)   [2] Nicene Creed.

them on our lips and fill our hearts with them. She wishes us to prepare for Christ's coming as if that nativity were going to be renewed before our eyes.

See also how, when she commemorates the coming of her Divine Spouse upon earth, she deploys her full liturgical splendors, makes a brilliance of altar-candles shine out to celebrate the birth of the "Prince of Peace,"[3] of the "Sun of Justice"[4] who, coming into the world, rises in our "darkness" to "enlighten every man."[5] She grants to her priests the privilege—one which is almost unique during the year—of offering the Holy Sacrifice of the Mass three times.

These feasts are magnificent; they are also full of charm. The Church evokes the memory of the angels singing songs of "Glory to the new-born Babe"; of the shepherds, simple souls who come to the manger to adore Him; of the wise men hastening from the East to render Him their adoration and offer Him rich gifts.

And yet, like every feast here below, this solemnity, even with the prolongment of an octave, is ephemeral. It passes. Is it therefore for a feast of one day, splendid though it be, that the Church demands of us so long a preparation? Certainly not! Why then? Because she knows that contemplation of this mystery contains a very special grace for our souls.

I said to you at the beginning of these talks that every mystery of Christ not only constitutes an historical fact that has occurred in time, but also contains its own special grace upon which souls ought to be nourished so as to live by it.

Well, what is the intimate grace within the mystery of the Nativity? What is that grace for the reception of which the Church takes so much care to dispose us? What fruit ought we to gather from contemplating the Christ Child?

The Church herself indicates this, in the first Mass of Christmas, that of midnight. After having offered up the bread and the

---

[3] Isa. 9:6.   [4] Malachi 4:2.   [5] See John 1, vv. 5, 9.

wine which a few moments later, at the Consecration, are going to be changed into the Body and Blood of Jesus Christ, she sums up her desires in this prayer: "Let the oblation of the festival we are celebrating today be acceptable to you, we beseech you, Lord; so that by your bountiful grace, by means of this most holy exchange, we may be found like unto Him in whom our substance is united to you"[6]—become sharers in that divinity to which, through the Word, our human substance is united.

We ask to have a share in that divinity. What occurs is like an exchange. By becoming incarnate, God took upon Himself our human nature, and in return He gives us a sharing in His divine nature.

That thought, so concise in form, is more explicitly expressed at the same stage of the Second Mass of Christmas Day: "May our offerings, we beseech you, Lord, prove suitable to the mysteries of the Nativity of which we sing today; that as this man who has been born into our human nature has at the same time shone gloriously upon us as God, so this earthly substance"—which He united to Himself—"may communicate to us that which in Him is divine."

To be made sharers in the divinity to which our humanity has been united in the Person of Christ, and to receive this divine gift through that very humanity—such is the grace attached to the celebration of the mystery of this day, Christmas Day.

You see, it is a human-divine exchange. The child born on Christmas Day is at the same time God, and the human nature that God takes to Himself from us is to serve as the instrument through which He communicates His divinity to us: "As this man who has been born into our human nature has at the same time shone gloriously upon us as God, *so*—in the same way—this earthly substance may *communicate to us* what is *divine*." Our offerings will be "suitable to the mysteries" signified by the birth on Christmas Day if—by our contemplation of the divine work

---

[6] *Secretum* of Midnight Mass.

at Bethlehem and our reception of the Eucharistic Sacrament—
we do share in the eternal life that Christ wishes to communicate
to us through His humanity.

"Oh, wondrous exchange," we shall sing on the octave day of
Christmas: "The *Creator* of human nature deigned to *take on a
human body and soul* and be born of the Virgin. He became man
without having a human father and *has bestowed on us His divine
nature.*"[7]

Let us pause for a few moments with the Church in wonder at
this exchange between creature and Creator, between heaven and
earth, an exchange that constitutes the very depth of the mystery
of the Nativity. Let us consider what its acts and its matter are—
under what form it in fact occurred. We shall then see what fruits
we derive from it—and see, also, what it engages us to.

1. **The first action of this exchange: the Eternal Word asks
   for a human nature from us so as unite Himself to it by a
   personal union: "The Creator ... taking to Himself a
   human body and soul."**

Let us transport ourselves to the cave at Bethlehem, let us
gaze on the child lying in the manger. What is that child in the
eyes of a profane person, of an inhabitant of the little town who
happens to go to the stable after the birth of Jesus?

Only a newly-born child; one whose life comes from a woman
of Nazareth. A son of Adam, as we all are, for his parents have
had themselves inscribed in the census registers; you'll be able to
follow the details of his genealogy, from Abraham to David, from
David to Joseph and to his mother. But this is only a man—or
rather, he will become a man, for at present he is only a child, a
feeble child whose life is maintained by a drop of milk.

That is how he appears to the senses, this little being upon his
bed of straw. Many of the Jews saw nothing else than that in

[7] Antiphon of Vespers for the octave day of Christmas.

Him. You will later hear his fellow-countrymen, astonished by His wisdom, ask themselves "Where did he get it from? Is not this the carpenter's son?"[8] "The carpenter's son" was all he had ever been in their eyes.

But to the eyes of faith, a life higher than human life animates this Child; He possesses divine life. What indeed does faith tell us about Him? What revelation does it give us?

What faith tells us that this Child is God's own Son. He is the Word, the Second Person of the Adorable Trinity, He is the Son who receives divine life from His Father, by a communication beyond human power to describe: "As the Father has life in Himself, even so He has given to the Son also to have life in Himself."[9] He possesses the divine nature, with all its infinite perfections. In the splendors of heaven, God begets this Son by an *eternal* begetting.

It is to this Divine Sonship of Christ in the heart's-embrace of the Father that our adoration is in the first place addressed. It is this that we extol at the Midnight Mass. In the Dawn Mass of Christmas, the Holy Sacrifice will celebrate the nativity of Christ according to the flesh—His birth at Bethlehem, of the Virgin Mary. Finally, the Third Mass of Christmas will be in honor of the coming of Christ into our souls.

The Night Mass, all-enveloped in mystery, starts with these words that are full of solemnity: *"Dominus dixit ad me: Filius meus es tu, ego hodie genui te"*—"The Lord has said to me: You are my Son, this day have I begotten you." That is the cry which escapes from the soul of Christ united to the Person of the Word and which reveals to the earth for the first time what heaven knows from all eternity. "This day" is first of all the "today" of eternity—and eternity has no dawn, no waning.

The Heavenly Father now contemplates His Incarnate Son. The Word stays no less God for having been made man. Having

[8] See Matt. 13:55; Mark 6:3; Luke 4:22.   [9] John 5:26.

become Son of Man, He remains Son of God. The first gaze that reposed on Christ, the first love with which He was surrounded— they are the gaze and the love of His Father: "As the Father has loved me..."[10] What contemplation and what love! Christ is the only Son of the Father; that is His essential glory; He is equal to and "consubstantial with" the Father, "God from God, Light from Light."[11] "Through Him all things came to be, not one thing had its being but through Him."[12] It is through this Son that time, the ages, have been created; He it is who "holds all things in being by the power of His word." It is He who "in the beginning drew the earth out of nothing, and the heavens are the work of His hands. They shall grow old, like a garment, they shall be changed, like a coat: but He—He is always the same and his years are eternal!"[13]

And this Word "was made flesh": *Verbum caro factum est.*[14]

Let us adore this Word, who became incarnate *for us*: "Christ is born for us, come let us adore Him."[15] One who is God took to Himself our humanity. Conceived by the mysterious working of the Holy Spirit in the womb of Mary, Christ was begotten from the most pure substance of the blood of the Virgin, and the life He has from her makes Him like to us: "The Creator of human nature deigned ... to be born of the Virgin. He became man without having a human father."[16]

That is what faith tells us: this Child is the Word of God, incarnate; He is the Creator of humankind, made man. If He needs a drop of milk to live on, yet His is the hand by which the birds of the air receive their food:

> *He suffers not the birds to starve*
> *Who on a little milk is fed.*[17]

---

[10] John 15:9.   [11] Nicene Creed.   [12] John 1:3 (Jerus.)
[13] See Hebr. 1, vv. 3, 10-12; the Epistle for the Third Mass of Christmas Day.
[14] John 1:14.   [15] Invitatory of the Matins of Christmas.
[16] Antiphon of Office, January 1st, *O admirabile commercium!*
[17] Hymn of Lauds for Christmas Day, *A solis ortus cardine.*

Look at this Child lying in the manger: eyes closed, He sleeps, He does not show outwardly all that He is. In appearance, He is simply like every other child. And yet at this moment of your seeing Him, in that He is God, in that He is the Word Eternal, He was judging souls who appeared before Him. As man, He is lying on the straw; as God, He is holding the universe in being and reigning in heaven: "He lies in the manger and in heaven He reigns."[18] This child, soon to start growing—"The child grew ... advanced in age"[19]—is He who is eternal and whose divine nature knows no change: "He is always the same and His years are eternal!" He who was born in the sphere of time is also He who is before all time. He who was made known to the shepherds and herdsmen of Bethlehem is He who, from nothing, has created the nations: "All nations are before Him as if they had no being at all."[20]

> To see the world's Creator there –
> Our Shepherd, were the shepherds led.

So, you see: to the eyes of faith, there are two lives in this Child; two lives indissolubly united in an ineffable manner. For the human nature belongs to the Word, by such a belonging that there is but one single Person, that of the Word—the Word who, by His own divine existence, holds the human nature in being.

Undoubtedly it is perfect, complete, this human nature of Christ: "*perfect man*":[21] nothing touching on its essence is lacking to it. This Child has a soul like ours; a body similar to ours; faculties—intellect, will, imagination, feelings—like ours. It is indeed one of us that His life on earth for thirty-three years will reveal; most authentically human. Sin, only, will be absent from His life: "It was right that He should in all things be made like unto His brethren,"[22] "in all things except sin."[23] Perfect in itself, this human nature will keep its own activity, its native splendor. Between these two lives of Christ—the divine, which He ever possesses by

---

[18] Twelfth response of Matins, octave of Christmas.   [19] Luke 2, vv. 40, 52.
[20] Isa. 40:17.   [21] Creed attributed to Athanasius.   [22] Hebr. 2:17.   [23] Hebr. 4:15.

His eternal birth in the heart's-embrace of the Father; the human, which He commenced to possess in the sphere of time by His incarnation in the womb of a virgin; between these two lives there is neither mixture nor confusion. The Word, in becoming man, remains what He is. He took to Himself from our race, the human race, that which He was not; but the divine in Him does not absorb the human: the human is not lessened by the divine. As I have said to you often, the union between the two natures is such that there is nevertheless but one single Person—the Divine Person, and the human nature belongs to the Word, is the Word's own humanity: "A wondrous mystery is revealed today: both natures receive something new; God becomes man, continuing to be what He had been, taking up what He had not been; there is neither mingling nor division of natures in Him."[24]

2. The second action of this exchange: by becoming incarnate, the Word brings to us, in return, a sharing in His divinity: "He ... has bestowed on us His divine nature."

So there you have, if I can so express it, one of the actions of this exchange. From us, God took to Himself our nature so as to unite it to Himself in a personal union.

What is the other action? What will God give us in return? Not that He owes us anything: "You have no need of my goods," said the Psalmist.[25] But as God does everything with wisdom, He could not have clothed Himself in our nature without a motive fully worthy of Himself.

What the Incarnate Word gives to humanity in return is an incomprehensible gift: it is a participation, a real and intimate participation in His divine nature: "He ... has bestowed on us His divine nature": *Largitus est nobis suam deitatem.*[26] In exchange for the humanity that He has taken to Himself, the Incarnate Word

[24] Antiphon of Lauds for the octave of Christmas.   [25] Ps. 15 (16):2.
[26] *O admirabile commercium!*

permits us to share in His divinity, He makes us participants in His divine nature: And thus is accomplished the most wonderful exchange we could ever celebrate.

As doubtless you know, this participation had already, as far back as the creation, been offered and given to Adam, the first man. The gift of grace, with all the splendid privileges in its train, made Adam God-like. But the sin of the first man, head of the human race, destroyed and made impossible on the creature's side this amazing participation.

It was so as to restore it that the Word became incarnate; it was so as to re-open the road to heaven, and give us a share in His eternal life, that God became man. For this Child, being God's own Son, possesses the divine life, like His Father and with His Father. In this Child "dwells all the fullness of the Godhead bodily";[27] in Him are amassed "all the treasures of wisdom and knowledge"[28]—all the treasures of divinity. But He does not possess them for Himself alone: He has an infinite desire to communicate to us the divine life that He Himself *is*: "I am the way, the truth and *the life*."[29] It is for this that He comes: "I came *that* they may have life."[30] It is for us that a Child is born; it is for us that the Son is given: "For there is a Child born *for us*, a Son given *to us*."[31] By allowing us to share in His condition of Son, He will make us children of God. "When the fullness of time came, God sent His Son, born of a woman ... that we might receive the adoption of sons."[32] What Christ is by nature, that is Son of God, we shall be by grace. The Word Incarnate, the Son of God made man, became author of our divine begetting: "The Savior of the world, who was born on this day, is the author *of our heavenly birth*."[33] This in such a way that, only-begotten Son though He be, He will become "the firstborn among many brethren."[34]

．　．　．

[27] Col. 2:9.　　[28] Col. 2:3.　　[29] John 14:6.　　[30] John 10:10.
[31] Isa. 9:6 (Jerus.); Introit of Third Mass of Christmas Day.　　[32] Gal 4:4-5.
[33] Postcommunion of Third Mass of Christmas Day.　　[34] Rom. 8:29.

Such are the two actions of the wondrous exchange that God effects between us and Him. He took to Himself our nature so as to communicate to us His divinity. He took to Himself a human life so as to give us a share in His divine life. He became man so as to make us gods, God-like: "God was made man, so that man might become God."[35] And His human birth becomes the means of our birth to the divine life.

In us also, there will henceforth be two lives. The one, the natural life that we have by our birth according to the flesh, but which, in God's sight, in consequence of original sin, is not only without merit but is—before baptism—stained fundamentally, making us enemies of God, worthy of deserved punishment. We are born "*filii irae*," "*children of wrath*."[36] The other life—supernatural, infinitely above the rights and demands of our nature. It is this life that God communicates to us by His grace, the Incarnate Word having merited it for us.

God the Father begets us to this life through His Word, the Word of Truth, and the infusion of His Spirit, in the baptismal font: "He has begotten us by the Word of truth";[37] "by means of the cleansing water of regeneration and renewal by the Holy Spirit."[38] It is a new life, which is added over-and-above, surpassing and crowning our natural life: "If any man is in Christ, he is *a new creature*."[39] It makes us children of God, brethren of Jesus Christ, worthy of one day sharing in His beatitude and His glory.

Of these two lives, which are in us as in Christ, it is the divine that ought to be the dominant one, albeit that in the Christ Child it was not yet made manifest, and that in us it remains always veiled beneath the homely, the unremarkable, outward appearance of our everyday existence. It is the divine life of grace that ought to rule and govern (and thus make pleasing to the Lord) all our natural activity, in this way divinized at its root.

---

[35] Sermon attributed to St. Augustine, no. 128 in the Appendix to his Works.
[36] Eph. 2:3.   [37] James 1:18.   [38] See Titus 3:5.   [39] 2 Cor. 5:17.

Oh, that contemplation of the birth of Jesus, and participation in this mystery by receiving the Bread of Life, might bring us to finish, for good and all, with everything that destroys or diminishes the divine life within us: sin, from which Christ, whose nativity has "put away our old man,"[40] came here to deliver us; all infidelity, all imperfection, all attachment to the merely created; immoderate caring for things that pass ("denying ... worldly desires"[41] instead); the shabby preoccupations of our vain self-love!

Oh, that such contemplation and participation might bring us to give ourselves to God entirely, according to the promises made at our baptism when we were born to divine life; might bring us to give ourselves up to the full accomplishment of all that He wills and of His good pleasure, as the Word Incarnate did when entering into this world: "Behold ... I come to do your will, O God";[42] might bring us to abound in those good works that make us pleasing to God: "an acceptable people, pursuing good works."[43]

The divine life brought by Jesus from the time of His birth would then no longer meet with any obstacles and it would freely blossom out for the glory of our Heavenly Father; "the teachings with which the Incarnate Word's new Light floods our faith" would then "shine forth in what we do";[44] and through all our works, born of grace, our celebration of the nativity of Christ would then respond worthily to the grandeur of the mystery and to the ineffable Gift given to us by it: "May our offerings prove suitable to the mystery of this day's Nativity."[45]

---

[40] Postcommunion of the Dawn Mass of Christmas. [*Translator's note*: the "old" man, (i.e. one's old self) as opposed to the "new" man regenerated by the sanctifying grace merited for us by Christ. Cf. St. Paul: "... stripping yourselves of the old man with his deeds, and putting on the new, him who is renewed ... according to the image of Him who created him": Col. 3:9-10 (Rheims). The Knox has: "You must be quit of the old self, and the habits that went with it..."]

[41] Titus 2:12 (Rheims); the Epistle of the Midnight Mass.   [42] Hebr. 10:7.

[43] Titus 2:14.   [44] Prayer of the Dawn Mass of Christmas.

[45] *Secretum* of the Dawn Mass of Christmas.

3. This exchange appears to us more wondrous still by the manner in which it operates. The Incarnation makes God visible so that we may be able to hear and imitate Him.

What completes the "wondrousness" of this exchange is the manner in which it takes place, the form in which it operates. How is it accomplished? How does this Child who is the Incarnate Word make us sharers in His divine life? By His humanity. The humanity that the Word took to Himself from us is to serve Him as instrument for communicating His divinity to us; and that for two reasons in which the Eternal Wisdom shines out on us infinitely. The humanity makes God visible, and it makes Him capable of suffering.

It makes Him *visible*.

Using the words of St. Paul, the Church at Christmas sings with such pleasure of this "appearing" of God among us: "The grace of God our Savior has appeared to all men,"[46] "The goodness and kindness of God our Savior has appeared,"[47] "A Light will shine upon us this day, for the Lord is born to us,"[48] "The Word was made flesh, and dwelt among us."[49]

The Incarnation effects this unheard-of marvel: men have seen God living in the midst of them.

St. John also is pleased to bring up this side of the mystery. "The Word of Life was before all things; and we have heard Him, we have seen Him with our eyes, we have looked upon Him, and our hands have touched Him. He, the Life eternally with the Father, is the same Life who has appeared to us, and we give testimony of Him. And Him whom we have seen and heard, we now proclaim to you, so that your joy may be complete."[50]

What a joy indeed to see God manifesting Himself to us, not in the dazzling splendor of His omnipotence, nor in the unutterable

[46] Titus 2:11 (Rheims); the Epistle for the Midnight Mass.
[47] Titus 3:4; the Epistle for the Dawn Mass.   [48] Introit of the Dawn Mass.
[49] John 1:14.   [50] See 1 John 1:1-4.

glory of His sovereignty, but under the veil of a humble, poor, weak, humanity that we can see and touch!

We might have been have been afraid of the redoubtable majesty of God: the Israelites prostrated themselves in the dust, full of terror and dread, when amid flashes of lightning God spoke to Moses on Sinai. We ourselves are attracted by the charms of One who is God become a *Child*. The Child in the manger seems to say to us: "You are afraid of God? You are wrong. He who sees me sees also the Father.[51] Do not follow your imagination, do not make up a God from the deductions of philosophy, do not ask science to make my perfections known to you. The real Almighty God is the God I am and reveal to you; the real God is I who come to you in poverty, humility and childhood, but who one day will give my life for you. I am the brightness of the glory of the Eternal Father, the image of His substance,[52] His only-begotten Son, God as He is God. In me you will learn to know His perfections, His wisdom and His goodness, His love for mankind and His mercy towards sinners.[53] Come to me, for, God as I am, I have willed to be man like you, and I do not reject those who draw near to me with trust."[54] Grant, Lord ... that "*as* the man born to us gloriously shone as our God..."

You may say to me: "But why did God thus deign to make Himself visible?" First of all, to instruct us: "Our Savior has appeared to all men, instructing us."[55] It is indeed God who will henceforth speak to us through His own Son: "God ... in these days has spoken to us by His Son";[56] we have but to listen to this beloved Son to know what God wants of us. The Heavenly Father tells us so Himself: "This is my beloved Son; hear Him";[57] and Jesus will take pleasure in repeating to us that His teaching is that of His Father: "My teaching is not my own, but His who sent me."[58]

---

[51] John 14.9.   [52] Hebr. 1:3.   [53] "He has shone in our hearts ... in the face of Christ Jesus": 2 Cor. 4:6.   [54] "... so this earthly substance may confer upon us what is divine": *Secretum* of the Dawn Mass of Christmas.   [55] Titus 2:11-12.   [56] Hebr. 1:2.   [57] Matt. 17:5; Mark 9:6; Luke 9:35.   [58] John 7:16.

In the next place, the Word made Himself visible to our eyes so as to become the example we ought to follow.

We have only to watch this Child grow, only to look at Him living in the midst of us, living like us, as a man, to know how we ought to live in the sight of God, as children of God; for everything He does will be pleasing to His Father: "I do always the things that are pleasing to Him."[59]

Being the Truth in His teaching of us, He will show us the Way by His example. If we live in His light, if we follow that Way, we shall have Life: "I am the Way, and the Truth, and the Life."[60] In that manner, by knowing God manifested in the midst of us, we shall be drawn towards the things which are invisible: "... that while we recognize God *visibly*, we may *by this* be drawn on by Him to the love of things invisible."[61]

4. The Incarnation makes God capable of suffering, capable of expiating our sins by His sufferings, and of healing us by His humiliations.

The humanity of Christ makes God visible; but above all—and it is here that the Divine Wisdom is shown to be "wondrous"—it makes God *capable of suffering*.

Sin which destroyed the divine life in us demanded a satisfaction, an expiation without which it was impossible for the divine life to be given back to us. Being merely created, man was not able to give this satisfaction for an offense of infinite malice,[62] and, on the other hand, Divinity is not able either to suffer or to expiate. God can only communicate His life if sin is expunged; and, by an immutable decree of Eternal Wisdom, sin can only be expunged if it is expiated in a manner equal to the sin. How was this problem to be resolved?

---

[59] John 8:29.   [60] John 14:6.   [61] Preface of the Mass for Christmastide.

[62] [*Translator's note*: Infinite, because Adam's sin, committed with a fully clear sight, was against the Infinite God.]

The Incarnation gives us the answer. Consider the Child of Bethlehem—this Child is the Word made flesh. The humanity that the Word makes His own is capable of suffering; and it is this humanity that will suffer, that will expiate. These sufferings, these expiations, which are the works of that humanity—very much its works—belong however, as the whole of that humanity itself does, to the Word. From that Divine Person they take on an infinite value which will suffice to redeem the world, to destroy sin, to make grace superabound in souls like a headlong and fructifying river: "The stream of the river makes joyful the city of God."[63]

O wonderful exchange! Let us not pause to try and find how God *might* have effected this; let us look at the way in which He brought it about in fact. The Word asked of us[64] a human nature so as to find in it the means to suffer, the means to expiate, to merit, to heap blessings upon us. It was through the flesh that man turned away from God; it is by making Himself flesh that God delivers man:

> *The Blest Creator, us to save,*
> *Put on the body of a slave;*
> *Flesh freeing flesh, a ransom paid*
> *Not to lose those whom He had made.*[65]

The flesh that clothed the Word of God would become, for all flesh, the instrument of salvation. "Oh, wondrous exchange!"

As you will not be unaware, we had to wait until the immolation of Calvary before the expiation would be complete: but, as St. Paul has told us, it was at the first moment of His incarnation that Christ expressed acceptance of the accomplishment of the will of His Father, acceptance of His offering Himself as a Victim for the whole human race: "Therefore in coming into the world, He says, 'Sacrifice and oblation you did not desire, but you have

---

[63] See Ps. 45 (46):5.   [64] [*Translator's note*: in the person of the Virgin Mary at the Annunciation.]   [65] Hymn for Lauds of Christmastide.

prepared *a body* for me. Then said I, Behold, I come ... to do your will, O God.'"[66] It was by this oblation that Christ began to sanctify us: "In accordance with this divine will we have been sanctified";[67] and it was as far back as the manger that He inaugurated the life of suffering that He willed to live for our salvation, an earthly life of which Golgotha was the appointed end, and which, by its destruction of sin,[68] restored friendship with His Father to us. The manger was undoubtedly only the first stage, but it contained at root all the others.

That is why, in her celebration of Christmas, the Church attributes our salvation to the Son of God's birth in the sphere of time, to that birth itself: "Almighty God, may the new birth of your only-begotten Son in flesh deliver us whom the old servitude holds captive under the yoke of sin."[69] That is why, from Christmas onwards, deliverance, redemption, salvation, eternal life, will be spoken of constantly. It is through His humanity that Christ, High Priest and Mediator, reunites us with God; and it is at Bethlehem that He appeared to us in that humanity.

See, also, how from the time of His birth He began to fulfill His mission.

What is it, in fact, that makes us lose divine life? It is *pride*. Because they believed they could become like God, "as gods, knowing good and evil,"[70] Adam and Eve lost—for themselves and their race—the friendship of God. Christ, the new Adam, buys us back—redeems us; restores us to God, through the *humility* of His incarnation. "Christ Jesus, though He was by nature God, did not consider being equal to God a thing to be clung to, but emptied Himself, taking the nature of a slave and being made like unto men."[71] He manifested Himself as man: "And appearing as man..."[72] What a humiliation that was! Later, it is true, the Church

---

[66] See Hebr. 10, vv. 5, 7; Ps 39 (40):8.   [67] Hebr. 10:10 (Knox).
[68] [*Translator's note*: original sin, which had closed heaven to the human race.]
[69] Prayer of the Third Mass of Christmas Day.   [70] Gen. 3:5.
[71] Phil. 2:6-7.   [72] Ibid., v. 7.

will exalt to highest heaven His resplendent glory as Victor over sin and death; but now, as He is on earth, Christ knows only abasement and weakness. When our eyes rest upon this little child whom nothing distinguishes from other little children, and we think that He is God, the Infinite God, "in whom are hidden all the treasures of wisdom and knowledge,"[73] we feel our soul pierced deeply, and our vain pride finds itself confounded in the face of such an abasement.

What things besides pride have lost us divine life? Our *refusal to obey*. Look at the Son of God, He gives us the example of a wonderful obedience. With the simplicity that we see in little children, He abandoned Himself into the hands of His parents; He let them touch Him, lift Him up and carry Him about as they wished. And all His childhood, all His adolescence, all His youth, are summed up by the Gospel in simply these words: He "was subject" to Mary and Joseph.[74]

What else? Our *covetousness*: "the lust of the eyes";[75] everything of outward show, everything that glitters, fascinates and seduces; the fundamental emptiness of the fleeting trifles we prefer to *God*. The Word was made flesh; but He was born into poverty and low estate: "Being rich, He became poor for your sakes."[76] Though He is "the King of the ages,"[77] though it is He who by one word drew out of nothing the whole of creation, who had only to "open His hand, and every living being was filled with blessing"[78]—it was not in a palace that He was born. His mother, having found no room at the inn, had to take refuge in a cave. The Son of God, Eternal Wisdom, *willed* to be born in nakedness and to lie upon straw.

If with faith and love we contemplate the Child Jesus in His crib, we shall see in Him the Divine Example of so many virtues; if we know how to lend the ear of our soul listen to what He tells

---

[73] Col. 2:3.   [74] Luke 2:51.   [75] 1 John 2:16.   [76] 2 Cor. 8:9.
[77] 1 Tim. 1:17.   [78] See Ps. 144 (145):16.

us, we shall learn a great number of things. If we run through the circumstances of His birth, we shall see how the humanity served the Word as an instrument not only for instructing us, but also for raising us up, for giving us life, for making us pleasing to His Father, for detaching us from the things that pass and from ourselves, for lifting us up to Himself.

Divinity puts on our mortal flesh; and thereby, as God lowers Himself to live a human life, so man is raised to divine things.[79]

5. We must participate in this exchange through faith. Those who receive the Word-made-flesh by believing in Him have the power to become children of God.

So therefore, whatever aspect of this exchange we bring the eyes of our faith to bear upon, whatever the details of it that we examine, it appears to us wonderful.

Is it not wonderful indeed, this childbirth by a virgin?—*Natus ineffabiliter ex virgine*, "Born of a virgin, beyond all telling."[80] "The mother has brought forth the King whose name is eternal; the joy of motherhood is hers and the honor of a virgin. Never has this been seen before, never will it be seen again."[81] "Daughters of Jerusalem, why marvel you at me? Truly divine is this mystery that you see in me."[82]

Wonderful this union—indissoluble yet without confusion—of divinity and humanity in the one person of the Word: *Mirabile mysterium*, "A wondrous mystery ... two natures are made new."[83] Wonderful this exchange, by the contrasts involved in its being effected. God allows us to share in His divinity, but the humanity that He took to Himself from us in order to communicate His

---

[79] St. Gregory, Homily I on the Gospels: "As Divinity accepted the weakness our flesh, so human flesh received the Light that pardoned it. Truly, God having suffered human things, man was thereby lifted up to divine things."

[80] Antiphon of Vespers for the Octave of Christmas.   [81] Antiphon of Lauds for Christmas Day.   [82] Antiphon for Feast of the Expectation of Our Lady, December 18th.   [83] Antiphon of Lauds in the Octave of Christmas.

divine life to us is a suffering humanity—He was "a man ... acquainted with infirmity,"[84] it was a humanity that would suffer death and, by death, would give us back life.

Wonderful, this exchange, in its source, which is nothing else than God's infinite love God for us. "God so loved the world that He gave His only-begotten Son."[85] Therefore let us abandon ourselves to joy and with the Church sing: "For to us a Child is born, *to us* a Son is *given*."[86] And how is He given? "In the likeness of sinful flesh."[87] Which is why the love that gave us Him thus in our humanity (this humanity that is susceptible of suffering) to expiate sin, is a love without measure: "Through the exceeding love with which God has loved us, He sent His Son in the likeness of sinful flesh."[88]

Wonderful, finally, in its fruits and effects. By this exchange, God gives us His friendship again; He restores to us the right to enter into possession of the eternal inheritance; He looks anew on humanity with love and pleasure.

Therefore joy is one of the feelings that are most evident in the celebration of this mystery. The Church constantly invites us to it, because she recalls the words of the angel to the shepherds: "I bring you news that will be for you a source of great joy ... for a Savior has been born to you."[89] It is the joy of deliverance, of inheritance regained, of peace rediscovered, and, above all, of men being given the sight of God Himself: "And He shall be called Emmanuel," God-with-us.[90]

But this joy will only be an assured joy if we remain firm in the grace that comes to us from the Savior and makes us His brethren. "O Christian," cried St. Leo, in a sermon the Church reads during the Holy Night, "recognize your dignity. And having been made a sharer in Divinity, take care not to fall away from so sublime a state."[91]

---

[84] Isa. 53:3.   [85] John 3:16.   [86] Isa. 9:6 (RSV, Cath.)   [87] Rom. 8:3.
[88] Antiphon for the Octave of Christmas.   [89] See Luke 2:10-11.
[90] See Isa. 7:14; Matt. 1:23.   [91] *Sermo* I on the Nativity.

"If you knew the gift of God," said Our Lord Himself.[92] If you knew who this "Son given to you" is! If, above all, we receive Him as we ought to receive Him! Let it not be said of us: "He came unto His own"—into His own domain—"and His own received Him not."[93] Through the fact of creation, we are all the domain of God; we belong to Him: but there are some of us who do not receive Him upon this earth. How many of the Jews, how many pagans, rejected Christ, because He appeared in a flesh susceptible of suffering! Souls sunk in the darkness of pride and of the senses: "The light shines in the darkness, and the darkness grasped it not."[94]

And how ought we to receive Him? By faith: "... to those who believe in His name."[95] It is to those who believing in His person, in His word, in His works, *have received this Child as God*, that it has been given, in return, to become themselves children of God: "*Ex Deo nati sunt*," "who have been born ... of God."[96]

Such, indeed, is the fundamental disposition we should bring, for this wonderful exchange to bear all its fruits in us. Faith, only faith, can make us know why and how it comes about. Faith alone makes us penetrate the depths of this mystery; it alone gives us a true knowledge of it, one that is worthy of God.

For there are a good many modes and degrees of knowledge.

"Ox and ass knew their God," wrote Isaiah in speaking of this mystery.[97] They saw the child lying in the manger. But what did they see? That which an animal can see: the form, the size, the color, the movement—a wholly rudimentary knowledge, not going beyond the realm of the senses. Nothing more.

The passers-by, the curious who have gone up to the stable, have seen the child; but for them he is like all other children.

[92] John 4:10. [93] John 1:11. [94] John 1:5.
[95] John 1:12. [96] See John 1:13.
[97] See Isa. 1:3: "The ox knows his owner, and the ass his master's crib."

They have not gone further than having this purely natural knowledge. Perhaps they have been struck by the beauty of the child? Perhaps they have pitied his destitution. But that feeling has not lasted at all, and indifference has resumed the upper hand before long.

Then there are the shepherds, simple-hearted men, illumined by a light from on high: "the glory of God shone round about them."[98] Assuredly they have understood more; they have recognized in this child the Messiah, promised and awaited—the "expectation of nations";[99] they have rendered him their homage, and their souls have for a long time been filled with joy and peace.

Likewise the angels looked upon the New-born, the Word-made-flesh. They saw in Him their God, and so this knowledge threw those pure spirits into amazement and wonder at so incomprehensible an abasement. For He did not will to unite Himself to *their* nature, but to human nature: "Nowhere does He take hold of angels: *but of the seed of Abraham He takes hold.*"[100]

What shall we say of the Virgin when she gazed on Jesus? So pure, so humble and tender her gaze, so full of happiness—to what depths of the mystery it penetrated! Impossible to express in words what lights Jesus's soul was flooding forth on His mother at that time, what sublime adoration, what perfect homage, Mary rendered to her Son, to her God, to all the states and all the mysteries of which the Incarnation is the substance and root.

There is finally (but it is something untellable) the gaze of the Father contemplating His Son, made flesh for mankind. The Heavenly Father saw that which never man, nor angel, nor Mary herself could comprehend: the infinite perfections of Divinity, hidden in a Child. And this contemplation was the source of an indescribable delight: "You are my beloved Son, in you I am well-pleased."[101]

. . .

---

[98] Luke 2:9.   [99] Gen. 49:10.   [100] Hebr. 2:16 (Rheims).
[101] Mark 1:11; Luke 3:22; Matt. 3:17; 17:5; 2 Peter 1:17.

When we contemplate the Word Incarnate at Bethlehem, let us rise above the senses, so as to look only with the eyes of faith. Faith makes us share here below in the knowledge the Three Divine Persons have of each other. There is in that statement no exaggeration at all. Sanctifying grace, indeed, makes us sharers in the divine nature. Well now, the activity of the divine nature consists in the knowledge and the love which the Divine Persons have of each other and for each other; and we share in that knowledge therefore. And just as sanctifying grace, coming to full flower in glory, will give us the right to gaze upon God as He sees Himself[102]—in that same way, on earth, in the darkness of faith, grace grants us to look upon the depths of the mysteries through the eyes of God: "The new light of thy glory has shone upon the eyes of our mind."[103]

When our faith is a living and perfect faith, we do not stop at the rind, at the outside of the mystery; we reach the inside of it so as to contemplate it with the eyes of God. We pass through the humanity of Christ so as to penetrate as far as the divinity which the humanity hides and reveals at the same time. We see the divine mysteries in the divine light.

And enraptured, astonished by so prodigal an abasement, the soul that is given life by this faith prostrates itself; delivers itself up whole and entire to give glory to our God who, for love of His creatures, veils in this way the native splendor of His unfathomable perfections. That soul adores Him, gives itself up to Him; truly knows no rest till it has yielded up everything to Him (a yielding-up *in return*, so as to complete the exchange God wishes to contract with the soul); till everything of itself, all of its activity, has been subjected to this "King of Peace"[104] who comes, "like a Bridegroom in His splendor,"[105] to save, to sanctify and, so to speak, to deify that soul.

.   .   .

[102] 1 John 3:2: "We shall see Him as He really is" (Jerus.)
[103] Preface of the Mass at Christmas.   [104] Antiphon of Vespers of Christmas Day.   [105] Magnificat antiphon of Christmas Day.

Let it, then, be with great faith that we approach the Child-God. We might wish to have been at Bethlehem to receive Him. But look—holy communion gives us Him with just as much reality, though our senses have a lesser perception of Him still. In the tabernacle, as in the crib, it is the same God, full of power; the same Savior, full of goodness.

If we wish it, the wondrous exchange still continues. For it is also through His humanity that, at the holy table, Christ infuses the divine life into us. It is by eating His flesh and drinking His blood, by uniting ourselves with His humanity, that we draw from the very source of eternal life: "He who eats my flesh and drinks my blood has life everlasting."[106]

So each day the union established between man and God at the Incarnation continues and is made closer. By giving Himself in holy communion Christ increases, in a faithful and generous soul, the life of grace.[107] He makes it develop more freely and come to flower with greater strength; even confers on the soul a promise of that eternal blessedness of which grace is the seed-germ, that eternal life where God Himself will communicate Himself to us in all plenitude and without veil: "That as the Savior of the world, born on this day, brings about our own rebirth to the life of God, so also may *He Himself* give us this life for ever."[108]

Our life in heaven will be the consummation—magnificent, glorious—of that exchange inaugurated at Bethlehem in the poverty and abasement of the Christmas crib.

---

[106] John 6:55.   [107] "O God, who through the holy exchange of this Sacrifice has made us partakers of the one supreme Divinity, grant we beseech thee that as we know thy truth, so we may follow it with worthy conduct": *Secretum* for the Fourth Sunday after Easter.

[108] Postcommunion for the Third Mass of Christmas Day.

CHAPTER EIGHT

The Epiphany

Introduction: God, Eternal Light, reveals Himself especially in the Incarnation.

Every time a soul finds itself in the smallest way in intimate contact with God, it feels itself enveloped in mystery: "Clouds and darkness are round about Him."[1] This mystery is the inevitable consequence of the infinite distance separating the creature from the Creator. On all sides, a finite being is surpassed by Him who, eternally, is the very plenitude of Being.

That is why one of the deepest characteristics of the Divine Being is its incomprehensibility and invisibility. It is a truly remarkable thing, this invisibility here below of the divine light.

"God is light," says St. John; He is infinite light, without clouds and darkness: "God is light, and in Him is no darkness." St. John is careful to note that this truth constitutes one of the very foundations of his Gospel: it is "the message we have heard from Him and announce to you."[2] But this light that bathes us all in its brightness, instead of revealing God to the eyes of our soul, hides Him. As with this Light, so with the sun; its very brilliance prevents us from gazing on it: He "dwells in light inaccessible."[3]

---

[1] Ps. 96 (97):2.   [2] 1 John 1:5.   [3] 1 Tim. 6:16.

154

And yet this Light is the Life of our soul. You will have noticed that in Holy Scripture the ideas of life and of light are frequently associated. When the Psalmist wishes to describe the eternal happiness of which God is the source, he says: "They shall be inebriated with the plenty of thy house; and thou shalt make them drink of the torrent of thy pleasure. For with thee is the fountain of *life*." And immediately he adds: "and in thy light *we shall see light*."[4] It is the same when Our Lord declares Himself "the light of the world." "He who follows me," He said (and there is more here than a mere juxtaposition of words) "does not walk in the darkness, but will have the *light of life*."[5] And this light of life proceeds from the light which in essence *is* life: "In Him was life, and the life was the light of men."[6] Our life in heaven will be to know the eternal light without veil, and to rejoice in its splendors.

Already, here below, God grants a participation in His light by endowing the human soul with intelligence: "The light of Thy countenance, O Lord, is signed upon us."[7] Reason is a true light for man. All the natural activity of man, if it is to be worthy of himself, ought to be directed primarily by that light which shows him the good to pursue—a light so powerful that it is even capable of revealing to man the existence of God and some of His perfections. St. Paul, writing to the faithful at Rome,[8] declares the pagans to be "without excuse" for not having known God by contemplating the world, the works of His hands. The works of God contain a trace, a reflection, of His perfections and thus, up to a certain point, declare the Infinite Light.

God has made another manifestation of Himself—a deeper one, and more full of mercy. It is the Incarnation.

The Divine Light, too bright to be shown to our feeble gaze in all its splendor, was veiled beneath the humanity—"through the veil (that is, His flesh)" is St. Paul's expression.[9] "The brightness

---

[4] Ps. 35 (36):9-10. [5] John 8:12. [6] John 1:4.

[7] Ps. 4:7. [8] Rom. 1:20. [9] Hebr. 10:20.

of eternal light"[10]—Light welling forth from Light, *Lumen de Lumine*, the Word clothed Himself in our flesh so that through that flesh we might gaze upon Divinity: "The new light of thy glory has shone upon the eyes of our mind."[11] Christ is God brought within our reach, showing Himself to us, in an existence authentically human. The veil of the humanity prevented the infinite and dazzling refulgence of Divinity from blinding us.

But for every soul of goodwill, rays come forth from this man which reveal that He is equally God. The soul enlightened by faith knows the splendors hidden behind the veil of this Holy of holies. In the mortal man who is Jesus, faith finds God Himself; and, finding God, drinks deep at the source of light, salvation and everlasting life: "Because, when thy only-begotten Son appeared in the substance of our mortality, He restored us with the new light of His immortality."[12]

This manifestation of God to men is a mystery so unheard-of, a work so full of mercy; so much does it constitute one of the characteristics of the Incarnation which are of its essence, that during the early centuries the Church had no feast-day to honor principally the Savior's birth at Bethlehem; she celebrated the feast-day of the "Theophanies," or the "Divine manifestations" in the person of the Incarnate Word—the manifestation to the Magi; the manifestation at Jesus's baptism on the banks of the Jordan; that at the marriage-feast at Cana when Jesus worked His first miracle. In passing from the Church of the East to that of the West, the feast kept its Greek name, *Epiphany*, or "manifestation"; but it had as its object almost exclusively the manifestation of the Savior to the Gentiles, to the pagan nations, in the persons of the Magi.

You know well enough the Gospel account of the coming of the Magi to Bethlehem, an account illustrated and popularized

[10] Wisdom 7:26.   [11] Preface of the Mass at Christmas.
[12] Preface of the Mass of the Epiphany.

by tradition.[13] I shall simply say a few words on the general significance of the mystery. Then, latching on to certain details, I shall indicate some of the numerous lessons it contains for our devotional life.

1. The manifestation to the Magi signifies the calling of the pagan nations to the light of the Gospel.

The Fathers of the Church saw in the summons of the Magi to Christ's cradle the calling of the pagan nations to the Faith. That is the very foundation of the mystery, explicitly indicated by the Church in the prayer by which she sums up the desires of her children at this Solemnity: "O God, who on this day didst reveal Thy only-begotten Son *to the Gentiles* through the guiding of a star..."

The Word Incarnate was first manifested to the Jews, in the persons of the shepherds. Why was that? Because the Jewish people were the Chosen People. It was from this people that the Messiah was to come—the Son of David. To this people had been made the magnificent promises the fulfillment of which constituted the Messianic reign; it was to this people that God had entrusted the Scriptures and given the Law—that Law of which all the elements were a figure of the grace Christ was to bring. It was fitting, therefore, that the Word Incarnate should manifest Himself first of all to the Jews.

At the crib, the shepherds, simple men of upright heart, represented the Chosen People: "I bring you good news of great joy ... there has been born to you today in the town of David a Savior..."[14]

Later on, in His public life, Our Lord would manifest Himself to the Jews by the wisdom of His teaching and the splendor of His miracles.

---

[13] Most writers place the coming of the Magi after the Presentation of Jesus in the Temple. Here we follow the order indicated by the Church who, in her liturgy, celebrates the Epiphany on January 6th and the Presentation on February 2nd. [14] Luke 2:10-11.

We shall notice, even, that He confines His preaching to the Jews alone. See, for example, when the Canaan woman, from the pagan region of Tyre and Sidon, asked Him to help her. How did Christ reply to the disciples who intervened in her favor? "I was not sent except to the lost sheep of the house of Israel."[15] For her (so to speak) to wrest from Jesus the grace she was imploring would require from that poor pagan a lively faith and a profound humility. When, during His public life, Our Lord sent His apostles to preach the good tidings as He had been doing, He said to them likewise: "Do not go in the direction of the Gentiles, nor enter the towns of Samaritans; but rather go to the lost sheep of the house of Israel."[16] Why this rather strange recommendation? Were the pagans excluded from the grace of the Redemption and from the salvation brought by Christ? No; but it was part of the divine plan to reserve to the apostles the evangelization of the pagan nations, after the Jews, by crucifying the Messiah, had definitively rejected the Son of God.[17] When Our Lord died on the cross, "the veil of the temple was rent in two,"[18] to show that the Old Covenant, between God and the Hebrew people alone, had ended.

Many of the Jews, indeed. had not wanted to receive Christ. The pride of some, the sensuality of others, had blinded their souls, and they did not want to accept Him as the Son of God. It is of them that St. John speaks when he says: "And the light shines in the darkness; and the darkness grasped it not," and "He came unto His own, and His own received Him not."[19] That is why Our Lord said to these unbelieving Jews: "The kingdom of heaven

---

[15] Matt. 15:24.   [16] Matt. 10:5-6.

[17] [*Translator's note*: The word "Jews" here should be taken as referring only to those particular persons within the Jewish authorities of Jesus's day, and the people who supported them, who did in fact "reject" Him. They, and their dispositions, are "known only to God," as the *Catechism of the Catholic Church* puts it. What is spoken of here certainly does *not* apply to the whole Jewish people. See para. 597 of the *Catechism* (headed "Jews are not collectively responsible for Jesus's death"); and article 4 of Vatican II's Declaration *Nostra Aetate*.]   [18] Matt. 27:51 (Rheims).   [19] John 1, vv. 5, 11.

will be taken away from you and will be given to a people yielding its fruits,"[20] to the Gentiles.

The pagan nations have been called to become the inheritance promised by the Father to His Son Jesus: "Ask of me, and I will give you the Gentiles for your inheritance."[21] Our Lord said, of Himself: "The good shepherd lays down his life for his sheep," immediately adding that His flock is not solely from among His own people: "Other sheep I have that at present do not belong this fold. Them also must I bring, and they shall hear my voice, and there shall be one fold and one shepherd."[22]

That is why, before ascending to heaven, He sent His apostles to continue His work and mission of salvation no longer among the lost sheep of Israel only, but among *all* peoples. "Go therefore, and preach to every creature, teach all nations ... I am with you until the end of the ages."[23]

Yet the Incarnate Word did not wait till His ascension to pour forth the grace of the good tidings upon the Gentiles. As early as His appearance upon earth, He invited them to His crib in the persons of the Magi. Eternal Wisdom, He wished in that way to show us He brought peace: "peace on earth among men of good will";[24] and, moreover, not only to those who were near Him, the faithful Jews represented by the shepherds, but also to those who lived far away from Him, the pagans represented by the Magi. In that way, as St. Paul said, "He Himself is our peace"; He it is who of the two peoples "has made both one."[25] Coming, He "announced the good tidings of peace to you who were afar off, and of peace to those who were near." He made both peoples one because He alone is the perfect Mediator through the union of His humanity to His divinity, and thus both peoples "have access in one Spirit"—in the one Holy Spirit—"to the Father."[26]

[20] Matt. 21:43. [21] Psalm 2:8. [22] See John 10, vv. 11, 16.
[23] See Matt. 28:19-20; Mark 16:15. [24] Luke 2:14.
[25] Eph. 2: 14. [26] Ibid., vv. 17-18.

The calling of the Magi and their sanctification signify the vocation of the Gentiles to faith and salvation. To the shepherds God sent an angel—for the Chosen People were used to the appearing of spirits from heaven. To the Magi who scrutinized the stars, He caused a marvelous star to appear. This star was a symbol of the interior illumination that enlightens souls, to call them to God.

Indeed, the soul of every adult is enlightened, at least once, like the Magi, by the star of a calling to eternal salvation. To all, light is given. It is a firm tenet of our faith that God wishes to save everyone: "God our Savior ... wishes *all* men to be saved and to come to the knowledge of the truth."[27]

On Judgment Day all without exception will, with a conviction produced by the evidence, declare the infinite justice of God and the perfect rightness of the judgments He makes: "You are just, O Lord, and your judgment is right."[28] Those whom God will banish far away from Himself for ever will recognize that they themselves have been the architects of their own loss.

Now, that would not be true if the damned had not had the possibility of knowing and accepting the divine light of faith. It is contrary not only to the infinite goodness of God but also to His justice, to condemn a soul because of that soul's invincible ignorance.[29]

Doubtless, the star that calls men to the Christian faith is not the same for all; it shines differently; but its luster is sufficiently visible for hearts of good will to be able to recognize it and see in it the sign of a divine call. In His providence, which is full of wisdom, God incessantly

---

[27] 1 Tim. 2:4.　　　　　　　　　　[28] Ps. 118 (119):137.

[29] [*Translator's note*: Taken on its own, this paragraph of Marmion's might seem to be interpreting the "necessity" of faith for salvation as referring to explicit faith in Christ and the Church. Based on the unquestionable fact that the goodness and justice of God would not condemn a soul for being in *invincible* ignorance, and on the further unquestionable fact that God desires the salvation of all without exception, Marmion is driven to say that everyone (he says every adult) "is enlightened at least once ... by the star of a calling to eternal salvation," such an illumination, it seems, as to negate that ignorance and give the individual an opportunity of "knowing and accepting the divine light of faith." But in his next succeeding paragraph and a later

varies His action—action which is as incomprehensible as Himself; He varies it according to the ever-active kindnesses of His love and the ever-holy demands of His justice. In this we ought, with St. Paul, to adore "the depth of the riches of the wisdom and the knowledge of God," and to declare that they infinitely surpass our mere created insight: "Who has known the mind of the Lord, or who has been His counselor?" "How incomprehensible are His judgments and how unsearchable His ways!"[30]

We have the happiness of having "seen the star" and of having recognized as our God the child in the manger. We have the happiness of belonging to the Church, of which the Magi were the first-fruits.

---

one, Marmion adds a modifying subtlety to what he has just said here. For each individual, he says, God "varies His action"; for each the light of the star "shines differently." "The manifestation of this calling," he says, "can take diverse forms, according to the designs of God, our character, the circumstances in which we live, the events in which we are involved." Hence, Marmion's eloquent reference to important personal moments of influx of light does not necessarily imply something as luminously explicit as a clear illumination about the truth of Christ and the Church.

Since Marmion's day, the Church has clarified and deepened her teaching on this matter (and Marmion's modifying words are nearer to this). *Lumen Gentium* 14 says that "they could not be saved who, *knowing that* the Catholic Church was founded as necessary by God through Christ, would refuse either to enter it, or to remain in it." (my emphasis). But then *Lumen Gentium* adds that "those who through no fault of their own do not know the Gospel of Christ or His Church, but who nevertheless seek God with a sincere heart, and, moved by grace, try in their actions to do His will through the dictates of their conscience as they know it [i.e. as they know His will]—those too may achieve eternal salvation." See also Pope John Paul's *Redemptoris Missio* (1990), 10.

Those words of *Lumen Gentium* are not an invitation to go easy on evangelization. Immediately following the words of *L.G.* 16 quoted above, the *Catechism of the Catholic Church* (para. 848) quotes the Decree *Ad gentes* of the same Church Council, Vatican II: "Although in ways known to Himself God can lead those who, through no fault of their own, are ignorant of the Gospel, to that faith without which it is impossible to please Him, the Church still has the obligation, and the sacred right, to evangelize all men." Pius XII wrote about "those who do not belong to the visible Body of the Catholic Church," and he stressed that "even though by an unconscious desire and longing they have a certain relationship with the Mystical Body of the Redeemer, *they still remain deprived of those many heavenly gifts and helps which can only be enjoyed in the Catholic Church*" (para. 103, my italics).]   [30] Rom. 11:33-34.

In the Office of the Feast of the Epiphany, the liturgy describes this calling to faith and salvation of the whole of humanity in the persons of the Magi as the wedding of the Church and her Spouse. Hear with what joy, in what magnificently symbolic terms taken from the prophet Isaiah, she proclaims the splendor of that spiritual Jerusalem that was to receive on her motherly breast the nations, now the inheritance of her Divine Spouse.[31] "Arise, shine brightly, O Jerusalem: for your light is come, and the glory of the Lord is risen upon you. Whilst darkness covers the earth, and a mist the people, the Lord shall rise upon you, and His glory shall be seen upon you. And the Gentiles shall walk in your light, and kings in the brightness of your rising. Lift up your eyes round about and see: all these are gathered together, they are come to you; your sons shall come from afar, and daughters shall rise up at your side. Then shall you see, and be radiant, and your heart shall thrill and be enlarged, for you shall see come to you the riches of the sea and the treasures of the nations."[32]

Let us offer God a ceaseless thanksgiving for having made us capable of "having a share in the inheritance of the saints in light, by rescuing us from the power of darkness and transferring us into the kingdom of His Son"[33]—that is to say, into the Church.

The call to faith is a very great benefit because it contains, in seed-germ, a calling to eternal bliss in the vision of God. That call, let us never forget, has been the dawn of all God's mercies in our regard. For man, all is summed up in fidelity to that calling; the purpose of faith is to bring us to the Beatific Vision.

We should not only thank God for this grace of our Christian faith; we should also, each day, make ourselves more worthy of it by safeguarding our faith against all the dangers it runs in this age of naturalism, indifference and human respect, and by living our life of faith with an unremitting fidelity.

.   .   .

---

[31] Epistle of the Feast.   [32] See Isa. 60:1-5.   [33] See Col. 1:13.

In addition, let us ask God to grant this precious gift of faith to all the souls who are still in "darkness and in the shadow of death"; let us ask the Lord that the star rise over them; that He Himself be the Sun—"the Orient" who visits them from on high, through His "loving-kindness"[34]

That prayer is very pleasing to Our Lord; it is asking Him, indeed, that He may be known and exalted as Savior of all mankind, and King of kings.

It is very pleasing, also, to the Father: for He desires nothing as much as the glorification of His Son. Let us, then, at this holy time, repeat often the prayer the Incarnate Word Himself put on our lips: *Our Father, who art in heaven*, O Father of Lights, *Thy kingdom come*—that kingdom of which your Son Jesus is head. May your Son be more and more known, loved, served, glorified, so that, in His turn, by manifesting you His Father to men, He may glorify you in the unity of the Holy Spirit who is common to you both: *"Father, glorify your Son, that your Son may glorify you."*[35]

2. The faith of the Magi, a prompt and generous one, is the model for ours.

If we now return to some of the details of the Gospel account, we shall see how rich in its teaching this mystery is.

I have told you that the Magi at Bethlehem represented the Gentiles in the call they were given to the light of the Gospel. The behavior of the Magi shows us the qualities our faith ought to have.

What is apparent, right at the beginning, is the generous fidelity of that faith. Look at it the whole thing. The star appears to the Magi. Whatever their country of origin—Persia, Chaldea, Arabia or India—the Magi, according to tradition, belonged to a priestly caste and devoted themselves to a study of the stars. It is more than probable that they were not ignorant of the revelation made to the Jews, of a king who would be their liberator and Lord

---

[34] Luke 1:78-79; Ps. 106 (107):14.   [35] John 17:1.

of the world. The prophet Daniel, who had specified the time of His coming, had had dealings with Magi.[36] Perhaps, even, Balaam's prophecy, that "a star shall rise out of Jacob"[37] was not unknown to them? However that may be, here is this marvelous star appearing to them. Its extraordinary brilliance striking their eyes, their attention is aroused at the same time as an interior grace of illumination enlightens their souls. This grace gave them a presentiment of the person and the prerogatives of Him whose birth the star was announcing; it inspired them to go and seek Him so as to pay Him their homage.

The fidelity of the Magi to the inspiration of grace is admirable. Not the slightest doubt seize their minds; raising no objections they feel compelled to put their purpose into operation immediately. Neither the indifference or skepticism of those around them, nor the disappearance of the star, nor the difficulties inherent in an expedition of that kind, nor the length of the journey nor the dangers it entailed—none of these things stop them. Without delay and with perseverance, they obey God's call. "We have seen *His* star in the East, and have come";[38] we set out as soon as it was shown to us.

In this the Magi are our model, whether it be a matter of a call to faith, or of our being called to perfection. There is, indeed, for each faithful soul a call to holiness: "I am the Lord your God; be holy because I am holy."[39] The Apostle Paul assures us that from all eternity there exists for us a divine decree, full of love, that contains this calling: the Father "chose us in Him," Christ, "before the foundation of the world that we should be holy and without blemish in His sight."[40] And for those whom He has thus called to holiness, "all things work together unto good"—for those "who are saints through His call."[41] The manifestation of this calling is

---

[36] [*Translator's note*: Daniel is said to have been himself a Magus.]
[37] Numbers 24:17.   [38] Matt. 2:2.   [39] Levit. 11:44.
[40] Eph. 1:4.   [41] Rom. 8:28.

for each one of us that person's "star." It can take diverse forms, according to the designs of God, our character, the circumstances in which we live, the events in which we are involved. But it shines in the soul of each one of us.

And what is the end-purpose of this appeal? For us, as for the Magi, it is that of leading us to Jesus. The Heavenly Father makes the star shine within us; for, as Christ Himself says, "No-one can come to me unless the Father who sent me draw him."[42]

If we listen faithfully to the divine appeal, if we press ahead generously, eyes fixed upon the star, we shall arrive at Christ who is the life of our souls. And whatever our sins, our faults, our miseries, Jesus will welcome us with kindness. He has promised this: "All that the Father gives to me"—attracts to me—"will come to me, and him who comes to me I will not cast out."[43]

The Father drew Mary Magdalene, a notorious sinner, to the feet of Jesus. And see how she, with a generous faith, straight away following the divine ray of the star gleaming in her unhappy soul, rushed into the banqueting-hall to manifest publicly to Christ her faith, her repentance and her love. Magdalene followed the star, and the star led Magdalene to the Savior: "Your sins are forgiven ... your faith has saved you; go in peace."[44] One who comes to me *I will not cast out.*

The lives of the saints and the experience of souls show that in our super-natural existence there are often decisive moments on which depend the whole worth of our interior life and sometimes our eternity itself.

Look at Saul on the road to Damascus. He is an enemy and relentless persecutor of the Christians, "breathing threats of slaughter" against all who bear that name. And see how the voice of Jesus makes itself heard. This is for Saul the "star," the divine call. He listens to the call, he follows the star: "Lord, what will

[42] John 6:44.   [43] John 6:37.   [44] Luke 7, vv. 48, 50.

you have me do?" What alacrity and what generosity! And from that moment consequently, having become a "chosen vessel"[45] he will live only for Christ.

Look, on the contrary, at that young man, full of goodwill, with an upright and sincere heart, who approaches Jesus and asks Him what he must do to gain eternal life. "Keep the commandments," our Divine Savior tells him. "Master," he replies, "I have kept them ever since I was a child," what is still lacking to me? At this, the Gospel says, "Jesus, looking upon him, loved him"; this look, full of love, was a ray of the star. Then see how the star is immediately manifested to the young man. Jesus said: "One thing is lacking to you. If you want to be perfect, sell whatever you have, and give to the poor, and you shall have treasure in heaven; and having done that, come, follow me." But this young man does not follow the star. "His face fell at the saying, and he went away sad, for he had a great many possessions." The words Our Lord spoke immediately afterwards were: "With what difficulty will they who trust in riches enter the kingdom of God!"[46] and some commentators see in those words a prediction of the loss of that soul.[47]

Thus, whether it be a matter of a call to faith or to holiness, we shall only find Christ and the life of which He is the source on condition that we are attentive to grace and perseveringly faithful in our seeking of union with God.

The Heavenly Father calls us to His Son through the inspiration of His grace; but He wishes that we, like the Magi, as soon as the star shines in our hearts shall leave all on the instant: our sins, the occasions of sin, bad habits, infidelities, imperfections,

---

[45] Acts 9, vv. 1, 6, 15.   [46] Mark 10:17-23; Matt. 19:16-23; Luke 18:18-24.

[47] [*Translator's note*: But as the disciples said among themselves "Who, then, can be saved?" and Jesus said to them "With men it is impossible, but not with God..." (Mark 10:26-27), it may be that those commentators are being too categoric in drawing such a conclusion about the young man.]

attachments to what is merely created. He wishes that, taking no account of either the criticism or opinions of men or the difficulties of the work to be done, we set ourselves at once to seek Jesus—whether we have lost Him through one mortal sin, or whether, possessing Him through sanctifying grace, we are called to a closer and more intimate union with Him.

Vidimus stellam: "Lord, I have seen *your* star, and I come to you. What will you have me do?"

3. Behavior of the Magi on the disappearance of the star.

It occasionally happens that the star disappears from our sight. Whether the inspiration of grace bears an extraordinary character, as was the case for the Magi, or whether—and this for us is the most frequent case—it is attached to the super-natural providence of everyday, the star sometimes stops showing itself; its light is hidden; the soul finds itself in spiritual darkness. What is then to be done?

Let us see what the Magi did when that occurred. The star showed itself to them only in the East and then it disappeared: "We have seen His star *in the East*." If it told them of the birth of the King of the Jews, it did not indicate to them the precise place where they could find Him. What was to be done? The Magi betook themselves to Jerusalem, the capital of Judea, the metropolis of the Jewish religion. Where better than in the holy city could they learn of that which they sought?

In the same way, when our star disappears, when divine inspiration does not at all make things clear for us, leaves us in uncertainty, God wishes us to have recourse to the Church, to those who represent Him among us, in order to learn from them the path we ought to follow. This is the plan of Divine Providence. When a soul is in doubt or difficulty on its journey to Christ, God loves to see it asking for light and direction from those whom He has established as His representatives in our midst: "He who hears you, hears me."[48]

Once again, look at Saul on the road to Damascus. To the call of Jesus, he cries out immediately: "Lord, what will you have me do?" What does Christ reply? Does He at that time make known His will to Saul directly? He could have done that since He had revealed Himself to him as the Lord. But He does not do that; He sends Saul back to His representatives: "Get up now and go into the city, and you will be told"—by another—"what you have to do."[49]

By submitting the aspirations of our souls to the control of those who have the grace and the mission of directing us in our seeking of union with God, we run no risk of going astray—and this, moreover, whatever be the personal merits of those who guide us. In the period when the Magi arrived at Jerusalem, the assembly of those who had authority to interpret the Holy Scriptures was composed in large part of unworthy elements; and yet God willed that it should be through their ministry and teaching that the Magi should officially be apprised of the place where Christ had been born. God, indeed, cannot allow a soul to be deceived when, with humility and trust, that soul addresses itself to the legitimate representatives of His sovereign authority.

Very much to the contrary, it will find light and peace. Like the Magi leaving Jerusalem, it will then see the star again, full of brightness and splendor, and, filled with joy like them also, that soul will again go forward on its way: "And when they saw the star they rejoiced exceedingly."[50]

---

[48] Luke 10:16.   [49] Acts 9:6 (Jerus.)   [50] Matt. 2:10.

4. Their faith at Bethlehem—how deep it was! Symbolism
   of the gifts they offered to the Child-God. The way for
   us to imitate them.

Let us now follow the Magi to Bethlehem. There especially
we shall see manifested the depth of their faith.

The wondrous star led them to the place where, at last, they
were to find Him they had so long been seeking. And what did
they find? A palace, a royal cradle, a long train of assiduous servants? No, the poor dwelling of some workman. They sought a
God, a king, and all they saw was a child on his mother's lap—not
a child transfigured by rays of light, such as the apostles would later see on Mount Tabor, but a little child, a child poor and weak.

Nevertheless, from this being, so frail in appearance, went
forth invisibly a divine power: "Power went forth from Him."[51]
He who had made the star rise so as to lead the Magi to His cradle was now enlightening them Himself; He filled their minds inwardly with light and their hearts with love. It was on account of
this that they recognized in this child their God.

The Gospel tells us nothing of their words, but it makes
known to us a sublime gesture of their perfect faith: "And falling
down they adored Him."[52]

The Church wishes us to associate ourselves with this adoration by the Magi. When, during Holy Mass, she gives us those
words of the Gospel account to read: "And falling down they
adored Him," she makes us bend the knee to show that we, too,
believe in the divinity of the child of Bethlehem.

Let us adore Him with deep faith. God the Father asks of us
that so long as we are still here on earth all the activity of our interior life shall tend towards a union with His Son in faith. Faith
is the light by which we can see God in the Virgin's Child, hear
the voice of God in the words spoken by the Incarnate Word, follow, in the actions of Jesus, the example of One who is God, take

[51] Luke 6:19, 8:46; Mark 5:30.   [52] Matt. 2:11 (Rheims).

to ourselves the infinite merits of One who is God, through the pains and the satisfactions made by One who is also a man and who suffered like us.

Through the veil of His humanity—humble, susceptible of suffering—the soul enlightened by a living faith always discerns God. Wherever that soul encounters this humanity, whether it be in the humiliations of Bethlehem, upon the roads of Judea, on the gibbet of Calvary, or under the Eucharistic appearances, that faithful soul prostrates itself before this humanity because it is the humanity of One who is God. Throwing itself at His feet, that soul listens to Him, obeys Him, follows Him, until such time as God shall be pleased to reveal His infinite majesty in the holy splendors of the Beatific Vision: until "we who already know you by faith, may see your glory face to face."[53]

The attitude of adoration we find in the Magi translated into eloquent language the depth of their faith. The gifts they offered are also full of meaning. The Fathers of the Church have insistently called attention to the symbolism of those gifts brought to Christ by the Magi. Let us, to conclude this talk, pause to consider how profound that symbolism is. It will be a joy for our souls, and food for our devotional life.

As you know, the Gospel tells us that "opening their treasures, they offered Him gifts of gold, frankincense and myrrh."[54] It is evident that in the thinking of the Magi these presents were to serve to express the feelings of their hearts as much as to honor Him to whom they brought them.

By examining the nature of these gifts, which they had prepared before setting out on their journey, we see that the divine light had already manifested to the Magi something of the surpassing dignity of Him whom they desired to see and adore. The nature of these gifts likewise indicates what sort of duties the Magi wished to fulfill in regard to the person of the King of

[53] Prayer of Mass of the Epiphany. [54] Matt. 2:11.

the Jews. The symbolism of the gifts, therefore, has reference both to Him to whom they were offered and to those who were presenting them to Him.

Gold, the most precious of the metals, is a symbol of royalty; and then again it is a mark of the love and fidelity that each person owes to his monarch.

Incense is universally recognized as a symbol of divine worship; it is offered to God alone. By preparing this gift the Magi showed that they wished to declare the divinity of Him whose birth the star was announcing, and to recognize that divinity by the supreme adoration which can be rendered only to God.

Finally, they had been inspired to bring myrrh to Him. What did they wish to indicate by this myrrh, which serves to dress wounds and embalm the dead? This gift signified that Christ was man, and a man susceptible of suffering, who would die one day. Myrrh symbolized also the spirit of penance and immolation that should characterize the life of disciples of the Crucified One.

In this way grace had inspired the Magi to bring presents to Him they were seeking. It should be the same as that for us. "We who listen to the account of the offerings of the Magi," says St. Ambrose, "let us draw forth from our treasures and make similar offerings." Every time we draw near to Christ, let us bring Him presents, as the Magi did—and magnificent presents, presents which (as theirs were) are worthy of Him to whom we offer them.

You may say to me perhaps: "We have no gold or frankincense or myrrh." True; but we have what is much better, we have treasures much more precious, and, moreover, the only ones that Christ, our Savior and King, looks forward to receiving from us. Are we not offering gold to Christ when, by a life full of love and of fidelity to His commandments, we declare that He is the King of our hearts? Are we not presenting frankincense to Him when we believe in His divinity and recognize it by our adoration and our prayers? By uniting our humiliations, our sufferings, our sorrows and our tears to His, aren't we bringing Him myrrh?

And if, by ourselves, we are lacking in these good things, let us ask Our Lord to enrich us with treasures that will be pleasing to Him. He possesses them to give to us.

That is what Christ Jesus Himself made St. Mechtilde understand, one Epiphany Day, after holy communion. "See," he said, "how I give you gold—my Divine Love; and incense—all my holiness and devotion; and, finally, myrrh—the bitterness of all I suffered in my Passion. I give you them as your own, to such a degree that you will be able offer them to me as gifts, as good things belonging to yourself."[55]

Yes, this is an extremely consoling truth, that we ought never to forget. The grace of divine adoption, which makes us brethren of Jesus and living members of His mystical body, gives us the right to take to ourselves His treasures so as to give them value as our own before Himself and His Father. You know, said St. Paul, the greatness and the power of "the grace of our Lord Jesus Christ—how, being rich, He became poor for your sakes, that by His poverty you might become rich."[56]

The replacement for poverty is Our Lord Himself; He is our riches, our thanksgiving. Enclosed within Him, eminently, are what the presents of the Magi signify. He is in His own person, and to perfection, the reality of the deep symbolism of the gold, frankincense and myrrh. Nothing at all better than Himself, therefore, could possibly be offered by us to His Heavenly Father in rendering thanks for the priceless gift of the Christian faith. God has given us His Son; and according to Jesus's own words, Infinite Being could not have shown His love for us in a more striking way: "God *so* loved the world"—so much did God love the world—"that He *gave* His only-begotten Son."[57] For, adds St. Paul, in giving His Son He has given all good to us: "How can He fail to grant us also all things with Him?"[58]

---

[55] *Le Livre de la grace spéciale*, Part I, Ch.8.   [56] 2 Cor. 8:9.
[57] John 3:16.   [58] Rom. 8:32.

But we owe to God, in return, a more than ordinary thanks-giving for this ineffable gift. What shall we give to God that will be worthy of Him? His Son Jesus. In offering His Son to Him, we give back to Him the Gift He has given to us: "We offer unto Thy Most Excellent Majesty, of Thy own gifts bestowed on us, a pure Victim, a holy Victim, an unspotted Victim...";[59] and no gift could be more pleasing to Him.

The Church, who knows the secrets of God better than any-one, knows this so well! On this day of the Epiphany, when her mystical nuptials with Christ began, she offers to God, not gold, frankincense and myrrh, but Him who is represented by those gifts, immolated on the altar and received in the hearts of His faithful: "Look graciously, we beseech thee, O Lord, upon the offerings of thy Church, by which gold, frankincense and myrrh are not now offered but He who by these same gifts was signified is sacrificed and received: Jesus Christ, thy Son, our Lord."[60]

Let us then, along with the priest, offer the Holy Sacrifice. Let us offer to the Eternal Father His Divine Son after having received Him at the holy banquet. But let us, through love, also offer our-selves with Him, that we may in everything do what His Divine Will shows us we should do. This is the most perfect present we could give to God.

The Epiphany continues still; it is prolonged through all the ages. "We also," says St. Leo, "should experience the joys of the Magi; for the mystery that was accomplished then should not stay confined to that day. By the munificence of God and the power of His goodness, our present times still enjoy the reality of which the Magi had the first-fruits."[61]

The Epiphany is renewed, indeed, when God makes the light of the Gospel illumine the eyes of pagans. Each time the Truth shines upon the sight of those who live in error, what is appearing is a ray of the star.

[59] Canon of the Mass.   [60] *Secretum* of the Mass of the Epiphany.
[61] St. Leo the Great, *Sermo* 35.

The Epiphany continues also in a faithful soul when the soul's love becomes more fervent and steadfast. Fidelity to the inspirations of grace—it is Our Lord Himself who says it—becomes the source of a living, a brighter, illumination. "He who loves me," said Christ, "*I will manifest myself to him.*"[62] Happy the soul who lives by faith and love! A manifestation of Christ Jesus, one ever new and ever more deep, will be produced in that soul; Christ will lead that soul into an ever closer understanding of His mysteries.

Holy Scripture compares the life of the just man to a luminous path, "like the light of dawn, which shines brighter and brighter until full day"[63]—until that day when all veils fall away, when all shadows disperse, when in the light of glory the eternal splendors of the Godhead appear. There, says St. John in that rather mysterious book, the Apocalypse, in which he describes the magnificences of the heavenly Jerusalem, "the city has no need of the sun or the moon to shine upon it," for the Lamb—Christ—is Himself the Light that illumines and rejoices all the elect.[64]

That will be the Epiphany of heaven.

"O God, who on this day didst manifest thine only-begotten Son to the Gentiles by the guidance of a star: graciously grant that we, who know thee now by faith, may be led on to contemplate the beauty of thy Majesty."[65]

---

[62] John 14:21.
[64] Apoc. 21:23, 22:5.

[63] Prov. 4:18 (RSV, Cath.)
[65] Prayer of Mass of the Epiphany.

CHAPTER NINE

THE VIRGIN MARY, AND THE MYSTERIES OF CHRIST'S CHILDHOOD AND HIDDEN LIFE

(The time after the Epiphany)

Introduction: The Divine Word took to Himself a human nature so as to unite it to Himself personally.

The mystery of the Incarnation can be summed up as an exchange between Divinity and our humanity, an exchange that is wonderful in all its aspects. In return for the human nature that He took to Himself from us, the Eternal Word grants us a share in His divine life.

It is indeed to be noted that it is we who gave the Word a human nature. God could have produced a humanity already fully established in its organic completeness (as was Adam on the day of his creation) and united that humanity to His Son. Christ would have truly been a man, because nothing that constitutes the essence of a man would have been foreign to Him; yet, in not joining Himself directly to us by a human birth, He would not, strictly speaking, have been of our race.

God did not choose to proceed in that way. What was the plan of Infinite Wisdom? That the Word should take the humanity He was to unite to Himself *from us*. Christ would thus be truly the "Son of Man"; He would be a member of our race: "born of a woman,[1] born "according to the flesh of the offspring of David."[2] When at Christmas we celebrate Christ's birth, we go back through the centuries to read there the list of His ancestors; we run through His human genealogy; and, going over the successive generations again, we see that He was born into the tribe of David, of the Virgin Mary: "... of her was born Jesus who is called Christ."[3]

God willed, as it were, to beg from our race the human nature that He destined for His Son in order to give us in return a participation in His divinity: "O wondrous exchange!"

As you know, God's very nature moves Him to infinite bounty: it is of the essence of good that it spreads beyond itself: *Bonum est diffusivum sui*, "Good is self-diffusive." Infinite Goodness is drawn in an infinite way to give itself. God is this limitless Goodness; revelation tells us that there are between the Divine Persons, from the Father to the Son, from the Father and the Son to the Holy Spirit, infinite communications which in God account for the whole of this *natural* tendency of God's Being to give itself.

But, beyond this natural communication of Infinite Good, there is another communication, emanating from His wholly *free* love for creatures. The fullness of the Being and the Good that is God has overflowed, outwardly, through love. And how has that come about? God willed first of all to give Himself in a wholly particular way to a created entity by uniting that created entity, in a personal union, to His Word. That gift of God to what is created is unique: it makes of this created being[4] chosen by the Trinity God's own Son: "You are my Son, this day have I begotten you."[5] This is Christ, this is the Word united personally, and in an indissoluble way, to a humanity, to a human nature, one in every way like ours, sin excepted.

---

[1] Gal. 4:4.   [2] Rom. 1:3.   [3] Matt. 1:16.

[4] [*Translator's note*: Christ, as man, has a created human body and a created human soul, united at the Incarnation to the uncreated Second Person of the Trinity, the Word.]   [5] Ps. 2:7.

He asked us for this human nature. "Grant me, for my Son, your nature," the Eternal Father asked of us in some way, "and I in return will give you, to that human nature first of all, and, through it, to every person of good will, a participation in my divinity."

For God does not thus communicate Himself to Christ[6] except by delivering Himself up, through Christ, to us all. The divine plan is that Christ receive the divinity in its fullness and that we, in our turn, draw from this fullness: "Of His fullness we have all received."[7]

Such is this communication of the goodness of God to the world: "God so *loved* the world that He *gave* His only-begotten Son."[8] Such is the wonderful arrangement of things that governs the "wondrous exchange" between God and humanity.

But *who in particular* would God ask to give birth to that human nature He wished to unite to Himself so closely, in order to make it the instrument of His graces to the world?

We have already given the name of that creature, whom all generations would proclaim as "blessed."[9] The human genealogy of Jesus climaxes with Mary, the virgin of Nazareth. To her, and through her to us, the Word asked for a human nature, and Mary gave it to Him. That is why thereafter we will see her as inseparable from Jesus and His mysteries. Wherever Jesus is, we will see her. He is *her* Son as much as He is the Son of God.

---

[6] [*Translator's note:* Marmion's language here is perhaps capable of being misunderstood. There was no purely created person to whom Divinity was then communicated; nor is Marmion saying or implying this. Rather, at the very moment of the Incarnation a created human nature was united to the Person of the eternal, uncreated, Word. It is in this sense that God communicated Himself to Christ—by the Second Person of the Trinity taking to Himself a human nature in becoming incarnate. As Marmion himself never tires of quoting: "What He [Christ] was [i.e. God], He remained; what He was not [i.e. man], He took to Himself."]

[7] John 1:16.   [8] John 3:16.   [9] Luke 1:48.

Nevertheless, though Jesus keeps His nature as Son of Mary wherever He is, it is above all in the mysteries of the infancy and hidden life that He reveals Himself under that aspect. Though Mary, wherever she is, occupies a unique place, it is in those mysteries that her role shows itself, exteriorly, in its most active form, and it is good that in the next few moments we should reflect upon her, for it is especially in the infancy and hidden life that her privilege of being Mother of God shines out brightly. And, as you know, that incomparable dignity is the source of all the other privileges of the Virgin.

Those who do not know the Virgin, those who do not have a real love for the mother of Jesus, risk not having a fruitful understanding of the mysteries of the human nature of Christ. He is the Son of Man, as He is the Son of God; those two characteristics He possesses are of His essence. Though He is Son of God by an eternal begetting beyond words to describe, He became Son of Man by being born of Mary in the sphere of time.

Let us reflect upon this virgin at her Son's side. In return, she will obtain for us the grace of arriving at a deeper understanding of these mysteries of Christ with which she is so closely united.

1. **How, in the mystery of the Annunciation to the Virgin, the exchange between the Divinity and humanity was concluded. "Mother of God."**

In order that the exchange God wished to contract with humankind might be possible, it was necessary that humankind should consent to it. That was the condition laid down by Infinite Wisdom.

Let us imagine ourselves at Nazareth. The "fullness of time" had come, says St. Paul, when God had determined to send His Son into the world, by making Him be born there, "born of a woman."[10] The angel Gabriel, messenger of God, brought heaven's

[10] Gal. 4:4.

proposals to the young virgin. A sublime conversation began, in which the rescue of the human race was to be decided. The angel starts by giving the virgin a salutation proclaiming her, on behalf of God, "full of grace."[11] And, indeed, not only is she immaculate, no stain upon her soul—the Church has defined that, alone of all creatures, she has been untouched by original sin—but as well as this, because she has been predestined to be the mother of His Son, the Heavenly Father has showered His gifts upon her. She is "full of grace"—not indeed as Christ will be "full of grace"; for He is this by right, and His fullness is of the divine fullness itself. Mary receives everything by way of participation, but to a measureless extent, one that correlates with the utterly surpassing office and dignity of being Mother *of God*.

"Behold," says the angel, "you shall conceive in your womb and bring forth a Son, and shall give Him the name 'Jesus,' Savior ... He shall be called the Son of the Most High ... and of His kingdom there shall be no end." "How shall this come about," replies Mary, "seeing that I am a virgin." (For she wishes to keep her virginity.) "The Holy Spirit shall come upon you, and the power of the Most High shall overshadow you; and that is why the Holy One, the fruit of your womb, shall be called Son of God." "Behold the handmaid of the Lord" is Mary's answer, "be it done to me as you say."[12]

At that solemn moment, the exchange is concluded. When Mary uttered that *Fiat* of hers, that "Let it be done to me," the whole of humanity had said to God, through her voice: Yes, O God, I accept: let it be so! And immediately "*the Word was made flesh.*" At that instant, the Word became incarnate within her by the operation of the Holy Spirit: Mary's womb became the Ark of the New Covenant between God and man.

When, in the *Credo*, the Church sings the words that recall this mystery: "He became incarnate of the Virgin Mary, and became man"—*Et incarnatus est de Spiritu Sancto et homo factus est*—she

[11] Luke 1:28.   [12] See Luke 1, vv. 31-35, 38.

requires her ministers to bend the knee as a sign of adoration. We too—let us adore this Divine Word who was made man for us in the womb of a virgin; let us adore Him all the more for further abasing Himself by taking, in St. Paul's phrase, "the form of a servant,"[13] the condition of a creature. Let us adore Him in union with Mary herself who, enlightened by light from on high, bowed down low before her Creator who had become her Son, and with the angels, marveling as they were at this infinite condescension towards humankind.

Next let us greet the Virgin; let us thank her for having given us Jesus. That we have Jesus, and the life He brought, we owe to Mary's having given her consent: "it was through her that we received the author of life, Jesus Christ."[14] To our thanks, let us add our joyous congratulations. Look at how the Holy Spirit Himself, through the mouth of Elizabeth—"And Elizabeth was filled with the Holy Spirit"[15]—saluted the Virgin on the morrow of the Incarnation: "Blessed art thou among women and blessed is the fruit of thy womb ... Blessed art thou for believing; the message that was brought to thee from the Lord shall have fulfillment!"[16] Blessed, for this faith in God's words made the Virgin become the mother of Christ. What praises comparable to those have ever been given by Infinite Being to one who is simply a creature?

Mary referred back to the Lord all the marvels worked within her. From the moment the Son of God had taken flesh in her womb, the Virgin sang in her heart a hymn full of love and gratitude. At the home of her cousin Elizabeth, she let the inner feelings of her soul overflow; she intoned that Magnificat which, in the course of the centuries, her spiritual children would repeat with her in praise of God for having chosen her from among all women: "My soul glorifies the Lord, and my spirit rejoices in God my Savior, because He has regarded the lowliness of His

---

[13] Phil. 2:7 (Rheims).   [14] Prayer of Office for January 1st.
[15] Luke 1:42.   [16] Luke 1, vv. 42, 45 (Knox).

handmaid ... For the Almighty has done great things to me, and holy is His name."[17]

Mary was at Bethlehem for the census ordered by Caesar Augustus, when, as St. Luke tells us, the time came for her to give birth. "And she brought forth her firstborn Son, and wrapped Him in swaddling clothes, and laid Him in a manger, because there was no room for them in the inn."[18] Who is this Child? He is Mary's Son, because it is of her that He has just been born.

But the Virgin beheld in this Child—who looked like all other children—God's own Son. Mary's soul was filled with immense faith; this faith, enclosed in her, surpassed the faith of all the just of the Old Testament, and that is why in seeing her Son she recognized her God.

This faith found its outward expression in an act of adoration. From the very first look she gave Jesus, the Virgin bowed low interiorly, in an adoration the depths of which are to us an unfathomable sea.

To this faith—such a living faith as it was!—to this adoration so profound, are to be added the intense joys-of-heart of a love beyond measure.

Human love, first. God is Love; and, so that we may have some idea of this Love, He gives a sharing in it to mothers. The heart of a mother, with her untiring tenderness, with the constancy of her solicitude, the inexhaustible delicacy of her affection, is a truly divine creation, although God has placed in it no more than a spark of His Love for us. Yet, imperfectly as the heart of a mother reflects the Love that He has for us, God gives us our mothers so that the love of a mother in some way represents it before us. He places our mother at our side, from the cradle onwards, to guide us, to guard us, especially in those first years during which we need tenderness so much.

[17] See Luke 1:46-49.   [18] Luke 2:6-7.

Going on from that, imagine the fondness with which the Holy Trinity fashioned the heart of the virgin chosen above all others to be the mother of the Word Incarnate. It pleased God to pour love into her heart, in forming it expressly to love this One who would be the God-made-man.

In the heart of Mary, the adoration of a creature towards her God was joined, in perfect harmony, with the love of a mother for her only Son.

The Virgin's super-natural love is no less marvelous. A soul's love for God, you know, is commensurate with that soul's degree of grace. What is it that, in *us*, prevents grace and love from developing? Our sins, our deliberate shortcomings, our intentional infidelities, our attachment to created persons and things. Each deliberate shortcoming narrows the heart, strengthens egoism. But the soul of the Blessed Virgin is one of complete purity; no sin has soiled it, not the shadow of a shortcoming has touched it; she is "full of grace." Far from encountering in her the least obstacle to the blossoming of grace, the Holy Spirit ever has found her heart wonderfully docile to His inspirations—which is why that heart of hers was so enlarged by love.

What must have been the joy of the soul of Jesus to feel Himself loved to such an extent by His mother! After the joy—to us, an incomprehensible, unimaginable joy—that he had received from the Beatific Vision and the infinite delight with which the Heavenly Father looked upon Him, nothing could have rejoiced Him as much as the love of His mother. In that love He found a more than abundant compensation for the indifference of those who did not wish to receive Him; He found in the heart of this young virgin a hearth-fire of love ever kept burning, one that He Himself stirred by each divine glance of His and by the interior grace of His Spirit.

Between these two souls there constantly occurred exchanges that made bright the union of this Son and this mother. From Jesus to Mary such gifts were given; from Mary to Jesus there was such reciprocity of giving, that, after the union of the Divine Persons and the hypostatic union of the Incarnation, one could not conceive of anything greater or deeper.

Let us draw near to Mary with a humble but complete confidence. Her Son being the Savior of the world, she enters into His mission too profoundly for her not to share the love He bears for sinners. "O Mother of Jesus," let us sing to her with the Church, "you gave birth to your Creator while remaining a virgin, succor this fallen race whom your Son, by taking to Himself a human nature, came here to raise up; have pity on the sinners whom your Son came on earth to redeem. It was for us, O Mary, in order to redeem us, that He deigned to descend from the eternal splendors into your virginal womb."[19]

2. Mary's Purification and the Presentation of Jesus in the Temple.

Mary will understand that prayer, for she is intimately associated with Jesus in the work of our redemption.

Eight days after the birth of her Son, she caused Him to be circumcised in accordance with Jewish Law; and it was at this time that she gave Him the name indicated by the angel—the name "Jesus," Savior, which points to His mission of salvation and His work of redemption.

When He was forty days old, the Virgin associated Him with the work of our salvation more directly and deeply still, by presenting Him in the Temple. She it is who was the first to offer up her Divine Son to the Father. After the oblation of Himself that Jesus, Supreme High Priest, made at the very moment of the Incarnation, and which He completed on Calvary, Mary's offering is the most perfect. It is in a different category to all the priestly acts of men; it surpasses them even, because Mary is the mother of Christ, whereas men are only His ministers.

[19] See Hymn, *Alma Redemptoris Mater*.

Let us contemplate Mary in that solemn act of the Presentation of her Son in the Temple at Jerusalem.

All the magnificent and minute ceremonial of the Old Testament converged on Christ; all of it was obscure symbol that was to find its complete reality in the New Covenant.

As you know, among the prescribed rituals that were binding on Jewish women who had become mothers was that of presenting themselves in the Temple some weeks after childbirth. The mother was to be purified from the legal stain she, in consequence of original sin, had contracted by the birth of the child. Further, if the child was the firstborn and a male, she had to present him to the Lord to be consecrated to Him as Sovereign Master of all creation: "Every firstborn male must be consecrated to the Lord."[20] However, the child could be "bought back" by an offering, large or otherwise—a lamb or a pair of pigeons—according to the family's financial position.

Most assuredly, these prescribed obligations did not bind either Mary or Jesus. Jesus was the supreme lawgiver of all the Jewish ritual; His childbirth had been miraculous and by a virgin; there was nothing but what was pure in His birth: "the *Holy One* to be born of you shall be called the Son of God."[21] Consequently, there was no need at all to consecrate Him to the Lord, seeing that He was God's own Son; and there was no need for any purification of her who had conceived through the Holy Spirit and remained a virgin.

But Mary, guided in this by the same Holy Spirit who is the Spirit of Jesus, was in perfect conformity with the feelings of her Son's soul. "O Father," Jesus had said on coming into the world, "You no longer wish for sacrifices and holocausts; they are insufficient to satisfy your adorable justice and to buy back sinful man; but you have given me a body to be immolated to you. Here I am; I wish in all things to do your will."[22] And what had the words of the Virgin been? "Behold the handmaid of the Lord, be it done to me as you say."

---

[20] Luke 2:23 (Jerus.); Exod. 13, vv. 2, 12.   [21] See Luke 1:35.

[22] See Hebr. 10:5-7; Ps. 39(40):7-8 (6).

It was for that reason that she wished to carry out this ceremony, showing thereby how deep her submission was. Therefore, with Joseph her husband, she brought there Jesus, her "firstborn Son," who would remain her only Son, but who was to become "the firstborn among many brethren"[23] who, through grace, would resemble Him.

When we meditate on this mystery, we are forced to say: "You are a hidden God, O Savior of the world!"—"a hidden God, the God of Israel, the Savior."[24] On that day of the Presentation Christ entered into the Temple for the first time, and it was into *His* Temple that He entered. This wonderful Temple, the admiration of the nations and the pride of Israel, in which were carried out all the religious rites and sacrifices of which God Himself had regulated the details, this Temple belonged to Him: for this Child, carried in the arms of a young virgin, is the King of kings and the Sovereign Lord: "The Lord ... shall come to *His* Temple."[25]

And how does He come? In the splendor of His majesty? As Him to whom all the sacrifices are alone due? No, He goes there absolutely hidden.

Listen to what the Gospel says. There must have been a bustling crowd on the approaches to the sacred building: merchants, Levites, priests, teachers of the Law. A small unnoticed group makes its way through them. These are the poor, for they are not leading a lamb, the offering of those who are rich; all they bring is two doves, the sacrifice of those in poverty. No-one takes any notice of them, for they have no train of servants. The great, the proud, among the Jews do not spare them a glance, and it requires the Holy Spirit to enlighten the old man Simeon and the prophetess

---

[23] Rom. 8:29. [*Translator's note*: The point with which Marmion ends (that Christ was to become the "firstborn of many brethren" by grace) is a central element of the *New* dispensation. It links up with what Marmion says in the preceding paragraph.]   [24] Isa. 45:15.   [25] Malachi 3:1.

Anna so that they recognize the Messiah. He who is the Savior promised to the world, the Light who is to shine before all the nations—the "salvation ... prepared before the face of all peoples"[26]—comes into His Temple as "a hidden God": "Truly, you are a hidden God!"[27]

Nothing of the feelings of Jesus's sacred soul was revealed outwardly, either. The light of His divinity remained hidden, veiled. But He renewed here, in the Temple, the oblation of Himself He had made at the moment of the Incarnation; He offered Himself to His Father to be "His thing," belonging fully to Him as of right: "He shall be called holy to the Lord"[28] It was like the offertory of the Sacrifice which was to be consummated on Calvary.

What took place at the Presentation was extremely pleasing to the Father, therefore. To the eyes of the profane, there was nothing special about this simple action that all Jewish mothers performed. But God received on that day infinitely more glory in this Temple than He had received up to then from all the sacrifices and all the holocausts of the Old Law. Why is that? Because on that day it was His Son Jesus who was offered to Him, and who Himself offered to Him an infinite homage of adoration, thanksgiving, expiation, supplication. It was a gift worthy of God. The Heavenly Father must have received with immeasurable joy this sacred offering; and the enraptured gaze of all the heavenly court been riveted upon this unique oblation. Now there was no longer a need for holocausts or the sacrifice of animals: the only Victim worthy of God had just been offered to Him.

And it was by the hands of the Virgin, of the Virgin full of grace, that this offering that was so pleasing to Him was presented. Mary's faith was perfect. Filled with the lights of the Holy Spirit, her soul understood the worth of the offering she made to God

---

[26] Luke 2:30-31.   [27] See Isa. 45:15   [28] Luke 2:23; Exod. 13:2.

at this time. Through His inspirations, the Holy Spirit harmo-
nized her soul with the interior dispositions of her Divine Son's
heart.

Just as she had given her assent in the name of the whole of
humanity when the angel announced to her the mystery of the
Incarnation, in that same way, on the day of the Presentation,
Mary offered Jesus in the name of the human race. She knew that
her Son is the King of glory, the new Light, begotten before the
daystar, the Lord of life and of death. That is why she presented
Him to God to obtain for us all the graces of salvation that her
Son was to bring to the world as the angel had promised, "O Sion
... Mary brings to you the glorious King of the new light; remain-
ing ever a virgin, she bears in her arms the Son begotten before
the daystar."[29]

Never forget, either, that He whom she thus offers is her own
Son, He whom she carried in her virginal and fruitful womb.
What priest, what saint, has ever presented the Eucharistic oblation to God in so close a union with the Divine Victim as was the
Virgin at that time? Not only was she united to Jesus through
feelings of faith and love (as we ourselves can be, though to an
infinitely lesser degree), but the bond that united her to Christ
Jesus was unique: Jesus was her own, the fruit of her womb. That
is why Mary, ever since she presented Jesus as the first-fruits of
the future Sacrifice, has so preponderant a share in the work of
our redemption.

And see how Christ Jesus wills to associate the Virgin Mother
of God with His own position as Victim, from that moment also.

That is what the old man Simeon—guided by the Holy Spirit,
with whom he was filled: "and the Holy Spirit was in him ... And
he came by inspiration of the Spirit into the temple"[30]—that is
what Simeon led up to. He recognized in this Child the Savior of

---

[29] Antiphon *Adorna* of the blessing of the candles on the Feast of the
Presentation, Candlemas Day.   [30] See Luke 2, vv. 25, 27.

the world: he took Him into his arms and sang out his joy at having at last seen with his own eyes the promised Messiah. After having extolled this Child as "a light of revelation to the Gentiles," a light that one day would show itself to all the nations, and a glory for the people of Israel, he gave back Jesus to His mother's arms, and, addressing Mary, said to her: "This Child is destined for the fall and for the rise of many in Israel, and for a sign that shall be contradicted. And your own soul a sword shall pierce, that the thoughts of many hearts shall be revealed."[31] These words were a foreshadowing of Christ's Sacrifice by the shedding of His blood on Calvary.

The Gospel tells us nothing of the feelings to which this prediction gave rise in the Virgin's pure heart. Can we believe it could ever disappear from her mind? St. Luke reveals to us later, about other events, that Mary "kept all these words in her heart."[32] Can we not already say the same of this scene, of this saying of Simeon's that was so unexpected to her? Yes, she kept the memory of these words that in their mystery were so terrible to her mother's heart. It was from that time on, and always, that her heart was pierced. But, in full accord with the feelings of the heart of her Son, Mary accepted being associated, so soon and so fully, with His Sacrifice.

Later on, we shall see her completing her oblation on the hill of Golgotha, as Jesus did. We shall see her stand upright— "standing by the cross of Jesus,"[33] *Stabat mater ejus*, offering her Son again, the fruit of her womb, for our salvation as, thirty-three years before, she had offered Him in the temple at Jerusalem.

Let us thank the Virgin Mary for having presented her Divine Son for us. Let us render fervent thanksgiving to Jesus for having offered Himself to His Father for our salvation.

At Holy Mass, Christ offers Himself anew. Let us present Him to His Father; let us unite ourselves with Him, like Him, in a

---

[31] Luke 2:32-35.   [32] Luke 2:51 (Rheims).   [33] John 19:25.

disposition of complete submission of our will to His Heavenly Father. Let us unite ourselves to the faith of the Virgin—how deep it was! It is through such true faith as this, and such fully faithful love, that our offerings will merit to be pleasing to God: "Grant that ... we may truly acknowledge Thee and faithfully love Thee,"[34] "...that the gifts we offer in the sight of Thy Majesty may be found worthy."[35]

3. Jesus is lost, when twelve years old.

In awaiting what was to happen when Simeon's prophecy came fully true, Mary would, even then, have her share of sacrifice.

She soon would flee to Egypt, into an unknown land, so as to remove her Son from the wrath of the tyrant Herod. She stayed there until, after the death of King Herod, the angel told Joseph that they must retrace the road they had taken and go back to Palestine. Thereupon the Holy Family went and settled at Nazareth. It was there that Jesus would live until he was thirty—so that He would be become known as "Jesus of Nazareth."

The Gospels have preserved for us only one incident of this period of Christ's life: Jesus found in the Temple, after being lost.

You know the circumstances that had taken the Holy Family to Jerusalem. The Child Jesus was twelve years old. That was the age when young Israelites were first subject to the rules prescribed by the Mosaic Law, notably that of going to the Temple three times a year, on the feasts of Passover, of Pentecost and of Tabernacles. Our Divine Savior who, by His circumcision, had willed to bear the yoke of the Law, accordingly went with Mary and His foster-father into the holy city. He was doubtless making that pilgrimage for the first time.

---

[34] Prayer for Blessing of the Candles.   [35] *Secretum,* Mass of the Presentation.

When He went into the Temple, no-one suspected that this young person was the God they worshipped there. Jesus was in that place, mingling with the throng of Israelites, taking part in the religious ceremonies, in the chanting of the psalms. His soul understood the significance of the sacred rites as never any creature would; it relished the deep impressiveness emerging from the symbolism of that liturgy the details of which God Himself had determined. Jesus was seeing, in figure, all that was to be accomplished by Him in person. This was an occasion He took to offer perfect praise to His Father, in the name of those present and of the whole of humanity. God the Father thereby received a homage infinitely worthy of Himself.

At the end of the feast, says the Evangelist (who must have had the account from the Virgin herself) the Child Jesus "remained in Jerusalem, and his parents did not know it."[36] At the time of the Passover, as you will understand, the number of Jews who were in the city was very considerable; and this gave rise to crowding and congestion such as one can hardly imagine. On the return, the "caravans"—the particular sets of pilgrims who would leave together—were formed with extreme difficulty, and it was not before well on in the day that people were able to get their bearings. Moreover, young persons could join this or that group in their caravan as they pleased; that was the custom. Mary believed that Jesus could be found with Joseph.[37] She therefore journeyed on, singing the sacred hymns. Above all she thought of Jesus, expecting to see Him again soon.

But what a distressing surprise she received when, rejoining the group where Joseph was, she found the Child was not there! "And Jesus? where is Jesus?" were the first words from both of them. "Where is Jesus?" Neither of them knew.

[36] Luke 2:43.   [37] [*Translator's note*: Mary's being separated from Joseph in the crowds appears to be Marmion's own dramatic reconstruction. Whilst it is quite possible, it is not found in the Gospel, which simply speaks of both Mary and Joseph believing that Jesus was in another part of the

When God wishes to lead a soul to the very heights of perfection and contemplation, He causes that soul to pass through great trials. Christ has said that when a branch, united to Him who is the Vine, bears fruit, then His Father "prunes" it: *Purgabit eum.* And why? "To make it bear even more."[38] These are hard trials consisting, as they do especially, of spiritual darkness, of feelings of being abandoned by God; they are trials by which the Lord "empties" the soul of itself, to make it worthy of a more intimate, higher, union.

The Virgin Mary certainly had no need of such trials: what branch was more fruitful, ever, seeing it was she who gave Divine Fruit to the world? But when she lost Jesus she knew those sharp sufferings that were to increase both her capacity to love and the extent of her merits. We cannot easily estimate the greatness of the suffering she underwent. To understand it we have to comprehend what Jesus was to His mother.

Jesus had said nothing; Mary knew Him too well to think that He had lost His way. If He had left His parents, it was because He had willed to do so. When would He return? Would she ever see Him again? Mary had not lived several years at Nazareth at the side of Jesus without being conscious that He had within Him an ineffable mystery. And for her at this time, that was the source of a quite unequalled anguish.

They had now to go and search for the Child. What days those days of searching must have been! God permitted that the Blessed Virgin be in darkness during those hours filled with anxiety. She did not know where Jesus was; she did not understand

---

returning caravan. But there appears to be a certain tradition to that effect. Husenbeth's *Life of the Blessed Virgin Mary* has the note: "St. Epiphanius and St. Bernard inform us that in these journeys the men went in companies separate from the women, and that St. Joseph and the Blessed Virgin did not feel uneasy at first at the disappearance of Jesus, and did not perceive it till the evening, when all the travelers assembled together."]   [38] John 15:2 (Jerus.)

why He had not forewarned His mother. Her sorrow was immense at being thus parted from the one whom she loved both as her Son and as her God.

The Gospel tells us that Mary and Joseph first looked for Jesus "among their relations and acquaintances,"[39] but no-one had seen Jesus. Their hearts full of disquiet, they then returned to Jerusalem and searched everywhere. Finally, after three days they found Him, as you know, in the Temple, seated in the midst of the teachers of the Law.

The Teachers of Israel used to meet in one of the rooms of the Temple to explain the Holy Scriptures; anyone could come and join a group of their disciples and hearers. That is what Jesus did. He had come there, into the midst of them, not in order to teach—the hour had not yet sounded when He presented Himself to all as sole Lord, come to reveal secrets from on high; He had come there, like other young Israelites, to "listen and ask questions" (these are the very words used in the Gospel).[40]

And what was the object of the Child Jesus in thus asking questions of the teachers of the Law? Doubtless He wished to enlighten them, to bring them, by His questions and answers and by the quotations He made from Scripture, to speak of the coming of the Messiah; to guide their researches in the direction of that subject, so that their attention should be awakened as to the circumstances of the promised Savior's appearing. That, it seems, was what the Eternal Father wished of His Son, a mission He gave Him to accomplish, and for which He caused Him to interrupt for a time His hidden and wholly silent life. And the Teachers of Israel "were astonished at His wisdom and His answers."[41]

Mary and Joseph, overjoyed at finding Jesus, went up to Him, and His mother said to Him: "Son, why have you done so to us?" It was not a reproach—the humble Virgin was too wise to dare to

[39] Luke 2:44 (Jerus.)   [40] Luke 2:46.   [41] Luke 2:47 (Rheims).

blame Him whom she knew to be God; it was rather a cry from the heart, betraying her feelings as a mother: "Your father and I have been seeking you sorrowing"—sorrowing, *dolentes*. And what was Christ's reply? "How is it that you sought me? Did you not know that I must be about my Father's business?"[42]

These words fallen from the lips of the Word Incarnate are the first that have been recorded by the Gospel. The whole person, the whole life, the whole of the work of Jesus, are summed up by those words. They speak expressly of His Divine Sonship, they point to His supernatural mission; and the whole of Christ's existence will be but a shining and magnificent commentary on them.

They also contain a precious teaching for our souls. I have said to you often: in Christ there are two "begettings": He is *Son of God* and *Son of Man*.

As "Son of Man," He was bound to observe the natural law and the Mosaic law which require children to show their parents respect, love and submission. And who has done so better than Jesus? He Himself would say later: "I have not come to destroy the Law, but to bring it to perfection."[43] Who is there that can look in His heart and find sincerer marks of human tenderness?

As Son of God, He has obligations to His Heavenly Father[44] that are higher than human ones, and which seem sometimes to be in opposition to the latter. His Father had made Him understand on that day that He should remain in Jerusalem.

By the words He uttered in those circumstances Christ wishes to tell us that when God asks us to do His will, we ought not to let ourselves be stayed from doing so by any human consideration. It is on such occasions that we must say: "I need to devote myself wholly to the things of my Heavenly Father."

St. Luke, who doubtless was recording a humble acknowledgement about it by the Virgin herself, tells us that she and Joseph

---

[42] Luke 2:48-49.   [43] See Matt. 5:17.

[44] [*Translator's note*: Obligations wholly of *love*.]

"did not understand" the words He spoke to them[45]—did not understand the depths of them. Mary well knew that her Divine Son could not act other than in a perfect way: but why, then, could He not have forewarned her? What she did not grasp was the relationship that existed between the way Jesus had acted and the interests of His Father. What place had the present conduct of Jesus in the program of salvation His Heavenly Father had given Him? That still escaped her.

But if at that time she did not perceive the whole import of it, she did not thereby doubt that Jesus was the Son of God. This is why she submitted in silence to the Divine Will that had just demanded of her love such a sacrifice. She "kept all these words in her heart."[46] It was in her heart that she kept them; that was the tabernacle where she adored the mystery of the words of her Son while waiting until full light should be given her.

4. The hidden life at Nazareth.

The Gospel tells us that, after having been found in the Temple, Jesus returned to Nazareth with His mother and St. Joseph, and that He remained there up to the age of thirty. And the sacred writer sums up the whole of that long period simply in these words: that He *"was subject to"* Mary and Joseph.[47]

So, out of a life on earth of thirty-three years, He who is Eternal Wisdom willed to spend thirty in silence and obscurity, in submission and in work.

There is in that a mystery, and a lesson of which many souls, devout as they are, have not grasped the full meaning.

For what is it a question of, indeed? The Word, who is God, was made flesh. On a certain day, after centuries of waiting, He who is infinite and eternal so abased Himself as to take on human form: He "emptied Himself, taking the form of a servant, being

---

[45] Luke 2:50.   [46] Luke 2:51 (Rheims).   [47] Luke 2:51.

born in the likeness of men."[48] Even though He was born of an immaculate virgin, the Incarnation constituted an immeasurable abasement for Him: "Thou didst not abhor the virgin's womb."[49] And why did He descend to this abyss? To save the world, by bringing Divine Light to it.

Now, save for rare beams that illumined some privileged souls: the shepherds, the Magi, Simeon and Anna, here we have this Light *hidden*. Voluntarily it was put under a bushel for thirty years, before shining out clearly for a period of hardly three years.

Is this not mysterious? Does it not disconcert our reason? Had we been aware of Jesus's mission, might we not have said to Him, as some of His kindred would later: "No-one does a thing in secret if he wants to be publicly known ... *manifest yourself to the world.*"[50]

But God's thoughts are not our thoughts, and His ways go beyond our ways. He who came to redeem the world wished first to save it by a life hidden from the eyes of the world.

For thirty years, in the workshop of Nazareth, the Savior of the human race did nothing but work and obey. All the work of Him who came on earth to instruct humanity, in order to give back the eternal inheritance to it, was the work of living in silence, and of obeying two creatures in the most ordinary of actions.

Oh truly, my Savior, you are a hidden God! Doubtless, O Jesus, you "advanced in age, in wisdom, in grace, before your Father and before men."[51] From the first moment of your entry into this world, your soul possessed the fullness of grace, all the treasures of knowledge and wisdom: but this wisdom and this grace only declared themselves little by little, were only manifested to the extent needed. You lived, to the eyes of men, a hidden God; your divinity was veiled behind the outward appearances of a worker in a carpenter's shop. O Eternal Wisdom, who, so that we might be drawn out of the abyss into which the prideful

---

[48] Phil. 2:7.   [49] Hymn, *Te Deum.*   [50] John 7:4.   [51] See Luke 2:52.

disobedience of Adam had cast us, willed to spend your days in a humble workshop and be obedient to creatures there, I adore you and bless you!

In the sight of His contemporaries, therefore, the life of Christ Jesus at Nazareth appeared as if it were the commonplace existence of a simple artisan. You can see how true that is because, later,[52] when Christ in His public life revealed who He was, the Jews of His homeland were so astonished by the wisdom of His words, the sublimity of His teaching, the greatness of His works, that they asked themselves: "Where did he get this wisdom, and how is he able to perform these miracles? This is the carpenter's son, isn't it; we have always known him; his mother is called Mary. Where, then, has he learnt all these things?" Christ was for them a stumbling-block, for up to then they had seen in Him only someone in a local workshop.

This mystery of the hidden life contains teachings that our faith ought to pick up with avidity.

First, nothing is great in the sight of God but what is done for His glory with the grace of Christ. We are only pleasing to God in the measure that we resemble His Son Jesus.

The Divine Sonship of Christ gives to the least of His actions an infinite value; Christ Jesus is not less adorable, or less pleasing to His Father, when He wields a chisel or plane than when He dies on the cross to save the human race. In us, sanctifying grace, which makes us adopted children of God, divinizes all our activity at its root and renders us worthy—albeit upon different grounds— of being looked on kindly by the Father as Christ is.

As you know, the most precious talents, the most sublime thoughts, the most generous and striking actions, are without merit for life eternal as soon as they cease to be vivified by sanctifying grace. This passing world can admire and applaud them; but eternity—which alone does not pass away—neither receives

[52] See Matt. 13:54-55; Mark 6:2-3.

nor takes account of them. "What does it profit a man," said Jesus, Infallible Truth, "if he gain the whole world"[53]—by force of arms, by charm of eloquence or by authority of knowledge—if, not having my grace, he is excluded from my kingdom, the only kingdom that will never end?

Look, on the other hand, at this poor man who earns a living laboriously, at this humble servant, of whom the world is unaware, at this beggar in the street, disdained by all. The commonness of their existence neither attracts nor retains anyone's attention. But they have the grace of Christ giving them life: and see how these souls delight the angels and are for the Father, for God, for Infinite Being self-subsistent, an uninterrupted object of love! These souls bear in themselves, through grace, the very features of Christ.

Sanctifying grace is the first source of our true greatness. It is what confers on our life, however commonplace and ordinary that life may appear, its genuine nobility, its imperishable splendor.

But this gift is a hidden one.

The kingdom of God is built especially in silence. It is, above all else, interior and hidden in the depths of the soul: "Your life is hidden with Christ in God."[54]

Undoubtedly grace possesses a power that almost always is expressed outwardly, by works of charity radiating from it; but the mainspring of its power is an entirely inner one. True intensity of Christian life is to be found in the deepest part of the heart; it is there that God dwells, adored and served in faith, recollection, humility, obedience, simplicity, toil and love.

Our outer activity only has stability and super-natural fruitfulness to the extent that it is linked to this interior life. We shall only truly radiate outwards fruitfully in the measure that the supernatural hearth-fire of our inner life is more ardently blazing.

[53] See Matt. 16:26.   [54] Col. 3:3.

What greater thing can we do here below than advance the reign of Christ in souls? What work is worth as much as that? What work excels it? It is the whole work of Jesus and the Church.[55]

We shall not succeed in this, however, by means other than those employed by our divine head. Let us be completely convinced of this—that we shall work more for the good of the Church, the salvation of souls, the glory of our Heavenly Father, in seeking first to remain united to God by our whole life being one of faith and of love of which He is the sole object, than by a devouring and feverish activity that allows us neither time nor leisure to meet with God again in solitude, recollection, prayer and detachment from ourselves.

Now, nothing so favors this intense union of the soul with God as does the hidden life. And that is why souls having an interior life, enlightened by a ray from on high, like so much to contemplate the life of Jesus of Nazareth: they find in it, along with a special charm, abundant graces of holiness.

5. The Virgin Mary's feelings during the years of the hidden life.

It is from the Virgin Mary especially that we shall succeed in having a share of graces Christ merited for us through His hidden life at Nazareth. No-one knows the fruitfulness of that life better than the humble Virgin, because on no-one more than her has such fruitfulness been lavished. For the mother of Jesus, those years must have been a spring ceaselessly flooding forth graces beyond price. You cannot think of it without being dazzled; you feel incapable of conveying such intuitions as you may have of it.

---

[55] This truth has been remarkably demonstrated and explained in a recent [1913] work which we strongly recommend to our readers—*L'âme de tout apostolat*, by Dom J.B. Chautard, Abbot of Sept-Fons (Paris, Téqui) [English translation by Rev. F. Girardey, C.SS.R., as *The Soul of the Apostolate*]. This work is addressed primarily to the clergy and members of religious orders, but it will be no less useful to all laypeople engaged in active works.

Let us reflect for a moment on what they must have been for Mary, those thirty years when so many things that Jesus did, so many of His words and actions, were revelations for her.

Doubtless there must have been things that were incomprehensible, even for the Virgin. No-one could live in continual contact with the Infinite, as she did, without sometimes feeling and touching mystery. But nevertheless, what abundant light was in her soul! what constant increase of love those ineffable dealings with One who is God, working under her eyes and obeying her, must have brought about in her immaculate heart!

Mary lived at Nazareth with Jesus in a union surpassing all one can say of it. They were truly one: mind, heart, soul, all of the Virgin's existence was in absolute accord with the mind, heart, soul and life of her Son. Her existence was, if I can put it this way, a *vibration*—a pure and perfect resonance, tranquil and wholly love-filled—of that same life of Jesus.

Now, what was it that in Mary was the source of this union and this love? It was her faith. The faith of the Virgin is one of her most characteristic virtues.

What wonderful faith that was, full of glorious abandon to the angel's words! The heavenly messenger announces to her an unheard-of, an astonishing mystery, a mystery to rock back nature upon its heels: that there be conceived, in a virginal womb, One who is God! And what does Mary reply? "Behold the servant of the Lord; let it be done unto me as you say."[56] It was because she gave to the angel's words the full assent of her mind that she merited to become the mother of the Incarnate Word: *Prius concepit mente quam corpore,* "she conceived in her mind before conceiving in her body."[57]

Mary's faith in the divinity of Jesus never wavered: she always saw in her Son Jesus *Infinite God.*

---

[56] See Luke 1:38.   [57] St. Augustine, *De Virgine; Sermo* CCXV, note 4; St. Leo, *Sermo* I on the Nativity of the Lord, c.1; St. Bernard, *Sermo* I on the Vigil of the Nativity.

And yet, to what trials was this faith not subject! Her Son is God; the angel said to her that He would occupy the throne of David, that He would save the world and that His kingdom would have no end. And look at how Simeon predicted to her that Jesus would be "a sign that shall be contradicted," that He would be an occasion of ruin as well as of salvation;[58] and then Mary had to flee into Egypt to remove her Son from the tyrannical fury of Herod; and then until He was thirty her Son, who is God, who had come here to redeem the human race, lived a life of toil, submission and obscurity in a poor workshop. Later, she would see her Son pursued by the hate of the Pharisees, see Him abandoned by His disciples, in the hands of His enemies, hanging on the cross, taunts heaped upon Him, engulfed in suffering. She would hear Him cry out to His Father: "My God, my God, why have you forsaken me?" But her faith remained unshakeable—it was even then, at the foot of the cross, that it shone out in all its splendor. Mary always recognized her Son as her God, and that is why the Church proclaims her the "faithful Virgin" par excellence: *Virgo fidelis*.

And this faith, which was the wellspring of all Mary's love for her Son, was what made her always remain united to Jesus, even during the sorrows of His Passion and death.

Let us ask the Virgin to obtain for us this firm and practical faith; a faith that finds completion in love and in the accomplishment of the divine will: "Behold the servant of the Lord; let it be done unto me as you say." These words sum up Mary's whole life; may they guide our own life too!

This ardent faith that was for the Mother of God a wellspring of love was also a source of joy. The Holy Spirit Himself taught us this when, through the mouth of Elizabeth, He declared the Virgin to be blessed because of her faith: "Blessed is she who has believed."[59]

---

[58] Luke 2:34.   [59] Luke 1:45.

It will be the same as this for us. St. Luke records that, after one of Jesus's discourses to the crowd, a woman lifted up her voice and cried out: "Blessed is the womb that bore you and the breasts that nursed you." And Christ replied: "Rather, blessed are they who hear the word of God and keep it."[60] Jesus does not contradict in any way the acclamation by this Jewish woman; was it not He who inundated His mother's heart with incomparable joys? He simply wished to show us where, for us as for her, the source of joys is to be found. The privilege of being Mother of God is unique; Mary is the honored creature who, from all eternity, God Himself chose for the astonishing mission of being the mother of His Son: that is the root of all Mary's greatness.

But Jesus wished to teach us that, just as the Virgin has merited the joys of being the Mother of God through her faith and love, we can partake, not of course in the glory of having brought Christ into the world, but in the joy of giving birth to Him in our souls. And how shall we obtain this joy? By "hearing the word of God and keeping it." We hear it through faith, we keep it by lovingly doing what it requires of us.

Such is, for us as for Mary, the source of true joy of soul; such is for us the way to happiness. If, after having disposed our heart to accept the teachings of Jesus, we obey His will and stay united to Him, we shall become as dear to Him—it is again He who declares it—as if we were for Him a mother, a brother, a sister: "Whoever does the will of my Father in heaven, he is my brother and sister and mother."[61]

What closer or more fruitful union than that could we ever desire?

---

[60] Luke 11:27-28.   [61] Matt. 12:50; Mark 3:35; Luke 8:21.

CHAPTER TEN

The Baptism and Temptation of Jesus
(*Lent*)

In the different mysteries of Christ Jesus on earth, Eternal Wisdom arranged events in such a way that the humiliations of the Incarnate Word were always offset by a revelation of His divinity. Christ thus appears to us in the truth of His divine nature as well as in the reality of His human condition.

The deep reason for this disposition of things by heaven is to aid and to exercise—both of these together—*our faith*, foundation of all the super-natural life. The astonishing abasements to which love made Christ descend give to faith its merit. The manifestation of His divine prerogatives gives to faith its support.

The mysteries of the birth and childhood of Jesus are marked by these contrasts of shadow and light which make our faith "reasonable" at the same time as leaving it free. Christ's public life was full of them, to the extent that the Jews would bitterly dispute among themselves on the subject of His personhood. To some, He seemed only like the son of a workman of Nazareth, whereas for others He could only be the One sent by the Most High to enlighten and save the world; He whom the prophets had foretold.

We shall again meet this supernatural disposing of things in those events by which, after thirty years of hidden existence, Christ started out on His public life—His baptism by John, the Precursor, in the waters of the Jordan, and His temptation in the desert.

Let us contemplate Jesus in these two mysteries that are closely linked. We shall see how wonderful the mind of Infinite Wisdom is, to what great lengths Christ, who is our model, willed to go before us on that road on which we all ought to follow Him in order to resemble Him.

1. By presenting Himself to John to receive the baptism of penance, Christ performed an action of deep humility.

As you know, God had given John, son of Zacharias and Elizabeth, the mission of being the forerunner charged with announcing to the Jews the coming of the Word Incarnate.

Impelled by divine inspiration, and after an altogether austere life, John in about his thirtieth year had begun his preaching on the banks of the Jordan. All his teaching was summed up in these words: "Do penance, for the kingdom of heaven is at hand."[1] To his pressing exhortations he added baptism in the river, so as thereby to show his hearers the necessity of purifying their souls to make them less unworthy of the coming of the Savior. This baptism was conferred only on those who recognized that they were sinners and confessed their misdeeds.

Well, one day when John was administering "baptism of repentance for the forgiveness of sins,"[2] Christ Jesus, His hour come to leave the obscurity of the hidden life so as to manifest the divine secrets to the world, mingled with the crowd of sinners and presented Himself along with them to receive the purifying ablution from John.

When a devout soul dwells on the thought that He who in this way declares Himself a sinner and presents Himself voluntarily to receive the baptism of penance is the Second Person of the

---

[1] Matt. 3:2 (Rheims).   [2] Mark 1:4; Luke 3:3.

Blessed Trinity, He before whom the angels veil their faces and sing: "Holy, holy, holy,"[3] that soul remains in confusion at so prodigious an abasement.

The Apostle Paul tells us that Christ is "holy, innocent, undefiled, set apart from sinners,"[4] and here is Christ Himself coming forward as one who is culpable, asking for a baptism of repentance for the remission of sins! What is the reason for this?

It is that, in all His states, the Word Incarnate fulfills a two-fold office, that of Son of God, by virtue of His eternal begetting, and that of head of the sinful human race whose nature He has taken to Himself, the race He came here to redeem.

It is His due, as Son of God, to sit at the right hand of His Father to receive the glory that comes to Him again in the splendor of heaven.

But as head of fallen humanity, having taken to Himself a flesh which is culpable with regard to its race, even though wholly pure in Him—"in the likeness of sinful flesh"[5]—He will only be able to enter into heaven at the head of His mystical body after having gone through the humiliations of His life and the sufferings of His Passion: "Did not the Christ have to suffer these things before entering into His glory?"[6]

Possessing the divine nature, says St. Paul, Christ "thought it not robbery to be equal to God"[7]—to declare Himself the equal of the Father in perfection; but "for us and for our salvation He came down from heaven,"[8] He descended to abysses of abasement; and, in virtue of this, His Father has exalted Him, giving Him this name of Jesus, Savior, a name that encompasses our redemption. In exalting His Son, He "has raised us up together with Christ, and seated us together in heaven's heights."[9] It is truly so as to precede us there that Christ entered into heaven: "Our forerunner Jesus has entered for us."[10]

Nevertheless, He would only enter there after having, by His

---

[3] Isa. 6:3.   [4] Hebr. 7:26.   [5] Rom. 8:3.   [6] Luke 24:26.
[7] Phil. 2:6 (Rheims).   [8] See Nicene Creed.   [9] See Eph. 2:6.   [10] Hebr. 6:20.

blood, paid off everything to Divine Justice for us: "It is His own blood ... that has enabled Him to enter, once for all, into the sanctuary; the ransom He has won lasts for ever."[11]

Christ indeed came to free us from the devil's tyrannical slavery, into the power of which humankind had fallen in consequence of the fall: "everyone who commits sin is a slave of sin."[12] He came to save us from the eternal punishments that Satan was empowered to inflict upon us in administration of God's justice: "... lest, perhaps, the adversary deliver you to the judge, and the judge deliver you to the officer."[13]

Now, the Word Incarnate, the God-man, effected our redemption only by voluntarily substituting Himself for us, by making Himself as one with our sin, to the point (as St. Paul says) that God accounted Him as though a living sin: "For our sake God made the sinless one into sin."[14]

Taking upon Himself our iniquities, He would take upon Himself also our chastisements; He would suffer abasement and humiliation beyond measure.

Such is the eternal decree.

You understand now why, from the beginning of His public life, from the moment He inaugurated His redemptive mission in a manifest way, Jesus submitted Himself to an action of profound humility, to a rite that ranged Him with sinners.

See, indeed, how when John, enlightened from on high, recognized in the one who had come to him the Son of God, the one of whom he had said: "He ... who is to come ... has been set above me, the strap of whose sandal I am not worthy to loose,"[15] he, John, was vehemently against conferring on Jesus the baptism of penance. He was for dissuading Him, saying: "It is I who should be baptized by you—and yet you come to me!" But what did Christ reply to him? "Let it be so now, for this is how it is befitting for us to fulfill all justice."[16]

---

[11] Hebr. 9:12 (Knox). [12] John 8:34. [13] Matt. 5:25 (Rheims).
[14] 2 Cor. 5:21 (Jerus.) [15] John 1:27. [16] See Matt. 3:14-15.

What is this justice? It consists in the humiliations of the adorable humanity of Jesus, which, by rendering supreme homage to Infinite Holiness, fully settles all our debts to Divine Justice. Jesus, just and innocent, takes the place of all the sinful race, "the Just for the unjust";[17] and, by His immolation, has become "the Lamb of God, who takes away the sin of the world":[18] the "propitiation for our sins ... those of the whole world."[19] It is thus that He "fulfills all justice."

When we meditate on these profound words of Jesus, let us humble ourselves along with Him; recognize our condition of being sinners; and, above all, renew the renunciation of sin that marked our baptism.

John, the Precursor, heralded that baptism—a baptism which would be superior to his, because it would be established by Christ in person: "I indeed baptize you with water, for repentance"—to arouse you to repent—"but He who is coming after me is greater than I ...He will baptize you with the Holy Spirit and with fire."[20] Exteriorly, the baptism Jesus instituted is a baptism by water, as was John's; but when it is conferred, at that same time the divine power of the Holy Spirit, who is a spiritual fire, purifies and transforms the soul interiorly: "... through the washing of regeneration, and renewal by the Holy Spirit."[21]

Let us, therefore, renew often our renunciation of sin. As you know, the distinctive quality of "baptized person" remains indelibly in the depths of our soul; and when we repeat the promises made at the time of our initiation, new strength comes forth from the baptismal grace, to make firm our power of resistance to everything that leads to sin—the suggestions of the devil and the allurements of the world and of the senses. It is thus that we can safeguard the life of grace within us.

[17] 1 Peter 3:18. [18] John 1:29. [19] 1 John 2:2.
[20] Matt. 3:11; Mark 1:8; Luke 3:16. [21] See Titus 3:5.

By that also, we shall witness to Christ Jesus our intense gratitude for His having borne the burden of our iniquities to free us from them. He "loved me," said St. Paul when he recalled this mystery of an infinite love; He "loved me and gave Himself up for me!"[22] May I live for Him, for His glory; not for myself, to satisfy my covetousness, my self-love, my pride, my ambition!— may "they who are alive ... live no longer for themselves, but for Him who died for them and rose again."[23]

2. **Christ Jesus is glorified on coming forth from the waters of the Jordan. How this testimony of the Eternal Father at the start of the public life of Jesus characterizes one of the aspects of His redemptive mission.**

"And when Jesus had been baptized, He immediately came up from the water. And behold, the heavens were opened, and He saw the Spirit of God descending in the form of a dove and coming upon Him. And at that same time, a voice from the heavens was heard, saying: 'This is my beloved Son, in whom I am well-pleased.'"[24]

That mysterious scene is but one particular example of the divine law that I indicated to you at the beginning of this talk. It is necessary that Christ be glorified as soon as, for our sakes, He suffers humiliation.

Jesus so far humbles Himself as to let Himself be mistaken for one of a crowd of sinners, and, immediately, the heavens open in praise of Him. He asks for a baptism of penance, of reconciliation; and behold, the Spirit of Love gives testimony that He reposes in Jesus with the fullness of His gifts of grace. Jesus acknowledges it as fitting that He be struck for the sake of divine justice; and behold, the Father proclaims Him to be the object of all His delight. "He humbled Himself ... Therefore God also has exalted Him."[25]

. . .

---

[22] Gal. 2:20.   [23] 2 Cor. 5:15.   [24] See Matt. 3:16-17.   [25] Phil. 2:8-9.

It is at this moment that the mission of Jesus as One sent from God is declared authentic. The witness by the Father gives the world an accreditation (so to speak) of His Son, and thus underlines one of the distinctive features of Christ's work in regard to us.

It is to be noted, indeed, that Christ's mission takes on a twofold aspect: it bears the character both of a redemption and of a sanctification. To redeem souls and then, the redemption accomplished, to infuse life into them—these two things together are the Savior's work. The two elements are inseparable, but distinct.

We find the seed of this in the circumstances that marked the baptism of Christ, which was the prelude to His public life.

Just now we saw how, by presenting Himself for a baptism of penance, the Word Incarnate witnessed to His role of Redeemer. He was to complete His work by the gift of the divine life that is His; He confers it on us by virtue of the merits of His Passion and death: "God sent into the world His only-begotten Son so that we could have life through Him";[26] "God so loved the world that He gave His only-begotten Son, that those who believe in Him may ...have eternal *life*."[27]

The source of eternal life is, in us, a light.

In heaven, it is the light of the Beatific Vision. In that light we live by the very life of God: "For with thee is the fountain of life; and in thy light we shall see light."[28]

Here below, the source of our super-natural life is likewise a light, the light of faith. Faith is a participation in the knowledge that God has of Himself, and this knowledge is communicated to the soul by the Incarnate Word. Faith becomes for us a light that guides us on all the paths we tread, and that is why it has to enliven all our super-natural activity: "The righteous man will live by faith."[29]

Well now, the foundation of this faith is the witness God the Father gives of His Son Jesus: "This is my beloved Son, in whom I am well-pleased."

[26] 1 John 4:9 (Jerus.)

[27] John 3:15.

[28] Psalm 35 (36):10 (9).

[29] Hebr. 10:38 (Jerus.)

Christ has been solemnly presented to the world as the One sent by the Father. All that He says to us will be an echo of the Eternal Truth that, in the heart's-embrace of the Father, He never ceases to contemplate: "The only-begotten Son ... He has revealed Him."[30] His teaching is not just His own, but is that of His Father who sent Him,[31] and Jesus will repeat it all to us. That is why, on the Last Day, He will be able to say to His Father: "I have finished the work you gave me to do"; and "I have made you known to the world."[32]

The words of Christ, the Word Incarnate, have not produced in all souls the light that should be for them the source of salvation and life. He is "the Light of the world," no doubt about that; but we need to follow this Light if we do not want to walk in darkness but to arrive at heaven and the Light that will be the source of our eternal life there: "He who follows me does not walk in the darkness, but will have the light of life."[33] Only by *receiving*[34] His Son do we please God.

In order to hear the words of Christ profitably, we have to be drawn by the Father: "All that the Father gives me will come to me."[35] Those not drawn by the Father do not listen to the voice of the Word: "The reason why you do not hear is that you are not of God."[36] And who are those whom the Father draws? Those who recognize in Jesus God's own Son: "They who believe that Jesus is the Christ are born of God."[37]

That is why the Father's public testimony to His Son after His baptism constitutes at the same time the starting-point for all the public life of Jesus, Word Incarnate, Light of the world—and also the very foundation of the whole of the Christian faith, and of our sanctification.

---

[30] John 1:18.   [31] John 7:16.   [32] See John 17, vv. 4, 6.   [33] John 8:12.

[34] [*Translator's note*: Marmion uses "receive," *recevoir*, in the same sense as in John 1:12: "to as many as received Him..."]   [35] John 6:37 (Jerus.)

[36] John 8:47.   [37] See 1 John 5:1.

Thus, this mystery of the baptism of Jesus, which marks the start of His public ministry, contains a resumé, as it were, of His whole mission here below.

By the humiliation He willed to undergo by receiving this rite of repentance "for the forgiveness of sins," a presage of His baptism of blood upon the cross, Christ "fulfilled all justice." From that moment, He renders to His Father's infinite perfections (perfections which had been insulted by sin) the supreme homage of the humiliations by which He effects our redemption.

In return, the heavens open; the Eternal Father authentically introduces His Son into the world; the glorious splendor revealed by this testimony heralds the mission the Word-made-flesh is about to inaugurate, the mission to enlighten souls; the Holy Spirit rests upon Him to mark the fullness of the gifts adorning His sacred soul and at the same time symbolizing an anointing with the grace that Christ is to communicate to the world.

Baptism, with faith in Jesus Christ, has become for us the sacrament of divine adoption and of Christian initiation.

It is conferred on us in the name of the Blessed Trinity—of that Trinity which was revealed to us on the banks of the Jordan.

Sanctified by contact with the humanity of Jesus, and united with "the Word of Truth,"[38] the water has the power to wash away the sins of those who detest their misdeeds and declare their faith in the divinity of Christ. It is baptism, not only by water "for the forgiveness of sins," but also by the Spirit who alone can "renew the face of the earth."[39] From being "children of wrath,"[40] as we were, it makes us children of God, thenceforth participating, with Jesus, although in lesser measure, in the Heavenly Father's delight.

And so much so, says St. Paul, that we have, by our baptism, shed ourselves of the "old" man (who descends from Adam), with

[38] James 1:18.   [39] Ps. 103 (104):30.   [40] Eph. 2:3.

his works of death, and put on the "new" man created in justice and truth (the soul regenerated by the Word and the Holy Spirit) who is unceasingly renewed in the image of Him who created him.[41]

As you can see: in the same way that baptism constitutes for Christ a resumé of the whole of His mission which is both a redemptive and a sanctifying one—in that same way it contains for us the seed of all the development of our Christian life with its twofold aspect of "death to sin" and "life lived for God."[42]

So true is this, that according to the Apostle Paul: "All you who have been baptized into Christ, have put on Christ Himself";[43] so true is it that we are united with Christ in all His mysteries.

Oh, the happy situation of faithful Christians! Oh, the senseless blindness of those who forget their baptismal promises! Oh, the terrifying destiny of those who trample them underfoot!

"For," said John the Baptist to the Jews, "already the axe is laid at the root of the trees; every tree that is not bringing forth good fruit will be cut down and thrown into the fire."[44] "Behold," he said also, "one mightier than I (that is, Christ) is coming... Winnowing fan in His hand, He will make clean His threshing-floor, and will gather the wheat into His barn; but the chaff He will burn in a fire that will never go out." "The Father loves the Son, and has given all things into His hand. He who believes in the Son"—by a faith put into practice—"has everlasting life; he who refuses to believe in the Son shall not see life, but the wrath of God rests upon him."[45]

[41] Col. 3:9-10; Eph. 4:22-24.   [42] See Rom 6:11.   [43] See Gal. 3:27.
[44] See Matt. 3:10-12; Luke 3:9, 16-17.   [45] See John 3:35-36.

3. Immediately after His baptism, Jesus is urged into the desert by the Holy Spirit, to undergo assaults by the devil there. Reasons for this mystery.

Hardly had Jesus been baptized, the Gospel tells us, than He was led into the desert by the Spirit. The sacred writers use different expressions to signify this action of the Holy Spirit. Jesus was "led," relates St. Matthew; "urged," says St. Luke; "borne away" into the desert, according to St. Mark.[46] What does this variety of terms indicate, if not the vehemence of the interior action of the Spirit upon the soul of Christ? And with what aim was He urged into the desert? "To be tempted by the devil." That is the explicit testimony of St. Matthew's gospel.

Isn't this strange? The Father has just declared that Jesus is His beloved Son; the Spirit of Love rests upon Jesus; and behold, immediately—*statim*—this Spirit hastens Him off to the desert, for Him to be exposed to the devil's suggestions there. What a mystery! What, then, can be the meaning of so extraordinary an episode in the life of Christ? Why is Christ making use of this at the beginning of His public life?

In order to understand the depths of it, and before seeing what the Gospel account says, we ought first to remind ourselves of the place in our spiritual life that temptation has.

The divine perfections demand that a creature, rational and free, be put to the test before being admitted to enjoy the future beatitude. It is necessary that here below such a creature be on trial before God, and that it renounce, freely, its own gratifications so as to recognize God's sovereignty and obey His law. The holiness and justice of God require this homage.

---

[46] Matt. 4:1; Luke 4:1; Mark 1:12. [*Translator's note*: I have followed Marmion's three French words, *conduit*, *pousse* and *emporte*. The English scriptural versions used in these pages have "led," except for the quotation from St. Mark, where the Knox has "sent" and the other versions "drove."]

Such a choice, glorious for the Infinite Being, is for us the foundation of that merit which the Lord rewards with the beatitude of heaven. The Council of Trent laid down that it is God who saves us, but in such a way that the salvation is both a gift of His mercy and at the same time the reward for our merits.[47] Eternal life will be our reward because, having had to choose, we will have repelled temptation in order to adhere to God: when trials came, we will have submitted to them so as to remain faithful to the divine will. Gold is tested in the furnace, and constancy amid temptation reveals a soul who is worthy of God.

Such the noble condition of every free creature.

The first to be put to the test were the angels. Though we do not know exactly what the test was, we do know that it was of a nature corresponding to the angelic mode of being.

As you know, the angels are creatures exclusively spiritual. Their actions are not measured by time, as ours are. Further, those actions of theirs possess a power, a wideness of range, and a profundity, to which no human action can attain.[48] Pure spirits, the angels do not reason at all. In us, the extreme excitability of our imagination, a sensitive faculty tied to the body's organism, presents a number of particular things to us for our choice as "good things," the variety of which slows up the action of our intellect and will. We go from one "good thing" to another; we afterwards return to one of them that perhaps at first we had decided to reject. It is not the same as this for the angels. In an angel, wholly spiritual by nature, hesitation has no place. In an

---

[47] "Hence, to those that work well unto the end and trust in God, eternal life is to be offered, both as a *grace* mercifully promised to the sons and daughters of God through Christ Jesus, and as a *reward* promised by God Himself, to be faithfully given to their good works and merits ... [God's] bounty toward all men is so great that He wishes the things that are *His gifts* to be *their merits*": Council of Trent, Sess. VI, cap.16.

[48] Obviously, we here speak of the order of nature.

angel, acts of intellect and of will take on a character of fullness, of fixity, of irrevocability, that confers on those acts an incomparable strength.[49]

No human existence, however prolonged, will attain, through the whole of its operations put together, either the power or the amplitude or the intensity of that one single act by which the angels, put to the test, made and fixed their choice.

That is why the fidelity of the good angels has been so pleasing to God; that is also why the revolt of the rebel spirits possesses a gravity that we cannot measure and of which we are not capable. Their profundity of understanding, which meant that they acted in full light of knowledge of what they were doing, imbued this unique sin with such thorough malice, that Divine Justice had to punish it by an immediate sentence of eternal damnation.

For us, acceptance of trials, resistance to temptation, take place step by step over our entire life; the struggle against corrupting allurements; patience with things willed or permitted by Providence that are in opposition to our desires—these are choices facing us every day: "The life of man upon earth is a warfare."[50]

But also, every day is a magnificent occasion for steadfast fidelity to God. A person who, from the time of first becoming conscious of his or her actions, till the moment of soul being separated from body, had never allowed in a deliberate sin; who, placed between God and temptations capable of turning that person away from Him, always had freely chosen the Divine Will—such a person would have given immense glory to God. And why? Because, each of that person's actions would have proclaimed only God as Lord. "Blessed that soul who could have transgressed the eternal law, and has not transgressed it; who could have done evil, and has done no evil at all."[51] For the Lord

---

[49] St Thomas, *De veritate*, q. XXIV, a.10 and 11.   [50] Job 7:1.

[51] See Ecclesiasticus (Sirach) 31:10.

will reward such a soul magnificently: "Well done, good and faithful servant ... enter into the joy of your Lord."[52]

The first man was put to the test. He hesitated; he gave in; he preferred above God that which was created and his own satisfaction. He drew the whole of his race into his rebellion, his fall and his punishment.

This is why it was necessary that a second Adam, representing all who will achieve their destiny, should go in the opposite direction to the first Adam. In His adorable wisdom, God the Father willed that Christ Jesus, our head and our model, should face temptation and, by His free choice, remain victorious so as to teach us to be so too. That is one of the reasons for this mystery.

Another, deeper, reason exists—one that provides a close link between this mystery and that of baptism.

What did Jesus say to John the Baptist when the latter was refusing to carry out his ministry of penance in regard to Jesus? "This is how it is befitting for us to fulfill all justice."[53] That justice, we saw, consisted for Jesus in submitting to the whole of the expiation decreed by His Father for the redemption of the human race: "to give His life as a ransom for many."[54] After the sin of Adam, the human race was in slavery to Satan, and it was from the hands of the prince of darkness that Christ Jesus had to save it. It was to "destroy the works of the devil"[55]—the devil's reign— that Christ appeared here below. That is why, from the time He received baptism, which marked Him as "the Lamb of God, who takes away the sin of the world,"[56] who rescues all the flock from the power of the devil, the Word-made-flesh entered into personal combat with "the prince of the world." That is why the Holy Spirit immediately urged Him into the desert, as of old they drove into the desert the scapegoat laden with all the sins of the people. "Jesus was led into the desert *to be tempted by the devil*."[57]

---

[52] Matt. 25:21 (Rheims).   [53] See Matt. 3:15.   [54] Matt. 20:28.
[55] 1 John 3:8.   [56] John 1:29.   [57] John 14:30.

4. The Gospel account of the temptation.

Let us now contemplate our divine head in the clutches of the prince of the rebel spirits.

As you know, Jesus remained in the desert for forty days and forty nights, in the midst of wild animals, in complete solitude, fasting unremittingly. That is the exact testimony of the Gospel: "During that time He ate nothing,"[58] "He was with the wild beasts."[59]

To understand properly this mystery of the temptation of Jesus, remember what I have told you so often: that Christ is completely like us: "It was right that He should in all things be made like unto His brethren."[60] Now, imagine to what a state of weakness a man would be reduced who had allowed Himself no food for forty days. Our Lord did not will to work a miracle that would have prevented His experiencing the effects of such fasting; and accordingly the Gospel tells us that at the end of that period He *"was hungry."*[61] And after the lapse of such a long period of time He would be bound to have been in a state of utter prostration. In just a moment we shall see how the devil seized the occasion to tempt Him.

Yet, though sharing our infirmities and feebleness, the sacred humanity of Jesus cannot experience sin: "...as we are in all things *except sin.*"[62] The soul of Jesus is not liable to ignorance, error, any moral failing.

Is there any need for me to add that neither does He feel any of the disordered movements that, in us, result from original sin or from habits of sin? If, for our sakes, Jesus submitted to hunger and exhaustion, He remains in Himself the Holy One of holy ones. What is the consequence of that doctrine? That the temptation that Christ can undergo does not attain to His soul and remains wholly exterior; He cannot be tempted except by the "princes and powers of the world of darkness, the evil spirits."[63]

---

[58] Luke 4:2 (Jerus.)   [59] Mark 1:13.   [60] Hebr. 2:17.
[61] Matt. 4:2.   [62] Hebr. 4:15.   [63] See Eph. 6:12.

Among those spirits, we have to think that the one who tempted Christ was endowed with particular power. But, marvelous as was his intelligence, he nevertheless did not know who Christ was. No created being can see God except in the Beatific Vision; the devil is bereft of that.

And at the same time he did not know the nub of the mystery—that in Christ was established a union of divinity with the humanity. Certainly he suspected something; he had not forgotten the malediction that had lain heavy upon him since God established eternal enmity between him and the woman who was to crush his head;[64] that is to say, destroy his power in souls. He could not have been unaware of the marvels that had been worked since the birth of Jesus; the account of the temptation shows that clearly. But his knowledge was uncertain. He wished by tempting Christ to find out, in a manner beyond doubt, whether it would be possible to triumph over Him. For he definitely took Christ to be an extraordinary being.

The tempter, then, approaches Jesus. The Gospel tells us that this is how it was: "the tempter came."[65] And seeing Jesus in a state of exhaustion, he seeks to make Him fall into a sin of gluttony. Not into a sin of great gluttony, by presenting delicious foods to Christ; the devil had too high an opinion of Him whom he was attacking to think that He might succumb to a suggestion of that sort. Instead, he puts the point to Jesus, who is faint with hunger, that if He is the Son of God He has the power to work miracles to satisfy this hunger. In saying that, the devil wished to push Jesus into bringing forward to an earlier time than His Father's hour the working of a miracle that would have a personal objective. "If you are the Son of God, command that these stones"—and he pointed to the pebbles at Jesus's feet—"become loaves of bread."[66] And what does Our Lord reply? Does He make known that He is the Son of God? No. Does He work the miracle proposed by the

---

[64] Gen. 3:15.   [65] Matt. 4:3.   [66] Matt. 4:3; Luke 4:3.

devil? No, again. He contents Himself with replying in some words of Scripture: "Man does not live on bread alone, but on every word that comes from the mouth of God."[67] Later, during His public life, when one day the Apostles bring food to Jesus and say: "Master, do have something to eat," He would give a similar reply: "I have food to eat that you do not know about.... My food is to do the will of Him who sent me."[68] That is what He says to the devil at the temptation. To appease His hunger, He will wait until the Father comes to His aid; He will not bring forward the time appointed by His Father for Him to show His power. When the Father speaks, He will hear the Father's voice.

Seeing himself repulsed, the devil understands that he has before him, if not the Son of God, at least a being of high sanctity. And so he will use a more dangerous weapon. He has a marvelous knowledge of human nature; he knows that those who have arrived at a high degree of perfection and of union with God are above the reach of the gross appetites of the senses, but that they can allow themselves to be seduced by the more subtle suggestions of pride and presumption. They can believe themselves to be better than others and can think that even if they voluntarily expose themselves to danger, God is bound to give them a wholly special protection because of their fidelity. The devil, therefore, tries to push Jesus in that direction. Using his spiritual power, he transports Jesus to the pinnacle of the temple and says to Him: "If you are the Son of God, throw yourself down. You, indeed, will be in no danger; for it is written that God has commanded His angels to bear you up upon their hands, lest you dash your foot against a stone."[69]

"If Jesus is the Son of God," His appearing from on high and descending in that way into the middle of the crowd that thronged the outer court of the temple—well, what a marvelous sign of His Messianic mission that would be, what an evident

---

[67] Matt. 4:4 (Jerus.); Luke 4:4.   [68] See John 4, vv. 31-32, 34.
[69] Matt. 4:5-6; Luke 4:9-11; Ps. 90 (91):12.

proof that God was with Him! To make his suggestion more appealing, the devil relies in his turn on God's words. But Jesus replies in superlative fashion, using another sacred text: "You shall not tempt"—by vain presumption—"the Lord your God."[70] This time, also, the devil is defeated. Snares have been set, but the Word of God is triumphant.

In his third and last assault, the spirit of darkness tries hard to conquer Christ. Taking Him up a high mountain, he shows Him all the kingdoms of the world, he unrolls before His eyes all their riches, all their splendor, all their glory. What a temptation to ambition, he thought, for this one here who believes Himself to be the Messiah! Though a price would have to be paid. It was all simply a further ruse by the devil to find out finally who this was that was resisting him so strongly. "All this is mine; yet I will give it to you if, falling down, you adore me," he said.[71] You know what Jesus's response was and the vigor with which He repulsed the sacrilegious suggestions of the evil one: "Get behind me, Satan! It is written: 'The Lord your God shall you worship, and Him only shall you serve.'"[72]

Now the prince of darkness knows himself to be entirely unmasked; he can do no more than take himself away. However, says the Gospel, he departed from Jesus *"for a while."*[73] The sacred writer thereby indicates that, during the public life, the devil will return to the attack. Through his fellow-fiends, if not in person, he will pursue Our Lord relentlessly. During the Passion, especially, he will be intent on the ruin of Jesus at the hands of the Pharisees: "This is your hour; this is the reign of darkness."[74] He will press them, and they will press the crowd, to demand that Jesus be crucified: "Away with him, away with him! Crucify him!"[75] But, you know, the death of the Savior on the cross was the decisive blow, precisely, that would destroy the devil's kingdom for ever. To

[70] Matt. 4:7; Luke 4:12.
[72] Matt. 4:10; Deut. 6:13.
[74] Luke 22:53 (Jerus.)

[71] See Matt. 4:9; Luke 4:6-7.
[73] Luke 4:13.
[75] John 19:15.

such extent does Divine Wisdom shine out everywhere in His works! "Eternal God, who established the salvation of mankind on the tree of the Cross ... *that he* [the devil] *who overcame by the tree, by the tree also might be overcome...*"[76]

The Gospel adds that after the tempter had left Him, "angels came and ministered to" Jesus.[77] That was a perceptible manifestation of the Father's glorifying of the Son for having so abased Himself as to submit, in our name, to the devil's attacks. The faithful angels appeared and served to Jesus the bread for which He had waited till the hour appointed by the providence of His Father.

Such is the Gospel account of the temptation of Jesus.

If Christ, the Incarnate Word, Son of God, willed to enter into combat with the evil spirit, shall we be surprised that the members of His mystical body have to do the same? So many people, even pious ones, think that temptation is a sign of being reproved by God. But, more often, it's just the opposite! Having become disciples of Jesus through baptism, we cannot be above our Divine Master.[78] "*Because* you were acceptable to God, *it was necessary* that temptation should prove you,"[79] put you to the test. It is God Himself who tells us that.

Yes, the devil can tempt us, and tempt us strongly, and tempt us when we most think we are safe from his shafts: at the time of prayer, after holy communion—yes, even at those hallowed times he can whisper to us thoughts contrary to faith, contrary to hope. He can urge our minds to independence in regard to God's rights, incite us to rebel. He can rouse in us all the evil passions. This he can do—and will not fail to do.

Once more, let us not be surprised at this; let us never forget that Christ, our model in all things, was tempted before we were; and was not only tempted but felt the touch of the spirit of darkness. He allowed the devil's hands to be laid on the sacred humanity.

[76] Preface of the Cross.   [77] Matt. 4:11.
[78] Matt. 10:24; Luke 6:40; John 13:16, 15:20.   [79] Tobias (Tobit) 12:13.

Above all, let us not forget that it was not only as Son of God that Jesus overcame the devil, but also as head of the Church. In Him and through Him we have triumphed, and still triumph, over the suggestions of the rebel spirit.[80]

This is, indeed, the grace that our Divine Savior won for us by this mystery; in it is to be found the source of our confidence when in trials and temptations. It only remains for me to show you how unshakeable that confidence should be, and how, through faith in Jesus Christ, we shall always find the secret of victory.

5. **Grace that Christ has merited for us by this mystery. Triumphing over temptation by staying united to the Word Incarnate. The promises of spiritual invulnerability set forth in the Psalm "You who dwell in the shelter of the Most High."**

The grace that the Word Incarnate has merited for us by undergoing temptation is the strength by which we in our turn get the better of the devil, come out victorious from the struggle we must necessarily undergo before being admitted to enjoy divine life in heavenly bliss. Christ Jesus has merited that those who are united to Him share in His impeccability—and share in the same measure as that of their union with Him.

We touch here the very center of the mystery.

We see in the Gospel that Christ was impeccable, inaccessible to the evil which is sin, to the least imperfection. But what is the source of that moral invulnerability of His?

The fundamental reason is that He is the very Son of God; as the Second Person of the Trinity He is Infinite Holiness and cannot succumb to evil.

Nevertheless, if we examine the humanity of Jesus in itself, we see that it is a created humanity as ours is; it is one that is like ours:

[80] "It was clearly appropriate that He should triumph over our temptations through His temptations": St. Gregory, *Homil.* XVI *in Evangel.*

union with the divinity did not remove in that humanity those weaknesses of body and soul which are compatible with His being the Son of God. Christ suffers hunger; He is overcome by fatigue; sleep weighs down His eyelids. Fear, sadness, anxiety, truly invade His soul. And yet, He has not in Him the shadow of an imperfection. If, therefore, the humanity of Jesus, *as such*, enjoys impeccability, it is because it is rooted in good in a marvelous way. Now, what are the means God uses in order to render the sacred soul of Jesus inaccessible to moral evil, to sin; in order to establish it in impeccability?

The means are: causing Jesus's humanity to "dwell in the shelter"—under the protection—"of the Most High":[81] *In adjutorio Altissimi.* Or, according to the more significant words of the original text, "in the secret sanctuary of the Most High." And what is this shelter, this sanctuary? It is the Beatific Vision.

As you know, the Beatific Vision is the blessed contemplation of God as He is in Himself. One to whom that grace is accorded can nevermore be separated from God, because he *sees* that God is the Sovereign Good, and that no particular "good," however vast it be, can be compared with God. Thenceforth, sin—which consists of turning away from the law of God, from God's will, or, what essentially comes to the same thing, turning away from God in order to adhere to a "good" one finds in oneself or in some created entity—is made radically impossible. In this blessed state where the intellect contemplates very Truth, there is no place for any ignorance, any illusion, any error. And the will, adhering to Absolute Good who comprises in Himself the fullness of all good, knows no hesitation, no weakening, no defection of any sort. The soul that has attained to this summit finds itself (to use theological language) perfectly "confirmed in grace."

. . .

[81] Ps. 90 (91):1 (St P)

This confirmation in grace is a consequence of our destiny; it admits of different degrees that are measured by the perfection and extent of this destiny.[82]

The humanity of Jesus was eternally destined to be united to the Eternal Word; and so from the very first instant of its existence the soul of Christ possessed, as a privilege resulting from this union, as a "co-natural" attribute, the Beatific Vision. Christ's soul was confirmed in grace to the highest degree, that is to say, in an *essential* and *absolute* impeccability. That is why we hear Our Lord, head of all achieving their planned destiny of glory, issue this challenge to the Jews: "Which of you can convict me of sin?"[83] We hear Him likewise say to His apostles, at the Last Supper: "Henceforth I will no longer speak much with you, for the prince of the world (the devil) is rising up against me, but nothing of him is in me."[84] Even as man, Christ Jesus is the holy one par excellence: "You alone are holy, Jesus Christ!"[85]

In heaven, the blessed have reached "the mature measure of the fullness of Christ";[86] they have attained to the full extent of the divine gift "according to the measure of Christ's bestowal";[87] they enjoy the Beatific Vision to the full degree of the grace that has been bestowed upon them. They participate in a complete way, each according to his or her degree, in the Divine Sonship of Jesus. That is why they remain, as He does, established for ever "in the secret sanctuary of the Godhead." That is eternal impeccability.

Here below, it is not yet given to us to dwell fully in that "shelter" of the Godhead. But what is it that, for us on earth, takes the place the Beatific Vision? It is faith. By faith, we have

---

[82] [*Translator's note*: As stated earlier, there is in the term *predestination*, as Marmion uses it, not the slightest denial of our wills being free to win heaven; no suggestion that God offers the inheritance of eternal beatitude to some and not all. But there are degrees of grace and of confirmation in grace (and degrees of beatitude, in the way that small and large vessels can both be full). And God, being outside time, has foreknowledge of how our individual free wills are in the event going to be exercised.]   [83] John 8:46.   [84] See John 14:30.

[85] *Gloria* of the Mass.   [86] Eph. 4:13.   [87] Eph. 4:7.

God always present: "we walk by faith."[88] This faith, by the light of which we walk, is the source of our union with Jesus, and is the root of our perfection: "Walk in my presence and be perfect."[89] In the measure that, through faith, we live a life of contemplation of God and remain united to Jesus Christ, in that same measure we become invulnerable to temptation.

Already, on earth, souls are met with who are so united to Christ, souls whose faith is so complete, that even in the present life they are confirmed in grace. For example, the most holy Virgin: she was predestined to a total exemption from sin, even original sin. That is a unique privilege: "Thou art all fair, O Mary, and there is in thee no stain of original sin."[90] St. John the Baptist was sanctified in his mother's womb, and the Fathers of the Church tells us that he was confirmed in divine grace. It was the same with the Apostles, after they had received the gift of the Spirit on the day of Pentecost.

God's gift of a share in this "confirmation in grace" is for all: and this share, as I have said, is in the measure of our life of faith. A soul who lives in habitual contemplation of God, through faith, draws continuously from that fount of life: "For with you is the fountain of life."[91] Such a soul participates in the union of Christ with His Father: "I in them, and you in me," and consequently also in the love the Father bears for His Son Jesus: "that the love with which you have loved me may be in them, and I in them."[92]

That is why God takes real delight in such souls; He protects them, makes them, little by little, invulnerable. All their enemies can attack them, but: "Though a thousand fall at your side, ten thousand at your right hand, you yourself will remain un-scathed."[93]: Such souls shall tread the demons underfoot; the whole universe can rise up around them, be unleashed against them, and they will say to God: "You are my protector, and my

---

[88] 2 Cor. 5:7. [89] Gen. 17:1 (St P)
[90] Antiphon, Feast of the Immaculate Conception. [91] Ps. 35 (36):10 (9).
[92] John 17, vv. 23, 26. [93] Ps. 90 (91):7 (Jerus.)

refuge,"[94] and God will deliver them from every ambush, every danger: "Because he hoped in me, I will deliver him."[95]

The Church, who is full of solicitude for her children, who knows what dangers they are always exposed to; who knows, on the other hand, what powerful graces of life the mysteries of the Word Incarnate and our union with Him bring us, recalls to us every year, at the beginning of Lent, the mystery of the temptation of Jesus. She wants us to live for forty days in a spirit of penance, seclusion, solitude and prayer, as He did.

At this same time she puts on our lips the whole of Psalm 90, which begins with those words I have just been explaining: "You who dwell in the shelter of the Most High..." It is, par excellence, the Psalm of confidence in the midst of struggle, trial and temptation.

The magnificent promises contained in it apply first to Christ Jesus, and in the next place to all the members of His Mystical Body in the measure of their life of grace and faith.

That is why the Church is not content with making us read this Psalm, in its entirety, in the Mass of the First Sunday of Lent; she also extracts verses of it which, every day during this long period, she causes us to read in her canonical office so as to keep constantly before our eyes our Heavenly Father's loving kindnesses: "He has given His angels charge over you, that they guard you in all your ways,"[96] "He rescues me from the net of the fowler...,"[97] "He will cover you with His pinions, and under His wings you will find refuge,"[98] "His truth will encompass you, like a shield ...you will not fear the terror of the night."[99]

What confidence such promises, recalled each day, can inspire in a soul! What assurance they give a soul for walking forward on the road of salvation—"Behold, now is the day of salvation!"[100]— surrounded by snares, crowded about with enemies, though he be. God is with this soul; and, says St. Paul, "With God on our

---

[94] Ps. 90 (91):2.   [95] Ibid., v. 14.   [96] See Ibid., v. 11.   [97] See Ibid., v. 3.
[98] Ibid., v. 4 (RSV, Cath.)   [99] See Ibid., vv. 4-5.   [100] 2 Cor. 6:2.

side, who can be against us?"[101] For, he adds, God "will not permit us to be tempted beyond our strength, but will protect us and, through His protection will grant us to prevail in our trials,"[102] to overcome temptation, to show Him our fidelity, source of merit and of glory. He will give to our temptation a happy issue.

6. Faith is the weapon of resistance par excellence.

You see how invincible the soul is who dwells in the sanctuary of the Godhead.

But never forget that we only reach that sanctuary through faith in Jesus Christ, our head and our model.

Indeed, the Psalmist says that, to protect us against the satanic javelins, God's *truth—Veritas ejus—*will encompass us like a shield. That is equally the thought of St. Paul, when he details the weapons with which the Christian should arm himself for the spiritual struggle: "In *every* encounter, taking up the shield *of faith*, with which you can extinguish *all* the fiery darts of the evil one."[103] St. Peter speaks no differently either: "The devil ceaselessly prowls around you like a roaring lion seeking a prey to devour." But it is through the strength of your faith that you will resist him: "*Resist him, steadfast in faith.*"[104]

You will have noticed that, in order to repulse the devil, Christ Jesus each time made appeal to the word of God, to Scripture. The same tactic will lead us to triumph.

When, therefore, the devil tempts you against faith, for example, remember the testimony of the Eternal Father that Jesus is His beloved Son; and remember that "they who believe that Jesus is the Christ have been born of God."[105] When the devil urges you to a lack of trust, repeat Christ's words: "No-one is good but God

[101] Rom. 8:31 (Jerus.) [102] See 1 Cor. 10:13. [103] See Eph. 6:16.
[104] See 1 Peter 5:9. [105] See 1 John 5:1.

only";[106] or else: "Come to me, all you who labor and are burdened, and I will give you rest,"[107] "I will not turn away those who come to me."[108] If the devil tries to deject you, through a remembrance of your faults and your sins, reply to him in the words of the Savior: "I have come to call sinners, not the just."[109] If the devil prompts in you thoughts of pride or ambition: "Whoever exalts himself will be humbled."[110] If he incites you to vengeance: "Blessed are the meek."[111] If he makes delusive joys glitter before your eyes: "Blessed are the pure."[112]

On each occasion, arm yourself with the words of the Word; they are a shield against which every satanic dart will break and fall useless to the ground.

Faith is the weapon par excellence. "I take it as certain," wrote St. Teresa of Avila, "that God will never allow the devil to deceive someone who, mistrustful of self in all things, would be ready (being of a faith so firm) to face a thousand deaths for the smallest revealed truth."[113]

It is faith which, at the hour of trial, at the moment of temptation, recalls to us God's sovereign rights to obedience from His creatures; His infinite holiness; the adorable demands of His justice; the indescribable sufferings by which Jesus expiated sin; the gratuitousness of grace; the necessity of prayer; the eternity of suffering with which God punishes sinners who have died unrepentant; the unending bliss which is His magnificent reward for the fidelity of a few years. Faith repeats all these truths to us; and, however formidable the enemy's arrows, however violent his promptings, however lengthy the fight, the soul whose faith is a living one finds in this faith, and in (what faith produces) union with Christ, the best support for the soul's resistance, the very principle of the soul's stability in good, the true secret of victory.

---

[106] Luke 18:19; Matt. 19:17; Mark 10:18.   [107] Matt. 11:28.
[108] See John 6:37.   [109] Matt. 9:13.
[110] Matt. 23:12; Luke 14:11; 18:14.   [111] Matt. 5:4.
[112] Matt. 5:8.   [113] St. Teresa, *Life, written by herself*, Ch. 23.

Blessed (it is God Himself who tells us so), blessed is the man who undergoes temptation, without having laid himself open to it; who passes through the fire, eyes of faith fixed upon the words and example of Christ, as upon the Divine promises. That soul will triumph even here below, later receiving the reward for its generosity and love: "*Blessed* is the man who endures temptation; for when he has been tried, he will receive the crown of life which God has promised to those who love Him."[114]

For, says St. Paul, Christ does not forsake His disciples in the struggle. A compassionate High Priest who has suffered temptation, He knows what being put to the test is, and can sustain us in the midst of the fight.[115] He helps us, through His grace, He aids us by His prayer. For us, He makes again at that time the request He made of His Father when He was about to undergo, but to emerge glorious from, the final assaults of the devil: "Father, I do not pray that you take them out of the world, but that you keep them from evil."[116]

And because we believe in, and do not want to turn away from, Christ, His Son; because, by prayer and mistrustful of ourselves, we place our hope in Christ alone; because He sees and loves us in His Son—"because they are yours," said Christ,[117] the Father will "deliver us from evil"; He will send His good angels to come to us invisibly to serve us.

It is, moreover, the magnificent promise which He Himself made to us through the mouth of the sacred writer, again in the beautiful ninetieth Psalm, that I wish to quote in ending this talk: "Because he hoped in me," says the Lord, "I will deliver him; I will protect him because he has known my name; he shall cry to me, and I will hear him; I am with him in tribulation, I will deliver him, and I will glorify him; I will fill him with length of days; and I will show him"—so that he will rejoice in it for ever—"my salvation,"[118] the salvation I alone can give him.

---

[114] James 1:12.   [115] Hebr. 2:18 (Jerus.)   [116] John 17:15.
[117] John 17:9.   [118] Ps. 90 (91):14-16.

CHAPTER ELEVEN

SOME ASPECTS OF THE
PUBLIC LIFE OF JESUS
(*Lent*)

Introduction: Variety of aspects of the public life.

St. John the apostle, at the conclusion of his Gospel, says that if a detailed account of "all the many other things that Jesus did" were to be given, "not even the world itself, I think, could hold the books that would have to be written."[1]

Now as we start this contemplation of the public life of Our Lord, we ought to return to the same thought. If we wanted to comment in detail on each of His sayings, to consider each of His deeds, explain each of His actions, the whole of our lifetime would not suffice.

That contemplation would certainly form a most pleasant occupation for our souls. But not being able to pause at each page of the Gospel, we shall seize upon only some characteristic features of this period of the Savior's life—enough to admire the extent to which the Eternal Wisdom and Mercy shine out in the mysteries of the Incarnation and our redemption.

We shall see first how Christ Jesus proclaimed and established the divinity of His mission and of His Person so as to lay the foundation of our faith. Next we shall contemplate the tireless

[1] John 21:25

stooping down to the aid of misery in all its forms by which, incarnate in His humanity, He revealed to the world the depth and the riches of His infinite goodness. The whole of this revelation will stand out in high relief, by contrast, when we consider the entirely just behavior of Our Lord towards the pride of the Pharisees.

There, amongst a thousand others, are three aspects of the public life of Jesus at which our souls can pause, to draw graces of light from them, and principles of life.

1. Testimonies by which Our Lord established His divinity.

At the baptism of Jesus, which marked the beginning of His public life, we heard the Father enthrone Christ as His "beloved Son."

The teaching of Jesus during the three years of His exterior ministry in the service of souls is but a ceaseless commentary upon that testimony. We shall see Christ manifest Himself, by His actions and words, not as *adopted* son of God, like one elect, chosen to fulfill a special mission before his people as were those who were simply prophets—but as God's own Son, Son by nature, possessing in consequence divine prerogatives, the absolute rights of Sovereign Being, and requiring from us faith in the divinity of His works and of His person.

When we read the Gospel, we see that Christ speaks and acts not only as a man, like unto us, but also as God, high above every created being.

For see: He says of Himself that He is greater than Jonah, than Solomon,[2] than Moses. As man, through being born of Mary, He is "Son of David," but He is also "the Lord, seated at the right hand of God,"[3] sharing in His eternal power and His infinite glory.

---

[2] "A greater than Jonah is here ... a greater than Solomon is here": Matt. 12:41:42; Luke 11:31-32.   [3] See Ps. 109 (110):1.

Thus, He declares Himself to be Supreme Lawgiver, by the same title of right as God the Father. Just as God gave the Law to Moses, so He establishes the legal code of the Gospel: "You have heard that it was said to the men of old... But I say to you..."[4] That is the formula repeated throughout the whole Sermon on the Mount. So much does He show Himself master of the Law, that He revokes parts of it on His own authority, when He pleases, with a complete independence, as being the one who instituted it and is Sovereign Master of it.

This power has no limits. Jesus forgives sins, a privilege only God enjoys, because it is only to God that the offense of sin is given. "Take courage, your sins are forgiven you," He says to a paralytic whom someone brings to Him.[5] The Scribes and Pharisees, scandalized to hear a man speak in this way, murmur amongst themselves: "Who can forgive sins, but God only?" But Jesus reads in their hearts these secret thoughts; and, to prove to those who contest it with Him that He possesses this Divine power not by delegation but by title of right which is His own and personal, He immediately works a miracle: "That you may know that the Son of Man has power on earth to forgive sins," (then He says to the paralytic) "Arise, take up your pallet-bed and walk."

This example is a characteristic one: Christ Jesus works His miracles on His own authority, of Himself. Except before the raising of Lazarus, when He asks His Father that the miracle He was about to work should enlighten the souls who were to be witnesses of it,[6] He never prays before manifesting His power as did the prophets. Instead, by a word, a gesture, by a single act of His will, He cures the lame, He makes paralytics walk, He multiplies loaves of bread, He calms the raging of the waves, He casts out demons, He raises the dead.

Lastly, so great is His power that He will come upon the clouds of heaven to judge every creature;[7] "all power in heaven

---

[4] Matt. 5, vv. 22, 28, 32, 34, 39, 44 (RSV, Cath.) Mark 2:5-12; Luke 5:20-25.

[5] See Matt. 9:2-7;

[6] John 11:42.

[7] Matt. 24:30-31; 26:64; John 5:25-30; 1 Peter 4:5.

and on earth" has been given to Him by His Father.[8] Like His Father, He promises life eternal to all who follow Him.[9]

Those words and those actions show us Jesus as the equal of God the Father, sharing in the supreme power of divinity, in its essential prerogatives, in its infinite dignity.

We possess more explicit testimonies.

You know the episode in which Peter declares his faith in his Master's Divinity: "You are the Christ, the Son of the living God." "Blessed are you, Simon Bar-Jona," Jesus says to him immediately after, "for flesh and blood has not revealed this to you"—it is not by following your own natural lights that you have arrived at this knowledge of my divinity; "it is my Father in heaven who has revealed it to you." And to indicate the greatness of this act of faith, the Savior promises Peter that He will make him the foundation of His Church.[10]

In front of His judges at the time of His Passion, Our Lord proclaims His divinity still more authoritatively. As President of the Great Council, Caiaphas says to the Savior: "I adjure you by the living God that you tell us whether you are the Christ, the Son of God." That is it, replies Jesus, "you have said it; and hereafter you will see the Son of Man seated at the right hand of the Almighty and coming upon the clouds of heaven." The Jews regarded as a divine privilege the seating of someone at the right hand of God, and for anyone to arrogate this prerogative to himself constituted a blasphemy punishable by death. That is why Caiaphas had no sooner heard Jesus's reply than he tore his garments as a sign of protest and cried out: "He has blasphemed; what further need have we of witnesses?" And all the others replied: "He has made himself liable to death." But rather than retract, Christ accepted His condemnation.[11]

· · ·

[8] Matt. 28:18.
[10] See Matt. 16:17-18.
[9] Matt. 19:28-29.
[11] See Matt. 26:63-66.

It is above all in St. John's Gospel[12] that we find on Jesus's lips testimonies which show a union between Him and His Father such as can only be explained by the divine nature, a nature He possesses indivisibly with the Father and the Spirit common to them both.

You will notice that, except when He was teaching His disciples the way to pray, Christ Jesus never says "Our Father." Always, in speaking of His connection with God the Father, He says: "the Father," "my Father," and in addressing His disciples: "your Father." Our Lord was careful to mark the essential difference which, in this matter, exists between Himself and other men. He is Son of God by nature; they are so only by adoption.

That is why His dealings with the Father are of a unique character; they can result only from His divine origin.

One day, He said in the presence of His disciples: "I thank you, Father, Lord of heaven and earth, for hiding these things from the learned and prudent, and revealing them to little children. Yes, Father, for that is what it pleased you to do. All things have been delivered to me by my Father; and no-one knows the Son except the Father; nor does anyone know the Father except the Son, and those to whom the Son chooses to reveal Him."[13] By saying this, the Word Incarnate shows us clearly that between Him and His Father there is such a perfect equality of understanding as to us is incomprehensible. This Son, Jesus, is so great and His Sonship so beyond words to describe, that only the Father, who is God, can know Him. And the Father is of such majesty, His Fatherhood a mystery so sublime, that only the Son can have knowledge of what the Father is. This knowledge so much surpasses everything to which the learning of created beings can attain, that no man can share in it unless a revelation of it is given him.

You see how Our Lord establishes clearly His divine union

---

[12] Many of these testimonies are read at the Lenten Masses, especially after Passion Sunday. [13] See Matt. 11:25-27.

with the Father. But this union is not limited to one of knowledge; it extends to all the works done outwards from the Trinity.

Look at when Jesus cures a paralytic, telling him to take up his
pallet-bed; it was on the day of rest. Wholly scandalized, the Jews
immediately reproach the Savior for not observing the Sabbath.
And what does Our Lord reply? To show that He is supreme Master of the law, by the same title of right as His Father, He replies
to the Pharisees: "My Father goes on working, and so do I"—I act
like Him and with Him. So well do His hearers understand that by
these words He claims to be God, that they seek to put Him to
death, "because, not content with breaking the Sabbath, he spoke of
God as his own Father, and so made himself God's equal." Far
from contradicting them, Our Lord confirmed their interpretation: "I tell you most solemnly, the Son can do nothing by Himself; He can only do what He sees the Father doing: and whatever
the Father does the Son does too. For the Father loves the Son
and shows Him everything He does Himself."[14] Read in the Gospel the continuance and development of these words: you will see
with what authority Christ Jesus declares Himself in all things the
equal of the Father, God with Him and like Him.

The whole of the discourse after the Last Supper and the whole
of the priestly prayer of Jesus at that solemn time are full of these
affirmations that show He is the very Son of God, having the
same divine nature, possessing the same sovereign rights, enjoy-
ing the same eternal glory: "I and the Father are one."[15]

2. How these testimonies are likewise the foundation of our faith in Jesus Christ.

If we now look for the reason why Christ thus attests to His divinity, we shall see that it is so as to lay the foundation of our faith.

That is a truth you know already; but so important is it, that
we ought never to stop contemplating it. For the whole of our

---

[14] John 5:16-20 (Jerus.)   [15] John 10:30.

super-natural life and all our holiness have faith as their basis, and our faith itself rests upon the testimonies that clearly establish the Savior's divinity.

St. Paul exhorts us to regard Our Lord as "the apostle and the high priest of the faith which we profess."[16] "Apostle" signifies one who is sent in order to carry out a mission; and St. Paul says that Christ is the apostle of our faith. How is that?

In an expression used by the Church, the Incarnate Word is "the Angel of Great Counsel"[17] who dwells in the divine splendors. And why is He sent? To reveal to the world "the mystery which has been hidden from eternity in God,"[18] the mystery of the salvation of the world by a God-man. That is the fundamental truth to which Christ was to bear witness: "For this was I born, and for this came I into the world, *that* I should give testimony to the truth."[19]

Thus, the great mission of Jesus, especially during His public life, was to manifest His divinity to the world: *Ipse enarravit*, "He has revealed Him."[20] All his teaching, all He did, all His miracles, had the object of establishing His divinity in the minds of those who heard Him. Take, for example, the events at Lazarus's tomb. Before raising His friend from the dead, Christ lifted up His eyes to heaven: "Father," He said, "I give you thanks that you have heard me. Yet I knew that you always hear me; but because of the people who stand around, I spoke, *that they may believe that you have sent me.*"[21]

There is no doubt that Our Lord instilled this truth only gently, little by little. So as not to come up against the monotheistic ideas of the Jews head-on, He only revealed Himself by degrees; but, with admirable wisdom, He made everything converge upon

---

[16] Hebr. 3:1 (Knox).   [17] Introit of the Third Mass of Christmas. [*Translator's note*: "Angel" here simply means "Messenger." God the Son came on earth to redeem the human race and bring the salvific message that is His teaching.]   [18] Eph. 3:9.   [19] John 18:37 (Rheims). [20] John 1:18.   [21] John 11:41-42.

that manifestation of His Divine Sonship. At the end of His life, when the minds of the upright were sufficiently prepared, He did not hesitate to acknowledge His divinity in front of His judges, at peril of His life. Jesus is the King of Martyrs, of those who by the shedding of their blood have professed their faith in His divinity. The first of such martyrs, He was delivered up and immolated for having declared Himself to be God's own and only Son.

In His final prayer at the Last Supper, He (so to speak) rendered account to His Father, rendered account of His mission; and He summed up everything in these words: "I have accomplished the work that you gave me to do." And what is its fruit? That His disciples, for their part, have accepted His testimony: they "have known with certainty that I came from you, and they have believed that you sent me."[22]

Therefore, this faith in the divinity of His Son is, according to the very words of Jesus, the work par excellence that God the Father requires of us: "This is the work of God, that you believe in Him whom He has sent."[23]

It was this faith that brought numerous sick their cure: "Let it be done to you according to your faith";[24] that brought Mary Magdalene forgiveness of her sins: "Your faith has made you safe; go in peace."[25] It was this faith that merited for Peter his being made the indestructible foundation of the Church; that rendered the apostles pleasing to the Father and made them the object of His love: "The Father ... loves you because you have loved me."[26]

It is this faith also that gives us the power to become children of God: "... to those who believe in His name";[27] that makes the divine springs of the grace of the Holy Spirit rush headlong into our hearts: "He who believes in me ... from within him there

[22] See John 17, vv. 4, 8.

[23] John 6:29.

[24] Matt. 9:29; Mark 5:34, 10:52; Luke 17:19.

[25] Luke 7:50 (Rheims).

[26] John 16:27.

[27] John 1:12.

shall flow rivers of living water";[28] that dispels the darkness of death: "...that whoever believes in me may not remain in the darkness";[29] that brings divine life to us: "... so that those who believe in Him may not perish, but have eternal life."[30]

It was for lack of this faith that the enemies of Jesus would perish: "If I had not come and spoken to them, they would have no sin. But now they have no excuse for their sin";[31] and that is why "he who does not believe is already judged, because he does not believe in the name of the only-begotten Son of God."[32]

You see how everything comes down to faith in Jesus Christ, the Eternal Son of God; it forms the basis of all our spiritual life, the deep root of all justification, the essential condition of all progress, the assured means of reaching the summit of all holiness.

Let us prostrate ourselves at the feet of Jesus and say to Him: O Christ Jesus, Incarnate Word, who came down from heaven so as to reveal to us the secrets that you, the only-begotten Son of God, ever contemplate "in the heart's-embrace of the Father,"[33] I believe and I acknowledge that you are God, as the Father is; His equal.[34] I believe in you; I believe in your works;[35] I believe in your person; I believe that you came from the Father,[36] that you are one with the Father;[37] that whoever sees you sees also Him.[38] I believe that you are "the resurrection and the life."[39] I believe this and, believing it, I adore you, and consecrate to your service the whole of my being, the whole of my activity, the whole of my life. I believe in you, Christ Jesus, but increase my faith.[40]

---

[28] John 7:38; Isa. 12:3: "You shall draw waters with joy out of the Savior's fountains."   [29] John 12:46.
    [30] John 3:15 (Knox).   [31] John 15:22.   [32] John 3:18.
    [33] See John 1:18.   [34] Phil. 2:6.   [35] John 14:12; 10:38.
    [36] John 17:8.   [37] John 10:30.   [38] John 14:9.
    [39] John 11:25.   [40] Luke 17:5.

3. **The human actions of the Incarnate Word declare the divine perfections. The human kindness in Christ is a revelation of His eternal love.**

If Christ reveals to the world the truth and teaching of His eternal Sonship, it is through His humanity that He manifests to us the perfections of His divine nature. True Son of God though He is, He loves to call Himself "the Son of Man": He gives Himself this same title on the most solemn of occasions when claiming most authoritatively the prerogatives of Divine Being.

Every time we find ourselves in contact with Him, indeed, we are in the presence of this sublime mystery: the union of two natures, the divine and the human, in one single and the same Person—without mingling or confusion of the natures, without division of the Person.

That is the initial mystery we ought to have always before our eyes when we contemplate Our Lord. Each of His mysteries makes either the unity of His adorable Person, or the truth of His divine nature, or the reality of His human condition, stand out in high relief.

One of the profoundest and most touching aspects of the plan of the Incarnation is that the divine perfections are manifested to men through the human nature. The attributes of God, His eternal perfections, are to us here below incomprehensible; they are beyond all our learning. But, by making Himself man, the Incarnate Word unveiled to the simplest minds the inaccessible perfections of Divinity, through words falling from His human lips, through acts done in His nature of man. In making our souls able to grasp them through actions perceptible to the senses, He charms us and attracts us to Him: "so that while we acknowledge God in visible form, we may through Him be drawn to the love of things invisible."[41]

It is especially during the public life of Jesus that this plan, full of wisdom and mercy, is declared and is carried into effect.

·   ·   ·

[41] Preface of the Nativity.

Of all the divine perfections, love is assuredly the one which, more than any other, the Word Incarnate takes pleasure in revealing to us.

To the human heart, a tangible love is necessary to make it catch a glimpse of Infinite Love—a Love much deeper than the tangible, but surpassing all our understanding. Nothing, indeed, captivates our poor hearts as much as contemplating how Christ Jesus, true God as well as true man, expresses in human acts the divine kindness. When we see Him pouring out inexhaustible treasures of compassion, never-failing riches of mercy, in profusion around Him, we can in some small measure gain an idea of that ocean of the divine kindness upon which the sacred humanity, for our sakes, will draw.

Let us dwell upon some features of it; they will show us clearly to what levels, sometimes astonishing ones, our Savior stoops down to alleviate human misery in all its forms, including that of our sins. And let us never forget that even then, when He bends down to us, He remains God's own Son, Himself God, the Almighty Being, the Infinite Wisdom who, fixing all things firmly in His truth, performs nothing but what is sovereignly perfect. That undoubtedly gives to the words of kindness He utters, to the works of mercy He carries out, an inestimable value that enhances them infinitely: but especially does it capture our souls by showing us how deeply charming is the heart of our Christ, of our God.

You know what the first miracle of the public life of Jesus was: the water changed into wine at the marriage-feast of Cana at the request of His mother.[42] For our human hearts, what a revelation, unforeseen, of the divine tenderness and niceness! Austere ascetics might be scandalized at seeing a miracle asked for or worked in order to cover up the lack of means of poor parents at a wedding banquet. And yet, that is what the Virgin had not the

[42] John 2:1-11.

slightest hesitation in asking for, and that is what Christ was so good as to carry out. Jesus let Himself be touched by the public embarrassment in which poor folk were about to find themselves. To spare them it, He worked a prodigious miracle. And that which His heart here discloses to us of human kindness and humble stooping-down to help is but the outward manifestation of a higher kindness, divine kindness, which is the source of the human one. For everything the Son does, the Father does equally.

A short time afterwards, in the synagogue at Nazareth, Jesus read out from Isaiah, applying it to Himself as the program of His work of love: "The Spirit of the Lord is upon me. By His anointing He has consecrated me to bring good news to the poor; He has sent me to heal the contrite of heart; to announce to the captives release, and sight to the blind; to set at liberty the oppressed, to proclaim the year of Divine salvation."[43]

"What you have just heard," Jesus added, "has this very day begun to be fulfilled."[44]

And, indeed, the Savior was from then on revealed to all as a King full of gentleness and kindness. I would need to quote from every page of Gospel if I wished to show you how misery, weakness, infirmity, suffering had the gift of touching Him, and in so irresistible a way that He could refuse them nothing. St. Luke carefully mentions to us that Jesus was moved with "compassion."[45] The blind, the deaf-mutes, the paralytics, the lepers presented themselves before Him; and the Gospel tells us that He "healed them all."[46]

He welcomes all, too, with untiring forbearance; He lets Himself be pressed-in, besieged on all sides, ceaselessly, even after the sun had set;[47] so much so that one day He was not able to have anything to eat.[48] Another time, on the shores of Lake Tiberius, He had to go into a boat so as to get clear of the crowds and, sit-

---

[43] See Isa. 61:1-2; Luke 4:16-19.   [44] See Luke 4:21.   [45] Luke 7:13.
[46] Luke 6:19 (RSV, Cath.)   [47] Mark 1:32-33.   [48] Mark 3:20.

ting on board, give out the word of God to them with greater freedom.[49] Elsewhere the crowds so congested the house where He was, that in order to enable a paralytic lying on a pallet-bed to gain entry and reach Jesus, the only thing the invalid's friends could do was to make an opening in the roof and lower him down through it.[50]

The apostles—well, they were often impatient, and the Divine Master took occasion of this to show them His own gentleness. One day, they wanted to keep away from Him the children people brought to Him; they, the apostles, found them tiresome. "Leave these little children alone," Jesus said to them; "do not stop them coming to me; for the kingdom of heaven is for such as these." And He stopped and put His arms around the children, and blessed them.[51] Another time the disciples, annoyed at how He had been received in a town of Samaria, asked Him: "Lord, do you want us to bid fire come down from heaven and consume them?" But Jesus immediately turned and rebuked them: "You do not know what spirit you are made of. The Son of Man came, not to destroy men's lives but to save them."[52]

So true is this, that He even works miracles to bring the dead back to life. Look at how at Naim He encounters a poor widow following the mortal remains of her only son, and weeping. Jesus sees her; He sees her tears; His heart, deeply touched, cannot bear this sorrow: "Do not weep!" He says. And immediately He commands death to yield up its prey: "Young man, I say to you, arise." And he who had been dead sat up, and Jesus gave him back to his mother.[53]

All these manifestations of the mercy and kindness of Jesus, which disclose to us the feelings of His heart as man, touch the inmost fibers of our being. In a form that we can grasp, they

---

[49] Mark 4:1.   [50] Mark 2:4.   [51] See Mark 10:13-16.
[52] See Luke 9:54-56.   [53] Luke 7:11-15.

reveal to us the infinite love of our God. When we see Christ at Lazarus's tomb, weeping, and we hear the Jews, who witnessed the sight, say: "See how he loved him,"[54] our hearts understand this silent language of Jesus's human tears, and we enter into the sanctuary of the Eternal Love they reveal: "He who sees me sees also the Father."[55]

And besides, how all that conduct of Christ's condemns our selfishness, our hardness, our coldness of heart, our indifference, our impatience, our rancor, our impulses of anger and revenge, our resentment towards our neighbor! We forget too often the Savior's words: "Every time you showed compassion to one of the least of my brethren, you did it to me."[56]

O Jesus, who has said: "Learn from me; I am gentle and humble of heart,"[57] make our hearts like unto yours. Following your example, may we be merciful, so that we ourselves may obtain mercy,[58] but especially in order that we, by imitating you, may become like our Father in heaven!

4. Merciful conduct of Christ towards sinners. The prodigal son. The Samaritan woman at the well. Mary Magdalene. The woman taken in adultery.

One of the deepest forms of human misery, sin, especially drew Christ's merciful heart. If there is a single feature that particularly strikes one in the conduct of the Incarnate Word during His public life, it is this strange preference He shows for His ministry to sinners.

The sacred writers tell us that "*many* publicans[59] and sinners were at table with Jesus and His disciples."[60] So habitual with Him was this conduct, that He became called "a friend of publicans

---

[54] John 11:36.   [55] John 14:9.   [56] See Matt. 25:40.
[57] Matt. 11:29 (Knox).   [58] Matt. 5:7.   [59] Tax-gatherers in the pay of the Roman rulers of Judea. Recruited from the common classes, they were regarded as despicable because of their exactions. They were ranked with robbers.   [60] Mark 2:15; Matt. 9:10; Luke 5:29.

and sinners."[61] And when the Pharisees showed themselves scandalized by this, Jesus, far from denying it, confirmed it and gave the deep reason for its being so: "It is not the healthy who need a physician, but they who are sick. I have not come to call the just, but sinners to repentance."[62]

In the eternal plan, Jesus is our elder brother, predestined to be "the firstborn among many brethren" who would be true images of Him.[63] He has taken our nature; a sinful nature by race but a pure one in His person. He came here "in the likeness of sinful flesh."[64] He knows that the great majority of human beings fall into sin and have need of forgiveness; that souls who are slaves to sin, souls who "sit in darkness and in the shadow of death,"[65] far away from God, would not understand a direct revelation of the divine; they will only be drawn to the Father through the sacred humanity's stooping-down to them. That is why a large part of His teaching and doctrine, and a multitude of acts of gentleness and forgiveness towards sinners, have the object of making these poor souls grasp something of Divine Mercy, how immense it is.

In one of His most beautiful parables—you know it, the parable of the Good Samaritan, Jesus unveils for us an authentic portrait of His Heavenly Father.[66]

Its immediate aim, however (as the Gospel indicates very clearly) is to explain His own stooping down to the aid of sinners. St. Luke tells us, indeed, that the Pharisees, murmuring at how the publicans and sinners were drawing near to Jesus to listen to Him, said: "This man welcomes sinners and eats with them." Upon which, to justify the way He acted, "He spoke to them this parable."[67]

---

[61] Matt. 11:19; Luke 7:34. [62] Luke 5:31-32; Matt. 9:12; Mark 2:17.
[63] Rom. 8:29. [64] Luke 1:79; Ps. 106 (107):10. [65] Rom. 8:3.
[66] The Church reads this parable to us on the Saturday following the Second Sunday in Lent. [67] Luke 15:1-3.

244 BOOK TWO: THE MYSTERIES OF CHRIST

In it, He shows first the extraordinary kindness of the father who forgets all the ingratitude, all the baseness, of the guilty one, so as to think of only one thing: his son was dead, and has returned to life; was lost and now is found.[68] That is why he has to rejoice, why he must, at once, prepare a feast.

Christ Jesus could have stopped the telling of His parable at that point if the only thing He had wanted to do was to make the mercy of the father of the family towards the prodigal son shine out brightly to our eyes. So vast is that mercy, indeed, that we could not conceive of anything greater. So touched are we, so amazed, that it holds all our attention, and more often than not we lose sight of the lesson Jesus wanted to give to the murmurers, those who were blaspheming his conduct towards sinners.

For He goes on with the parable by describing to us the odious attitude of the elder son who refuses to share in the general joy by sitting down at the feast prepared for his brother.

Jesus wanted not only to make known to the Pharisees how unfeeling their proud conduct was, and how despicable the scandal they gave, but also to teach them that He, our elder brother, far from avoiding contact with His repentant brothers the publicans and sinners, sought them out and took part in their feasts. For "there will be more rejoicing in heaven over one sinner who repents than over ninety-nine righteous persons who need no repentance."[69]

On its own, the parable of the prodigal son constitutes a magnificent revelation of the Divine Mercy. But it pleased our Savior to illustrate this teaching and underline this doctrine by acts of kindness that delight us and move us profoundly.

You know the conversation Jesus had with the Samaritan woman.[70] It was at the start of Christ's public life. Our Lord was going from Jerusalem into Galilee. Having a long distance to cover, He had set out in the early morning, and around the hour of noon

---

[68] Luke 15:32.   [69] Luke 15:7 (RSV, Cath.)
[70] John 4:5-29; various translations or paraphrases given.

had arrived near Sychar, a town of Samaria. The Holy Gospel tells us that Jesus was "weary"; He was tired, as we ourselves would have been after having completed a considerable portion of a journey. And He sat down on the edge of the well—the well of Jacob situated in that place.

All the actions of the Word Incarnate are invested with something that is so beautiful in its simplicity. There is a complete absence of any pose, of any affectation. Wholly God as He is, Jesus is also (if I can put it this way) very human in the full and noble sense of the word: *Perfectus Deus, perfectus homo,* "God completely, and man completely."[71] We indeed recognize Him as one of us.

He sits, then, on the well-side, while His disciples go to fetch some food from the town nearby. But He—what had He come there to do? simply take a spot of rest, await the return of the disciples? No, He had also come to seek a strayed sheep, to save a soul.

Christ Jesus had come down from heaven to redeem souls: "Christ Jesus ... gave Himself as a ransom for all."[72] For thirty years He had had to repress the ardor, that burning ardor, of His zeal for souls. There is no doubt that He worked, He suffered, He prayed for them; but He did not go to them. Now the hour had come when His Father willed Him to undertake the preaching of the truth and the revelation of His mission, in order to gain souls. Our Lord went to Sychar to save one soul whose destiny that had been from all eternity.

And who was this soul? Most certainly there were in that locality many to be met with who were less corrupted than this sinner He wished to save; and yet it was she that He waited for; He knew all the dissoluteness, all the shameful things about this poor woman, and it was to her, in preference to all others, that He was about to manifest Himself.

---

[71] Creed attributed to St. Athanasius.   [72] 1 Tim. 2:6 (RSV, Cath.); Matt. 20:28; Mark 10:45.

So, this sinner arrives, carrying her pitcher to draw water from the well-spring. Immediately Christ addresses some words to her. And what does He say? Does He at once reproach her for her bad behavior, speak of the punishments her disorderly life deserves? Not at all; a Pharisee would have spoken in that way; but Jesus acts quite differently. He takes the occasion of their surroundings to enter into conversation with her: "Give me water to drink."

The woman looks at Him, astonished. She has just recognized that the one who speaks to her is Jewish. Now, the Jews despised the Samaritans and the latter detested the inhabitants of Judea— the Jews, St. John tells us, "have no dealings with the Samaritans." "How is it that you, a Jew, ask a drink of me, a Samaritan woman?" she says to Our Lord. And He, seeking to rouse a holy curiosity in her, replies: "If you knew the gift of God, and who it is who says to you 'Give me to drink,' you perhaps would have asked of Him, and He would have given you living water."

This poor creature, sunk in the life of the senses, understands nothing about spiritual things. She is more and more astonished, she asks herself how her interlocutor could give her water, since he lacks the means of drawing any; and what water could be better than the water of this well to which the Patriarch Jacob used to come, to quench his thirst—he and his sons, and his flocks. "Are you greater than our father Jacob?" she asks Christ. In his reply, Jesus insists: "Everyone who drinks of this water will thirst again, but whoever drinks of the water that I shall give him shall never thirst: it shall become in him a fount of living water, springing up unto life everlasting." "Lord, give me this water," replies the woman.

The Savior then lets her understand that He knows of the dissolute life she leads. This sinner, whom grace is beginning to enlighten, sees that she is in the presence of someone who reads the heart, to its depths: "Sir, I see that you are a prophet." And, all at once, her soul is touched and rises up towards the light. "Ought we to worship God on this mountain here, or rightly at

Jerusalem?" That, as you know, was a perpetual subject of dispute between Jews and Samaritans.

Christ Jesus sees arising in this soul, in the midst of her corruption, a glimmer of good will—enough for Him to bestow on her a greater grace. For as soon as He sees straightforwardness and sincerity in a search after truth, He brings light; He is happy to reward this desire for good, and for justice.

Therefore, He is about to make to this soul a twofold revelation. He teaches her that the hour has come for true worshippers in spirit and in truth as the Father seeks. And He manifests Himself to her as being the Messiah whom the Father has sent: "*I, who speak with you, am He*"—a revelation He had not yet made to anyone, not even the disciples.

Is it not remarkable that these two great revelations were made for the very first time to a miserable creature of sin who had no other title to be the object of such a privilege than her need for salvation and a little bit of goodwill?

This woman returned from there justified; she had received the grace of faith. She "left her water-jar" and went away into the town to tell everyone: "I have met the Messiah!" Her first action was to make known "the gift of God" which had been imparted to her with such liberality.

Meanwhile, the disciples had returned with some food. They offered it to their Master: "Rabbi, eat." What does Jesus reply to them? "I have food to eat of which you do not know. My food is to do the will of Him who sent me."[73] And what is the will of the Father? That all "come to the knowledge of the truth" that leads to salvation.[74]

It is with this that Christ Jesus occupies Himself. The will of His Father is that Jesus shall bring to Him the souls the Father wishes to save; shall show them the way, shall reveal to them the truth, and thus lead them to life: "All that the Father gives to me

[73] John 4, vv. 31-32, 34.　　　[74] 1 Tim. 2:4.

shall come to me, and him who comes to me I will not cast out."[75] That is the whole work of Jesus.

The sinful woman at Sychar had nothing that distinguished her from others, unless it be the depth of her misery. But she was attracted to Christ by the Father; and then the Savior received her, enlightened her, sanctified her, transformed her, and made her His apostle: "She who comes to me I will not cast out." For "this is the will of my Father who sent me, that I should lose none of those He has given me, but that I should raise them up"[76]—by grace here below, while awaiting the Last Day when they will be "raised up" in glory.

The Samaritan was one of the first women raised up to grace by Jesus. Mary Magdalene was another—but how much more glorious!

"A woman in the town who was a sinner..."[77] It is thus that the Gospel begins her story;[78] by an affirmation of her sinfulness. For applying herself to sin was Mary Magdalene's profession—as a soldier's profession is that of living under arms, as that of a politician the directing of a country's destinies. Her dissoluteness was notorious. Seven devils, a symbol of the abyss into which she had fallen, made their dwelling in her soul.[79]

One day, Christ had been invited to the home of Simon the Pharisee. Hardly had He sat down at table, when this sinful woman, carrying an alabaster vase filled with perfume, burst into the room where the feast was being held. Approaching Jesus, she threw herself at His feet and, weeping, bathed them with her tears, dried them with the hair of her head, kissed them and poured the perfume upon them.

As soon as she had come in, the Pharisee, quite scandalized, said to himself: Oh! if he knew the kind of woman this is, he

---

[75] John 6:37.   [76] See John 6:39.   [77] Luke 7:37.

[78] The liturgy for the Thursday after Passion Sunday contains a reading of this episode.   [79] Luke 8:2.

would not have tolerated her being at his feet; he is certainly no prophet: "If this man were a prophet, he would surely have known who and what sort of woman this is who is touching him, for she is a sinner." And Jesus, "answering"—note this word; the Pharisee had said nothing out loud, but Jesus *replies* to his inner thoughts, and puts a question to Simon, one you know well. There were two insolvent debtors whose debts their creditor canceled: which of the two would love him more? "The one, I suppose, to whom he forgave more," replied Simon.[80] "You have judged rightly," was Jesus's rejoinder. Then, turning towards Mary Magdalene: You see this woman—this woman who is indeed a sinner, whom you have despised in your heart—"if great sins have been forgiven her, she (as she had just shown) has also greatly loved."[81]

Mary Magdalene the sinner had become a triumph of the grace of Jesus, one of the most magnificent trophies of His Precious Blood.

This compassion of the Incarnate Word towards sinners is so far-reaching that sometimes He seems to forget the rights of His justice and His holiness. Jesus's enemies were so well acquainted with His compassion, that they went so far as to set traps for Him on that very ground.

Here they are now, bringing to Christ an adulterous woman; impossible to deny the crime or diminish its gravity: the Gospel tells us that this guilty person had been caught in the very act, and the Law of Moses ordained that she be stoned. The Pharisees, knowing of Jesus's kindness, counted on His absolving this woman, and that would be putting Himself in opposition to their law-giver. "What, therefore, do you say?" they asked Jesus.

But if Jesus is goodness itself, He is also Eternal Wisdom. First, He says nothing to His accusers' perverse demand for an answer, but they insist. And Our Lord then says to them: "Whoever is without sin among you, let him be the first to cast a stone at her."

---

[80] Luke 7:36-44 (RSV, Cath.)   [81] Luke 7:47 (Knox).

Returned in their own coin, this reply abashes them; and they can no longer do anything but go away from Him, one after the other.

Jesus stays, alone with the guilty woman. There remain only great misery and great mercy, in the presence of each other. And now, mercy stoops down to misery: "Woman, where are your accusers? Has no-one condemned you?" "No-one, Lord." "Neither will I condemn you. Go on your way; and from now on, sin no more."[82]

Jesus's kindness appeared so excessive to certain Christians of the early Church, that this episode was suppressed in several manuscripts of the first few centuries; but it is entirely authentic, and its insertion in the Gospel was willed by the Holy Spirit.

All these examples of Jesus's goodness of heart are but manifestations of a higher love: the Heavenly Father's infinite love for poor sinners. Never forget that in what Jesus does as man we must see a revelation of that which, with the Father and the Spirit common to them both, He accomplishes as God. Jesus receives sinners and forgives them—and this is very God who, in human form, bends down towards them, and welcomes them into the heart of Eternal Mercy.

5. The Savior's mercy is the principal source of our confidence. How this confidence is made firmer by penitence.

The revelation of Divine Mercy by Christ Jesus is the principal source of our confidence.

What happens at all those moments of grace when, in the light which God gives us, we catch a glimpse of the abyss of our sins, our miseries, our nothingness, is that, seeing ourselves so defiled,

[82] See John 8:3-11. We read this episode on the Saturday following the Third Sunday in Lent.

we say to Christ as St. Peter did: "Depart from me, O Lord, for I am a sinner"[83]—How could it be possible for you to enter into close union with a soul as touched by sin as I am? Seek, rather, souls that are noble, pure, souls privileged by grace. I myself am too unworthy to dwell so near to you.

But let us remember that Christ Himself said: "I have come to call sinners, not the just."[84] And look, indeed: did He not call Matthew to the rank of apostle—Matthew the publican and sinner? And whom did He appoint as leader of His Church, as head of that Body He willed to be "without spot or wrinkle or any such thing ... holy and without blemish,"[85] for the sanctification of which He came here to give the whole of His Precious Blood? Was it John the Baptist, sanctified while still in his mother's womb, confirmed in grace, and of so high a perfection that he was taken for Christ Himself? No. Perhaps John the Evangelist, the chaste disciple—he whom Jesus loved with a quite special love, who alone among the disciples remained faithful to Him all the way to the foot of the cross? Again, no. Whom, then, did He choose? Knowingly, deliberately, Our Lord chose a man who was to desert Him. Is this not remarkable?

In His divine foreknowledge, Christ knew everything in advance of its happening; and when He promised Peter that He would build His Church upon him, He knew that Peter, wholly admirable as was the spontaneity of his faith, would deny Him. Despite all the miracles worked in front of his eyes by the Savior, despite all the graces he had received from Him, despite the glory he had seen shining forth from the humanity of Christ on Mount Tabor—despite all this, on the very day of his First Communion and of his ordination, Peter cursed and swore: "I do not know the man!"[86]

And it is he that Jesus chose, in preference to all the others. Why is that?

---

[83] See Luke 5:8.
[85] Eph. 5:27 (RSV, Cath.)
[84] Matt. 9:13; Mark 2:17; Luke 5:32.
[86] Matt. 26:72-74.

Because His Church would be composed of sinners. Except the most pure Virgin Mary, we are all sinners; we all have need of Divine Mercy. And that is why Christ willed that the head of His Kingdom on earth should be a sinner, one whose fault would be recorded in Holy Scripture with all the details that show his cowardice and his ingratitude.

Look again at Mary Magdalene. We read in the Gospel that some women followed Jesus on His apostolic journeys, to minister to His needs and those of His disciples. Among all these women, whose devotion was tireless, whom did Christ most single out? Magdalene. "Wherever in the whole world this gospel is preached, this that she has done shall be told in memory of her."[87] He wished the sacred writer to hide nothing of the transgressions of this sinner; but He wished also that we should read that He had accepted the presence of Magdalene at the foot of the cross, by the side of His mother, the Virgin of virgins;[88] and that He reserved for her, Magdalene, His first appearance after His resurrection: "He appeared first to Mary Magdalene."[89]

Once again, why this stooping down to sinners so much? *In laudem gloriae gratiae suae,* "unto the praise of the glory"—the triumphant glory—"of His grace."[90] Such, indeed, is the greatness of divine forgiveness that it raised to one of the highest levels of holiness a sinner fallen into the abyss: "Deep calleth on deep."[91] "He met a woman lost to morals," said an author of the early centuries, "He made her"—through the depth of her penitence—"purer than a virgin."[92]

God wills that no-one shall glory in his own justice—"it is the gift of God, not the outcome of works, lest anyone may boast,"[93]

---

[87] See Mark 14:8-9. [*Translator's note:* "This that she has done": the anointing of His head "in preparation for burial." Marmion firmly identifies Mary of Bethany with Mary Magdalene.]   [88] John 19:25.   [89] Mark 16:9.
[90] Eph. 1:6.   [91] Ps. 41 (42):8.   [92] These words are found in one of the sermons attributed to St. John Chrysostom.   [93] Eph. 2:9.

but that all should give glory to the power of His grace and the wideness of His mercy: "for His mercy endures for ever."[94]

Our miseries, our faults, our sins we are acquainted with, well enough. But what we do not know—souls "of little faith"![95]—is the value of the blood of Jesus and the power of His grace.

Our confidence is drawn from its fountainhead, which is the infinite mercy of God towards us. And penitence is one of the strongest means of increasing that confidence.

The extreme willingness of God to forgive sinners cannot serve as motive for remaining in sin or falling again into sin after having been delivered from it. "Does it follow that we ought to go on sinning, to give still more occasion for grace? God forbid!" says St. Paul.[96] Ransomed from sin by the death of Christ, we ought no longer to return to sin.

You will have noticed that in forgiving the adulterous woman, Jesus gives her a grave warning: "Sin no more."[97] He says the same to the paralytic, adding the reason: "Behold, you are cured: sin no more, lest something worse befall you."[98] It is indeed as Jesus Himself said: "When the unclean spirit has gone out of a soul, he comes back, with other spirits more wicked than he, to lay siege to it; and if he makes himself master of it, the last state of that soul is worse than the first."[99]

Penitence is the required condition for receiving God's pardon and for safeguarding it within us. Look at Peter: he had sinned, and sinned gravely. But the Gospel recounts that he also "wept bitterly" over that sin.[100] Later, he had to wipe out his denials by a threefold protestation of love: "Yes, Lord, you know that I love you."[101] Again, look at Mary Magdalene, for she, besides being one of the most magnificent trophies of the grace of Christ, is at

[94] Ps. 135 (136):1 and throughout.   [95] Matt. 8:26; 14:31; 16:8; Luke 12:28.   [96] Rom. 6:1-2 (Knox).   [97] John 8:11.   [98] John 5:14.
[99] See Matt. 12:45; Luke 11:26.   [100] Luke 22:62.   [101] John 21:15-17.

the same time a splendid symbol of penitent love. What did she do? She immolated to Christ the most precious thing she had. What was that? Her flowing hair, which was her ornament, her glory (for a woman, wearing her hair long is "a glory," St. Paul says),[102] but of which she had made use to attract souls, to set a traps for them, to deprave them. And now she employs it—to do what? To wipe the Savior's feet. Like a slave, she degrades, publicly, in the sight of guests at table who were acquainted with it, what up to then had been her pride. This is a penitent love—self-sacrificing but, by the self-sacrifice, attracting and keeping the treasures of Mercy: "if great sins have been forgiven her, she has also greatly loved."

Yet whatever may be a soul's relapses into sin, we ought never to despair of it. "How many times should I forgive my neighbor?" St. Peter asked Our Lord. "Seventy times seven,"[103] replied Jesus, indicating by that an infinite number of times.

Here below, this inexhaustible measure in regard to repentance is that of God Himself.

To make complete the account I have just given you of Christ Jesus's kindness and stooping-down in love to us, I wish to add to it a trait that gives a finishing touch to the "humanizing" of Him and discloses to us one of the most touching aspects of His tenderness: Christ's affection for Lazarus and his two sisters at Bethany.

In all the public life of the Word Incarnate, we perhaps encounter nothing that so brings us close to him, and Him close to us, as the intimate picture of His relationship with His friends who lived in this little village. Our faith tells us that He is the Son of God, God Himself; but this friendship at our level reveals to us (it seems to me more than any other manifestation) His quality of being "Son of Man."

The sacred writers have barely sketched for us the picture of this holy affection; but what they have left us is enough for us to

---

[102] 1 Cor. 11:15.   [103] Matt. 18:22.

glimpse what it contained for Him of endless delight. Thus St. John tells us that "Jesus loved Martha and her sister Mary, and Lazarus."[104] They were His friends and the friends of His apostles; speaking of Lazarus to the apostles, He calls him "our friend"— "Lazarus, our friend."[105] The Gospel adds: "It was Mary who anointed the Lord with costly perfume, and wiped His feet dry with her hair."[106]

The house at Bethany was the home[107] that Christ, the Word Incarnate chose, here below, as a place of rest, and was the scene of that holy friendship of which He, the Son of God, deigned to give us the example. Nothing is more charming to our human hearts than the sight of that interior, unveiled for us by the Holy Spirit in the tenth chapter of the Gospel of St. Luke. Jesus is truly the honored, but very intimate, guest at that fireside. He must have been a frequent visitor to the house, considering that one day Martha, waiting on Him and very busy, dared to ask Him to intervene in a little domestic quarrel with her sister Mary who was quietly sitting at the feet of Jesus to enjoy the Savior's words. "Lord, do you not care that my sister is leaving me to do the serving all by myself? Please tell her to help me."[108] And, far from taking offense at such familiarity, which in a way included Him in the reproach made by Martha to her sister, Christ does intervene, and settles the matter by deciding in favor of her who symbolizes prayer and divine union: "Martha, Martha," He said, "you worry and fret about so many things, yet only one thing is needful. It is Mary who has chosen the better part; it will not be taken away from her."[109]

When we are present in spirit at this delightful scene, we feel in our hearts that Jesus is truly one of us: "it was right that He should in all things be made like unto His brethren."[110] We feel that in His person there is borne out that revelation which Eternal

---

[104] John 11:5.   [105] Ibid., v. 11.
[106] See John 11:2.   [107] [*Translator's note*: While in Judea.]
[108] Luke 10:40 (Jerus.)   [109] See Luke 10:40-42.   [110] Hebr. 2:17.

Wisdom makes to the world: "My delight is to be with the children of men."[111] We experience this feeling also: "No other nation has gods that draw near to it as our God draws near to us."[112]

Christ Jesus is truly "Emmanuel,"[113] God living among us, where we live, with us.

6. Severe behavior of Christ towards the hypocritical pride of the Pharisees.

The life of Jesus is a manifestation of the perfections of God, of the prodigalities of His supreme kindness and of the fathomless depths of His mercies. It is in the Word Incarnate that God discloses to us His inner "character": He "has shone in our hearts" ...in "the face of Christ Jesus."[114] Christ is "the image"— the visible image—"of the invisible God";[115] His words and His actions are the authentic revelation of the Infinite Being.

Now, our seeing Christ's character from His words and actions, and our idea of God, will be incomplete if, whilst meditating on Jesus's tireless stooping-down to the aid of all forms of misery, sin included, we neglect to examine also His conduct towards that form of human malice which is the one most contrary to divine nobleness and kindness, and which is summed up in a single word: phariseeism.

You know who the Pharisees were. After the return from exile in Babylon, some zealous Jews had put everything into the work of neutralizing foreign influence, perilous for the orthodoxy of Israel. Above all, they had striven to restore to a place of honor the rules prescribed by the Law of Moses, and to preserve the purity of those rules.

That zeal, worthy of every praise and showing high ideals, unfortunately degenerated, little by little, into a fierce fanaticism and

---

[111] See Prov. 8:31.   [112] Deut. 4:7 (Knox).   [113] Matt. 1:23; Isa. 7:14.
[114] 2 Cor. 4:6.   [115] Col. 1:15.

a cult of the text of the Law, carried to extremes. A class of Jews was formed, called the Pharisees—that is, the "ones set apart," separate from all foreign contact and from all dealings with those who did not observe their "traditions."[116]

Indeed, interpreting the Law with an uncommon refinement of casuistry, the Pharisees added to the Law an infinite number of rules, prescribed orally, that made it impracticable for most of the time and, in many of the provisions, puerile and ridiculous. Two points, the detail of which was the object of their endless discussions, attracted their attention especially: the observance of rest on the Sabbath day, and the legal and ritual purifications. More than once, in the Gospel, we see them laying blame upon the Savior on these points.

They had fallen into a formalism of great narrowness. Without caring about the interior purity of the soul, they were attached to the exterior observance, material and paltry, of the letter of the Law. That was the whole of their religion and of their perfection. A deep moral obliteration had resulted from this. These "pure" ones neglected weighty precepts of the natural law, in order to dwell on absurd details founded on their personal interpretations. Thus, under the pretext of not breaking the Sabbath rest, they taught that on the Sabbath day, one could neither care for the sick nor give alms to the poor, and we see them reproaching the disciples of Jesus for not observing the Sabbath because they rubbed ears of corn with their hands in order to eat them![117]

This exaggerated formalism necessarily led them to pride. They themselves being the authors of many of the prescribed rules, they likewise believed themselves to be architects of their own holiness. They were the "ones set apart," the pure, whom

[116] To the Pharisees, affiliated to their sect, are to be likened the Scribes. They were especially engrossed in the text of the Law and its interpretation and observance. Sharing the errors of the Pharisees, they were associated with them in the maledictions heaped upon the latter by the Savior.

[117] Luke 6:1-2; Matt. 12:1-2; Mark 2:23-24.

nothing soiled had touched. Hence, what was there about themselves that could cause anyone to reproach them? Were they not perfectly "correct," all down the line? And so they had an esteem for themselves that was extremely disordered. An immense pride drove them to seek avidly the front seats in the synagogues, the places of honor at the banquets to which they were invited, the salutations and applause of the crowd in the public places.[118]

This pride was displayed even in the sanctuary. You know the parable in which Christ depicts this odious ostentation so marvelously well.[119] Our Divine Savior contrasts the humility of the publican who dared not lift up his eyes to heaven because of his sins, and the self-satisfaction of the Pharisee who stood and gave thanks to God that he was "not like the rest of men" because of his exact observance of the details of the Law, and who, so to speak, claimed from God a complete approbation of his conduct.[120]

What made a number of the Pharisees contemptible was that to this pride was added a deep hypocrisy. In consequence of the multitude of prescribed rules they established, and that Our Lord Himself declares intolerable, "insupportable,"[121] many of them only attained a name for the holiness on which they prided themselves by habitually concealing their faults and failings behind a feigned appearance of it, by making the text of the Law be subject to unfaithful interpretations. In this way, they could infringe the Law whilst keeping up appearances in the eyes of the populace who admired them.

For their authority and their influence were considerable. People thought of them as interpreters and guardians of the Law of Moses. Parading a deep regard for every exterior practice of their observance, they imposed on the multitude, who considered them to be holy persons.

---

[118] Luke 20:46.   [119] Luke 18:9-14.   [120] In another series of talks (*Christ, the Ideal of the Monk*, Ch. 11, *Humility*) we have commented in detail on this parable which throws a powerful light upon the characteristics that our relations with God should bear.   [121] Matt. 23:4 (Rheims); Luke 11:46.

And so they took offense at everything that could lessen this ascendancy of theirs. From the very beginning of the public life of Jesus, they started to oppose Him. Besides, Christ did not attach His teaching to their school of thought: the doctrine He preached, the actions with which He underlined it, were the complete opposites of their opinions and conduct. His extraordinary willingness to concern Himself with publicans and sinners, rejected by them as impure; His independence with regard to the Law of the Sabbath, He saying that He is the Sovereign Lord of the Sabbath;[122] the miracles by which He showed His love for the people—these things could not fail to move them to anger.

Sinking further into their blindness bit by bit, and in spite of the warnings of Jesus Himself, they set traps for Him; they asked Him for a "sign from heaven"[123] in proof of His mission; they brought to Him the woman taken in adultery, seeking to place Him in opposition to the Law of Moses.[124] Trying to ensnare Him, they asked Him: "Is it lawful to pay tribute money to Caesar, or not?"[125] Everywhere, all through the pages of the Gospel, you can see them, filled with hate against Jesus, trying their best to destroy His authority with the crowds, to turn His disciples away from Him, to deceive the people in order to prevent Christ from fulfilling His mission of salvation.

More than once Our Lord warned His disciples to beware of the Pharisees' hypocrisy;[126] but at the end of His public ministry He, the Good Shepherd who brought the truth to His flock and was soon to give His life for them, wished to unmask completely these wolves who presented themselves under the outward appearances of holiness so as to dupe simple souls and lead them to their ruin.

Speaking solemnly in His Sermon on the Mount, Christ had

[122] Matt. 12:8; Mark 2:28; Luke 6:5.　　　　[123] Matt. 16:1.
[124] John 8:3-9.　　[125] See Matt. 22:15-22; Mark 12:13-17; Luke 20:20-26.
[126] Luke 12:1; Matt. 16:11.

astonished His Jewish audience by the revelation of a doctrine
that went against their inveterate instincts and their ancient prejudices. He had proclaimed before all of them that the blessed
ones in His Kingdom are the poor in spirit, the meek—the gentle
of heart, those who mourn, those who hunger and thirst for justice. He had declared that it is the merciful, the pure of heart, the
peacemakers, who are the true children of the Heavenly Father,
and that the deepest blessedness is that of being the object of
persecution because of Him.[127]

This doctrine, which forms the Gospel's "Magna Charta" of
the poor, the little, the humble, is the antithesis of what the Pharisees were preaching by word and example.

That is why we hear Our Lord pronounce against them a series
of eight maledictions which form a counterpart to the eight beati-
tudes by way of contrast. Read them in their entirety in the Gospel,
where they take up a whole page,[128] and you will see with what
indignation Christ, infallible Truth and the Life of souls, puts the
crowd and His disciples on guard against teaching and conduct
that turn people away from the kingdom of God, that cover up
cupidity and false zeal, that alter the truth of the Law and its re-
quirements, that establish a religion which is wholly one of appearance, that are contented with a purity wholly on the surface,
under which corruption and a persecuting hate lurk deceivingly.

"Woe upon you, Scribes and Pharisees, you hypocrites that shut
door of the kingdom of heaven in men's faces; you will neither
enter yourselves, nor let others enter when they would."[129]

"Woe upon you, Scribes and Pharisees, you hypocrites that
swallow up the houses of widows, under cover of your long prayers
there. Your sentence will be all the more terrible for that."[130]

"Woe upon you, Scribes and Pharisees, you hypocrites that will

[127] Matt. 22:15-17.   [128] Matt. 23:13-33.   [129] Matt. 23:13 (Knox). By en-
cumbering the road to heaven by the multitude of their intolerable require-
ments, and especially by turning away souls from Christ. [These are Marmion's
explanatory notes]   [130] See Matt. 23:14.

take care to pay the tithe for a leaf of mint or dill or cumin but neglect the weightier duties of the Law: justice, mercy, good faith. You should have done those weightier things, while not leaving the other ones undone. Blind guides, you filter water so as not to swallow a gnat, and then gulp down a camel!"[131]

"Woe upon you, Scribes and Pharisees, you hypocrites that scour the outward part of cup and dish, but leave the inside full of extortion and uncleanness."[132]

"Serpents, brood of vipers, how can you escape being condemned to hell?"[133]

What a contrast, on the part of Our Lord, between these violent denunciations, this vehement invective—and His attitude to the biggest sinners, to the Samaritan woman, to Mary Magdalene, to the woman taken in adultery, all of whom He forgives without a word of reproach; towards criminals like the good thief, to whom He promises heaven![134]

What causes this difference? Seeing that Christ Jesus is so ready to stoop down to the aid of sinners, why does He heap such terrible anathemas on the Pharisees, publicly?

It is because every form of weakness, of misery, when it is humbly recognized and acknowledged, attracts the compassion of His heart and the mercy of His Father: "As a father has compassion on his children, so the Lord has compassion on those who fear Him." For He knows "the stuff of which we are made..."[135]

Whereas pride, especially spiritual pride like the sin of the fallen angels, excites the indignation of the Lord: "God resists the proud."[136]

---

[131] See Matt. 23:23-24. The Law forebade the eating of all unclean animals; the Pharisees, exaggerating this requirement, drank nothing that had not been scrupulously filtered, and at the same time they neglected other things prescribed by the Law.   [132] See Matt. 23:25. The Pharisees avoided with ridiculous care the smallest stains of a purely legal kind, but did not take care to avoid sin, which defiles the soul.   [133] Matt. 23:33 (Jerus.)   [134] Luke 23:43.
[135] Ps. 102 (103):13-14 (St P and Knox).   [136] James 4:6; 1 Peter 5:5.

Now, the spirit of the Pharisees is the epitome of everything that is odious and hypocritical in pride. And those who are "proud in the conceit of their heart ... the rich"—rich in their own estimation—are sent away, empty-handed, from the presence of the Lord for ever.[137]

It is to be noted that phariseeism takes many forms. Our Lord did not come down on the Pharisees only because of their hypocritical pride which hid corruption under a cloak of perfection: "whited sepulchers" which appear clean on the outside, but within are filled with corruption and iniquity.[138]

He also reproached them for having substituted a formalism of human origin for the eternal law of God. The Pharisees were scandalized to see Jesus cure the sick on the Sabbath day; they took offense at the apostles not complying, before meals, with all the puerile series of legal ablutions which they, the Pharisees, had invented and in which they made the whole purity of man consist. Placing all sanctity in the minute observance of the traditions and practices that had issued from their own brain, they neglected even the weightiest precepts of divine law. Thus, according to them, one could, by uttering some simple words, consecrate goods or money to the service of the Temple and make them inviolable thereby; so that the devout Pharisee was no longer able to use them even to pay his debts or to provide for the needs of his parents who were in want. That, in the very words of the Savior, was to "have made void the commandment of God by your tradition."[139]

This formalism, wholly of human invention, which deprived religion of its true nature and diminished it, and this false conscience, were so repugnant to the nobleness of heart and sincerity of Jesus, that He unmasked and condemned these things outspokenly. What judgment did He bring to bear on this casuistry

---

[137] Luke 1, vv. 51, 53.   [138] See Matt. 23:27.
[139] Matt. 15:1-9; Mark 7:1-13.

indeed? "I say to you that unless your justice exceeds that of the Scribes and Pharisees, you shall not enter the kingdom of heaven."[140]

What a revelation of the inner character of God! What a manifestation of His way of judging and weighing up men! What a valuable light these bitter reproaches addressed to the Pharisees throw upon the notion of what perfection really is!

In the Sermon on the Mount, Christ shows us the summits of true perfection. In His condemnation of phariseeism, He discloses to us the abysses of false piety, of which the Pharisees were the exact type.

There is no snare of the devil more to be feared, nor one more deadly, than that of making some form of phariseeism pass for the holiness demanded by the Gospel. In this, the prince of darkness attacks even souls who seek perfection; he obscures their inner eye, through the appearances of a virtue that is wholly formalistic being substituted for the truth of the Gospel. Far from making progress in this way, one remains unfruitful before God. "Every tree that my Father has not planted will be rooted up."[141] That is the inexorable sentence of Jesus against the breed of the Pharisees.

You see in this matter how important it is to distrust our own feelings, our own lights; how important it is to base our holiness—not upon such or such a practice or devotion which we choose ourselves and which can be excellent, not upon such or such a thing prescribed by a religious rule we profess (its observance can be suspended by a higher law, such as the law of love of neighbor for example), but above all else, and in very first place, upon the fulfilling of God's law: the natural law, the Ten Commandments, the Commandments of the Church, our civil duties. All piety which does not respect this hierarchy of duties should be suspect to us; all asceticism not governed by the commands and the teaching of the Gospel cannot have come from the Holy

[140] Matt. 5:20. [141] Matt. 15:13.

Spirit who inspired the Gospel. "Only those," says St. Paul, "who are led by the Spirit of God are truly children of God."[142]

So wide is the tenderness of Jesus that at the very hour when He heaps terrible maledictions on the Pharisees and forewarns them of divine anger, the Gospel shows Him to us as deeply moved. The thought of the chastisement that is to fall upon the holy city for having rejected the Messiah through listening to these "blind men,"[143] draws from His sacred heart accents of anguish.

"Jerusalem, Jerusalem, you that kill the prophets, and stone those who are sent to you! How often would I have gathered your children together, as a hen gathers her young under her wings, but you would not!" And alluding to the Temple, which He would no longer enter, for it was the eve of His Passion, He added: "Behold, your house is left to you desolate. For I say to you, you shall not see me henceforth, until you shall say: 'Blessed is He who comes in the name of the Lord!'"[144]

So long as we are here below, the appeals of Eternal Kindness are unceasing: "*How often would I...*" But let us not be among those who, by continued squandering of grace, and the habit of deliberate sin, even though it be venial, harden themselves to the point of no longer understanding those appeals: "*But you would not!*" Let us beware of driving out the Holy Spirit from the temple of our soul by willed and obstinate resistance. God would then abandon us to our blindness: "Behold, your house is left to you desolate." Mercy is never lacking to a soul; it is the soul that, being lacking towards mercy, provokes justice.

Let us rather seek to remain faithful, not with a fidelity which limits itself to the letter, but one that has its source in love, and its support in our trust in a Savior who is full of kindness. Then,

---

[142] See Rom. 8:14. A development of these ideas may be found in the chapter headed *Truth in Charity* in our work *Christ, the Life of the Soul.*
[143] Matt. 15:14.   [144] Matt. 23:37-39.

whatever be our weaknesses, our miseries, our deficiencies and the faults that escape us, the day will dawn when we shall bless for ever Him who appeared on earth with a face that has our human features. He came to cure us of our infirmities, to ransom us from the abyss of sin. It is He also who will crown for ever the gifts of His mercy and His love within us. "Bless the Lord, O my soul ... He pardons all your iniquities, He heals all your ills."[145]

---

[145] Ps. 102 (103), vv. 1, 3-4 (St P)

CHAPTER TWELVE

On the Summit of Tabor
(*Second Sunday of Lent*)

Introduction.

The life of Jesus on earth is, in its very details, of such significance that we can never exhaust all its depths; a single saying from the Incarnate Word, from Him who is always in the heart's-embrace of the Father,[1] is a revelation so great that it can suffice as an ever-living source of salutary life. We see this in the lives of the saints: one word from Him has often been enough to convert a soul totally to God. His sayings come from heaven; hence their fruitfulness.

It is the same with the smallest of His actions; they are for us models, lights, sources of grace.

In the preceding talk I have endeavored to show you some of the aspects of His public life, sufficient to give you a glimpse of that which is ineffably divine, and also inexpressibly human, in that period of three years. To my great regret, I have had to leave on one side many of the Gospel narratives, to pass over in silence many scenes recounted by the sacred writers.

However, there is one page, a unique page and extraordinary to such a degree, a mystery so full of grandeur and at the same

[1] John 1:18.

time so fruitful for our souls, that it merits having a whole talk devoted to it. It is the Transfiguration.[2]

I have said to you often that nothing should be dearer to us than our belief in the divinity of Jesus: first, because nothing is more pleasing to Him; and next, because this belief is at once the basis and foundation, the center and the crowning, of the whole of our interior life. Well, the Transfiguration is one of those episodes in which, particularly, the splendors of this divinity shine forth to human eyes.

Let us, then, meditate upon the Transfiguration with faith, but also with love. The more our faith is a lively faith, the greater will be the love with which we draw near to Jesus in this mystery—and, also, the wider and deeper will be our capacity to be filled inwardly by His light and invaded by His grace.

Christ Jesus, Eternal Word, Divine Master, you who are "the brightness of the Father's glory and the image of His substance,"[3] who yourself have said: "If anyone love me, I will manifest myself to him,"[4] make us love you with fervor, so that we may receive from you a more intense light on your divinity. For it is in your divinity that the secret of eternal life is to be found; in knowing that our Heavenly Father is the one true God, and that you, Jesus Christ His Son, are His anointed one, sent here below to be our King and the High Priest of our salvation.[5] Enlighten the eyes of our soul by a ray of that divine splendor which on Mount Tabor shone forth, so that our faith in your divinity, our hope in your merits, and our love for your adorable person be both strengthened and increased.

---

[2] The Church provides for the Gospel account of the Transfiguration to be read to us twice: on the Second Sunday of Lent, to strengthen our resolve to bear the Lenten mortifications through a distant view of the glory Christ promises us by His Transfiguration; and a second time on August 6th, the Solemnity devoted solely to honoring the manifestation of the divine splendor in Jesus on Mount Tabor.   [3] See Hebr. 1:3.   [4] See John 14:22-23.   [5] See John 17:3.

1. The Gospel account of the Transfiguration.

Let us first go through the account in the Gospels. After that we will apply ourselves to penetrating its meaning.

It is the last year of the public life of Jesus. Up to then, Our Lord has made only rare allusions to His future Passion; but, says St. Matthew, "Jesus began to show His disciples that He must go to Jerusalem and suffer many things from His enemies, and be put to death, and on the third day rise again." And He added: "There are some of those standing here who will not taste death till they have seen the Son of Man appear in the glory of His kingdom."[6]

A few days after this prediction, our Divine Savior took along with Him some of His disciples. They were the three apostles chosen for the purpose: Peter upon whom, a few days before, He had promised He would found His Church;[7] James who was to be the first martyr from among the Twelve Apostles; and John, the disciple Jesus loved especially. Christ Jesus had already chosen them to be witnesses of His raising of Jairus's daughter from the dead;[8] and now He led them up a high mountain to be witnesses of an even deeper manifestation of His divinity. As you know, Tradition sees that "high mountain" to have been Mount Tabor. It rises, isolated and about 2,000 feet high, several leagues to the east of Nazareth. It is covered with rich vegetation; from its summit you can see in all directions.

It is there, to that high place, far from the noise of earth— *seorsum*, "by themselves"[9]—that Jesus went with His disciples. As He did habitually, He entered into prayer; it is St. Luke who gives us that detail: He "went up the mountain to pray." And as He prayed, He was transfigured. "The appearance of His countenance was changed, and His raiment became a radiant white."[10] He was wholly encompassed by a divine atmosphere.

---

[6] See Matt. 16, vv. 21, 28. [7] Matt. 16:18. [8] Mark 5:37; Luke 8:51.
[9] Matt. 17:1; Mark 9:1. [10] Luke 9:28-29.

When Jesus began to pray, the apostles let themselves fall asleep. But then a bright light awakened them, and they saw Jesus resplendent, and at His side Moses and Elijah, conversing with Him. And Peter was filled with such joy at seeing the glory of Jesus that, quite beside himself, "not knowing what he said," he cried out: "Master, it is good for us to be here"[11]—O Lord, it is good to be with you; may this be the end of those battles with the Pharisees, of weariness, of journeys and traveling about, of humiliations and snares set for you; let us stay here, "let us set up three tents, one for you, and one for Moses, and one for Elijah,"[12] and we will remain here with you. This place where they were—they could almost believe they were in heaven, so resplendent was the glory of Jesus, so much did the sight of Him satisfy their hearts.

While Peter was still speaking, a luminous cloud covered them, and from this cloud came a voice that said: "This is my beloved Son, in whom I am well-pleased; hear Him."[13] Straight away the apostles, filled with awe and reverence, threw themselves down in adoration before God.

But a moment afterwards Jesus came near and touched them, and said: "Arise, and do not be afraid." And "lifting up their eyes, they saw no-one but Jesus only":[14] *Neminem viderunt nisi solum Jesum.* They saw Jesus as they had seen Him some little time before, when He was climbing up the mountain with them; they saw Jesus as they were accustomed to seeing Him—Jesus known as "the carpenter's son of Nazareth"; Jesus who, not long after that, would die upon a cross.

---

[11] Luke 9:33; Matt. 17:4; Mark 9:4 (5).   [12] Ibid.
[13] Matt. 17:5.   [14] Matt. 17:8.

2. Significance of this mystery for the apostles who were witnesses of it: Christ wished, by the manifestation of His divinity, to forearm them against the "scandal" of His Passion.

That is the mystery as it is described in the Holy Gospel. Let us now see what its meaning is.

For everything in the life of Jesus the Incarnate Word is full of significance. Christ, if I can so express it, is the great Sacrament of the New Law. What is a sacrament? In the wide sense of the word, it is the outward sign of an inward grace; and one can therefore say that Christ is the great Sacrament of all the graces that God has given to humanity. As St. John the apostle wrote: "The Word was made flesh... And we saw His glory—glory as of the only-begotten of the Father—full of grace and truth"; and he immediately added: "Of His fullness we have all received,"[15] it is from this fullness that we must draw everything. Christ Jesus gives us all graces as God-man, because He has merited them, and because the Eternal Father has constituted Him sole High Priest and Supreme Mediator. Christ gives us these graces in all His mysteries.

I have said to you that the mysteries of Our Lord ought to be for us objects of contemplation, of admiration, of worship. They ought also to be like sacraments which, in the measure of our faith and love, produce in us the particular grace each indicates.

And that is true of all Jesus's circumstances, of every one of His deeds. For though Christ is always the Son of God, though in all He says and does He glorifies His Father first and foremost, we ourselves are no longer out of His thoughts ever; and to each of His mysteries He attaches a grace that is there to help us reproduce in ourselves His divine traits, so as to make us resemble Him.

So that is why Christ Jesus wants us to understand His mysteries, to go deeper into them—with reverence, of course, but

[15] John 1, vv. 14, 16.

also with confidence; wants us above all, as members of His mystical body, to live super-naturally by the interior grace that He wished to attach to them by living them before us and for us.

This is what St. Leo the Great, in speaking of the Transfiguration, says to us: "The Gospel account, which we have just heard with our bodily ears, and which has touched the inward hearing of our minds, invites us to seek out the meaning of this great mystery."[16] Being able to fathom the significance of the mysteries of Jesus is a precious grace: "And eternal life is this: to know you, the only true God, and Jesus Christ whom you have sent."[17] Our Lord said Himself to His disciples: "To you it is given to know the mystery of the kingdom of God, but to the rest in parables."[18]

So important is this grace for our souls, that the Church, guided in this by the Holy Spirit, has made it the very object of her request in the postcommunion of the Feast: "Grant, we beseech thee, Almighty God, that we may understand with purified minds the most holy mystery of the Transfiguration of thy Son, which we now solemnly celebrate."[19]

Let us, then, see the significance of this mystery.

First, its significance for the apostles, as it was in the presence of three of them that the mystery took place.

Why was Christ transfigured before their eyes? St. Leo, again, tells us this very clearly: "The principal object of this transfiguration was to remove from the hearts of the disciples the scandal of the cross. The humiliation of a Passion willingly accepted would

---

[16] *Sermo* 51, for the Saturday before the Second Sunday in Quadragesima. Part of this beautiful sermon forms the Lessons of the Second Nocturn of the Feast of the Transfiguration.   [17] John 17:3 (Jerus.)

[18] Luke 8:10; Matt., 13:11; Mark 4:11.   [19] In passing, one may note that this request forms also the object of the postcommunion of the Feast of the Epiphany, that other "manifestation" of the divinity of Jesus. The same idea is emphasized in the postcommunion of the Mass of the Ascension.

no longer trouble their faith, after the transcendence of the hidden mystery of the Son of God had been revealed."[20]

The apostles, living in close touch with their Divine Master and, moreover, remaining imbued with the prejudices of their race concerning their destiny of a glorious Messiah, could not accept the idea that Christ might suffer. Look at St. Peter, the prince of the apostles. A short time before, in the presence of them all and in their name, he had declared a firm belief in the divinity of Jesus; "You are the Christ, the Son of the living God."[21] The love he bore for Our Lord, and the conceptions, still earthly ones, that he retained about His reign made him reject the idea of the death of his Master. And so when Christ Jesus, a few days before the Transfiguration, had spoken openly to His disciples about His approaching Passion, Peter was upset. Taking Jesus on one side, he protested: "God forbid, Lord, that this should happen to you!" But our Divine Savior immediately reprimanded His apostle: "Get behind me, satan" ("satan" meaning "adversary"), "you who want to put obstacles in the path of the one who sent me; you have no feelings for the things of God, your thoughts are only human ones."[22]

Thus Our Lord foresaw that His apostles would not be able to bear His being humiliated; that His cross would be for them an occasion of their falling-away. These three apostles whom He chose to be present at His transfiguration, He was shortly afterwards to take again, in preference to the others, to witness His weakness, anguish and immense sadness in His agony in the Garden of Olives. He wished to forearm them against the scandal[23] His state of humiliation would then cause to their faith. He wished to strengthen their faith through His transfiguration. How so?

First, by the mystery itself. During His mortal life, Christ Jesus had the appearance of a man like all other men: "being found in

---

[20] *Sermo* 51, op. cit., p. 271.   [21] Matt. 16:16.   [22] See Matt. 16:22-23.
[23] [*Translator's note*: "Scandal," from *scandalum*, cause of stumbling; a stumbling-block to their faith.]

human form,"[24] as St. Paul says. So very true is this, that many of those who saw Him took Him for an ordinary man. Even His near relatives, "His own"—that is, those whom the sacred writer, according to the expression of that time, calls "the brethren of the Lord,"[25] His cousins—hearing such extraordinary doctrine from Him, accused Him of being mad.[26] Those who had known Him at Nazareth, in Joseph's workshop, were astonished and asked themselves where all this wisdom came from: "Is not this the carpenter's son?"[27]

There is no doubt that there was in Jesus a divine power, a wholly inner power, that was manifested by his miracles: "Power went forth from Him and healed all."[28] There was, as it were, a fragrance of His divinity escaping from Him and attracting the crowds. We read in the Gospel that it sometimes happened that the Jews, plain and worldly as they were, went three days without eating in order to be able to follow Him around.[29]

But in Him, outwardly, the divinity was veiled beneath the infirmity of mortal flesh. Jesus was subject to the varied and ordinary conditions of human life. He knew bodily weakness, was susceptible to suffering. He was subject to hunger, thirst, weariness, struggle, flight from His enemies. That was the Christ of every day; that was the humble existence of which the apostles were daily witnesses.

And now, look—on the mountain they see Him transfigured: His divinity shines out, in all its power, through the veil of His humanity. Jesus's face is resplendent like the sun: "His garments," says St. Mark, "became shining, exceedingly white as snow, as no fuller on earth can whiten."[30] Through this marvel, the apostles comprehend that Jesus is truly God; the majesty of His divinity fills them, the eternal glory of their Master is completely revealed.

And now, more: Moses and Elijah appear at Jesus's side, to converse with Him and to adore Him.

[24] Phil. 2:7(8) (RSV, Cath.)   [25] John 7:3.   [26] Mark 3:21.
[27] Matt. 13:55.   [28] Luke 6:19.   [29] Matt. 15:32.   [30] Mark 9:2.

For the apostles as for the Jewish faithful, as you know, Moses and the prophets epitomized everything. Moses was their law-giver; the prophets are here represented by Elijah, one of the greatest of them. In these two persons, the Law and the prophets came to that mountain to attest that Christ is indeed the Messiah, prefigured and foretold. Thenceforth, the Pharisees can attack Jesus, disciples of His can leave Him, but the presence of Moses and Elijah is a proof to Peter and his companions that Jesus respects the Law and is in accord with the prophets; He is indeed the One sent from God, the "one who was to come."

Finally, to crown all the testimonies, to complete the giving of evidence upon the divinity of Jesus, the Eternal Father makes His voice heard. God the Father proclaims that Jesus is His Son, is God like Himself. Thus, everything unites to consolidate the apostles' faith in Him whom Peter has recognized as "the Christ, the Son of the living God."

3. **Threefold grace that this mystery contains for us: it strengthens our faith; it indicates in a special way our super-natural adoption; it makes us worthy of one day sharing in Christ's eternal glory.**

The disciples of Jesus had at that time perhaps not penetrated the full greatness of this scene, or the full depth of the mystery of which they were the privileged witnesses. It was enough that they had been forearmed against the scandal of the cross; that is why Christ "cautioned them, saying: 'Tell the vision to no-one, till the Son of Man has risen from the dead.'"[31]

Later, after the Resurrection, when the Holy Spirit on the day of Pentecost had confirmed them in their high position of apostles, then it was that, through the voice of Peter, they disclosed the splendors they had seen. Peter, the head of the Church, he who

[31] Matt. 17:9; Mark 9:8.

had received from the Word Incarnate the mission of strengthening the faith of his brethren,[32] announced that the majesty of the Lord had been revealed; that Jesus "has received from God the Father honor and glory" on the holy mountain.[33] Peter, the chief shepherd, gives this vision as authority for exhorting his faithful, and us among them, not to waver in their faith.

For it was for us also that the Transfiguration took place. The disciples chosen to be its witnesses, said St. Leo, represent the whole Church; it was to her, as well as to the apostles, that the Father spoke in proclaiming the divinity of His Son and commanding us: "Hear Him."

The Church, in the collect of the Feast, has summed up perfectly the precious teaching of this mystery. For us, as for the apostles, the Transfiguration confirms our faith: "O God, who in the glorious Transfiguration of thine only-begotten Son didst confirm the mysteries of the faith by the testimony of the fathers..." Next, our adoption as children of God is signified by this mystery in a wonderful way. Finally, the Church asks the Father that He graciously make us "co-heirs with the King of glory," sharing His eternal triumph.

The Transfiguration strengthens our faith.

What, indeed, *is* faith? It is a mysterious sharing in God's self-knowledge, in God's knowledge of God as Father, Son and Holy Spirit. The Father, in knowing Himself, begets from all eternity a Son like unto Him, equal to Him. "This is my beloved Son, in whom I am well-pleased." These words are the greatest revelation God could ever make to earth. They are like a very echo of the life of the Father. The Father, in being what He is—Father—lives to beget His Son. This generating of a Son—a generating that has neither beginning nor end—constitutes the very property of being "the Father." In eternity we shall see with astonishment, wonder

[32] Luke 22:32.

[33] 2 Peter 1:16-18; the Epistle of the Feast of the Transfiguration.

and love this "procession," this proceeding, of the Son begotten in the heart's-embrace of the Father. This procession is eternal: "You are my Son, this day have I begotten you."[34] This "today" is the eternal "now" of eternity.[35]

When He tells us that Jesus is His beloved Son, the Father reveals to us His life; and when we believe in this revelation we share in the knowledge of God Himself. The Father knows the Son in the splendors without end. As for us, we know Him in the darkness of faith as we await the clear light of heaven. The Father declares that the child of Bethlehem, the adolescent of Nazareth, the preacher in Judea, the executed criminal of Calvary, is His Son, His beloved Son. Our faith is from believing this.

In the spiritual life, it is an excellent thing always to have before the eyes of our heart, so to say, this testimony by the Father. Nothing can sustain our faith as powerfully. When we read the Gospels, or a Life of Our Lord, when we celebrate His mysteries, when we go to visit the Blessed Sacrament, when we prepare to receive Him in our heart by holy communion, or adore Him there after having received Him—in the whole of our life, in short, let us try to have habitually before us those words: "This is my beloved Son, in whom I am well-pleased."

And let us say then: "Yes, Father, I believe it, and I want to repeat after you: This Jesus who is in me through faith, through holy communion, is your Son; and because you have said it, I believe it; and because I believe it, I adore your Son, so as to render Him homage, and through Him, in Him, to render likewise to you, O Heavenly Father, in union with your Spirit, all honor and glory."

Such a prayer is extremely pleasing to our Father in heaven; and when it is genuine, pure, frequent, it makes us an object of

---

[34] Ps. 2:7.   [35] [*Translator's note*: Words are inadequate to describe this. Concerning the mode of the eternal "begetting," St. Gregory Nazianzen wrote: "Let the doctrine be honored silently; it is a great thing for you to know the fact; the mode, we cannot admit that even angels understand..."]

the Father's love; He envelops us in the delight He takes in His own Son Jesus. Our Lord Himself has told us: "The Father loves you because you have loved me, and have believed that I came forth from God,"[36] that I am His Son. And what a blessing it is for a soul to be an object of the love of the Father, that Father from whom "every perfect gift" comes down,[37] who gladdens hearts.

It is likewise very pleasing to Jesus. He values what proclaims His divinity and our having faith in that divinity, a faith living, strong and deep, one secure against every assault. "Blessed is he who is not scandalized in me"[38]—who, despite the lowering involved in my Incarnation, the humble labor of my hidden life, the attacks and the blasphemies of which I am ceaselessly the object, the struggles that my disciples and my Church have to endure; who, despite all this, remains firm in his faith in me, and is not ashamed of me.

Look at the apostles during the Passion of Jesus; their faith was weak, they ran away. Only St. John followed His Divine Master to Calvary. And we know that after the Resurrection, when on behalf of Christ Himself Mary Magdalene and the other holy women came to say that they had seen Him, risen, they did not believe it, they said it was just women's tales, gossip.[39]

Again, look at the two disciples on the road to Emmaus; Our Lord had to join them, and, "beginning ... with Moses and all the Prophets, He interpreted to them all the things in the Scriptures that referred to Himself," showing them that it was necessary that the Christ "suffer these things before entering into His glory."[40]

Let us, then, believe firmly in the divinity of Jesus; let us never allow that faith to be shaken. To sustain it, let us recall to mind the testimony of the Eternal Father at the Transfiguration. There, our faith will find one of its best supports.

. . .

[36] See John 16:27.   [37] James 1:17.   [38] Matt. 11:6; Luke 7:23.
[39] Luke 24:11.   [40] Luke 24:25-27.

The prayer of the Feast says next that "the voice that came down from a bright cloud didst marvelously show beforehand our completed adoption."

The Eternal Father makes known to us that Jesus is His Son; but, as you know, Jesus is also "the firstborn among many brethren."[41] Having taken our human nature, He grants us, by grace, a sharing in His Divine Sonship. He being God's own Son by nature, we are children of God by grace. Jesus is one of us by His incarnation; and He makes us resemble Him by conferring on us a participation in His divinity, in such a way that we are no longer separate from Him, but with Him make up a single mystical body. That is divine adoption: "that we should be called children of God; and such we are."[42]

In declaring that Jesus is His Son, the Father declares that those who share, through grace, in His, the Father's, divinity are likewise His children, albeit by a different title to be so. It is through Jesus, the Word Incarnate, that this adoption is given to us: "He has begotten us through the Word of Truth," *Genuit nos veritatis*.[43] And by adopting us as His children, the Father gives us the right of one day sharing in His divine and glorious life. That is the "completed adoption," *adoptio perfecta*.[44]

On God's part, it is completed: for all God's works are marked with the seal of an Infinite Wisdom: "O Lord ... you have made all things in wisdom."[45] See, indeed, what riches God has heaped upon His adopted ones so as to make this gift incomparable: sanctifying grace, the infused virtues, the gifts of the Holy Spirit, the helps He grants us every day; the whole of this domain that here below constitutes for us the super-natural order. And, to guarantee us all these riches, there are the Incarnation of His Son, the infinite merits of Jesus which are applied to us in the Sacraments, the Church with all the privileges that her title "Spouse of Christ" confer on her. Yes, this adoption, on God's part, is perfect, completed.

---

[41] Rom. 8:29.   [42] 1 John 3:1.   [43] See James 1:18.
[44] Collect of the Feast of the Transfiguration.   [45] Ps 103(104):24.

But on our part? Here below, completed this adoption cannot be. Since the day when adoption was given to us through baptism, it always goes on developing; it is a seed-germ that has to grow, an outline needing to be filled-in, a dawn that has to reach its noonday. Its perfection we attain when, after we have been perseverantly faithful, our adoption shines forth in glory: "If we are children, we are heirs as well; heirs of God and co-heirs with Christ."[46]

That is why the Church ends the prayer of the Feast by asking that we attain the "perfect," completed, adoption which will only be effected in the glory of heaven: "Be pleased to make us co-heirs with this King of glory, and graciously grant that we partake of that same glory."

In the Transfiguration we see, indeed, a revelation of our future greatness. That glory which encircles Jesus is to become our portion. Why is that? Because He gives to us, as His members, the right to share in the inheritance He possesses as God's own Son.

That is the thought of St. Leo. "By this mystery of the Transfiguration, a providence no less great has founded the hope of the Church. The whole Body of Christ, which is to say, the souls who form His mystical body, can at this present time recognize what a transformation will be accorded it. The members can have assurance that one day they will be made sharers in the honor which in the head of that body shone forth."

Here below, by grace, we are children of God; but what, in consequence of this adoption, we one day shall be, we do not yet know: "Now we are children of God," but "it has not yet appeared what we shall be."[47] The day will come when, lightning having lit up the earth and made it shake and tremble to its foundations,[48] the just, in the words of Jesus Himself, "will shine forth like the

---

[46] Rom. 8:17 (Jerus.)   [47] 1 John 3:2.
[48] Ps. 76 (77):18; Introit of the Feast of the Transfiguration.

sun in the kingdom of their Father."[49] Their bodies will be glorious, like that of Christ upon Mount Tabor; the same glory as reflects on the humanity of the Word Incarnate will transfigure our bodies. St. Paul tells us expressly: Christ "will refashion the body of our lowliness, conforming it to the body of His glory."[50]

Doubtless we should not think that Christ on the holy mountain had all the magnificence of light with which His humanity now shines in heaven. It was barely a ray of it, but so resplendent that it ravished the disciples with delight.

Whence, therefore, did this wonderful radiance come? From Christ's divinity. It was a flowing-forth of the divinity upon the sacred humanity, a radiation of the hearth-fire of Eternal Life that ordinarily was hidden in Christ but which at this hour made His sacred body shine with a marvelous splendor. It was not a borrowed light, coming from outside, but truly a reflection of that immeasurable majesty that Christ contained and kept hidden in Himself. For love of us, Jesus during His earthly existence habitually hid His divine life beneath the veil of His mortal flesh; He prevented it from overflowing in a continuous light that would have blinded our weak eyes. But at the Transfiguration, the Word gave leave to the eternal glory to project its splendor upon the humanity that He, the Word, had taken.

That shows us that our holiness is nothing other than our resemblance to Christ Jesus: not a holiness of which we ourselves can be the first source, but one that is a flowing of divine life into us.

By the grace of Christ, this holiness has been like a light which has begun to shine within us,[51] from the time of our baptism which inaugurated our transformation into an image of Jesus. Here below, indeed, holiness is but an interior transfiguration

---

[49] Matt. 13:43. [*Translator's note*: This is at the General Judgment on the Last Day, when the bodies of those who have died will be joined to their souls again.]   [50] Phil. 3:21.   [51] 2 Peter 1:19; "a light shining in a dark place."

modeled upon Christ. The Father "has destined us to become conformed to the image of His Son."[52] By our fidelity to the action of the Spirit, this image grows little by little, develops, is perfected, until we attain the Light of eternity. Then, the transformation will become evident, in the sight of the angels and the elect. This will be the supreme ratification of a completed adoption that will make spring forth within us an inexhaustible fount of joy.

4. **Means of arriving at the glorious state presaged by the Transfiguration: listening to Jesus, the beloved Son of the Father: "Hear Him."**

Such is the glorious state that awaits us, because that is the glorious state of our head, Jesus, of whom we are the members: a wonderful state which the Transfiguration on the mountain makes us glimpse, and proposes to our faith as an object of hope.

But, you will ask me, what ought we to do to attain that? What road ought we to follow so as to arrive at that blest glory of which we see one ray in the transfiguration of our Divine Savior?

There is only one such road, and it is the Father who will show it us. The Father, who adopts us, who calls us to the celestial inheritance for us to share His beatitude, to participate one day, endlessly, in the fullness of His life—the Father Himself, in this same mystery, indicates to us the way: "This is my beloved Son, in whom I am well-pleased."

It is true that we have already heard these words at Jesus's baptism; but at the Transfiguration the Father adds to them something new, containing the whole secret of our life: "Hear Him." It is as if, in order to make us arrive at Him, the Father refers this to Jesus. And such indeed is the Divine plan.

Being the Son of God, living always in the heart's-embrace of the Father, Jesus, the Word Incarnate, makes known the divine

---

[52] Rom. 8:29.

secrets: "He has revealed Him."[53] He is "the true light that enlightens every man who comes into the world";[54] where He shines,
there is no darkness. To hear Him is truly to hear the Father who
calls us, because Jesus's doctrine has not come from Him alone;
it is the doctrine of the Father who sent Him.[55] Everything He
teaches, His Father bade Him reveal to us: "All things that I have
heard from my Father I have made known to you."[56] He is the
only road that henceforth leads to the Father: "No-one comes to
the Father but through me."[57] In times past, and frequently, God
spoke by Moses and the prophets; but now He only speaks to us
by His Son.[58]

And look: in order to make us understand this very clearly,
Moses and Elijah disappeared when the voice of the Father told
us to listen to His Son: "And after the voice (of the Father) had
spoken, Jesus was found alone."[59] He alone is thenceforth the
one Mediator; He alone fulfills the prophecies and is the Law in
Himself. He substitutes realities for what were only figures and
predictions; He replaces the Old Law, wholly one of servitude,
by the New Law, wholly one of adoption and love. To be a child
of the Eternal Father, to attain adoption, completed and glorious, we have only to listen to Jesus: "My sheep hear my voice."[60]

And when does He speak to us? He speaks to us in the Gospel;
He speaks to us by the voice of the Church, of our shepherds; by
that of occurrences and trials; by the inspirations of His Spirit.

But listening to Him properly needs silence; needs our retir-
ing often, as Jesus did at the Transfiguration, to a solitary place;
seorsum, "by ourselves." It is certainly true that Jesus is to be
found everywhere, even in the tumult of a big city; but one only
listens to Him well within a soul that is quieted and surrounded
by silence; one only understands Him well in prayer and praying;

[53] John 1:18.   [54] John 1:9.   [55] John 7:16.
[56] John 15:15.   [58] John 14:6.   [58] Hebr. 1:1-2.
[59] Luke 9:36 (Jerus.)   [60] John 10:27.

"as He prayed..."[61] It is then above all that He reveals Himself to the soul, so as to attract that soul to Him, to transfigure that soul in Him. At the time when we are praying, let us think that the Father is showing us His Son: "This is my beloved Son." Let us at that time adore Him with a profound reverence, a lively faith and an ardent love. And at that time also we shall hear Him who alone has words of eternal life: "Lord, to whom shall we go? You have words of everlasting life."[62]

Let us listen to Him through faith, through that acceptance of everything He tells us: Yes, Lord, I believe it because you tell us it; you are always in the heart's-embrace of the Father: you see the divine secrets in the splendor of Eternal Light. We for our part believe what you reveal. Faith is for us is that lamp of which the apostle, a witness of your Transfiguration, speaks; the lamp which lights up the darkness to guide us: "a lamp shining in a dark place."[63]

It is in that light surrounded by darkness that we walk; and, despite that same darkness, we should walk valiantly. Listening to Jesus is not only listening with our bodily ears; we listen also with the ears of our heart. Our faith should be a practical one, expressing itself through works worthy of a true disciple of Jesus, conformed to the spirit of His Gospel; what St. Paul calls works "to please God"[64]—a phrase the Church has herself repeated[65] when on our behalf she asks God that we be worthy children of our Heavenly Father.

And this, despite temptations, despite trials, despite sufferings. Let us not listen to the voice of the devil: his suggestions are those of a prince of darkness. Let us not allow ourselves to be carried away by the prejudices of the world: the world's maxims deceive. Let us beware of allowing ourselves to seduced by the

---

[61] Luke 9:29.   [62] John 6:69.   [63] 2 Peter 1:19; the Epistle of the Feast of the Transfiguration.   [64] 1 Thess. 4:1; the Epistle for the Second Sunday of Lent.

[65] "We humbly beseech thee, Almighty God, that we ... may worthily serve thee by lives well-pleasing to thee" (Postcommunion of Second Sunday in Lent).

enticements of the senses: satisfying them brings the soul nothing but trouble.

It is Jesus alone that we must listen to and follow. Let us give ourselves up to Him through faith, trust, love, humility, obedience, *abandon* to Him. If our soul is closed to the noises of earth, to the tumults of the passions and of the senses, the Word Incarnate will become the Master of our soul little by little; He will make us understand that the true joys, the deepest joys, are those which are found in serving Him. The soul that has the happiness of being admitted, like the privileged apostles, into the Divine Master's intimacy will sometimes experience the need to cry out like St. Peter: "Lord, it is good for us to be here."

Undoubtedly, Jesus will not always lead us to Tabor—there where it is "good to be"; He does not always give us feelings of consolation. If He does give us them, we must not spurn them, for they come from Him. We must accept them humbly, but without seeking them again for ourselves or becoming attached to them. St. Leo notes that Our Lord did not reply to Peter when the latter suggested setting up some tents to establish a lasting dwelling in that place of beatitude. Not that He condemned the idea, says St. Leo, but that then was not the time for it. As long as we are still here below, it is more often to Calvary that Jesus leads us—that is to say, through what is opposed to our own will, through trials, temptations.[66]

For, look, what did He talk about with Moses and Elijah on the mountain? Of His divine prerogatives, of His glory that was enrapturing the apostles? No; He spoke about His approaching Passion, of the excess of His sufferings that astonished Moses and Elijah as much as they were dazed by the excess of His love. It is through the cross that Jesus conducts us to life; and because He knows we are weak in trial, He wished by His transfiguration to show us what glory we are called to share with Him, if we re-

---

[66] St. Leo, *Sermo* 51, 5 (On the Transfiguration).

main faithful: "joint heirs of Christ, provided, however, we suffer with Him that we may also be glorified with Him."[67] Here below it is not the time for repose, but the time for toil, effort, struggle, patience.

Let us remain faithful to Jesus, despite everything. He is the Son of God, equal to God the Father—that we know. His words do not pass: He is the Eternal Word. Well, He affirms that those who "follow Him" will attain to "the light of life."[68] Happy are the souls who listen to Him, who listen to Him alone and listen to Him always, without doubting His words, without letting themselves be disturbed by the blasphemies of His enemies, without letting themselves be overcome by temptations, without letting themselves be disheartened by trials![69] "For our present light affliction, which is for the moment, prepares us for an eternal weight of glory that is beyond all measure,"[70] says St. Paul. We do not know what weight of glory is reserved for us because of the least of our sufferings borne in union with Christ Jesus. "God is faithful";[71] and in all the vicissitudes they pass through, God will infallibly guide those faithful souls to the transformation which makes them resemble His Son.

And so, our transfiguration into Jesus comes about little by little, interiorly, until the day when it will be revealed, radiant in that company of the elect who bear the sign of the Lamb, and whom the Lamb transfigures because they are His.

Our Lord Himself has promised us this. "The world shall rejoice," He said before left us, "and you shall be sorrowful"[72]—you here below shall be in affliction, in trials, as I myself was before entering into my glory: "Did not the Christ have to suffer these things before entering into His glory?"[73] That is necessary; it is the way of my Providence; but "take courage,"[74] have confidence;

---

[67] Rom. 8:17.   [68] John 8:12.   [69] St. Leo, Ibid., 8.   [70] 2 Cor. 4:17.
[71] 1 Cor. 10:13; 1:9; 2 Thess. 3:3.   [72] John 16:20.
[73] Luke 24:26.   [74] John 16:33.

"I am with you all days, even unto the consummation of the world."[75] At present, your faith welcomes me every day in the mystery of my self-abasement, but I shall come one day in the full revelation of my glory. And you, my faithful disciples—you will enter into my joy, you will have part in my glory, for you are one with me. Did I not ask my Father at the time when I paid the price for this through my sacrifice?—"Father, *I will* that where I am, they also whom you have given me may be *with me;* in order that they may behold my glory"—the glory that I received from you before the creation of the world.[76] For you whom I call my friends; you to whom I have confided the secrets of the divine life as my Father ordained; you who have believed and have not left me—you will live with my life. A life that is full, a joy that is perfect, because it will be my own life and my personal joy that I shall give you; my life and my joy as Son of God: "so that *my own joy* may be in you, and your joy be *complete.*"[77]

---

[75] Matt. 28:20.   [76] John 17:24.   [77] John 15:11 (Jerus.)

CHAPTER THIRTEEN

"Christ Loved the Church, and Delivered Himself Up For Her"

(*Palm Sunday*)

Introduction.

In giving us an account of the Transfiguration, St. Luke brings up this detail: that Moses and Elijah talked with Jesus about His death.[1]

So therefore, at the very time that for His favored disciples Christ is raising a corner of the veil that hides the splendors of His divinity from the sight of the multitude, He is speaking of His Passion and death. That might seem strange, might it not? And yet, where Christ is concerned there is nothing there which cannot be explained.

The Passion marked the culminating point of the work He came to carry out here below. For Jesus, it was the hour when He consummated the sacrifice that was to give infinite glory to His Father, redeem humanity and re-open to mankind the wellsprings of eternal life. Therefore Our Lord, who was devoted wholly to doing the will of His Father, ardently desired from the first moment of His incarnation to see what He called "His" hour come: "His hour,"[2] the hour par excellence. "I have a baptism"—a baptism of blood—"to be baptized with, and how distressed I am until it is accomplished!"[3]

---

[1] Luke 9:31.   [2] John 13:1.   [3] Luke 12:50.

Jesus longed for the hour to sound when He would be plunged in suffering and would undergo death in order to give us life.

He does not wish to bring that hour nearer, of course; Jesus is fully submissive to the will of His Father. St. John notes more than once that the Jews sought to take Him by surprise and put Him to death; but always Our Lord escaped, even through a miracle, "because His hour had not yet come."[4]

But when the hour did sound, Christ delivered Himself up with the greatest ardor, though He knew in advance all the sufferings that were to overtake His body and His soul. "I have greatly desired to eat *this* Passover with you before I suffer."[5] It had come at last, the hour so long awaited.

Let us contemplate Jesus at that hour. This mystery of the Passion is ineffable, and everything about it is great, to the smallest detail; as moreover are all things in the life of the God-man. Here especially we are at the doors of a sanctuary we cannot enter except with living faith and deep reverence.

A passage of the letter of St. Paul to the Ephesians sums up the essential points we must consider in this mystery. "Christ," he says, "loved the Church"—and "delivered Himself up for her"—"that ... she might appear before Him in all her glory, not having spot or wrinkle or any such thing, but holy and without blemish."[6]

The very mystery of the Passion is indicated by those words. Jesus delivered Himself up in person. And what made Him deliver Himself up? Love is the deep reason for this mystery: He "loved the Church." And the fruit of that oblation of the whole of Himself, through love, is the sanctification of the Church: "That He might sanctify her,"[7] that she might be "holy and without blemish."

Every one of those truths revealed by the apostle has within it treasures of light and fruits of life for our souls. Let us look at them for a few moments. We shall then see how we should participate in the Passion of Jesus so as to draw upon those treasures and gather those fruits.

---

[4] John 7:30; 8:20.   [5] Luke 22:15.   [6] See Eph. 5:29.   [7] Ibid.

1. **Love is the driving-force that made Christ undergo the sufferings of the Passion.**

St. Paul tells us that "Christ loved the Church."

"The Church" here signifies the kingdom of those who, as the same apostle also says,[8] were to form the mystical body of Jesus. Christ loved this Church, and it is because He loved her that He delivered Himself up for her. This love is what commanded the Passion.

To be sure, it was first and above all for love of His Father that Jesus willed to undergo the death of the cross. He Himself said so explicitly: "That the world may know that I love the Father"[9] I carry out the Father's will, which is that I deliver myself up to death.

Look at Christ Jesus during His Agony in the Garden. For three hours long, anxiety, sadness, fear, anguish, rain down on His soul like a torrent; they assail it to the point that the blood escapes from His sacred veins. What an abyss of sorrows there was in that Agony! And what did Jesus say to His Father? "Father, if it is possible, let this cup pass away from me." Does this mean that Christ no longer accepted the will of His Father? Oh, most certainly He accepted it! But this prayer was a cry from the faculty of feeling of poor human nature when it is crushed by aversion and suffering: at that time, He was above all a man *sciens infirmitatem*, "acquainted with infirmity."[10] Our Lord felt a frightful burden of agony weigh down upon His shoulders. He wished us to know this, and that is why He uttered this prayer.

But listen to what He immediately added: "Yet, Father, let your will be done, not mine."[11] In this we have the triumph of love. Because He loves His Father, He put His Father's will above all else and agreed to suffer everything. Note that the Father could, had He so wished in His eternal designs, have cut short the sufferings of Our Lord, have changed the circumstances of His death; but He did not so wish. In His justice, He required that, in

---

[8] 1 Cor. 12:27: "You are the Body of Christ, member for member"; Eph. 1:23; 4:12; 5:23.   [9] John 14:31.   [10] Isa. 53:3.   [11] See Matt. 26:39; Mark 14:36.

order to save the world, Christ should deliver Himself up to all these sorrows. Did that will diminish Jesus's love? Certainly not; He does not say: "My Father might have arranged these things differently." No, He says: "Let your will be done, not mine."

Thenceforth He went on with His sacrifice, to the end. Minutes after His Agony, at the moment of His arrest, when St. Peter wanted to defend Him and struck with his sword one of those who came to seize his Master, what did the Savior immediately say to Him? "Put your sword back in its scabbard; am I not to drink the cup that the Father has given me?"[12]

So therefore, it is above all His love for His Father that made Christ accept the sufferings of the Passion. But, also, it is the love that He bears for us.

At the Last Supper, when the hour for accomplishing His sacrifice sounded, what did He say to His apostles assembled around Him? "Greater love no man has than this, that a man lay down His life for His friends."[13] And Jesus was about to show to us this love that surpasses all other loves, for, says St. Paul, "Christ died for us all,"[14] "when we were still enemies."[15] What greater indication of love could He have given us? None.

Thus it is that the Apostle Paul never ceases to proclaim that Christ "loved us and delivered Himself up for us,"[16] that He "loved me and gave Himself up for me."[17] And "delivered" and "gave"—in what measure? As far as death itself.

What enhances this love infinitely is the sovereign liberty with which Christ Jesus offered Himself: "He was offered because it was His own will."[18] The following two things He said tell us how voluntary the acceptance by Jesus of His Passion truly was. Did He not say one day, when speaking of the Good Shepherd

---

[12] John 18:11 (Jerus.)
[13] John 15:13 (RSV, Cath.)
[14] 2 Cor. 5:15 (Knox).
[15] Rom. 5:10 (Jerus.)
[16] Eph. 5:2.   [17] Gal. 2:20.
[18] Isa. 53:7.

who gives His life for His sheep: "For this reason the Father loves me, because I lay down my life that I may take it up again"—take it up again on the day of my resurrection. And: "No-one takes it from me, but I lay it down of myself. I have the power to lay it down, and I have the power to take it up again."[19]

And see how what He said came true. At the time of His arrest, He asked those who wished to seize Him: "Whom do you seek?" "Jesus of Nazareth." "I am he." At the words "I am he," they "drew back and fell to the ground."[20] He had but to ask, He told them, and His Father "would promptly send me more than twelve legions of angels to my defense."[21] He added: "I sat daily with you in the temple teaching, and you did not lay hands on me."[22] He could have made the same thing as happened before happen now; but He did not wish it, because now "His hour" had come. See Him before Pilate. He avowed that the power the Roman governor had to condemn Him to death came only from His Father: "You would have no power over me were it not given you from above."[23] Had he wished, he would have been able to deliver Himself out of Pilate's hands, but because it was the will of His Father, He abandoned Himself to an unrighteous judge: He "yielded Himself to him who judged Him unjustly."[24]

That liberty with which Jesus gave His life was entire. And it is one of the most wonderful perfections of His Sacrifice, one of the aspects of it that touch our human hearts most deeply. "God so loved the world that He gave His only-begotten Son";[25] and Christ loved His brethren to the extent that He voluntarily delivered up the whole of Himself in order to save them.

---

[19] John 10:17-18.   [20] John 18:4-6.   [21] Matt. 26:53 (Jerus.)
[22] Matt. 26:55; Mark 14:49; Luke 22:53.   [23] John 19:11.
[24] 1 Peter 2:23.   [25] John 3:16.

2. Christ delivered Himself up completely to sorrow and to death.

All was perfect in Jesus's Sacrifice: both the love that inspired it and the liberty with which He accomplished it. Perfect also in the gift offered: Christ offered up *Himself*.

Christ offered up the whole of Himself: His soul and His body were broken, crushed by sorrows: there are no sorrows that He has not known. If you read the Gospel attentively, you will see that Jesus's sufferings were so extensive that all the members of His sacred body were stricken, that all the fibers of His heart were lacerated by the ingratitude of the crowd, by the desertion of those who were His own, by the sorrow of His mother; and that His sacred soul had to undergo all the humiliations that could be heaped on any man. In Him, Isaiah's prophecy came true to the letter: "Many were astonished on seeing Him, so much was He disfigured... no shapeliness or beauty to attract our eyes... like a leper, He seemed to us,"[26] entirely unrecognizable.

I was speaking to you just now about the agony in the Garden of Olives. Christ, who exaggerates nothing, discloses to His apostles that His innocent soul is then oppressed with so piercing and so bitter a sadness that it is capable of making Him die: "My soul is sorrowful even unto death."[27] What an abyss! One who is God, Infinite Power and Beatitude, finds Himself overwhelmed by sadness, fear and anxiety: "He began to feel dread and to be exceedingly troubled,"[28] "to be saddened."[29] The Word Incarnate knew all the sufferings that were about to inundate Him during the long hours of His Passion. That sight aroused in His natural feelings all the repulsion that one who was merely created would have experienced. In the divinity to which it was united, His soul saw clearly all the sins of men, all the outrages committed against God's holiness and infinite love.

---

[26] See Isa. 52:14; 53:2-4.   [27] Matt. 26:38 (Rheims); Mark 14:34.
[28] Mark 14:33.   [29] Matt. 26:37.

He had taken upon Himself all these iniquities, it was as if He were clothed in them; He felt weighing on Him all the anger of divine justice: "I am a worm, and no man: the reproach of men, and the outcast of the people."[30] He foresaw that for many men His blood would be shed in vain, and this sight raised the bitter suffering of His sacred soul to its highest pitch. But, as we have seen, Christ accepted everything. He gets up now, leaves the garden and advances to meet His enemies.

It is here that there begins for Our Lord that series of humiliations and sufferings we can hardly attempt to describe.

Betrayed by the kiss of one of His apostles, pinioned by the soldiery like a malefactor, He is taken to the high priest. There, in face of the false accusations uttered against Him, "He kept silence."[31]

He did not speak, except to declare that He is the Son of God: "You have said it. I am."[32] This avowal of the divinity of Christ is the most solemn one that could ever be made: Jesus, King of martyrs, died for having avowed His divinity, and all the martyrs would give their life for the same reason.

Peter, the head of the apostles, had followed His Divine Master from a distance; he had promised never to desert Him. Poor Peter! You know how, three times, he denied Jesus. That, without any doubt, was for our Divine Savior one of the deepest griefs of that terrible night.

The soldiers guard Jesus and heap on Him insults and bad treatment. Not being able to bear His gaze that is so gentle, they blindfold Him in derision; they give Him insolent slaps on the face. Vilely, they dare to soil with their foul spittle that adorable face the angels never gaze on but with rapture.

The Gospel next shows us how Jesus, when morning comes, is brought back before the high priest, and then dragged from tribunal to tribunal; treated by Herod as a fool—He, Eternal Wisdom;

[30] Ps. 21 (22):7.   [31] Mark 14:57-61; Matt. 26:60-63.
[32] Matt. 26:64; Mark 14:62.

scourged on the orders of Pilate. Pitilessly the executioners strike their innocent victim, whose body is soon no more than one big wound. And yet that cruel scourging is not enough for these men who are no longer men; they thrust a crown of thorns on Jesus's head, they mock and jeer at Him.

The lax Roman governor imagines that the hate of the Jews will be satisfied by seeing Christ in such a pitiable state; He presents Him to the crowd: *Ecce homo,* "Behold the man!"[33] Let us look at this moment on our Divine Master, plunged into that abyss of suffering and ignominy, and let us think that the Father, too, is presenting Him to us and saying to us: "This is my Son, the splendor of my glory—but struck now because of the wickedness of my people."[34]

Jesus hears the cries of this populace in a rage, who prefer a brigand to Him and who, in return for all His benefits, are demanding His death: "Crucify him, crucify him!"[35]

Therefore the sentence of death was pronounced, and Christ, carrying His heavy cross on His bruised shoulders, began His journey to Calvary. What sorrows were still reserved for Him! The sight of His mother whom He loved so tenderly, and whose immense affliction He understood better than anyone; the stripping of His clothing; the piercing of His hands and feet; the burning thirst. Then, the spiteful sarcasm of His most mortal enemies: "So you would destroy the Temple and rebuild it in three days! Then save yourself," and then we will believe you. "He saved others ... he cannot save himself."[36] Finally, His abandonment by His Father whose holy will He had always done: "Father, why have you forsaken me?"[37]

Truly He had drunk the cup to the dregs, He had made come true to the last iota, that is to say, to the smallest detail, what had been foretold of Him. And so, when everything had been accom-

[33] John 19:5. [34] See Isa. 53:8. [35] John 19, vv. 6, 15.
[36] Matt. 27:40-42 (Jerus.); Mark 15:29-32; Luke 23:35.
[37] See Matt. 27:46; Mark 15:34.

plished, as He had drained to the depths all the sorrows and all the humiliations, He could utter His *Consummatum est*. Yes, "everything had been completed"; He had now only to yield up His soul to His Father: "And bowing His head, He gave up His spirit."[38]

When the Church, during Holy week, reads us the account of the Passion, she interrupts it at this point, to adore in silence.

Like her, let us prostrate ourselves; let us adore this Crucified One who has just yielded up His last breath; He is truly the Son of God: "True God from true God."[39] Let us, above all, take part on Good Friday in the solemn Adoration of the Cross which, in the mind of the Church, is to make reparation for the numberless outrages with which the Divine Victim was overwhelmed by His enemies on Golgotha. During this touching ceremony, the Church puts on the lips of the innocent Savior some moving exclamations; they apply literally to the people who killed their God, but we can take the words in a sense that is wholly spiritual: they will make lively feelings of compunction arise in our souls. "O my people, what have I done to thee? or in what have I grieved thee? Answer me.... What more ought I to have done for thee that I have not done? I planted thee as my finest vineyard, and thou hast become exceeding bitter to me: for in my thirst thou gavest me vinegar to drink, and with a lance thou hast pierced thy Savior's side.... For thy sake I scourged Egypt with its firstborn, and thou hast scourged me... I led thee out of Egypt, drowning Pharaoh in the Red Sea, and thou hast delivered me to the chief priests.... I opened the sea before thee, and thou with a spear hast opened my side.... I went before thee in a pillar of cloud, and thou hast led me to the judgment-hall of Pilate.... I fed thee with manna in the desert, and thou hast beaten me with blows and scourges.... I gave thee a royal scepter, and thou hast given me a crown of thorns for my head.... I lifted thee up with great power, and thou hast hanged me upon the gibbet of the cross"!

[38] John 19:30. [39] Nicene Creed.

Let our hearts be touched by these reproaches of one who is God, suffering for men. Let us unite ourselves to that obedience, so full of love, which led Him to the immolation of the cross: "He humbled Himself, becoming obedient to death, even to death on a cross."[40] Let us say to Him: "O Divine Savior, who has suffered so much for love of us, we promise you to do our utmost to sin no longer. Through your grace, O adorable Master, make us die to all that is sin, to all attachments to sin, to every inordinate attachment to the created,[41] that we may live only for you."

For, as St. Paul says, the love Christ has shown us by dying for us "*urges* us" to this: "that they who are alive may live no longer for themselves, but for Him who died for them."[42]

3. How, by His immolation, Christ sanctifies the Church.

Christ's Sacrifice, began at the Incarnation, has been completed. From the pierced side of Jesus spring forth streams of living water to purify and sanctify the Church: "Christ loved the Church, and delivered Himself up for her, that He might sanctify her, cleansing her" so that she would be "holy and without blemish."[43] That is the perfect fruit of this perfect immolation. By one single and sole oblation, Christ brought to perfection, for ever, those sanctified in the whole course of time: "For by one offering He has perfected for ever those who are sanctified."[44]

How has Christ, by His oblation, sanctified the Church?

As you know, our sanctification essentially consists in a participation in the divine nature by sanctifying grace. This grace makes us children of God, God's friends, justified in His sight, heirs to His glory.

---

[40] Phil. 2:8.   [41] [*Translator's note:* Using a shorthand phrase in general use, Marmion refers to attachment "to creatures," *à la créature*. This phrase is close to what an old litany calls "all irregular adherence to this world." The translation used here, and in not dissimilar phrases earlier in this book, draws on what is its generally intended signification, in an effort to avoid misunderstanding.]

[42] See 2 Cor. 5:14-15.   [43] Eph. 5:26-27.   [44] Hebr. 10:14.

Through sin, we are deprived of grace, enemies of God, excluded from the beatitude of heaven.

By His Sacrifice, Christ has destroyed sin, and given us back grace. As St. Paul expressed it, Christ, by letting Himself be nailed to the cross, tore up our sentence of condemnation and of death: "canceling the decree against us,"[45] "reconciling us"[46] for ever with His Father.[47]

Let us not forget, indeed, that Christ stood in the place of the whole of humanity. He united Himself to a sinful race, although sin had never touched Him personally; He was like us in all things, sin excepted.[48] But He bore on His shoulders the sins of all mankind: "the Lord hath laid on Him the iniquity of us all."[49] He took the place of us all, and has made satisfaction for us all by virtue of this. Through love, Christ made Himself liable for our sins jointly with us; and we, through grace, have become able to enjoy the advantage of His satisfactions.[50]

Further, Christ has merited for His Church all the graces necessary for her to form the oganized body willed by Him, one "not having spot or wrinkle ... holy and without blemish."

The value of these merits is, indeed, infinite. Why is that? Is it because His sufferings, as vast and as deep as they could possibly

---

[45] Col. 2:14. [46] See Rom. 5:10. [47] [*Translator's note*: Marmion must not be supposed to be advancing the notion of universal individual *eternal* salvation since the Redemption. Anyone who thinks that for a moment has only to read Marmion's blunt words on hell in *Christ, the Life of the Soul*, following Our Lord's blunt words and warnings in the Gospels. The Redemption was of the whole human race. After the Fall and before the Redemption, no member of the human race was eligible for the eternal beatitude of heaven. After the Redemption—now—every human being is so eligible. That is the point Marmion is now making; heaven (which after the Fall was closed) is now open to everyone, through Christ's Sacrifice on Calvary. But whether a given individual attains to the eternal beatitude of heaven depends on the exercise of that person's free will in the present life; and more particularly, and crucially, on the state of the individual's soul at the moment of death.] [48] Hebr. 4:15.
[49] Isa. 53:6. [50] [*Translator's note*: Marmion, in both parts of this sentence, uses the word *solidaire*—a legal metaphor or analogy.]

have been, knew no limits? Certainly; but He who, through them, merited for us is One who is God; and though He suffered them in His human nature, those sorrows, and the merit they created, belong to One who is God; that is why their worth is limitless.

Christ Jesus has therefore merited for all our graces and all our lights: His death has re-opened for us the gates of life, has transported us from darkness into light:[51] it is the cause of our salvation and of our holiness: "He became to all who obey Him the cause of eternal salvation."[52]

The sacraments, which are the channels by which grace and divine life reach our souls, have their value only through Jesus's Sacrifice. If we are today in a state of grace, to what do we owe it? To our baptism. And our baptism—what has merited *its* fruits? The death of Christ Jesus. It is the same with the Sacrament of Penance; we are washed clean in the blood of the Savior. The power of the sacraments is drawn from the cross; they have efficacy only in continuity with the Holy Passion of Christ.

Leader and head of the Church, Christ has merited for her the abundance of graces that make her beautiful and glorious. The zeal of the apostles, the strength of the martyrs, the constancy of confessors of the faith, the purity of virgins—all are nourished by the blood of Jesus. All the favors, all the gifts that gladden souls; even the unique privileges showered upon the Virgin Mary, were bought by this Precious Blood. And how infinite, this price that was paid! No grace at all is beyond our hoping if our appeal is to our High Priest and Mediator.

It comes to this: that in Jesus we have everything. In Him, nothing is lacking of what is needed for our sanctification: "with Him plentiful redemption."[53] His Sacrifice, offered for all, has given Him the right to communicate to us everything He has merited.

Oh, if we only understood that in Him we have everything! That His infinite merits are ours! If only we had an absolute

---

[51] Col. 1:12-13.   [52] Hebr. 5:9.   [53] Ps. 129 (130):7.

confidence in those merits! During His mortal life Jesus said to the Jews, and repeats now to us: "And I, if I be lifted up from the earth, will draw all things to myself"[54]—once I have been lifted up upon the cross, my power will be such that I can lift up to myself all those who have faith in me. Those who, of old, in the desert, looked upon the bronze serpent lifted up by Moses were cured of the bite-wounds that had smitten them because of their sins.[55] So also they who look at me with faith and love merit to be drawn to me, and I will lift them up to heaven. I, who am God, have consented, for love of you, to be nailed to a cross, like one accursed.[56] In return for this humiliation I have power to draw you to me, to purify you, to adorn you with my grace, and to lift you up to heaven where I now am. I came from heaven; I have ascended to heaven after having offered my Sacrifice; I have power to make you enter there with me, for in this I am your Forerunner. I have power to unite you with me in so intimate a way that "no-one will ever steal from me" anyone whom the Father gave me,[57] whom I redeemed with my Precious Blood. "I give them eternal life; they will never be lost."[58]

"Lifted up from the earth, I will draw all things to myself." When we look at the crucifix, let us think of this infallible promise of our Supreme High Priest, a promise that is the source of absolute confidence. For if Christ died for us "when we were His enemies,"[59] what graces of pardon, of sanctification, can He refuse us now that we detest sin, now that we seek to detach ourselves from inordinate attachment to created beings, from attachment to ourselves, in order to please Him alone?

O Father, draw me to your Son! O Christ Jesus, Son of God, draw me, the whole of me, to you!

---

[54] John 12:32. [55] Num. 21:8-9. [56] Deut. 21:23; Gal. 3:13.
[57] John 10:28-29 (Jerus.) [58] Ibid., v. 28. [59] See Rom. 5:10.

4. Necessity for us to commune with the sufferings of Jesus. Different ways in which this participation can take place: contemplating, with faith, Christ in His Passion; being present at the Holy Sacrifice of the Mass which reproduces the oblation of Calvary; uniting our sufferings with His. Strength that Christ has merited for us to carry our cross with Him.

The death of Jesus is the source of our confidence. But for it to be fully efficacious, we ought ourselves to participate in His Passion. On the cross, Christ Jesus took the place of us all; but though He suffered for all of us, He only applies the fruits of His immolation to us if we associate ourselves with that Sacrifice of His.

How can we take part in the Passion of Jesus? In several ways.

The first is to contemplate Christ Jesus with faith and love, in the stages of His sorrowful journey to Calvary.

Every year, during Holy Week, the Church re-lives with Jesus, day by day, hour by hour, all the phases of that mystery of her Divine Spouse who shed His blood. She places before all her children the spectacle of these sufferings that have saved humanity. In former times, servile work was forbidden during those holy days. All proceedings had to be adjourned, all trade was suspended; legal pleading was not allowed at all. The thought of the God-man redeeming the world by His sorrows occupied all minds, moved all hearts. At present, how many souls, saved by the blood of Christ, pass those holy days in indifference! Let us be all the more faithful in contemplating the different episodes of this sacred mystery in union with the Church. We shall find it a source of priceless graces.

The Passion of Jesus holds such a place in His life, it is so much His work, He has attached so much value to it, that He has willed that the memory of it be recalled among us, not only once a year during the solemnities of Holy Week, but each day. He has Himself instituted a Sacrifice to perpetuate through the ages the memory and the fruits of His oblation on Calvary. It is the Sacrifice of the Mass: *"Do this in remembrance of me."*[60]

To be present at this Holy Sacrifice or to offer it with Christ constitutes an intimate and very efficacious participation in the Passion of Jesus.

On the altar indeed, as you know, is reproduced the same Sacrifice as on Calvary. It is the same High Priest, Jesus Christ, who offers Himself to His Father through the hands of the priest at the altar. It is the same Victim; the only difference is in the manner of His being offered. We sometimes say: "Oh, if only I had been at Golgotha with the Virgin and St. John and Mary Magdalene!" But faith puts us in the actual presence of Jesus immolating Himself on the altar; He renews, in a mystical manner, His Sacrifice, so as to give us a share of His merits and His satisfactions. We do not see Him with our bodily eyes; but faith tells us that He is there, and for the same ends as those for which He offered Himself on the cross. If we have a living faith, it will make us prostrate ourselves at the feet of Jesus who is immolating Himself; it will unite us to Him, to His feelings of love for His Father and for mankind, and to His hatred of sin. It will make us say with Him: "Behold, I come to do your will, O God."[61]

We shall especially enter into these sentiments if, after having offered ourself, with Jesus, we unite ourself to Him by sacramental communion. At that time Christ gives Himself to us, as the one who comes to expiate and destroy sin within us. On the cross He made us die with Him to sin: "With Christ I am nailed to the cross,"[62] says St. Paul. At those supreme moments Christ has not separated us from Him; He has granted us to overthrow within us the reign of evil, which caused His death, in order that we may have part in the holy and irreproachable assembly of the elect: "without spot or stain."

. . .

[60] Luke 22:19; 1 Cor. 11:24. [61] Hebr. 10:7; Ps. 39 (40):8-9.
[62] Gal. 2:19 (Rheims).

Finally, we can also associate ourselves with this mystery by bearing, for love of Christ, the sufferings and adversities that, in the designs of His providence, He gives us to undergo.

When Jesus made His way to Calvary, bowed under His heavy cross, He fell down beneath its weight—He, *Virtus Dei*, "the Strength of God";[63] we see Him humiliated, weak, prostrate on the ground, He is incapable of carrying His cross. This was a homage His humanity rendered to the power of God. Had He so willed, Jesus, in spite of His weakness, could have carried His cross all the way to Calvary; but at that moment His divinity wills, for our salvation, that His humanity shall feel weakness, in order that it merit for us the strength to bear our sufferings.

To us also God gives a cross to carry, and everyone thinks his own cross to be the heaviest. We ought to accept our cross without argument, without saying "God could have changed this or that circumstance of my life." Our Lord told us: "If anyone wishes to come after me"—wants to be my disciple—"let him … take up his cross, and follow me."[64]

In that generous acceptance of *our* cross, we shall find union with Christ. For note well, that in carrying our own cross, we truly take our share of that of Jesus. Consider what is recounted in the Gospel. The Jews,[65] seeing their victim becoming weak, and fearing He would not have the strength to reach Calvary, stopped Simon of Cyrene upon the way, and forced him to help the Savior.[66] As I have just said to you, Christ, had He so willed, could have drawn on His divinity for the necessary strength, but He consented to be helped. He thereby wished to show us that each of us ought to aid Him to carry His cross. Our Lord says to us: "Accept that part of my sufferings which, in my divine prescience, on the day of my Passion, I reserved for you."

[63] See 1 Cor. 1:24.   [64] Matt. 16:24; Mark 8:34; Luke 9:23.
[65] [*Translator's note*: It was in fact the Roman soldiers.]
[66] Matt. 27:32; Mark 15:21.

How could we refuse to accept, from the hands of Christ, this sorrow, this opposition to our wishes, that adversity? to drink a few drops from the cup which He Himself presents to us, and from which He has drunk first? Let us therefore say to Him: "Yes, Divine Master, I accept this share, with all my heart, because it comes from you." Let us therefore take hold of it, as Christ took hold His cross, for love of Him and in union with Him. We shall sometimes feel our shoulders sag beneath the burden; St. Paul confesses that certain hours of his existence were so full of worry and annoyances that he was "weary even of life"[67] But, like the great apostle, let us look at Him who so loved us that He delivered Himself up for us. At those hours when the body is tortured, or the soul crushed, or the mind lives in darkness, or the deep action of the Holy Spirit in His purifying operations makes itself felt, let us unite ourselves to Christ with more love still. Then the power and the unction of His cross will be communicated to us, and we shall find there, along with strength, that peace and that inner joy which knows how to smile in the midst of suffering: "I overflow with joy in all our troubles," declares St. Paul.[68]

Those are graces Our Lord has merited for us. Indeed when He mounted to Calvary aided by the Cyrenean, Christ Jesus, God-man, thought of all those who in the course of the centuries would help Him carry His cross by accepting their own. He at that time merited for them inexhaustible graces of strength, resignation and self-surrender that would make them say, as He did: "Father, let your will be done, not mine!" How so?

There is here an essential truth on which we ought to meditate.

The Word Incarnate, head of the Church, took hold of His share of sorrows, the greatest share; but He wills to leave a share of suffering to the Church, which is His mystical body. St. Paul makes us understand this, by words which are profound, even though they seem strange: "What is lacking in the sufferings of Christ I fill up in my flesh for His body, which is the Church."[69]

---

[67] 2 Cor. 1:8. [68] 2 Cor. 7:4. [69] Col. 1:24.

Is, then, anything lacking in the sufferings of Christ? Certainly not. They were superabundant, immense; and their merit is infinite: "with Him plentiful redemption." Nothing is lacking in the sufferings by which Christ has saved us. Then why does St. Paul speak of a "filling-up" that he himself must bring? St. Augustine gives us the answer: "The whole Christ," he says, "is formed of the Church united with its head, who is Christ. The leader has suffered everything He was to suffer; what remains is that the members, if they wish to be worthy of their leader, shall in their turn bear their share of sorrows."[70]

We have, then, as members of Christ, to join in His sufferings. Christ has reserved for us a participation in His Passion; but in doing so He has placed by the side of the cross the strength necessary to carry it. For, says St. Paul, Christ, because He Himself has experienced suffering, has become for us a High Priest full of compassion.[71]

5. The Passion does not end the cycle of the mysteries of Jesus. By His sufferings, Christ merited to enter into eternal glory. That law is likewise ours: if we share the sorrows of Jesus on the cross, we shall partake also of His glorious life: "I go to prepare a kingdom for you."

There is more still. We having obtained the grace to carry our cross with Him, Christ Jesus likewise grants us to share in His glory, after having been associated with His sufferings: "if we suffer with Him, that we also may be glorified with Him."[72] For us as for Him, this glory will be in the measure of our "passion." The glory of Jesus is infinite, because He, being God, has in His Passion gone to the utmost degree of suffering and humiliation. And it is because He has so deeply abased Himself that God has given Him such glory: "Therefore God the Father has exalted Him."[73]

[70] *Enarrat. in Ps.* 86 (87):5.   [71] Hebr. 2:17-18; 4:15; 5:2.
[72] Rom. 8:17.   [73] Phil. 2:9.

The Passion of Jesus, indeed, as important as it was in His life, as necessary as it is to our salvation and our sanctification, does not end the cycle of His mysteries.

When reading the Gospel you will have observed that when Our Lord speaks of His Passion to the apostles, He always adds that He will "on the third day rise again."[74] These two mysteries are equally linked together in the thought of St. Paul, whether he is speaking of Christ alone or alluding to the mystical body. Well, the Resurrection marks for Jesus the dawn of His life in glory.

That is why the Church, when she commemorates solemnly the sufferings of her Spouse, mingles accents of triumph with her feelings of compassion. The vestments of black or violet, the stripping of the altars, the "lamentations" taken from Jeremiah, the silencing of the bells, witness to the bitter desolation gripping the heart of her His spouse on those anniversary days of the great drama. And what hymn does she make ring forth at that time? A song of triumph and of glory, the *Vexilla Regis*:

> Abroad the royal banners fly,
> Now shines the Cross's mystery ...
>
> O lovely and refulgent Tree,
> Adorned with purpled majesty ...
>
> Blest Tree, whose happy branches bore
> The wealth that did the world restore ...
>
> That which the prophet-king of old
> Hath in mysterious verse foretold
> Is now accomplished, as we see
> God rule the nations from a Tree.
>
> O Trinity, we praises sing
> To Thee, from whom all graces spring;
> Celestial crowns on those bestow
> Who conquer by the Cross below.

[74] Matt. 16:21; 17:22; 20:19.

And, from another hymn:

> Sing, my tongue, the Savior's glory,
> Tell His triumph, far and wide;
> Tell aloud the famous story
> Of His body crucified;
> How upon the cross a victim,
> *Vanquishing in death*, He died.[75]

The cross represents the humiliations of Christ; but since the day when Jesus was nailed to it, it occupies a place of honor in our churches. Instrument of our salvation, the cross became for Christ the price of His glory: "Did not the Christ have to suffer these things before entering into His glory?"[76]

It is the same as that for us. Suffering has not the last word in the Christian life. After having shared in the Passion of the Savior, we partake of His glory also.

On the very eve of His death, Jesus says to His disciples: "You are they who have continued with me in my trials"; and He immediately adds that, in return, He prepares for them a kingdom, as His Father has prepared one for Him: "As my Father appointed a kingdom for me, so do I appoint for you."[77] This divine promise applies equally to us. If we have stayed with Jesus in His trials, if with faith and love we have often contemplated His sufferings, Christ will come, when our last hour sounds, to take us with Him that we may enter into the kingdom of His Father.

The day will arrive, sooner than we think, when death will be close to us. We shall be stretched out on our bed, without movement. Those around us will be looking at us, silent in their powerlessness to help us. We shall no longer have any vital contact with

---

[75] [*Translator's note:* The *Pange lingua*, by Fortunatus (as is the *Vexilla Regis*). It is not to be confused with the *Pange lingua* of St. Thomas Aquinas, sung on Maundy Thursday.]   [76] Luke 24:26.   [77] Luke 22:28-29 (RSV, Cath.)

the outside world; our soul will be one-to-one[78] with Christ. We shall know then what "staying with Him in His trials" is; we shall understand Him when He says to us, supreme and decisive, in that agony which is now ours: "You never left me in my agony; you accompanied me when I went to Calvary to die for you. Here I am now; I am near you, to help you, to take you with me. Do not be afraid, have confidence, I am here!": "It is I, fear not."[79] We shall then repeat, in full assurance, the words of the Psalmist: O Lord, though the very shadow of death surrounds me already, I "fear no evil, for you are with me."[80]

---

[78] [Translator's note: Marmion's expression is seul-à-seul, "alone together."]
[79] Luke 24:36 (Rheims); John 6:20.   [80] Ps. 22 (23):24 (RSV, Cath.)

CHAPTER FOURTEEN

IN THE STEPS OF JESUS, FROM THE PRAETORIUM TO CALVARY

(Holy Week)

Introduction.

The Passion constitutes the "Holy of holies" of the mystery of Jesus. It is the crowning point of His public life, the summit of His mission here below, the work to which all the others converge, or from which they draw their value.

Every year, during Holy Week, the Church commemorates its different phases, in detail. Every day, in the Sacrifice of the Mass, she renews for us the memory of it and the reality of it, in order to apply its fruits to us.

To this central act of the liturgy there is added a pious practice which, though not part of the official public worship oganized by the Spouse of Christ, has become very dear to souls because of the abundant graces of which it is the source. It is the devotion to the Passion of Jesus in the very well-known form of "the Way of the Cross."

The immediate preparation made by the Savior for His oblation as High Priest on Calvary was the carrying of His cross, from the Praetorium to Golgotha, weighed down with sorrows and opprobrium.

The Virgin Mary and the first Christians must, more than once, have devoutly retaken that road He took, watering with their tears the places sanctified by the sorrows of the God-man.

You know also with what enthusiasm and fervor the faithful of the West in the Middle Ages undertook the long and arduous pilgrimage to the Holy Places, in order to venerate there the way that had been stained with the Savior's blood. Their piety was nourished by a fruitful source of priceless graces. Returned to their own land, they had it at heart to preserve the memory of the days they had spent at Jerusalem in prayer. Especially from the fifteenth century onwards, this led, almost everywhere, to reproductions being made of the sanctuaries and "stations" of the Holy City. The piety of the faithful was thus able to be satisfied by spiritual pilgrimages renewed at will. Subsequently, in relatively recent times, the Church enriched this practice by attaching to it the same indulgences as are gained by those who at Jerusalem follow the "Stations of the Cross."

1. **Why contemplation of the sorrows of the Word Incarnate is sovereignly fruitful for souls. No detail is negligible in the Passion of Christ, Son of God and object of the Father's delight. Jesus particularly manifests His virtues in the course of His Passion: ever living, He produces in us the perfection we contemplate in Him during His immolation.**

This contemplation of the sufferings of Jesus is very fruitful. I am convinced that outside the Sacraments and liturgical acts, there is no practice more useful for our souls than the Way of the Cross made with devotion. It is of sovereign super-natural efficacy. Why is that?

First, because the Passion of Jesus is His work par excellence; almost all its details were prophesied; there is no other mystery of Jesus of which the circumstances were foretold so carefully by psalmist and prophets. And when one reads the Gospel account of the Passion, one is struck by the attention Jesus gives to the "fulfilling" of that which has been foretold of Him. At the Last Supper, if He permits the presence of Judas the traitor it is "that the Scripture may be fulfilled."[1] To the Jews who have come to lay hold of Him, He Himself says that He is freely delivering Himself up to them to fulfill "the Scriptures of the prophets."[2] On the cross, says St. John, "Jesus, knowing that all things were now accomplished, *that* the Scripture might be fulfilled, said

---

[1] John 13:18.   [2] Matt. 26:56.

'I thirst.'" John is relating how the Savior calls to mind the psalmist's prediction about Him: "In my thirst they gave me vinegar to drink."[3] For even that prophecy to be accomplished —at that very time, in all its detail—Jesus cries out "I thirst"; and having attached "a sponge full of vinegar" to a stick of hyssop, they put it to His mouth.[4] Nothing in this is small or negligible, because all these details mark the actions of this One who is the God-man.

The Father is well-pleased by all these things done by Jesus. He contemplates His Son with love not only when Christ is in all the brightness of His glory on Tabor, but also when Pilate shows Him to the crowd, crowned with thorns and become the outcast of humanity. The Father envelops His Son in gazes of infinite pleasure and no less in the ignominy of the Passion than in the splendors of the Transfiguration: "This is my beloved Son, in whom I am well-pleased." And what is the reason for this?

That Jesus during His Passion honors and glorifies His Father in an infinite measure, not only because He is the Son of God but also because He abandons Himself to all that justice and love of His Father asks of Him. He has been able to say, in the course of His public life, "I do always the things that are pleasing to Him,"[5] and that is particularly true of those hours when, in order to recognize the rights of Divine Majesty outraged by sin and to save the world, He delivered Himself up to death, and death on a cross: "that the world may know that I love the Father."[6] The Father loves Him, with a love that has no limits, because He gives His life for His sheep and because, through His sufferings and satisfactions, He merits for us all the graces that give back to us friendship with God: "*For this reason* the Father loves me, *because* I lay down my life."[7]

We also ought to love to meditate on the Passion because it is there too that Christ makes His virtues shine out. He possesses all the virtues in His soul, but the occasion for manifesting them came

---

[3] Ps. 68 (69):22 (21).   [4] John 19:28-30 (Rheims).   [5] John 8:29.
[6] John 14:31.   [7] John 10:17.

especially at His Passion. His immense love for His Father, His charity towards mankind, His hatred of sin, His forgiveness of injuries, His patience, His gentleness, His strength, His obedience to legitimate authority, His compassion—all these virtues shine out in an heroic way during the days of His sorrows.

When we contemplate Jesus in His Passion, we see the Exemplar of our life, the model—admirable and at the same time accessible—of those virtues of compunction, abnegation, patience, resignation, abandon to God's will, charity, gentleness, that we ought to practice in order to become like our divine head: "If anyone wishes to come after me, let him deny himself, and take up his cross, and follow me."[8]

There is a third aspect which too often we forget, but which nevertheless is of extreme importance. When we contemplate the sufferings of Jesus He grants us, according to the measure of our faith, the grace to practice the virtues He revealed during those sacred hours. How so?

When Christ lived on earth, there emanated from His divine person an all-powerful strength which cured bodies, enlightened minds and gave life to souls: "Power went forth from Him and healed all."[9]

Something analogous happens when we put ourselves into contact with Jesus by faith. Christ surely bestowed special graces on those who, with love, followed Him on the road to Golgotha or were present at His immolation. He still maintains that power now. And when, in a spirit of faith, so as to feel for Him in His sufferings and to imitate Him, we follow Him from the Praetorium to Calvary and take our place at the foot of the cross, He gives us those same graces, He makes us partakers of the same favors. Never forget that Christ Jesus is not a model who is dead and inert. Ever living, He produces super-naturally, in those who draw near to Him with the required dispositions, the perfection they behold in His person.

At each Station of the Cross, our Divine Savior presents Himself to us in His threefold character of Mediator who saves us by His merits;

---

[8] Matt. 16:24; Mark 8:3-4; Luke 9:23; 14:27.   [9] Luke 6:19.

perfect Model of sublime virtues; and Efficacious Cause who can effect within our souls, by His divine omnipotence, the virtues of which He gives us the example.

You may say to me that these characteristics can be found in all the mysteries of Jesus Christ. This is true; but in what plenitude do we find them in the Passion, which is par excellence the mystery of Jesus!

That is why, if for several moments each day, suspending your work, abandoning your preoccupations, silencing in your heart the noise of all things created, you accompany the God-man on the road to Calvary with faith, humility and love, with a real desire to imitate the virtues He manifests in His Passion, then be assured that your souls will receive choice graces that will transform them little by little into a resemblance of Jesus, and of Jesus crucified. Now, is it not in such a resemblance that St. Paul places the whole of sanctity?

It is enough, in order to gather the precious fruits of this practice, as it is for gaining the numerous indulgences with which the Church enriches it, that you pause at each Station of the Cross and there meditate on the Passion of the Savior. No formula of prayer is prescribed, no form of meditation is imposed—not even meditation on the subject to which the specific "station" alludes. Full liberty is left to the taste of each person and the inspiration of the Holy Spirit.

2. Meditations on the "stations" of the Way of the Cross.

Let us now make together the Way of the Cross. The "considerations" I shall give you at each station (I need hardly say this) have no other aim than to aid meditation. Each can take from them what he wishes; each can vary these considerations and affections following the aptitudes and needs of his soul.

Before beginning, let us remember what St. Paul advises: "Have this mind in you which was also in Christ Jesus... He humbled Himself, becoming obedient to death, even to death on a cross."[10] The deeper we enter into the dispositions that the heart of Jesus had in treading

---

[10] Phil. 2, vv. 5, 8.

the way of sorrows: love for His Father, charity towards mankind, hatred of sin, humility, obedience, the more our souls will be filled with graces and lights, because the Eternal Father will see in us a more perfect image of His Divine Son.

My Jesus, you went on that journey for love of me, carrying your cross. I wish to make that journey with you and in the way you did. Imbue my heart with the feelings that overflowed from your heart during those sacred hours. Offer to your Father for me the Precious Blood you shed then for my salvation and my sanctification.

I. Jesus is Condemned to Death by Pilate

Jesus stands before the Roman Governor.[11] He stands there because He, the Second Adam, is the head of the whole race that He is about to redeem by His immolation. The first Adam had, by His sin, merited death: "For the wages of sin is death."[12] Jesus, innocent, but laden with the sins of the world, is to expiate them by His Sacrifice, by the shedding of His blood. The chief priests, the Pharisees, His own people, surround Him like furious bulls.[13] Above their clamors our sins cry out and tumultuously demand the death of the just man: "Crucify him, crucify him!" The lax Roman Governor hands the Victim over, to be nailed to a cross: "He handed Him over to them to be crucified."[14]

What does Jesus do? Although He is standing there because He is our head; although in St. Paul's phrase He "bore witness"[15] to the truth of His doctrine, and to the divinity of His person and of His mission, He nevertheless humbles Himself interiorly before the judgment pronounced by Pilate: "You would have no power at all over me were it not given you from above."[16] In this earthly power, unworthy but legitimate, Jesus sees the majesty of His Father. And what does He do? He delivers Himself up, more than *being* delivered up: He "yielded Himself up to him who judged Him unjustly."[17] He abases Himself by obeying the judgment even to the extent of death; He voluntarily accepts, for our sakes, so as to give us life, the sentence of condemnation: "He was

[11] Matt. 27:11.   [12] Rom. 6:23.   [13] Ps. 21 (22):13 (12).
[14] John 19:15-16.   [15] 1 Tim. 6:13.   [16] John 19:11.   [17] 1 Peter 2:23.

offered because it was His own will."[18] Just as the disobedience of one man, Adam, brought in its train the fall of a great number, so the obedience of one man, Christ Jesus, established them in justice.[19]

We should unite ourselves with Jesus in His obedience, accept everything our Heavenly Father places on our shoulders, through whatever persons—a Herod or a Pilate—from the moment their authority is legitimate. From now on let us, in expiation of our sins, accept death together with all the circumstances with which it may please Providence to surround it; let us accept it as a homage rendered to Divine Justice and Holiness, outraged as they have been by our sins. United to the death of Christ Jesus, our death will become "precious in the sight of the Lord."[20]

My Divine Master, I unite myself to your Sacred Heart in its perfect submission and complete abandonment to the will of the Father. May the power of your grace produce in my soul that spirit of submission which will deliver me up, without reserve or murmur, to the good pleasure from on high, to everything it shall please you to send me at the hour when I must depart this world.

II. JESUS IS LADEN WITH HIS CROSS.

Pilate then handed Jesus over to be crucified, and they led Him forth, "Himself bearing the cross."[21] Jesus had made an act of obedience, He had delivered Himself up to the will of His Father; and now the Father shows Him what it is that obedience places upon Him: it is the cross. He accepts it as coming from the hands of His Father, with all the sorrows and ignominies it entails. At that moment Jesus accepted the increase of suffering brought by this heavy load on His bruised shoulders, and the unspeakable tortures that would be inflicted upon His members, upon His sacred limbs, at the time of His crucifixion. He accepted the bitter sarcasm, the hate-filled blasphemies, with which His worst enemies, in their apparent triumph, would deluge Him as soon as they saw Him hanging on the infamous gibbet. He accepted the agony

---

[18] Isa. 53:7.   [19] Rom. 5:19.   [20] Ps. 115 (116):15.   [21] See John 19:17.

of the three hours on the cross, the abandonment by His Father. We ourselves can never fathom the abyss of affliction to which our Divine Savior consented when He received the cross. At that moment also, Christ Jesus, who took the place of us and who was about to die for us, accepted the cross for all His members, for each of us: "Truly He has borne our infirmities and carried our sorrows."[22] To His own sufferings He united, at this same time, all the sufferings of His mystical body, making them draw from that union their value and their reward.

Let us therefore accept our cross in union with Him, so as to be worthy disciples of this divine head. Let us accept it without raising objections or murmuring. Heavy as was the cross which His Father had laid upon His shoulders, did it diminish Jesus's love for His Father, His confidence in Him? Quite the contrary. "Shall I not drink the cup that the Father has given me?"[23] Let it be so with us also. "If someone wishes to be my disciple, let him take up his cross, and follow me." May we not be among those whom St. Paul calls "enemies of the cross of Christ."[24] Let us rather take up our cross, the one God lays on our own shoulders; in the generous acceptance of this cross we shall find peace. Nothing so gives peace to a soul who suffers as this entire abandon to God's good pleasure.

My Jesus, I accept all the crosses, all the contradictions of my will, all the adversities that the Father has destined for me. May the unction of your grace give me the strength to carry those crosses with the same abandon that you have shown us in receiving your cross for our sakes: "God forbid that I should glory save in the cross of our Lord Jesus Christ"[25]—save in a participation in your sufferings.

III. Jesus Falls the First Time.

He will be "a man of sorrows, and acquainted with infirmity."[26] That prophecy of Isaiah is accomplished to the letter. Jesus, exhausted by His sufferings of soul and body, sinks down beneath the weight of the cross: the Almighty falls from weakness. This weakness of Jesus does

[22] See Isa. 53:4.   [23] John 18:11.   [24] Phil. 3:18.   [25] Gal 6:14.   [26] Isa. 53:3.

honor to His divine power. By it, He expiates our sins, He atones for the rebellions of our pride, and lifts up a world incapable of saving itself: "O God, who in the humility of your Son didst raise up a fallen world..."[27] More, He merited for us at that time the grace to humble ourselves for our sins, to acknowledge our falls, to confess them sincerely. He merited for us the grace of strength to aid our weakness.

In the presence of Christ prostrate before His Father, let us detest those times when our vanity and our ambition assert themselves; let us acknowledge the extent of our weakness. As much as God puts down the mighty, so does a humble avowal of our weakness attract His mercy: "As a father has compassion of his children, so ... the Lord knows the stuff of which we are made."[28] Let us cry out to God for mercy in those moments when we feel ourselves weak in face of the cross, of temptation, of the accomplishing of the divine will: "Have mercy on me, O Lord, for I am weak."[29]

O Christ Jesus, prostrate before your cross I adore you. "Power of God,"[30] you show yourself overwhelmed with weakness in order to teach us humility and put our pride to shame. O High Priest all-holy, who have gone through our trials so as to be able to sympathize with us in our infirmities,[31] do not abandon me to myself, for I am nothing but weakness. May your strength dwell in me[32] so that I do not succumb to evil.

IV. JESUS MEETS HIS AFFLICTED MOTHER.

For the Virgin Mary the day had come when the prophecy made by Simeon was in her to come fully true: "A sword shall pierce your own soul."[33] In the same way that on an earlier occasion she had united herself to Jesus in offering Him in the Temple, now she wishes more than ever to join her feelings with His and to share His sufferings at this hour when Jesus is about to complete His Sacrifice. She betakes herself to Calvary where she knows her Son is to be crucified. On the

---

[27] Prayer of Second Sunday after Easter.   [28] See Ps. 102 (103):13-14.   [29] Ps. 6:3.
[30] 1 Cor. 1:24.   [31] Hebr. 4:15.   [32] 2 Cor. 12:9.   [33] Luke 2:35 (Jerus.)

way there, she meets Him. What an immense sorrow to see Him in that frightful state! They look at each other, and deep calls to deep— the abyss of suffering of Jesus and the abyss of compassion of His mother. What is there that she would not do to help Him?

This encounter was at the same time a source of sorrow and a cause of joy for Jesus. A sorrow, in seeing the profound desolation into which His very sad state was plunging the soul of His mother; a joy, in the thought that His sufferings were paying the price of all the privileges that had been, and would be, showered on her.[34]

That is why He hardly pauses. Christ had the tenderest heart there could possibly be. At the tomb of Lazarus He shed tears; He wept over the misfortunes that would be coming upon Jerusalem. Never did son love his mother as much as He did; when He encountered her so desolate on the road to Calvary it must have moved Him in every fiber of His heart. And yet, He continues His journey to the place of His execution, because that is the will of His Father. Mary associates herself with this feeling; she knows that all things have to be accomplished for our salvation; she takes her part in the sufferings of Jesus by following Him all the way to Golgotha, where she will become co-redemptrix.

Nothing of the human ought to hold us back in our onward journey to God; no natural love ought to put a shackle on our love for Christ. We must continue further in order to stay united to Him.

Let us ask the Virgin, in her contemplation of Jesus's sufferings, to associate us with her, and to give us a share of the compassion she showed for Him, so that we may thereby obtain a hatred of sin which has required such an expiation. It has occasionally pleased God to imprint on the bodies of some saints, like St. Francis of Assisi, the stigmata of the wounds of Jesus, so as to manifest in a form perceptible to the

---

[34] [*Translator's note*: It is the Church's teaching that the privileges given to Mary in view of her destiny to conceive and bring forth Christ, including her being preserved from stain of original sin from the first moment of her own existence, are entirely derived from the Redemption and were applied to her by the Trinity in anticipation of the Redemption.]

senses the fruit produced by contemplation of the Passion. We ought
not to desire those exterior marks; but we ought to ask that an image
of the suffering Christ be imprinted in our hearts. Let us beg the Virgin
for this special grace:

> Holy Mother, pierce me through,
> In my heart each wound renew
> Of my Savior crucified.[35]

O Mother, behold your Son; through the love that you bear Him
may a remembrance of His sufferings accompany us wherever we go.
It is in His name that we seek this; to refuse it to us would be to refuse
it to your Son Himself, seeing that we are His members. O Christ
Jesus, behold your mother; for her sake, grant that our hearts be with
you in your sorrows, so that we come to resemble you.

V. SIMON OF CYRENE HELPS JESUS TO CARRY HIS CROSS.

"As they went out, they came across a man from Cyrene, named
Simon, and commandeered him to carry Jesus's cross."[36] Jesus is exhausted. The Almighty though He be, He wishes His sacred humanity,
laden with all the sins of the world, to bear the weight of justice and
expiation. But He wishes us to help Him carry His cross. Simon represents us all, and it is all of us that Christ asks to share His sufferings:
we are only His disciples on that condition. "If anyone wishes to
come after me"—to walk in my footsteps—"let him take up his cross,
and follow me." The Father has decided that a share of sorrows be left
to the mystical body of His Son, that a portion of expiation be undergone by His members: "What is lacking in the sufferings of Christ,"
said St. Paul, "I fill up in my flesh for His body."[37] Jesus wishes it also,
and it was so as to signify this divine decree that He accepted the help
of the Cyrenean.

But also, He merited for us at that moment the grace of strength to
endure trials generously; He has put in His cross the unction that makes

[35] Hymn, *Stabat Mater*.   [36] See Matt. 27:32; Mark 15:21.   [37] Col. 1:24.

ours tolerable—for in carrying our cross it is indeed His cross we carry. He unites our sufferings to His sorrow, and by that union He confers on them an inestimable value, the source of great merits. Our Lord said to St. Mechtilde: "As my divinity drew to itself the sufferings of my humanity, and has made them its own (and this is the dowry of a spouse), so also will I transport your pains into my divinity; I will unite them to my Passion and make you share in the glory my Father conferred on my sacred humanity as the return for all its sufferings."[38]

This is what St. Paul makes us understand in his letter to the Hebrews, so as to encourage us to bear all things for love of Christ: "Let us run with perseverance the race that is set before us, eyes fixed on Jesus, the guide and perfector of our faith." He "who for the joy set before Him, despising ignominy, suffered the cross and merited thereby to be seated at the right hand of the throne of God."[39] "Consider Him who endured from sinners such hostility against Himself, so that you may not grow weary or fainthearted."[40]

My Jesus, I accept from your hand the particles you detach for me from your cross. I accept all the vexations, the contradictions, the pains, the sufferings you permit or which it pleases you to send me; I accept them as my share of expiation. Unite with your unspeakable sufferings that little which I do; for it is from your sufferings that mine draw all their merit.

VI. A Woman wipes the Face of Jesus.

Tradition tells us a woman,[41] moved by compassion, went up to Jesus and, stretching out her hand, wiped His adorable face with a piece of cloth.

Of the suffering Jesus, Isaiah had foretold that He would have in Him "no shapeliness or beauty to attract our eyes ... whereupon we

---

[38] *The Book of Special Grace*, Part II, Ch. 31.   [39] See Hebr. 12:1-2.
[40] Hebr. 12:3 (RSV, Cath.)   [41][*Translator's note:* This is how Marmion expresses it. She is generally called "Veronica," a reference to the tradition that the cloth with which she wiped Christ's face had thereafter a "true image" of His face upon it.]

esteemed Him not."[42] The Evangelist tells us that the soldiers gave Him insolent slaps, that they spat on His face: and the crown of thorns made blood flow down onto His sacred countenance. Christ Jesus willed to suffer all that to expiate our sins; He willed to heal us by the bruises His divine face received: "By His bruises we are healed."[43]

Being our elder brother He gave back to us, by substituting Himself for us in His Passion, the grace which makes us children of God. We ought to resemble Him, seeing that that is the very shape of the destiny willed for us: "to become conformed to the image of His Son."[44] How is that? Totally disfigured as He was by our sins, Christ in His Passion remained the Beloved Son, the object of all His Father's delight. We resemble Him in this if we keep within us sanctifying grace which is the source, the basis, of our likeness to God. We resemble Him also by practicing the virtues He manifested during His Passion, by sharing His love for His Father and for souls, His patience, His fortitude, His forbearance, His gentleness.

O Heavenly Father, in return for the bruises your Son Jesus willed to suffer for us, glorify Him, exalt Him, give Him that splendor He merited when His adorable face was disfigured for our salvation.

VII. JESUS FALLS A SECOND TIME.

Let us consider our Divine Savior sinking down once more beneath the weight of the cross. God had placed on His shoulders all the sins of the world: "The Lord has laid on Him the iniquity of us all."[45] Those were *our* sins that weighed Him down: He saw them all, in their multiplicity and detail; he accepted them as His own, to the point that, in the very words of St. Paul, He appeared to be no more than *living sin*: "For our sake God made the sinless one into sin."[46] As the Eternal Word, Jesus is all-powerful; but He wished to experience all the weakness of a humanity weighed-down. This wholly voluntary weakness honors the justice of His Heavenly Father, and merits strength for us.

---

[42] See Isa. 53:2-3.   [43] Isa. 53:5.   [44] Rom. 8:29.
[45] Isa. 53:6.   [46] 2 Cor. 5:21 (Jerus.)

Let us never forget our infirmity; let us never give way to pride. However great the progress we may believe ourselves to have made, we always remain weak for carrying our cross behind Jesus: "Without me you can do nothing."[47] One thing only becomes our strength—the divine power that flows from Jesus: "I can do all things in Him who strengthens me";[48] but that divine power is only given us if we beseech it often.

O Jesus, made weak for love of me, weighed down beneath the burden of my sins, give me the strength that is in you, so that you alone will be glorified by my works!

VIII. JESUS SPEAKS TO THE WOMEN OF JERUSALEM.

"Now there was following Him a great crowd of the people, and of women who were bewailing and lamenting Him. But Jesus, turning to them, said: 'Daughters of Jerusalem, do not weep for me, but weep for yourselves and for your children. For behold, days are coming in which people will say, "Blessed are the barren, and the wombs that never bore"... Then they will cry out to the mountains, "Fall upon us"... For if the green wood is treated like this, what will happen to the wood that is dry?'"[49]

Jesus knows the ineffable demands of His Father's justice and holiness. He recalls to the daughters of Jerusalem that this justice and this holiness are adorable perfections of the Being of God. He Himself is "a High Priest, holy, innocent, undefiled, set apart from sinners,"[50] He is doing no more than substituting Himself for them; and yet, see with what severe blows Divine Justice strikes Him! If this Divine Justice requires of Him so extensive a reparation, what on the Last Day will be the punishment of the guilty who up to then have obstinately refused to unite to Christ's sufferings their own part of the expiation?[51]

---

[47] John 15:5.   [48] Phil. 4:13.   [49] See Luke 23:27-31.   [50] Hebr. 7:26.

[51] [*Translator's note*: This echoes Marmion's above quotation of Christ's words about the green wood and the dry (Luke 23:31). *A Catholic Commentary on Holy Scripture* describes those words as "a parable picturing a man so set on kindling a fire that instead of seeking dry sticks he uses green and damp wood; its application is to the

"It is a fearful thing to fall into the hands of the living God."[52] On that Day, the disorder of human pride will be so deep, and the anguish of those who have wanted nothing to do with God will be so terrible, that those hapless ones, banished far from God for ever, will gnash their teeth in despair; they will ask "the hills to cover them,"[53] as if they were able to escape from the fiery shafts of a justice the entire fairness of which, on the evidence, they will acknowledge.

Let us implore the mercy of Jesus for that dread day when He will come, no longer as a Victim bowed under the weight of our sins, but as Sovereign Judge to whom the Father has given "all power in heaven and on earth."[54]

O my Jesus, have mercy on me! O you who are the Vine, grant that I remain united to you through grace and my good works, so that I bear fruit that is worthy of you; so that I do not become, through my sins, a dead branch, good only for being cut off and cast into the fire.[55]

IX. JESUS FALLS A THIRD TIME.

God, said Isaiah, in speaking of Christ during His Passion, willed to bruise Him with suffering: "to bruise Him in infirmity."[56] Jesus was weighed down by Justice. We shall never, even in heaven, be able to measure what that was for Jesus, what it was to be subjected to the shafts of Divine Justice. No creature has borne the weight of it in all its fullness; not even the damned have. But the sacred humanity of Jesus, united to that Divine Justice by direct contact, has borne all its power and all its rigor. That is why, as a Victim who has delivered Himself up to all its blows, He is broken by the exhaustion that this Holy Justice makes weigh upon Him.

O my Jesus, teach me to detest sin which obliges Justice to demand from you such an expiation! Grant that I unite to your sufferings all

---

present circumstances: seeing that to all appearances divine justice now falls upon an innocent person [the Innocent who in fact bears the sins of the guilty], how will it be when the turn of the guilty comes?"]   [52] Hebr. 10:31.   [53] Luke 23:30.
[54] Matt. 28:18.   [55] John 15:6.   [56] Isa. 53:10 (Rheims).

my own pains, so that through them I may erase my wrongdoings and make satsifaction, even here below.

X. Jesus is Stripped of His Garments.

"They divide my garments among them, and for my raiment they cast lots."[57] That is the prophecy of the psalmist. Jesus now is stripped of everything and left in the nakedness of absolute poverty. Not even does He have His clothes at His command, for as soon as He is lifted up on the cross, the soldiers share them out between them, casting lots for His tunic.[58] Jesus, under impulse of the Holy Spirit,[59] abandons Himself to His executioners as Victim for our sins.

Nothing is so glorious for God, or so useful for our souls, as to unite an absolute and unconditional offering of ourselves to that which Jesus made at the moment when He abandoned Himself to the executioners to be stripped of His garments and nailed to the cross, in order by His deprivation to give us back the riches of His grace: "that by His poverty you might become rich."[60] That offering of ourselves is a true sacrifice; that immolation to the divine will is the foundation of the whole spiritual life. But for it to acquire the whole of its value, we must unite it to Jesus's offering, for it is through that oblation that we have all been sanctified.[61]

O my Jesus, accept the offering I make to you of the whole of my being, join it to that which you made to your Heavenly Father at the moment you arrived at Calvary; strip me of all attachment to what is created and to myself!

XI. Jesus is Nailed to the Cross.

"They crucified Him, and with Him two others, one on either side, and Jesus between them."[62] Jesus delivers Himself up to His executioners: "as a lamb dumb before its shearer, so He did not open His

---

[57] Ps. 21 (22):19 (18) (Jerus.)   [58] John 19:24.   [59] Hebr. 9:14.
[60] 2 Cor. 8:9.   [61] Hebr. 10:10.   [62] John 19:18 (RSV, Cath.)

mouth."[63] The torture of this crucifixion by nails through hands and feet is inexpressible. Above all, who could speak of the feelings of the sacred heart of Jesus in the midst of these torments? He must have repeated, doubtless He did repeat, those words He said when coming into this world: "Father, you wish there to be no more holocausts of animals, they do not suffice for recognizing your holiness; but you have given me a body, and, behold, here I am!"[64] Jesus continuously sees the face of His Father, and with immeasurable feelings of love He delivered up His body so as to atone for all the insults given to Eternal Majesty, He became "obedient to death." And to what death did He submit? Even "death on a cross";[65] they crucified Him between two thieves. Why was that? Because "it is written, 'Cursed be every one who hangs on a tree,'"[66] on a gibbet. He willed to be "reputed with the wicked"[67] in order to give recognition to the sovereign rights of Divine Holiness.

He delivered Himself up for us also. Jesus, being God, saw us all at that moment; He offered Himself up to redeem us, because it was to Him, High Priest and Mediator, that the Father had given us.[68] What a revelation of Jesus's love for us! "Greater love no-one has, than that he lay down his life for his friends."[69] He could not have gone further than He has: He loved to the ultimate, "to the end."[70] And this love is also the love of the Father and of the Holy Spirit, for they are but one.

O Jesus, "who, in obedience to the will of your Father, and with the co-operation of the Holy Spirit, has by your death given life to the world; deliver me by your most holy Body and Blood from all my iniquities and from all evils; make me always cleave to your Commandments and never suffer me to be separated from you."[71]

---

[63] Acts 8:32; Isa. 53:7.

[64] See Hebr. 10:5-7; Ps. 39 (40):8.

[65] Phil. 2:8.

[66] Gal. 3:13 (RSV, Cath.); Deut. 21:23.

[67] Isa. 53:12; Mark 15:28; Luke 22:37.

[68] John 17:9.

[69] See John 15:13.

[70] John 13:1.

[71] Ordinary of the Mass, Prayer before Communion.

XII. Jesus Dies on the Cross.

"And Jesus cried out with a loud voice and said, 'Father, into your hands I commend my spirit.' And having said this, He expired."[72]

After three hours of indescribable sufferings, Jesus dies. The only oblation worthy of God, the unique sacrifice that redeems the world, is accomplished: "For by one offering He has perfected for ever those who are sanctified."[73]

Christ Jesus promised that when He was "lifted up from the earth," on the cross, He would "draw all things to myself."[74] We are His by a twofold title: as creatures brought into being out of nothing, by Him and for Him; and as souls redeemed by His precious blood:[75] One single drop of blood from Jesus, God-man, would have sufficed to save us, for in Him everything is of infinite value. But, among so many other reasons, He wished His blood to be poured out to the last drop, and His Sacred Heart to be pierced to show us the extent of His love. And it is for us all that He shed His blood: each one of us can in all truth repeat the ardent words of St. Paul: He "loved me and gave Himself up for me."[76]

Let us ask Him to draw us to His sacred heart by virtue of His death on the cross; let us ask that we die to our self-love, to our own will—sources, both, of so many infidelities and sins, and that we live for Him who died for us. Since it is to His death that we owe the life of our souls, is it not entirely just that we should live only for Him? that "they who are alive" should "live no longer for themselves, but for Him who died for them"?[77]

O Father, glorify your Son hanging on a gibbet. Since He humbled Himself even unto death, death on a cross, raise Him high. May the name you have given Him be exalted; may every knee bend before Him; may every tongue confess that your Son Jesus lives henceforth in your eternal glory![78]

---

[72] Luke 23:46. [73] Hebr. 10:14. [74] John 12:32. [75] Apoc. 5:9.
[76] Gal. 2:20. [77] 2 Cor. 5:15. [78] Phil. 2:11.

XIII. The Body of Jesus is Taken Down from the Cross and Given to His Mother.

The bruised body of Jesus is given back to Mary. We cannot imagine the sorrow of the Virgin at that moment. Never did mother love her child as Mary loved Jesus; her mother's heart was fashioned by the Holy Spirit to love this One who is God-man. Never did human heart beat with more tenderness for the Word Incarnate than Mary's heart did. For she was "full of grace" and her love encountered no obstacle at all to its opening-forth to fullness of bloom.

Then too, she owed all to Jesus; her immaculate conception, the privileges that make her a unique creature, had been given her in anticipation of the death of her Son. What unutterable sorrow was hers when she received in her arms the blood-stained body of Jesus!

Let us throw ourselves down at her feet to ask her pardon for our sins that were the cause of so much suffering. "O Mother, fount of love, make me understand the intensity of your sorrow, so that I share your affliction. Make my heart be afire with love for Christ my God, so that my only purpose is to please Him!"

> Can the human heart refrain
> From partaking in her pain,
> In that Mother's pain untold?...
>
> O thou Mother! fount of love!
> Touch my spirit from above,
> Make my heart with thine accord:
>
> Make me feel as thou hast felt;
> Make my soul to glow and melt
> With the love of Christ my Lord.[79]

---

[79] Hymn *Stabat Mater*.

XIV. The Body of Jesus is Laid in the Tomb.

Joseph of Arimathea, having taken the body of Jesus down from the cross, "wrapped it in a winding-sheet, and laid it in a tomb fashioned out of the rock," one in which no-one had ever yet been buried.[80]

St. Paul says that Christ had to be like unto us in all things.[81] Even in His tomb Christ is one of us: He was entombed, says St. John, in a shroud with the spices; "that is how the Jews prepare a body for burial."[82] But the body of Jesus, united to the Word, was not to "see corruption";[83] it remained in the tomb for barely three days, and, by His own power, Jesus came forth from the tomb, resplendent with life and glory, and "death shall no longer have dominion over Him."[84]

The Apostle tells us also that by our baptism we have been entombed with Christ so that we may die to sin: "All we who have been baptized into Christ Jesus have been baptized into His death."[85] The waters of baptism are like a sepulcher where we should leave sin behind, and from which we come forth animated by a new life, the life of grace. The sacramental power of our baptism lasts for ever. By uniting ourselves, through faith and love, to Christ entombed, we renew that grace of dying to sin so as to live only for God.[86]

Lord Jesus, may I bury in your tomb all my sins, all my iniquities, all my infidelities. Through the power of your death and burial, give me the grace to renounce, more and more, everything that separates me from you. Grant that I may renounce Satan, the maxims of the world, my self-love. By the power of your resurrection, may I henceforth follow your example and live only for the glory of your Father.

---

[80] Luke 23:53 (Knox).   [81] Hebr. 2:17.   [82] John 19:40 (Knox).
[83] Acts 2, vv. 27, 31; Ibid. 13:35; Ps. 15 (16):10.   [84] Rom. 6:9.
[85] Rom. 6:4.   [86] Rom. 6:11.

CHAPTER FIFTEEN

"If You Have Risen With Christ..."

(*Easter*)

Introduction: The Church calls the Resurrection of Jesus "Holy." Twofold element constituting holiness.

The whole of the mystery of Christ during the days of His Passion can be summed up in these words of St. Paul: "He humbled Himself, becoming obedient to death."[1] We have seen the extent to which Christ abased Himself; He sounded the very depths of humiliation, He chose the death of one "accursed," as was written: "Cursed be every one who hangs on a tree."[2]

But these abysses of ignominy and suffering into which Our Lord was willing to descend were equally abysses of love; and this love has merited for us the mercy of His Father, has merited for us all the graces of salvation and sanctification.

If the word "humiliation" sums up the mystery of the Passion, there is one phrase, also from St. Paul, which in relation to Christ summarizes exactly His Resurrection: *Vivit Deo*, "He lives unto God."[3] "He lives": there is for Him henceforth only life, perfect and glorious, with no bodily weakness, no prospect of death: Christ "dies no more, death shall no longer have dominion over Him";[4] a life entirely for God, more than ever consecrated to His Father and His Father's glory.

.   .   .

---

[1] Phil. 2:8.   [2] Gal. 3:13; Deut. 21:23.   [3] Rom. 6:10.   [4] Rom. 6:9.

In her litanies, the Church applies certain designations to some of the mysteries of Jesus. She says of the Resurrection that it is "holy": "By your Holy Resurrection..." What is the meaning of that? Are not all the mysteries of Christ Jesus "holy"? Oh, certainly! He Himself, to begin with, is the Holy One par excellence: "You alone are holy," we sing in the *Gloria* of the Mass. And all His mysteries are holy. His birth is holy: "the Holy One that shall be born of you...," said the Angel Gabriel to Mary.[5] His life is altogether holy: "I do always the things that are pleasing" to the Father;[6] and, as you know, there was nobody able to convict Christ Jesus of sin.[7] His Passion was holy: it is true that it was for the sins of mankind that He died, but the Victim was wholly sinless; it was the spotless Lamb. The High Priest who immolated Himself was "holy, innocent, undefiled, set apart from sinners."[8]

Why then, out of all the mysteries of Jesus, is the Resurrection called "holy" by the Church?

Because it is in this mystery that Christ particularly fulfills the conditions of holiness; because this is the principal mystery that puts into high relief those elements precisely constituting human holiness, holiness that finds its model and its source in Christ. Because, true though it is that He is the "way"[9] and the "light"[10] throughout all His life, and that He gives us the example for all the virtues compatible with His divinity—it is in the Resurrection that Christ is above all the Exemplar of *holiness*.

What, then, are the constituent elements of holiness? Holiness can be epitomized for us by two elements: negatively, a distancing of oneself from all sin, detachment from all that is merely created; and positively, a total and firm belonging to God.

Well, as we shall see, these two characteristics are to be found especially in Christ's Resurrection, to a degree, a highest point, that was not manifested before His coming forth from the tomb. Even though the Word Incarnate had throughout the whole of His

[5] See Luke 1:35. [6] John 8:29. [7] John 8:46. [8] Hebr. 7:26.
[9] John 14:6.   [10] John 8:12.

existence been the "Holy One" par excellence, it is above all in His Resurrection that He reveals Himself to us under this aspect of holiness, in resplendent brightness. And that is why the Church sings: *Through your holy resurrection...*

Let us therefore contemplate this mystery of Jesus coming forth, living and glorious, from the sepulcher; we shall see how the Resurrection is the mystery of the triumph of life over death, of what is heavenly over what is earthly, of the divine over the human; and that, in highest degree, it actualizes the ideal of all holiness.

1. The Risen Christ is exempt from all human infirmity.

What was Christ Jesus before His Resurrection?

He was God and man. The Eternal Word had espoused a nature that belonged to a sinful race. There is no doubt at all that this humanity, this human nature of His, did not contract any sin; but it submitted itself to the bodily infirmities compatible with His divinity, infirmities which, in us, are often the results of sin: "Truly, He bore our infirmities, and carried our sorrows."[11]

Look at Our Lord during His mortal life. In the manger he was a little, weak, child, one who needed His mother's milk to sustain His life. Later, He experienced fatigue: "Jesus ... wearied as He was from the journey, was sitting at the well";[12] it was an actual fatigue that He felt in His limbs. Sleep—not feigned, but real—closed His eyelids: the apostles had to wake Him when the boat He slept in was tossed about by a storm.[13] Hunger He knew: "He was hungry."[14] Thirst, too: "I thirst";[15] and suffering. He experienced interior distress also; in the Garden of Olives fear, worry, anguish, sadness, swooped down on His soul: "He began to feel dread,"[16] "to be exceedingly troubled,"[17] "to be sorrowful... my soul is sorrowful, even unto death."[18] Lastly, He underwent death: "He gave up His spirit."[19]

---

[11] See Isa. 53:4.   [12] John 4:6.   [13] Matt. 8:24-25; Mark 4:38; Luke 8:23-24.
[14] Matt. 4:2; Luke 4:2.   [15] John 19:28.   [16] Mark 14:33.
[17] Ibid.; Matt. 26:37.   [18] Matt. 26:37-38 (Rheims).   [19] John 19:30.

Thus did He share in our weaknesses, our infirmities, our sorrows. Sin alone, and everything that is the source or moral consequence of sin, was unknown to Him: "it was right that He should in all things be made like unto His brethren ... in all things except sin."[20]

But after Resurrection, all these infirmities have disappeared. There is no longer in Him any drowsiness, any fatigue, any infirmity of any kind. Our Lord no longer experiences anything of that kind; it is a complete separation from everything that is weakness. Is His body no longer real, then? Certainly it is real. It is indeed the body He received from the Virgin Mary, the body that suffered death on the cross.

See how Christ Himself showed this to them, emphatically. On the evening of His Resurrection, He appeared to His apostles. They "were startled and panic-stricken, and thought they saw a spirit. And He said to them: 'Why are you disturbed, and why do doubts arise in your hearts? See my hands and feet, that it is I myself. Feel me and see; for a spirit does not have flesh and bones, as you see I have.' And having said this, He showed them His hands and His feet."[21] Thomas was not there at the time. "We have seen the Lord," the other disciples say to him on his return. Thomas does not want to believe anything; he remains skeptical. "Unless I see in His hands the print of the nails," he says, "and put my finger into the place of the nails, and put my hand into His side, I will not believe." Eight days afterwards, Jesus appeared to them again, saying "Peace be to you!" Then He said to Thomas: "Put your finger here, and see my hands; and put out your hand, and place it in my side; and be not faithless, but believing."[22]

In this way, Jesus made His apostles verify the reality of His risen body; but it is a body henceforth freed of all earthly infirmities. This body is agile, matter is no barrier to it at all; Jesus comes forth from a tomb hewn out of the rock, the entrance to which is

[20] Hebr. 2:17, 4:15.   [21] Luke 24:37-40.   [22] John 20:24-27 (RSV, Cath.)

closed by a heavy stone; He presents Himself in the midst of His disciples in a room with closed doors: "the doors where the disciples gathered had been closed for fear of the Jews."[23] His taking food with His disciples was not because He experienced hunger, but because by sharing the disciples' meal He wished, in His mercy, to confirm the reality of His Resurrection.

This risen body is henceforth immortal; it died but once:[24] "Christ, having risen from the dead, now dies no more, death shall no longer have dominion over Him."[25] The body of the risen Jesus no longer is subject to death or to the conditions of time: it is free from all the servitudes, all the infirmities taken by it in the Incarnation; it is no longer susceptible of suffering; it is spiritual, living in sovereign independence of these things.

It is here that we see exhibited in Christ the first element of holiness:[26] a separation from all that is dead, all that is earthly, all that is merely created; a liberation from all weakness, all infirmity, all susceptibility to suffering. On the day of His Resurrection Christ Jesus leaves behind in the tomb the winding-sheets that are a symbol of our infirmities, our weaknesses, our imperfections; He comes forth triumphant from the sepulcher; His liberty is complete, He is animated by a life that is intense, perfect, a life that gives vibrancy to all the fibers of His being. In Him, Life absorbs everything that was mortal.

2. Magnificent fullness of "life for God" in Christ Triumphant.

To be sure, we shall see the Risen Christ still touching earth. From love for His disciples, in a stooping-down to help the weakness of their faith, He consents to appear to them, to talk with them, to share their meal; but His life is above all a celestial one: *Vivit Deo*: "the life that He lives, He lives unto God."[27]

---

[23] John 20:19.   [24] Rom. 6:10.   [25] Ibid., v. 9.

[26] [*Translator's note*: "holiness": insofar as concerns the application of this term for us created beings, Marmion clearly is thinking of the perfect, the completed, holiness of heaven.]   [27] Rom. 6:10.

We know almost nothing of this celestial life of Jesus on the morrow of His resurrection; but that it was a wonderful one, who can doubt?

He has proved to His Father how much He loved Him by giving His life for mankind. All is now paid off, all is expiated; Justice, satisfied, no longer requires expiation from Him; friendship is reestablished between mankind and God; the work of redemption has been accomplished. But the heart's-binding[28] of Jesus to His Father—this continues, livelier and fuller than ever. The Gospel tells us nothing of that homage of adoration,[29] of love, of thanksgiving, that Christ was then rendering to His Father; but St. Paul sums all up by his *Vivit Deo*: Jesus lives for God.

That is the second element of holiness: the adhering, the belonging, the consecration to God. It will only be in heaven that we shall understand how fully Jesus lived for His Father in those blessed days; it was certainly with a perfection that delighted the angels. Now that His sacred humanity is free of all the necessities, is liberated from all the infirmities, of our earthly condition it delivers itself up more than ever before to the Father's glory. The Risen Christ becomes an infinite source of glory for His Father; there is no longer any weakness in Him; everything in Him is light, strength, beauty, life. Everything in Him sings an uninterrupted song of praise.

[28] [*Translator's note*: This is a free rendering of Marmion's French word *religion*, which has its root in the Latin *religare*, "to bind."]

[29] [*Translator's further note*: Marmion's word "adoration" stems from the fact that Christ is man as well as God. At the Incarnation the Son, equal to the Father, took flesh, became man: Christ is one Person, having two natures and wills, the divine and the human. In the light of that, there is nothing inaccurate in saying that *as man*, in the exercise of His human will, the eternal co-equal Son expresses His complete filial "given-ness" in the form of adoration *in His human nature*. His human adoration is, as it were, a translation into human terms of its transcendent divine "archetype" in His divine relationship to the Father as Son. See further Marmion's explicit references, in the next two paragraphs, to Christ's "humanity," "human nature," enveloped and penetrated (as Marmion puts it) by the divine life.]

Let mankind gather together into its being every kingdom of creation so as to recapitulate there the hymn of everything created; and what shall we then say of the unceasing song the humanity of Christ in glory, Supreme High Priest, triumphant over death, sings to the Trinity? This song, a perfect expression of the divine life which evermore envelops and penetrates in all its power and splendor the human nature of Jesus, is ineffable.

3. **Baptism inaugurates within us the Paschal grace. Teaching of St. Paul. How Christians, through distancing themselves from all sin and detaching themselves from all that is merely created, should imitate, throughout the whole of their lives, the spiritual liberty of Christ in glory.**

Such is the life of the Risen Christ. It is the model for our lives, and Christ has merited for us the grace of living, as He does, "for God," of being associated with His risen state. Not that it is by His Resurrection that He has merited it; it was in breathing His last that Christ came to the end of His mortal existence. Since then He can no longer merit; everything He has won for us has been through His Sacrifice, inaugurated at the Incarnation and completed by His death on the cross.

But His merits remain for us after His glorious coming forth from the tomb. See how Christ Jesus wished to keep the scars of His wounds: He shows them to His Father in all their beauty, as titles to communication of His grace: He "lives always to make intercession" for us.[30]

As you know, it is from being baptized that we share in this grace of the Resurrection. St. Paul affirms this to us: "We were buried with Him by means of baptism into death, in order that, just as Christ has arisen from the dead through the power of the Father, so we also may walk in newness of life."[31]

---

[30] Hebr. 7:25.   [31] See Rom. 6:4.

The holy water into which we are plunged at baptism[32] is, according to the apostle, a figure of the sepulcher. In coming forth from it, the soul is purified from all sin, all stain, set free from all spiritual death and clothed in grace, the source of divine life; in the same way that Christ, coming forth from the tomb, casts aside all infirmity so as thenceforth to live a perfect life.[33] That is why, in the early Church, baptism was administered only on Easter Night, and at Pentecost which closes Eastertide. We shall understand almost nothing of the liturgy of Easter Week if we do not have before our eyes the solemn conferring of baptism which took place then.

We are therefore risen with Christ, through Christ, for He has an infinite desire to communicate His glorious life to us. And what is needed to respond to this divine desire and become like the Risen Jesus? That we live in the spirit of our baptism. That, renouncing everything in our lives that is corrupted by sin, we more and more make the "old" self "die";[34] that everything within us be mastered and ruled by grace. The whole of sanctity for us is to be found in that; in separating ourselves from sin, from occasions of sin, detaching ourselves from what is merely created, from everything that is earthly, in order to live in God and for God with the greatest fullness and the greatest possible stability.

This work, inaugurated at baptism, is one pursued during the whole of our lives. Christ, it is true, dies but once; He has thereby granted us to die to all that is sin, as he did. But we—we must "die" each day, for we still retain in us the roots of sin, and the old enemy works ceaselessly to make them spring up again. To destroy these roots within us, to guard ourselves against all infidelity, against all created things loved for themselves; to exclude from

[32] [*Translator's note*: Marmion is thinking of baptism by immersion as practiced by the early Church. Today, of course, immersion has been replaced by the pouring of a little water on the head.]

[33] See, in *Christ, the Life of the Soul,* the talk on *Baptism: Sacrament of Adoption and Initiation: Death and Life* (Book II, Ch. 2).   [34] Rom. 6:6.

our actions not only every culpable motive but motives that are purely natural; to keep our heart free with a spiritual freedom—all this is the first element of our holiness, the one which Christ shows us fulfilled in Himself by that sovereign and admirable independence in which His risen humanity lives.

There, indeed, is one of the most significant aspects of the grace of Easter. St. Paul puts it in high relief, in very expressive terms. "Purge out the old leaven, that you may be a new dough"; for since "Christ our Passover"—our Paschal Lamb—has been sacrificed, you have become unleavened bread. "Therefore let us keep festival, not with 'the old leaven'"—not with the leaven of malice and wickedness—"but with the unleavened bread of sincerity and truth."[35]

That pressing exhortation of the Apostle Paul forms the Epistle of the Mass of Easter Day itself. It must seem obscure to a number of present-day Christians, and yet it is this passage, in preference to all others, that the Church, in summary of what our conduct should be, has chosen for the day of our celebrating the mystery of the Resurrection. Why that choice?

It is because it signifies clearly, though with profundity, what fruit the soul should gather from this mystery. What, then, do those words mean?

You know that among the Israelites, when the Feast of the Passover was approaching—the Feast bringing to the minds of the Hebrews the great anniversary of the "passing" of the destroying angel[36]—they had to remove from their houses every sort of leaven; and then, on the day of the Feast, after having sacrificed the paschal lamb, they ate the lamb with unleavened bread—that is, bread made without leaven, unfermented.[37]

All that was only a figure or symbol of the true Pasch, the Christian Pasch. "Purge out the old leaven," "you must be quit, now, of the old self"[38] born in sin; quit of its lustful desires,

---

[35] 1 Cor. 5:7-8.
[37] Exod. 12, vv. 8, 15.
[36] Exod. 12:26-27.
[38] Eph. 4:22 (Knox).

which you have renounced by your baptism. At that time of baptismal regeneration, you shared in the death of Christ which made sin die within you; you became, and you ought to remain, through grace, "a new dough," a new paste—which is to say "a new creature,"[39] a "new man,"[40] after the example of Christ, come forth glorious from the sepulcher.

That is why, like the Jews who when the time of the Pasch came abstained from all leaven in order to eat the paschal lamb, we Christians who wish to share in the mystery of the Resurrection, who wish to unite ourselves with Christ, the Lamb sacrificed and risen from the dead for us, should no longer live in a state of sin, should guard ourselves against those evil desires which are like a leaven of malice and wickedness: "Do not let sin reign in your mortal body."[41] We should preserve in us the grace which will make us live in the truth and sincerity of the divine law.

Such is the teaching St. Paul makes us hear on the very day of Easter, a teaching that points especially to the first element of our holiness: to renounce sin and every human motive that can, like an "old leaven," corrupt our actions; and—as regards all sin and every created entity—to live in that spiritual freedom which appeared so strongly in the Risen Christ.

We ask Jesus Himself for this grace in the following stanza which is repeated in each of the hymns of Paschaltide: *Quaesumus auctor omnium...*

> Creator Lord of everything,
> As now with Paschal joy we sing,
> Your people, who before you bend,
> From all attacks of death defend![42]

We ask Christ to preserve His people—that people whom "He has purchased with His own blood"[43] so that, St. Paul says, they might be a people "acceptable" to Him[44]—we ask Christ to preserve

---

[39] 2 Cor. 5:17.   [40] Eph. 4:24.   [41] Rom. 6:12.   [42] Hymn of Vespers, Matins and Lauds (Monastic Breviary).   [43] Acts 20:28.   [44] Titus 2:14.

them, from what? From every attack of spiritual death, which is to say from all sin, from everything that can lead to sin, from everything that tends to destroy or weaken in us the life of grace. So defended, we can form part of that body He wills to be holy and irreproachable: "that she might be holy and without blemish."[45]

4. Complete belonging to God: our "living for God"; the effecting of this in our soul.

The second element of holiness, the one moreover that gives to the first its *raison d'être* and its value, is *belonging to God*, devotedness to God; what St. Paul calls living for, or unto, God.[46]

This "life for God" embraces an infinite number of degrees. It supposes in the first place that one is entirely separated from every mortal sin: between mortal sin and divine life there is absolute incompatibility. Next there is distancing of oneself from venial sin, from the roots of sin, from every merely natural motive, and detachment from all that is merely created. The more complete the separation is, the more are we liberated, the more are we spiritually free, and the more also can the divine life develop and expand within us. In measure as the soul frees itself from the merely human, it opens itself to the divine, it tastes heavenly things, it lives with the life of God.

In this blessed state, the soul is not only free from every sin; it now acts solely under the inspiration of grace, solely from a supernatural motive. And when that motive extends to all its actions; when, through an impelling of habitual and steadfast love, the soul relates everything to God, to the glory of Christ and that of His Father, then this is fullness of life within the soul, this is holiness: the soul "lives for God."

You will notice that during Eastertide the Church speaks often to us of life, not only because Christ, by His resurrection, has conquered death, but above all because He has re-opened to souls

---

[45] Eph. 5:27.   [46] Rom. 6:11. [*Translator's note*: The Rheims has "a life unto God." The Knox version has "a life that looks towards God."]

the springs of life eternal. It is in Christ that we find that life: "I am ... the Life."[47] That is why, frequently also, the Church during those blest days causes to be read to us again the parable of the Vine. "I am the Vine," said Jesus, "you are the branches. If you dwell in me, and I in you, you will bear much fruit; for without me you can do nothing."[48] It is necessary for us to dwell in Him, and He in us, in order that we may bear much fruit.

How so?

Through His grace, through the faith we have in Him, through the virtues of which He gives us the example and we imitate. When, having renounced sin, we die to ourselves, as the grain of wheat dies in the ground before producing its fruitful wheat-ears;[49] when we simply act under the inspiration of the Holy Spirit and in conformity with the commandments and maxims of the gospel of Jesus, then it is the divine life of Christ that blossoms in our souls, it is Christ who lives in us: "I am alive; or rather not I; it is Christ that lives in me."[50]

Such is the ideal of perfection: being "alive to God in Christ Jesus."[51] We cannot arrive there in one day; holiness, inaugurated at our baptism, is only effected little by little, by successive stages. Let us strive to act in such a way that every Easter, every day of that blest period which extends from the Feast of the Resurrection until Pentecost, produces in us a more complete death to sin, to the merely created, and a more vigorous and abundant increase in Christ's life within us.

Christ has to reign in our hearts, and everything that is within us has to submit to Him. What does Christ do since the day of His triumph? He lives and reigns glorious, in God, in the heart's-embrace of the Father. He "lives and reigns with you and the Holy Spirit, one God for ever and ever."[52] Christ only lives where He reigns, and He lives in us to the degree that He reigns in our soul. He is King, as He is High Priest. When Pilate asked Him whether

---

[47] John 14:6. [48] See John 15:4-5. [49] John 12:25. [50] Gal. 2:20 (Knox).
[51] Rom. 6:11. [52] Ending words of liturgical prayers to the Father.

He was a king, Our Lord replied to him: "You have said it; I am a king," but "My kingdom is not of this world."[53] The kingdom of God is within us.[54] Christ's rule over us has to take place every day with greater fullness: it is what we ask of God the Father: "Thy kingdom come!" Oh, may that day come, Lord, when you will truly reign within us through your Christ!

And why is that not yet so? Because so many things in us: our self-will, our self-love, our natural activity, are not yet submissive to Christ, because we have not yet done what the Father desires: "Thou hast put all things under His feet,"[55] the psalmist declared, the feet of Christ. That is one part of the glory the Father wishes to give henceforth to His Son Jesus: He "has exalted Him and has bestowed on Him the name that is above every name, so that at the name of Jesus every knee should bend," that all in creation should be submissive to Him: in heaven, on earth and in hell.[56] All, too, in each one of us—our will, our intellect, our imagination, our energies.

He come within us as King on the day of our baptism; but His rule is disputed by sin. When we destroy sin, infidelity, attachment to what is merely created, because we live by faith in Him, in His word, in His merits, because we seek to please Him in all things—then Christ is Master, then He reigns in us as He reigns in the heart's-embrace of the Father; He lives in us. He can say of us to His Father: "See this soul in whom I live and reign, Father, that your name be hallowed."

Such are the profoundest aspects of the grace of Easter: detachment from all that is human, earthly, created; a complete belonging to God through Christ. The resurrection of the Word Incarnate becomes for us a mystery of life and of holiness. Christ being our head, God has raised us from the dead "*together with Christ.*"[57] We should therefore seek to reproduce in ourselves the features that mark His risen life.

---

[53] John 18, vv. 37, 36.   [54] Luke 17:21.   [55] Ps. 8:8(6) (RSV, Cath.)
[56] Phil. 2:9-10.   [57] Eph. 2:5.

It is to this that St. Paul exhorts us with so much insistence during these days of Easter. "If you have risen *with* Christ," he says— *CONsurrexistis*; if you wish Christ to give you a share in the mystery of His resurrection, if you wish to enter into the feelings of His sacred heart, if you wish to "eat the Pasch" with Him and one day share in His triumphant glory, then "seek the things that are above"—give your affections to the lasting things of heaven; detach yourselves from "the things that are on earth," which are fleeting: honors, pleasures, riches. "For you have died and your life is hidden with Christ in God."[58] And, just as the Risen Christ dies no more, but lives for ever for His Father, so die to sin yourselves and live for God through the grace of Christ: "Consider yourselves also as dead to sin, but alive to God in Christ Jesus."[59]

5. **How this twofold Paschal grace is strenthened in us: by contemplating the mystery and by Eucharistic communion.**

You will now ask me how we can strengthen this Paschal grace within us.

First by contemplating this mystery with great faith. Look, when Christ Jesus, appearing to His disciples, bade Thomas the doubting apostle to put his finger in the scars He had kept of His wounds, what did He say to him? "Be not faithless, but believing." And when Thomas then adored Him as his God, Our Lord added: "Blessed are those who have not seen and yet believe"[60]—you have believed in me, Thomas, because you have seen and touched me; but blessed are those who have believed without having seen.

Faith puts us in contact with Christ. If we contemplate this mystery with faith, Christ produces in us the grace He produced when He appeared to His disciples as Risen Lord. He lives in our souls; and, ever living, He ceaselessly acts within us, in conformity with the degree of our faith and according to the particular grace

---

[58] Col. 3:1-2. [59] Rom. 6:9-11. [60] John 20:27-29 (RSV, Cath.)

of each of His mysteries. It is recounted in the Life of St. Mary Magdalene de Pazzi that one Easter Day, being at table in the refectory, she had an air so happy and joyous, that a novice who was serving her could not prevent herself from asking the cause of this. "It is the beauty of my Jesus that gives me such joy," she replied: "I see Him present in the hearts of all my sisters." "Under what form?" the novice asked her. "I see Him," answered the Saint, "risen and glorious as the Church describes Him this Easter Day."[61]

It is above all by sacramental communion that we now take into ourselves the fruits of this mystery.

Whom do we receive, indeed, in the Eucharist? Christ—the Body and Blood of Christ. But note that, though it is true that sacramental communion rests upon the immolation of Calvary, and on the immolation of the altar which reproduces that of Calvary, it is nevertheless with Christ's glorified flesh that we communicate. We receive Christ as He is *now*—that is to say, glorified in highest heaven, and possessing, in all its plenitude of splendor, the glory of His Resurrection.

He whom we thus receive is truly the very source of our holiness; He cannot fail to give us a share in the grace of His "Holy Resurrection." In this, as in all things, it is of His fullness that we all receive.[62]

In our days still, Christ, ever living, repeats to each soul the words He spoke in the presence of His disciples at the time when, in the Paschal season, He was about to institute His Sacrament of Love: "I have longed to celebrate *this* Pasch with you."[63] Christ Jesus desires to make real within us the mystery of His resurrection. He lives above all that is earthly, delivered up entirely to His Father; and He wishes, for our joy, to draw us with Him into that same flow of love. If, after having received Him in holy communion, we let Him have total power to act, He will give to our

---

[61] *Life* by Father Cepari, French translation, Ch. 18.
[62] John 1:16.   [63] See Luke 22:15.

lives, through the inspirations of His Spirit, that steadfast orientation towards the Father which is the essence of holiness. And this, in such a way that all our thoughts, all our aspirations, all our activity, are directed our Father in Heaven.

It is you, O Divine Risen One, who come within me—you who, having expiated sin by your sufferings, have conquered death by your triumph; who, henceforth glorious, live only for your Father. Come within me "to destroy the works of the devil,"[64] to bring about the overthrow of sin and of my infidelity. Come within me to increase my detachment from everything that is not you. Come, to make me a sharer in that superabundance of perfect life which now overflows from your sacred humanity. With you, I shall sing then a song of thanksgiving to your Father who, on this day of your Resurrection, has crowned you with glory and honor as our leader and head.[65]

These aspirations are the same as those of the Church in one of her prayers where, after holy communion, she sums up the graces she entreats from God for her children: "We beseech thee, O Lord, that we be cleansed from our old nature, and that thy Sacrament, which we reverently take, may transform us into a new creature."[66]

And the Church wishes this grace to remain in us, even when the time of holy communion has passed, and after the Paschal solemnities have come to an end: "Grant, we beseech thee, Almighty God, that the power of the Easter Sacrament we have received may ever remain in our soul."[67] It is a permanent grace, one which gives us the power, in the words of St. Paul, to be renewed "day by day,"[68] ceaselessly; to increase in us the life of Christ, by drawing nearer and nearer to a resemblance of the glorious traits of our divine model.

---

[64] 1 John 3:8.
[66] Postcommunion of the Wednesday of Easter Week.
[67] Postcommunion of the Tuesday of Easter Week.

[65] Ps. 8:6(5).

[68] 2 Cor. 4:16.

6. The Resurrection of the Body completes the manifestation of the greatness of this glorious mystery. Joy which union with the Risen Christ creates in our soul; the Easter *Alleluia*.

In indicating the two aspects of the mystery of holiness which the resurrection of Jesus ought to produce in our hearts, we have not exhausted the riches of the Paschal grace.

God is so magnificently lavish in what He does for His Christ, that He wills that the mystery of the resurrection of His Son shall extend not only to our souls but also to our bodies. We shall rise again, we too. That is a dogma of the Faith. We shall rise again bodily, like Christ, with Christ. How could it be otherwise?

As I have said to you often, Christ is our head; we form with Him one mystical body. As Christ is risen—and He is risen in His human nature—it must be that we, His members, shall partake of the same glory. For it is not only through our soul, it is also through our bodies, it is through our whole being, that we are members of Christ. A union most intimate binds us to Christ. If, therefore, He is risen glorious, the faithful who, by His grace, are part of His mystical body will be united with Him in His resurrection.

Listen to what St. Paul says on this subject. "Christ has been raised from the dead, the first-fruits of those who have fallen asleep"[69]—He represents the first-fruits of a harvest; after Him the harvest is to follow. "For as by a man"—Adam—"came death, by a man also comes the resurrection of the dead. For as in Adam all die, so in Christ shall all be brought to life."[70] God, he further says in more vigorous language, has brought us to life in His Son—"brought us to life *together with Christ* ... in Christ Jesus."[71]

[69] [*Translator's note*: We do not remain unconscious between our individual deaths and the resurrection of the bodies of all. On our deaths, our fully conscious souls go either to heaven, or to the temporary cleansing-place (or cleansing-*state*) of purgatory; or to hell. On the coming of Christ on the Last Day, the bodies of all will be resurrected and joined to their souls.]

[70] See 1 Cor. 15:20-22.   [71] Eph. 2:5-6.

How so? It is because, through faith and grace, we are living members of Christ, we share in His states, we are one with Him. And as grace is the source of our glory, those who are, through grace, already saved *in hope*, are already also—in principle—risen in Christ.

That is our faith and our hope.

But "now our life is hidden with Christ in God." Now, in our present life, grace does not produce its effects of clarity and splendor which will be its completion in glory—just as Christ, before His resurrection, held back the glorious radiance of His divinity and allowed the three disciples to see only a reflection of it on the day of the Transfiguration on Tabor. Our interior life here below is known only to God; it is hidden to the eyes of men. Further, if through our spiritual freedom we strive to reproduce in our souls the characteristics of the risen life of Jesus, it is nevertheless a labor which still operates in a flesh that is wounded by sin and subject to the infirmities of time. We shall only arrive at that holy freedom at the price of a struggle ceaselessly renewed and faithfully sustained. We, too, must suffer so as to enter into glory, as Christ in person said to the disciples at Emmaus: "Did not the Christ have to suffer these things before entering into His glory?"[72] We are, said the Apostle Paul, sons of God. "But if we are sons, we are heirs also ... joint heirs with Christ, provided, however, we suffer with Him that we may also be glorified with Him."[73]

May these celestial thoughts sustain us through the days still remaining for us to spend here below. Yes, the time will come when "there shall be no mourning, or crying or pain any more"; God will "wipe away every tear" from the eyes of His servants who have become co-heirs with His Son. He will make them sit down at the eternal feast He has prepared to celebrate the triumph of Jesus and of those whose elder brother Jesus is.[74]

[72] Luke 24:26.   [73] Rom. 8:17.   [74] See Apoc. 21:4.

If every year, during Lent and Holy Week, we are faithful in sharing the sufferings of Christ, every year also the celebration of the mystery of Easter, by making us contemplate the victory of Jesus victorious over death, makes us partake more fruitfully and more abundantly of His divine condition of being risen; it increases our detachment from everything that is not God, it enlarges the divine life within us, through grace, faith and love. At the same time, it enlivens our hope: for, says St. Paul, "when"—at the Last Day—"Christ, *your life*," and head, shall appear, then, because you share in His life, "you too will appear *with Him* in glory."[75]

This hope fills us with joy, and that is because the mystery of Easter, by being a mystery of life, strengthens our hope—since it is also eminently a mystery of joy.

The Church shows this during Eastertide by multiplying the *Alleluia*,[76] a cry of elation and happiness, borrowed from the liturgy of heaven. She had excluded it during Lent, so as to manifest her sadness and commune with the sufferings of her Spouse. Now that Christ is risen, she rejoices with Him, she takes up again, with a new fervor, this joyous exclamation that sums up all the ardor of her feelings.

Let us never forget: we make but one with Christ Jesus; His triumph is our triumph; His glory is the source of our joy. Let us, also, with our Mother the Church, say the *Alleluia* often, to show Christ our joy at seeing Him triumph over death, and to thank the Father for the glory He gives His Son. The *Alleluia* which the Church tirelessly repeats during the fifty days of the Paschal season is like an ever-renewed echo of that prayer with which she ends Easter Week: "Grant us, we beseech thee, O Lord, ever to rejoice in these Paschal mysteries, that the work of our renewal may continue and bring us to everlasting bliss."[77]

[75] Col. 3:4.   [76] Meaning "God be praised!"
[77] *Secretum* of the Saturday of Easter Week.

CHAPTER SIXTEEN

"And Now, Father, Glorify Your Son"
(*The Ascension*)

Introduction.

After His resurrection, Christ remained for only forty days with His disciples. St. Leo says that "those days were not spent inactively."[1] By his repeated appearances to the apostles, by His talks with them, "speaking of the kingdom of God,"[2] Jesus filled their hearts with joy; He strengthened their faith in His triumph, His person, His mission. He also gave them His last instructions[3] for the establishment and oganization of the Church.

Now that the mission of His stay on this earth had been fully concluded, the hour had come for Him to return to His Father. The divine "giant"[4] had completely run His course here below: "I have ... finished the work that you gave me to do."[5] He was now going to experience in all their fullness the profound joys of a marvelous triumph: the Ascension to heaven completed gloriously the earthly life of Jesus.

Of all the Feasts of Our Lord, I dare to say that, in a certain sense, the Ascension is the greatest, because it is the supreme glorification of Christ Jesus. Holy Church calls this Ascension "wonderful" and "glorious";[6] and all the way through the Divine Office of the Feast she causes us to hymn the magnificence of this mystery.

---

[1] *Sermo* I, on the Ascension of the Lord, c. 2. [2] Acts 1:3. [3] Acts 1:2.
[4] Ps. 19:6(5). [5] John 17:4 (Jerus.) [6] *Secretum*, Mass of the Ascension.

Our Divine Savior had asked His Father to be glorified with that glory which He possesses, through His divinity, in the eternal splendors of heaven: "Father, glorify me with yourself, with the glory that I had with you before the world existed."[7] The victory of the Resurrection marked the dawn of that personal glorification of Jesus: "This is the glorification of Our Lord Jesus Christ, the beginning of which He entered upon at His resurrection."[8] Dawn come to full noon is the wondrous Ascension: "So then the Lord, after He had spoken to them, was taken up into heaven, and sits at the right hand of God."[9] That is the Father's glorification of the humanity of Christ above all the heavens.

Let us therefore say a few words on this glorification; on what the grounds of it are for Jesus, on the special grace it brings us. The Church sums up these points in a prayer for the Mass of the Ascension: "Grant, we beseech thee, Almighty God, that we who believe thy only-begotten Son, our Redeemer, to have this day ascended into heaven, may ourselves live there in spirit."

That prayer witnesses first to our faith in this mystery. By recalling the titles given to Jesus, of "only-begotten Son" and "Redeemer," the Church indicates the reasons for her Spouse's ascending to heaven. Finally, she points to the grace for our souls that is attached to this mystery.

1. **Magnificent splendor of the triumph of Jesus in His ascension to the right hand of the Father.**

The mystery of the Ascension of Jesus Christ is represented to us in a manner that accords with our nature: we contemplate the sacred humanity rising up from the earth and going up visibly towards heaven.

For the last time Jesus assembled together His disciples. He led them in the direction of Bethany, to the summit of the Mount

---

[7] John 17:5.   [8] St. Augustine, *Tractatus in Johann.*, CIV, 3.   [9] Mark 16:19.

of Olives. He renewed their mission of preaching the Gospel to the whole world, promising to be with them always, through His grace and the action of His Spirit.[10] Then, after having blessed them, He ascended above the clouds, through His own divine power and that of His glorious soul, and disappeared from their sight.[11]

But this material ascension, real as it was, marvelous as it may appear, is at the same time the sign of an ascension of which the apostles themselves on the hilltop would not see the conclusion—an ascension more wonderful still, though beyond our understanding. Our Lord "ascends ... above all the heavens,"[12] beyond all the choirs of angels, to rest only at God's right hand: "He ascended into heaven, and is seated at the right hand of the Father."[13]

You understand that this expression "at the right hand of" the Father is only figurative and is not to be taken literally. God the Father, being a spirit, has nothing of the bodily. But Holy Scripture,[14] and the Church in her Creeds, employ the expression to point to the sublimity of the honors, and the majesty of the triumph, accorded to Christ in the sanctuary of the divinity.

Similarly, when we say that Jesus "is seated," we mean to signify that He has entered for ever into possession of that eternal repose which His glorious battles have merited. That repose, though, in no way excludes the unceasing exercise of the full power the Father has communicated to Him for ruling, sanctifying and judging all mankind.

St. Paul, in his letter to the Ephesians, has extolled in magnificent terms this divine glorification of Jesus. God the Father, he says, has displayed the "working of His mighty power which He

[10] He remains also by His Real Presence in the Sacrament of the Eucharist.
[11] Luke 24:50-51; Acts 1:8-11.   [12] Eph. 4:10.   [13] Apostles' Creed, Nicene Creed, *Quicumque* (Athanasian Creed).   [14] Ps. 18 (19):2(1) ("the work of His hands"); Mark 16:19 ("at the right hand of"); Eph. 1:20; Col. 3:1.

has wrought in Christ in raising Him from the dead, and setting Him at His right hand in heaven above every Principality and Power and Virtue and Domination[15]—in short, above every name that is named, not only in this world, but also in that which is to come. And all things He made subject under His feet, and Him He gave as head over all the Church."[16]

Henceforth Christ Jesus is and remains for every soul the only source of salvation, of grace, of life, of blessing. Henceforth, says the Apostle, His name is so great, so resplendent, that "at the name of Jesus every knee should bend of those in heaven, on earth and in hell, and every tongue should confess that the Lord Jesus Christ lives and reigns in the glory of God the Father."[17]

And see, indeed: since that blest hour, the unnumberable multitude of the elect in the heavenly Jerusalem, whose eternal Light is the Lamb that was slain, throw their crowns at His feet, prostrate themselves before Him, and proclaim in a mighty choir, like the sound of the sea, that He is worthy of all blessing, of all glory, because their salvation and their beatitude have their beginning and their end in Him.[18]

Since that hour, over the whole face of the earth, every day, the Church, during the holy action of the Mass, makes her praises and her supplications ascend from her altars to Him who alone can sustain her in the fight, because He is the one and only source of all strength and all power: "You are seated at the right hand of the Father: receive our prayer. For you alone are the Holy One, you alone are the Lord, you alone are the Most High, Jesus Christ, with the Holy Spirit, in the glory of God the Father."[19]

Since that hour also, the princes of darkness—from whom the conquering Christ wrested their prey for ever: "Ascending on

---

[15] [*Translator's note*: ranks of angels.]   [16] Eph. 1:20-22.
[17] See Phil. 2:10-11.   [18] Apoc. 7:9; 3:12; 21:2; Hebr. 12:22; Apoc. 21:23; 5:12; 4:10; 14:2; 4:11; 22:13.   [19] *Gloria* of the Mass.

high, He led captivity captive"[20]—have been filled with terror at the very name of Jesus, and been forced to flee, their pride brought low, before the victorious sign of His cross.

Such is the splendor of the triumph into which the humanity of Jesus entered, for ever, on the day of His wonderful ascension.

2. Principal reasons for this marvelous exaltation of Christ: He is the Son of God; and He had been engulfed in the ignominies of the Passion.

You will now ask me what the reasons are for this supreme exaltation of Jesus, of this immeasurable glory that has become the possession of His sacred humanity.

We can sum them all up by two principal reasons. The first is that Jesus Christ is God's own Son; the second is that He had been engulfed in humiliation in order to redeem us.

Jesus is God and man. As God, He fills with His divine presence heaven and earth. It is therefore as man that He ascended to the right hand of the Father. But the humanity of Jesus has been united to the Person of the Word, it is the humanity of one who is God. As such, it is entitled as of right to divine glory in the eternal splendors.

During the mortal life of Christ—save on the day of the Transfiguration—that glory was veiled, hidden. The Word wished to unite Himself to a humanity feeble like our own; one capable of suffering, one subject to infirmity, pain and death.

We have seen that Jesus entered into possession of that resplendent glory as from the very dawn of His resurrection. His humanity from then on is glorious, no longer susceptible to suffering. But He still remained here below, a corruptible place where death reigns. For Him to attain the summit of that glory,

---

[20] Eph. 4:8 (Rheims); Ps. 67 (68):19. [*Translator's note:* He led with Him to heaven, as captives of His love, a multitude of souls who before had been in captivity.]

for it to reach its full brightness, the Risen Jesus needed a place that corresponded fittingly to His new condition; He needed the heights of heaven, from where thenceforth His glory and His power could in their fullness radiate upon the whole society of the elect and the redeemed.

God-man, Son of God, equal to His Father, Jesus is entitled to sit at His right hand, and to share with Him, in all their splendor, the infinite beatitude and the omnipotence of Sovereign Being.[21]

The second reason for this supreme glorification is that of its being a recompense for the humiliations Jesus underwent for love of His Father and charity towards us.

I have said to you often: In coming into this world, Christ delivered Himself up wholly to the will of the Father: "Behold, I come to do your will, O God."[22] He agreed to carry out to its full consummation the program of humiliations prophesied; to drink to the dregs the bitter cup of suffering and ignominies untold. He humbled Himself, even to the malediction of the cross. And why all that? "That the world may know that I love the Father,"[23] that I love His perfections and His glory, His rights and those things He wills.

And see why. "*Therefore*"—note this word which I have taken from St. Paul, it indicates the reality of the motive—therefore, because of which, the Father "has exalted Him above all that is in heaven, on earth and in hell."[24]

Battle over, a prince of the earth in his jubilation will reward the valiant captains who have defended his prerogatives, won

---

[21] If we consider the humanity of Jesus *of its nature,* then since that nature is a created one, its being "seated at the right hand of God" clearly does not mean that it has equality with Divine Being in its *essential* glory. What it signifies is a sublime and unparalleled participation in Infinite Beatitude and Power. [22] Hebr. 10:7-9; Ps.39 (40):8(7-8).

[23] John 14:31. [24] See Phil. 2:9-10.

victory over the enemy and extended by their conquests the bounds of his kingdom.

Is not this what happened in heaven on the day of the Ascension, but with incomparable splendor? Jesus, with sovereign fidelity, had accomplished the work His Father had asked of Him: "I do always the things that are pleasing to Him,"[25] "I have accomplished the work that you have given me to do."[26] Abandoning Himself to the blows of Justice, He had descended, a holy Victim, into abysses of sorrow and disgrace beyond our understanding. And now that all was expiated, paid off, redeemed, now that the powers of darkness were defeated; now that the perfections of the Father were recognized and His rights avenged, now that the gates of the kingdom of heaven were re-opened to the whole human race, what a joy it was for the Heavenly Father (if we dare so stammer in describing such mysteries) to crown His Son after the victory over the prince of this world! What divine delight in calling the sacred humanity of Jesus to enjoyment of the splendors, the beatitude and the power of an eternal exaltation!

And so much more because at the time He was completing His sacrifice, Jesus in person had asked the Father for this glory that was to extend the glory of the Father Himself: "Father, the hour has come! Glorify your Son, that your Son may glorify you."[27]

Yes, Father, the hour has come. Your Justice has been satisfied by expiation; may it also be so through the honors accruing to your Son Jesus because of that love of you that He manifested in His sufferings. O Father, glorify your Son! Make firm His reign in the hearts of those who love Him; bring again beneath His scepter the souls who have turned away from Him; draw to Him those who, sitting in darkness, do not yet know Him! Father, glorify your Son, so that in His turn your Son glorify you by manifesting to us your divine being, your perfections, your wishes! Father, "glorify your Son, that your Son may glorify you."

---

[25] John 8:29.   [26] John 17:4.   [27] John 17:1. The Church causes these words to be read at the Mass of the Vigil of the Ascension.

But the Father has already replied to us: "I have glorified it, and I will glorify it again."[28] And we can hear Him repeat to Christ Himself those solemn words foretold by the Psalmist: "Ask of me, and I will give you the Gentiles for your inheritance, and the utmost parts of the earth for your possession,"[29] "Sit at my right hand: until I make your enemies your footstool."[30]

The divine works are alive with ineffable and secret harmonies, the unique character of which charms faithful souls.

Look at this: where did Christ begin His Passion? At the foot of the Mount of Olives. There, during three long hours, His sacred soul—foreseeing, in the Divine Light, the sum of afflictions and insults that were to constitute His Sacrifice—was a prey to sadness, worry, aversion, fear, anguish. We shall never know what terrible agony was undergone by the Son of God in the Garden of Olives. Jesus suffered there in anticipation (and, as it were, in short compass) all the sorrows of His Passion: "Father, if it is possible, let this cup pass away from me..."[31]

And where did our Divine Savior inaugurate the joys of His ascension? Jesus, Eternal Wisdom—who in this, let us not forget, makes but one with His Father and the Holy Spirit—willed and chose that it should be from the summit of the same mount as had witnessed His sorrowful abasement that He should go up to heaven. There, on the same Mount of Olives where it had burst down on Jesus like an avenging torrent, Divine Justice crowned Him with glory and honor.[32] On that same mount which in the horror of darkness had preluded for Him the mighty combat, there arose the radiant daybreak of an incomparable triumph.

"*Per admirabilem ascensionem tuam...*"[33] Is not our Mother the Church, right in extolling as "wonderful" the ascension of her divine head?

---

[28] John 12:28 (RSV, Cath.) [29] Ps. 2:8. [30] Ps. 109 (110):1.
[31] Matt. 26:39. [32] Hebr. 2:9. [33] Litany of the Saints.

3. Grace that Christ gives us in this mystery; we enter
heaven with Him as members of His mystical body.

Such is the mystery of the Ascension of Jesus: the sublime glorification of Christ at the right hand of God, above all that is created.

Jesus came from the Father: "I came forth from the Father," and now He returns to the Father after having accomplished His mission here below: "I ... go to the Father."[34] He had "rejoiced like a giant to run the course"; He had left the heights of heaven, the sanctuary of divinity; from heaven was His "going forth"; and He goes up again to the summit of all things, to enjoy there divine glory, divine beatitude and divine power. "His circuit is to the height,"[35] ascending to heaven from where He came.

In regard to what, properly speaking, is divine about this triumph, it is the exclusive privilege of Christ, God-man, the Word Incarnate. Jesus alone as Son of God, as Redeemer of the world, has the right to this infinite glory. That is why St. Paul says: "To which of the angels has the Father ever said, 'Sit at my right hand'?"[36]

Our Lord Himself expressed an identical thought in talking with Nicodemus: "No-one," said Jesus, "ascends to heaven except He who has descended from heaven: the Son of Man who is in heaven."[37] Jesus is the Son of Man through His incarnation; but in becoming incarnate He remains the Son of God, who is always in heaven. Descended from heaven, from the heart's-embrace of the Father, to take upon Himself our nature, Christ ascended back there as to His natural abode. To Him alone, true Son of God, does it belong as of full right to ascend there into the presence of the Father, to have part in the sublime honors owed to Divinity; they are reserved for Him only: "No-one ascends to heaven except He who has descended from heaven."

. . .

[34] John 16:28. [35] See Ps. 18 (19):6-7. [36] See Hebr. 1:13. [37] John 3:13.

And we—may we not also enter into heaven? Are we to remain excluded from that abode of glory and beatitude? Do we not have part in the ascension of Jesus? Oh, certainly we have! But, you know, it is through Christ and in Christ that we shall enter heaven.

How so? Through baptism, which makes us children of God. Our Lord revealed this in that same talk with Nicodemus: "Unless a man be born again of water and the Holy Spirit, he cannot enter the kingdom of God."[38] It is as if He said: "There are no means of entering into heaven if you are not reborn of God; there is one eternal birth in the heart's-embrace of the Father; it is mine. By full right, I ascend to heaven, because I am God's own Son, begotten in the holy splendors; but there is another category of children of God: those who are 'born ...of God,'[39] through baptism."[40]

These are children of God, and consequently, says St. Paul, "heirs" of God: "If we are sons, we are heirs also: heirs indeed of God and joint heirs with Christ,"[41] in consequence sharing in His own eternal heritage.

Making us children of God, baptism makes us also living members of the mystical body of which Christ is the head. St. Paul is so explicit on this! "You are the body of Christ, member for member"[42]—each on his own part. And, more vividly still:

[38] See John 3:5.   [39] John 1:13.   [40] [*Translator's note*: See paragraphs 1257-1261 of the *Catechism of the Catholic Church* as to the necessity of baptism, but noting para. 1260 which contains the words: "Every man who is ignorant of the Gospel of Christ and of His Church, but seeks the truth and does the will of God in accordance with His understanding of it, can be saved. It may be supposed that such persons would have *desired Baptism explicitly* if they had known its necessity." There is, I think, no need to interpret the "ignorance" referred to as signifying *total* ignorance: for the minds of persons who genuinely do God's will as they see it may be clouded as to the necessity of baptism by water. Para. 1260 develops the Church's teaching as to "baptism of desire," which is a wider concept than explicit desire for baptism. Para. 1257 says: "God has bound salvation to the sacrament of Baptism, but He Himself is not bound by His sacraments."]   [41] Rom. 8:17.   [42] 1 Cor. 12:27.

"No-one ever hated his own flesh; on the contrary he nourishes it and cherishes it, as Christ also does the Church: because we are members of His body, made from His flesh and from His bones."[43]

Now, the members share in the glory of the head, and the joy of one person is reflected on the whole body. That is why we share in all the treasures Christ possesses; His joys, His glories, His beatitude become ours.

Such is the marvel of Divine mercy. "God, who is rich in mercy," cries the Apostle, "by reason of His very great love wherewith He loved us even when we were dead through sin, brought us to life together with Christ (for it is by grace that you have been saved), and raised us up with Him, and together seated us with Him in heaven, that He might show in the ages to come the infinite riches of His grace, through kindness towards us in Christ Jesus."[44]

And as everything the Father does, the Son does in like manner,[45] Christ Jesus draws our humanity up with Him, to seat it in glory and beatitude. That is the great action of Jesus, the magnificent exploit of this "divine giant": that, through His sufferings, He re-opens the gates of heaven to fallen humanity, and brings it, in train of Him, to heaven's splendors: "Thy only-begotten Son our Lord set at the right hand of thy glory the substance of our frail human nature, which He had taken to Himself,"[46] "Who ... was taken up into heaven, that He might grant to us to be sharers in His own divinity."[47]

When Christ ascended to heaven, says St. Paul, a whole procession of holy souls, a glorious conquest, entered there with Him: "He led captivity captive." But these just ones who escorted Jesus in His triumph were only the first-fruits of innumerable harvests. There will be a ceaseless ascension to heaven, until the day when Jesus's kingdom shall have attained the measure of its fullness.

---

[43] Eph. 5:30.   [44] See Eph. 2:4-7.   [45] John 5:19.
[46] *Communicantes*, Mass of the Ascension.   [47] Preface, Mass of the Ascension.

"Christ's ascension is therefore ours also; the glory of the head founds the hope of the body. On that holy day, not only did we receive assurance of entering again into possession of eternal glory; we already penetrated into the heights of heaven with Christ Jesus."[48] "The wiles of the old enemy tore us away from the first abode of bliss; the Son of God; by *incorporating* us in Him, placed us at the right hand of His Father."[49]

How we understand the chorus of thanksgiving the elect sing in praise of the Lamb who was slain for mankind! How we understand that acclamation, that adoration, they ceaselessly offer to Him who by indescribable torments paid for their bliss without end!

The hour of this glorification has not yet sounded for us. But in awaiting that hour of being united to the choir of the blest, we ought, in thought and by holy desires, to dwell in heaven where Christ our head lives and reigns for ever.

On earth we are but visitors and strangers in search of our homeland. As members of the city of the saints and of the household of God, we ought, through faith and hope, to live there already: "Our citizenship is in heaven,"[50] says St. Paul.

That is also the grace the Church makes us ask of God on this solemnity of the Ascension: "Grant, we beseech thee, almighty God, that we who believe thy only-begotten Son our Redeemer to have this day ascended into heaven, may ourselves live in mind of heavenly things."[51] In the postcommunion of the same Mass, we ask "that what we receive in visible mysteries we may enjoy in its invisible effect." Through holy communion, we are united to Jesus; and in coming to us, Our Lord grants us to share in hope the glory He enjoys in reality. He gives us the very pledge of it: "a pledge of future glory is given to us."[52]

Oh, let us say to Him, draw us along in train of you, magnifi-

---

[48] St. Leo, *Sermo* I, On the Ascension of the Lord, c. IV.   [49] Ibid.
[50] Phil. 3:20.   [51] Prayer of the Mass of Ascension Day.
[52] Antiphon of Vespers of Corpus Christi, *O sacrum convivium*.

cent and almighty Triumpher: "Draw me in your footsteps, let us run."[53] Grant us to ascend to heaven with you, to dwell there by faith, hope and love! May we detach ourselves from all things of earth, which are fleeting, so as to seek only the truly good things which are lasting! Enable us "to be in heart where we know your sacred humanity has ascended bodily"![54]

4. Feelings of deep joy to which this glorification of Jesus gives rise in us.

The ascension of Jesus gives rise to multifarious feelings in the faithful soul that contemplates it with devotion. Even though Christ no longer merits now, His Ascension nevertheless has the power of producing efficaciously the graces it signifies or symbolizes. It strengthens our faith in the divinity of Jesus; it increases our hope through the sight of the glory of our head. By animating us to observe His commandments—this observance being the basis of our merits, which themselves are the source of our future beatitude—it makes our love more ardent. It engenders in us admiration for so marvelous a triumph, and gratitude for the sharing in it that Christ gives us. Raising our souls towards heavenly realities, it brings alive in them detachment from things that are passing. "If you have risen with Christ, seek the things that are above, where Christ is seated at the right hand of God ... not the things that are on earth."[55] It gives us patience with the adversities of here below. For, as St. Paul says, if we have shared the sufferings of Christ, we shall be associated also with His glory: "sharing His sufferings so as to share His glory."[56]

There are, nevertheless, two feelings that I want to dwell on for a few moments, because, springing as they do in particular abundance from devout contemplation of this mystery, they are singularly fruitful for our souls. These are joy and confidence.

---

[53] Song of Songs 1:4(3) (Jerus.)   [54] St. Gregory, *Homil.* XXIX on the Gospels, c.11.   [55] Col. 3:1-2.   [56] Rom. 8:17 (Jerus.)

First, why does it *rejoice us*?

Our Lord Himself said to His apostles before leaving them: "If you loved me, you would indeed rejoice that I am going to the Father."[57] To us also, Christ says these words. If we love Him, we shall rejoice at His glorification; we shall rejoice that, having run the full course, He ascends to the right hand of His Father, to be exalted there in the highest heavens, to enjoy there, after His toils, His sufferings and His death, an eternal repose in immeasurable glory. A happiness such as for us is incomprehensible envelops and possesses Him for ever in the heart of Divinity; supreme power is given to Him over every creature.

How can we not be rejoiced that full justice has, in full plenitude, been rendered to Jesus by His Father?

See how much the Church, in her liturgy, invites us to celebrate with joyousness this exaltation of her Spouse, our God and our Redeemer.

Sometimes she urges all the nations to ring out the fullness of their joy in repeated hymns: "Oh, clap your hands, all you nations; shout unto God, with the voice of exultation!"[58] "God goes up with shouts of joy; the Lord goes up with trumpet blast."[59] "The Lord has reigned over all the nations; God sits on His holy throne."[60] "Glorify the King of kings, and sing praises to God!"[61]

At other times, she calls upon the angelic powers: "Lift up your gates, O ye princes"—princes of heaven—"and the King of Glory shall enter in." Astonished, the angels ask: "Who is this King of glory?" It is "the Lord, who is strong and mighty: the Lord mighty in battle." And the celestial spirits repeat: "Who is this King of glory?" It is "the Lord of hosts; He"—He alone —"is the King of glory."[62]

---

[57] John 14:28.   [58] Introit of Mass of Ascension Day; Ps. 46 (47):2 (1).
[59] Antiphon of Mass of Ascension Day; Ps. 46 (47):6.
[60] Antiphon, Mass of Sunday within the Octave of the Ascension; Ps. 46 (47):9.
[61] Antiphon of Lauds of Ascension Day.
[62] Ps 23. (24):7-10; alternative invitatory, Lauds of Ascension Day.

Then, finally, at other times, in a language full of poetry taken from the psalmist, she addresses Jesus Himself: "Be exalted, O Lord, in your strength! We will sing and praise your power."[63] "Your glory shines in the heights of heaven."[64] "You who make the clouds your chariot; who walk upon the wings of the winds."[65] "You are clothed with majesty and glory, robed in light as with a cloak."[66]

Yes, let us rejoice! Those who love Jesus experience a deep and intense joy in contemplating Him in the mystery of His ascension, in thanking the Father for having given such glory to His Son, and in felicitating Jesus at His being the object of it.

Let us rejoice, as well, that this triumph and glorification of Jesus is ours also.

"I ascend to my Father who is also your Father, to my God who is also your God."[67] Jesus simply precedes[68] us: He does not separate Himself from us, He does not separate us from Himself. His entering into His glorious kingdom is so as to prepare a place for us there: "I go to prepare a place for you."[69] He promises to return one day: "I am coming again, and I will take you to myself; that where I am, there also you may be."[70] And so we are already, by rights, in the glory and felicity of Christ Jesus; we shall be there one day in reality. Has He not asked this of His Father? "Father, *I will* that where I am, they also whom you have given me may be with me."[71] What power there is in that prayer, and what sweetness in that promise!

Let our hearts be given up wholly to this joy, this intimate and altogether spiritual joy. Nothing dilates our souls so much as this feeling, nothing makes us go more generously forward along the running-track of obedience to the Lord's precepts: "I have run

[63] Ps. 20 (21):14 (RSV, Cath.)

[64] See Ps. 8:2 (this and the preceding in First Vespers of Ascension Day)

[65] Ps. 103 (104):3 (RSV, Cath.)   [66] Ps. 103:1 (Rheims). Ps. 103 (104):2 (St P)

[67] See John 20:17.   [68] [*Translator's note*: In the 1926 edition from which this translation is made, the French verb is given as *posséder*, but the first edition has *précéder*, which is clearly right.]   [69] John 14:2.

[70] Ibid., v. 3.   [71] John 17:24.

the way of your commandments, when you enlarged my heart."[72] During these holy days of Ascensiontide, let us repeat often to Christ Jesus the ardent aspirations of the hymn of the Feast: "Be our joy, O you who will one day be our reward; and may all our glory dwell in you, for ever and ever":

> Oh, be our joy—thou who will be
> Our prize throughout eternity:
> Our future glory now in store
> In thee, O Christ, for evermore![73]

5. Why an unshakeable confidence should likewise animate us on this solemnity of the Ascension: Christ enters the Holy of holies as Supreme High Priest and remains there as our one and only Mediator.

To this deep joy we should join an *unshakeable confidence.* Above all, that confidence is based on the all-powerful standing Christ has with His Father, not only as invincible King inaugurating His triumph, but as Supreme High Priest interceding for us after having offered to His Father an oblation of infinite value. Now, it was on the day of His ascension that Jesus, in an altogether special way, began this unique mediation.

There is here an aspect of the mystery, a very interior one, on which it will be supremely useful for us to pause for a few moments. St. Paul, who revealed it to us in his epistle to the Hebrews, himself declares it ineffable, or "difficult to explain."[74] Following the great apostle, I am nevertheless going to try to give you some idea of it. May the Holy Spirit make us understand how marvelous the works of God are.

St. Paul first of all brings to mind the rites of the most solemn sacrifice of the Old Testament. Why does he do this? Doubtless because his letter was addressed to some Jews. It was necessary

---

[72] Ps. 118 (119):32.   [73] Hymn of Vespers and Lauds (Monastic Breviary).
[74] Hebr. 5:11.

to speak to them in a way they could understand. But there was a deeper reason. What was it? The Apostle himself discloses it. It is the very intimate relationship, established by God, between the ancient ceremonial and the Sacrifice of Christ. And what is that relationship?

As you know, God in His eternal foreknowledge embraces the whole series of the centuries. Further, being Infinite Wisdom, He disposes all things with perfect measure and equilibrium. Well, He willed that the principal events which marked the history of the Chosen People, and the sacrifices which He laid down as the religion of Israel, should be so many incomplete types, so many obscure symbols, of the magnificent realities that were to succeed them as soon as the Incarnate Word appeared on earth: "Now all these things happened to them as a type,"[75] "a shadow of things to come."[76]

That is why, from the very start, the Apostle lays stress on the sacrifices of the Jews. It was not for the pleasure of establishing a simple comparison that would help his hearers understand what he was expounding. It was because the Old Testament presaged, in sketchy outline, the splendors of the New Law established by Christ Jesus.

St. Paul calls to mind also what the structure was of the temple at Jerusalem, all the details having been determined by God Himself. There was, he said, a first or outer "tabernacle" called the holy place; the priests entered there at all times for the services of worship. But, beyond a veil, there was a second tabernacle called the Holy of holies, in which were the golden Altar of Incense and the Ark of the Covenant.[77]

This "Holy of holies" was the most august place on earth. It was the center towards which the whole religion of Israel converged, towards which the thoughts of all the Jewish people were directed and their hands lifted in supplication. And why was

[75] 1 Cor. 10:11.   [76] Col. 2:17.   [77] Hebr. 9:2-4.

that? Because it was there that God made His wholly special dwelling, the place of which He had promised, "My eyes and my heart shall be there always."[78] It was there that He received homage, blessed the vows and granted the prayers of Israel. It was there that He entered, so to say, into contact with His people.

But this contact, as you know also, was only established through the high priest as intermediary. So formidable, indeed, was the majesty of this tabernacle where God dwelt, that only the supreme high priest of the Jews could enter there, and entry was forbidden to all others on pain of death. The high priest went in there clothed in priestly vestments, wearing upon his breast the mysterious "rationale," an assemblage of twelve precious stones on which were engraved the names of the twelve tribes of Israel. It was only in this symbolic way that the people had access to the Holy of holies.

Moreover, it was only once a year that the high priest himself could go beyond the veil into this tabernacle that was so holy; and even then he needed to have sacrificed, outside the tabernacle, two animals—one for his own sins, the other for the sins of the people. He sprinkled with their blood the "propitiatory" where God's majesty reposed, while the Levites and the people thronged the court of the temple. This solemn sacrifice, through which once a year the high priest of the Jewish religion offered to God, in the Holy of holies, the homage of all his people and the blood of victims for sin, constituted the highest and most august act of his priesthood.

And yet, as I have told you following St. Paul, all that was only type or figure; the outer tabernacle "is symbolic for the present age."[79] And what imperfections there were in these symbols! So ineffectual was this sacrifice, that it had to be renewed

---

[78] 3 Kings, 9:3.   [79] Hebr. 9:9 (RSV, Cath.) [*Translator's note*: That is to say, under the Old Covenant. The outer sanctuary is "a parable-image of the pre-Messianic ... time" (*A Catholic Commentary on Holy Scripture*).]

each year. So imperfect was this high priest, that he lacked the power to give entrance to the inner sanctuary to the people he represented; whilst he himself could only enter it once a year, and under the protection, so to speak, of the blood of victims offered for his own sins.

Where, then, are the realities? Where, then is the sacrifice, perfect and unique, which will replace for ever these repeated and ineffectual offerings?

We find these realities—and with what fullness!—in Christ Jesus.

Christ, said St. Paul is the Supreme High Priest, but a High Priest "holy, innocent, undefiled, set apart from sinners, and become higher than the heavens."[80] He "entered into a sanctuary not made by the hands of men" (that is, not of this creation),[81] but "into the heavens,"[82] into the sanctuary of the Godhead: "reaching even behind the veil."[83] Like the high priest, He has entered there bearing the blood of the victim. What victim? Animals, as under the Old Covenant? Oh, no; this blood is nothing else than "His own blood,"[84] His Precious Blood of infinite value, shed "outside" the sanctuary of heaven, that is to say upon earth, and poured forth for the sins, no longer solely of the people of Israel but of humankind. He enters in through the veil, that is to say by means of His sacred humanity. It is through this veil that the way to heaven is henceforth open to us: "a new and living way which He inaugurated for us through the veil (that is His flesh)."[85] The final point is that he enters there, not once a year but "once and for all," *semel*;[86] for, His Sacrifice being complete and of infinite worth, it is unique and suffices to obtain for ever the perfection of those He wills to sanctify: "By one offering He has perfected for ever those who are sanctified."[87]

---

[80] Hebr. 7:26.   [81] See Hebr. 9, vv.11, 24.   [82] Hebr. 4:14.   [83] Hebr. 6:19.
[84] Hebr. 9:12.   [85] Hebr. 10:20. [*Translator's note*: The sacred humanity, which veils the divinity of Christ, is also the way through the veil which formerly barred heaven from mankind.]   [86] See Hebr. 9:11.   [87] Hebr. 10:14.

But (and it is in this above all that the divine work is wonderful, that the reality goes beyond the figure), Christ does not enter there alone. Our High Priest takes us with Him, not in a symbolic way but in reality, for we are members of His "fullness,"[88] as the Apostle says.

Before He came, no-one could enter heaven; this prohibition was symbolized by the formidable interdict against going through the veil into the Holy of holies. It was the Holy Spirit Himself who made it known, as St. Paul testifies: "The Holy Spirit signified by this that the way into the Holies was not yet thrown open..."[89]

But Christ Jesus, through His death, has reconciled humankind with His Father. He has torn up with His pierced hands the decree of our expulsion.[90] And that is why when He died the veil of the temple, as you know, was rent in twain, "torn in two from top to bottom."[91] What did this wonder signify? Not only that the Old Covenant with the Jewish people had ceased, that the symbols thenceforth gave place to a higher and more efficacious reality, but, as well as this, that Christ was opening the gates of heaven and giving us entry to the eternal inheritance.

On the day of His ascension, Christ, Supreme High Priest of the human race, took us with Him, by right and hope, to heaven.

Never forget that it is only through Him that we can enter there; no-one can enter into the Holy of holies except with Him. No created being can have the joy of eternal bliss except in train of Jesus; it is the worth of His merits that gains us the infinite beatitude. For all eternity we shall say to Him: "O Christ Jesus, it is through you, through your blood poured out for us, that we are before the face of the Father; it is your Sacrifice, your immolation, that merits for us, at every instant, our glory and our beatitude. To you, O Lamb that was slain, be all honor, all praise, all thanksgiving!"

· · ·

[88] Eph. 1:23.   [89] Hebr. 9:8.   [90] Col. 2:14.   [91] Matt. 27: 51.

While we await Christ's coming to seek us as He has promised, He is "preparing a place for us," and especially does He help us by His prayers.

For what does He do in heaven, this Supreme High Priest? St. Paul replies to us: Christ has entered into heaven "to appear *now* before the face of God on our behalf."[92] His Priesthood is eternal, never-ending. Consequently, His mediation is eternal also. And what infinite power there is in His being heard always!

He is there, in the presence of His Father, ceaselessly presenting to His Father that Sacrifice of which His wound-scars, that He has willed to keep, are an everlasting reminder. He is there, living always "to make intercession" for us.[93]

High Priest who is always heard, He repeats, for us, His priestly prayer at the Last Supper: "Father, I pray for them... They are in the world... Guard those you have given me... I pray for them, that they may have my joy made full in themselves... Father, I will that where I am, they also whom you have given me may be with me; so that they may behold my glory, which you have given me ... so that the love with which you have loved me may be in them, and I in them."[94]

How could these sublime truths of our faith fail to make an inexhaustible confidence arise within us? Souls of little faith, what is there for you to fear? What can you not hope for? Jesus prays for us, always! Why, said St. Paul, if in former times the imperfect blood of animal-victims purified the flesh of those on whom it was sprinkled, how much more shall the blood of Christ who offered Himself unblemished to God "cleanse your conscience from dead works"—from the works of sin—"so that you may serve the living God?"[95]

---

[92] Hebr. 9:24. [93] Hebr. 7:25. See pages 99 ff. above, what we have said about the oblation of Christ in heaven.

[94] See John 17, vv. 9, 11, 13, 24, 26. [95] See Hebr. 9:13-14.

Let us, then, have an absolute confidence in the Sacrifice, the merits and the prayer of our High Priest. On that day of His ascension, He entered into heaven; and, along with His triumph, inaugurated His unceasing mediation. He is the beloved Son in whom the Father is well-pleased. How can He not be heard after having, by His Sacrifice, manifested such love to His Father? He "was heard because of His reverent submission."[96]

O Father, look upon your Son; look at His wounds: "Look on the face of your Christ";[97] and, through Him, in Him, grant us one day to be where He is, so that—through Him also, in Him and with Him—we may render you all honor and glory!

6. We depend upon Christ, so as to be "delivered from evil" in the midst of the sorrows and trials of the present life.

When you go to communion, during these holy days of Ascensiontide, let your soul abandon itself to thoughts of joy and confidence.

By uniting yourself to Jesus Christ you incorporate yourself in Him; He is in you, and you in Him; and you are before the face of the Father. True, you do not see Him. Yet, by faith, you know yourselves to be in His presence, with Jesus who has taken you to Him. You are with Jesus in the heart's-embrace of the Father, in the sanctuary of Divinity. This is for us the deep grace of the Ascension—sharing, by faith, the ineffable inner life that Jesus has with His Father in heaven.

It is recounted in the Life of St. Gertrude that one day, on the solemnity of the Ascension, when she received the Sacred Host from the hand of the priest, she heard Jesus say to her: "Here I am; I did not come to say goodbye to you, but to take you with me to heaven and present you to my Father."[98] Leaning on Jesus, our soul is powerful, because Christ gives us part in all His riches

---

[96] Hebr. 5:7.   [97] Ps. 86 (87):10.
[98] *The Herald of Divine Love*, Book 4, Ch. 36.

and treasures: "Who is this that cometh up from the desert, flowing with delights, leaning upon her Beloved?"[99] In spite of our miseries and our weaknesses, let us never be afraid to approach God. By the grace of our Savior, and with Him, we can always be in the heart's-embrace of our Heavenly Father.

Let us lean upon Christ Jesus, not only in prayer but in all we do, and we shall be strong. Though we can do nothing without Him—"Without me you can do nothing,"[100] we can with Him do everything: "I can do all things in Him who strengthens me."[101] We find in Him both the source of a great confidence and the most efficacious motive for fidelity and patience in the midst of the sorrows, disappointments, trials, sufferings, that we must undergo on earth until our exile ends.

At the time His mortal life was drawing to a close, Jesus addressed to His Father a touching prayer for His disciples whom He was soon to leave: "Holy Father ... when I was with them, I guarded them myself. Now that I am about to return to you ... I do not pray that you take them out of the world, but that you keep them from evil."[102]

What a wholly divine solicitude is expressed in this prayer! Our Lord has said it for us all. And it inspired the Church, who enters always into the feelings of her Spouse, to include this prayer in the Mass of Ascension Day: "Accept, O Lord, the gifts we offer to thee in memory of the glorious Ascension of thy Son: and mercifully grant that we may be freed from present perils, and attain unto life eternal. Through the same Jesus Christ our Lord..."[103] Why is that prayer of Jesus taken up again by the Church?

Because there are obstacles standing in the way of our going to God; and these obstacles all come down to sin which turns us away from God. Our Lord asks that we be delivered from evil—

---

[99] Song of Songs, 8:5. [100] John 15:5. [101] Phil. 4:13.
[102] See John 17, vv. 12-13, 15. [103] *Secretum*, Mass of the Ascension.

that is, from sin which, by estranging us from our Heavenly Father, is the only real evil: "That you keep them from evil." Left to ourselves, to our native infirmity, we cannot avoid obstacles, but we shall be able to if we lean upon Christ. On this day of His Ascension He went up to heaven, victorious over Satan and the world: "Take courage, I have overcome the world,"[104] Satan "has no power over me."[105] Our Lord entered, as all-powerful High Priest, into the divine sanctuary: He has appeared "by the sacrifice of Himself."[106] Through holy communion, He lets us share His power and His triumph. That why we ought so much to lean upon Him.

With Christ offering His merits to His Father for us, there is no temptation we cannot conquer, no difficulty we cannot surmount, no adversity we cannot endure, no insane joy from which we cannot detach ourselves. In waiting to rejoin Jesus in heaven (or rather, waiting till He calls us there Himself, since He is "preparing a place" for us), let us live there, by faith in the limitless power of His prayer which is always heard; by hope of one day being sharers of His bliss; and by love that delivers us up joyously and generously to the faithful and entire accomplishment of His will and His good pleasure.[107] It is thus that we shall participate fully in this wonderful mystery of the glorious Ascension of Jesus: "living in mind of heavenly things."

---

[104] John 16:33.   [105] John 14:30 (Jerus.)   [106] Hebr. 9:26.
[107] "Grant us ever to have a will devoted to Thee, and to serve Thy Majesty with a sincere heart": Collect of Mass of Sunday within the Octave of the Ascension.

CHAPTER SEVENTEEN

The Mission of the Holy Spirit

(Pentecost)

Introduction: The way in which the visible mission of the Holy Spirit to the Apostles enters into the whole cycle of the mysteries of Jesus.

"If you loved me," said Christ to His apostles, "you would rejoice that I am going to my Father."[1]

For those who love Christ, the Ascension is indeed an inexhaustible source of joy. It is the supreme glorification of Jesus in highest heaven; it is the fulfillment of that prayer of Christ: "Father, glorify me with yourself, with the glory that I had with you before the world existed."[2] We are joyous in contemplating our Redeemer and head, God's Son, Jesus, seated at the right hand of His Father after having accomplished, in the self-abasements of His incarnation and the humiliations of His death, His mission of salvation here below.

But Our Lord did not only say to His apostles that they ought to rejoice at His ascension. He also said that His ascension would be to their advantage: "It is expedient for you that I depart. For if I do not go, the Consoler will not come to you; but if I go, I will send Him to you."[3]

---

[1] See John 14:28.   [2] John 17:5.   [3] See John 16:7. [*Translator's note:* Marmion here uses "Consoler," *Consolateur,* rather than "Advocate" (or "Paraclete," from the Greek, which can mean either).]

Every word uttered by the Word Incarnate is "spirit and life," as He Himself said: "The words that I have spoken to you are spirit and life."[4] They are weighty and deep, sometimes mysterious; some of them are difficult to understand, their depths not really fathomable except in prayer. The words of Jesus we have just heard on the subject of His departure from the earth are in that category.

"It is expedient for you that I depart."[5] What? How can it be good for the apostles that Jesus should go, that He should leave them in order to ascend to His Father? Is He not for them the source of all good things, the cause of every grace? Is He not "the Way, the Truth and the Life"? Has He not said, "No-one comes to the Father but through me"? How, then, can it be expedient for the apostles that Jesus should leave them?

Might they not have replied to Him in all truth: O Divine Master, do not say that! We have no need of anyone else, you are sufficient for us: "To whom shall we go?"[6] With you, have we not all graces? Then, "stay with us."[7]

But the words of the Divine Master had been precise: "I speak the truth to you"—*Veritatem dico.* "It is expedient for you that I depart..." He was saying: I cannot stay here any longer, it is time for me to return to my Father: but my leaving will be advantageous to you. Why was that? So that He could send them the Holy Spirit.

And there is the mystery. It is a mystery we are about to contemplate, in so far as that is possible for us. For everything in this is super-natural, and faith alone can guide us.

Although in this talk it is of the Holy Spirit that we shall constantly be speaking, we are about to see how this Spirit's visible mission to the disciples—a mission constituting the particular subject of the Solemnity of Pentecost—pertains to Jesus, in His

[4] John 6:64.   [5] John 16:7.   [6] John 6:69.   [7] Luke 24:29.

divine nature (as it pertains also to the Father), and that consequently it enters into the whole cycle of His mysteries.

First because Christ Jesus *prayed* for this mission; He made it the object of a wholly special prayer. Our Lord said to His disciples at the Last Supper: "I will ask the Father and He will give you another Consoler to dwell with you forever, the Spirit of Truth."[8]

Next, Jesus *promised* His apostles to send them this Spirit. "When the Consoler has come, whom I will send you from the Father, the Spirit of Truth who proceeds from the Father, He will bear witness concerning me."[9] "If I go, I will send Him to you."[10]

Moreover, He has *merited* this mission. By His prayer, as by His Sacrifice, Christ Jesus has obtained from His Father the bestowal on them of this Spirit of truth, love, strength and consolation. Every grace has been purchased by the prayer and immolation of the Savior—as is wonderfully confirmed by the coming of this Spirit so powerful and so full of kindness that Jesus Himself declares Him His equal, in whom the apostles will find another Himself!

Finally, and above all, I do not need to remind you that the sending of the Holy Spirit to the apostles had no other purpose than to *achieve the establishment of the Church.* Jesus had founded this Church upon Peter, but He wished to leave to the Holy Spirit (and we shall shortly see why) the careful task of perfecting it. Indeed, before His Ascension, when at table with His apostles, He charged them not to leave Jerusalem but to wait for the Spirit.[11] The coming of this Spirit was to serve for the glorification of Jesus; but at the same time the Spirit would fill them with strength so that they could "be witnesses to me in Jerusalem, and in all Judea, and Samaria, and even to the uttermost part of the earth."[12] These are the very words of Christ Jesus.

[8] See John 14:16-17.   [9] See John 15:26.   [10] John 16:7.
[11] Acts 1:4.   [12] Acts 1:8 (Rheims).

So then, you can see that this mission of the Holy Spirit to the apostles truly pertains to Jesus. So true is this, that St. Paul calls the Holy Spirit "the Spirit of Christ."[13] That is why we cannot go through the cycle of Christ's mysteries without contemplating this marvelous work which took place ten days after the Ascension.

Let us ask the Holy Spirit Himself to make known to us who He is, and of what His mission and work on the day of Pentecost consists. "Come, Spirit of Truth, enlighten our minds, so that there be kindled in our hearts the flames of love of which you are the infinite Hearth-Fire."

1. Who, within the Trinity, the Holy Spirit is.

We cannot understand the words of Jesus on the subject of the Holy Spirit unless we first remember what Revelation makes known to us of the life of this Spirit within the Blessed Trinity. You are aware of this mystery already;[14] but in contemplating it anew our faith will find there an increase of joy. Let us, then, enter with profound reverence into the sanctuary of the Godhead.

What does faith tell us? That there are in God: the Father, the Son and the Holy Spirit; three distinct Persons in one and the same unity of nature.

As you know, the Father does not proceed from anyone; He is the Wellspring without Wellspring, the first Source of all the interior life in God, the first Origin of all the ineffable communications within the Trinity. Knowing Himself, the Father begets by an Infinite Word one unique and perfect Son, to whom He communicates all that He is, except the property of being Father, which is personal to Himself: "As the Father has life in Himself, even so He has given to the Son also to have life in Himself."[15] The Son is equal in everything to the Father; He is the congruent

---

[13] Rom. 8:9; cf. 1 Peter 1:11; and Acts 16:7 has "the Spirit of Jesus."

[14] See the talk *The Holy Spirit, Spirit of Jesus* in our work *Christ, the Life of the Soul* (Book I, Ch. 6).   [15] John 5:26.

expression,[16] the perfect image, of the Father; He possesses with Him the same divine nature. The Father and the Son give themselves, each to the other, with a perfect love, and it is from this giving of love, by the Father to the Son and the Son to the Father, that, in a mysterious way, there proceeds the Holy Spirit, the Third Person of the Trinity. The Holy Spirit closes the cycle of the interior processes in God; He is the completion of the divine communications within the adorable Trinity.

As you know also, there is between these distinct Persons no superiority or inferiority; it would be a serious error to suppose such a thing. All three are equal in power, in wisdom, in goodness, because all three possess equally, in an indivisible manner, one and the same divine nature with all its infinite perfections. And that is why all our praise is addressed, at the same time, to the Father and to the Son and to the Holy Spirit: *Gloria Patri et Filio et Spiritui Sancto*.

Nevertheless, though there is between them neither inequality nor dependence, there is an order of nature, of origin, that indicates the communications themselves. The fact that the Son "proceeds" from the Father presupposes the Father as First Source—without there being any inequality of time, however.[17] The "proceeding" of the Holy Spirit presupposes the Father and the Son, of whom He, the Spirit, is the mutual gift.

That is a way of speaking we cannot reject. Jesus wishes all His disciples to be baptized "in the name of the Father, and of the

[16] [*Translator's note*: "congruent": Marmion's word is *adéquate*, used in the philosophical sense of "equal in magnitude"—here infinite in being and magnitude, and, like the Father and the Spirit, without beginning.]

[17] [*Translator's note*: Because none of the three Persons had any beginning. The Son's proceeding from the Father is from all eternity, as is the Holy Spirit's proceeding from the Father and the Son. That it is mind-numbingly difficult for us to place the concept of origin and proceeding in a setting of *no beginning* is because, living in time as we do here below, the concepts we are used to are geared to time and not eternity.]

Son, and of the Holy Spirit."[18] Those are the very words of the Word Incarnate; they contain a reality the depths of which are beyond our comprehension. But because they are the words of Jesus, we ought to respect inviolably the order between the Persons of the Trinity. As much as, in our doctrine and prayer, we ought to safeguard intact the unity of nature of the Three, as much also ought we to acknowledge the distinction between the Persons—a distinction based on the communications they have between themselves and on their mutual relations. There is, at one and the same time, equality and order; there is identical perfection and also distinction between their properties as Persons.

These truths constitute an ineffable mystery, about which we cannot speak without stammering. However, Our Lord has willed to reveal to us the existence of this mystery; He willed to make this revelation to us in His last discourse with His disciples, on eve of His death, "that your joy may be made full."[19] He even says to us that if we are His friends, it is because He has made known to us these secrets of God's inner life,[20] in this time of waiting before we rejoice in them in eternal bliss. And why would He have revealed them to us, those secrets, if He had not judged—He, Eternal Wisdom—that the revelation would be of benefit to us?

But note this too. That order of source, of origin, which exists in the ineffable communications of the Persons between themselves and is the very basis of the distinction between them, is something that God has revealed not only by His words. He has willed also to manifest it in His works.

Jesus tells us, in the Gospel, that "this is everlasting life, that they may know you, the only true God, and Him who you have sent, Jesus Christ."[21] He says often that His Father has sent Him. This word "sent," frequently employed by Christ Jesus, marks the distinction between the Persons. It is the Father who "sends"; it is

---

[18] Matt. 28:19.   [19] John 15:11.   [20] John 15:15.
[21] John 17:3; other passages containing "sent" include John 3:17; 4:34; 6:29.

the Son who is "sent." The order of origin which exists *from all eternity in heaven* between the Father and the Son is therefore manifested in *time*. For Christ at the same time, when speaking of His Father, says: "I and the Father are one";[22] and, addressing His Father: "All things that are mine are yours, and yours are mine."[23]

Jesus employs the same term, "send," in speaking of the Holy Spirit. He says to the apostles that *the Father* will send the Holy Spirit in His, Jesus's, name,[24] He says also that *He, Jesus,* will send Him: "If I go, I will send Him to you."[25] You see, then, that it is the Father and the Son who send. So speaks Jesus of the Spirit: and Our Lord wishes to indicate thereby the order that exists in God in the "proceeding" of the Holy Spirit.

2. Reasons why the descent of the Holy Spirit on the apostles did not take place until after the Ascension.

We here touch on the deep reason why Jesus said to His apostles that when He returned to heaven He would send the Spirit.

Christ Jesus in His divine nature is, with the Father, the Source from which the Holy Spirit proceeds. The gift of the Holy Spirit to the Church and to souls is a priceless grace, seeing that this Spirit is Divine Love in person. But, as I said to you just now, this gift, this sending, like every other grace, was merited for us by Jesus. It is the fruit of His Passion; Christ purchased it by the sufferings endured in His sacred humanity. Was it not, therefore, equitable that this grace should have been given to the world only when that humanity of Christ, through which it had been merited, had been glorified? This exaltation of the humanity in Jesus was not accomplished in its fullness, did not attain its full flowering, until the day of the Ascension. Only then did that

---

[22] John 10:30.   [23] John 17:10. Inasmuch as He is a Divine Person; for the humanity of Jesus, considered in itself, as a *nature,* is created and consequently inferior. It is in this sense that Jesus says elsewhere: "The Father is greater than I" (John 14:28).   [24] John 14:26.   [25] John 16:7.

sacred humanity enter definitively into possession of the glory which returned to it by twofold title as humanity united to the Son of God and as victim offered to the Father so as to merit every grace for souls. Seated at the right hand of the Father in the glory of heaven, the humanity of the Incarnate Word would thus be associated with the "sending"—by the Father and the Son—of the Holy Spirit.

We understand now why Our Lord Himself said to His apostles: "It is expedient for you that I depart. For if I do not go, the Consoler will not come to you; but if I return to my Father I will send Him to you." It is as if He said: "I have merited this grace for you by my Passion; and, for it to be given to you, it is necessary that my Passion shall be succeeded by my glorification. When the glory that returns to me has been given to me by my Father, when I am seated at His right hand, *then* I will send you the Spirit of consolation."

The Fathers of the Church[26] add another reason, relating to the disciples.

Jesus one day addressed these words to the Jews: "He who believes in me, as the Scripture says, 'From within him there shall flow rivers of living water.'" St. John the Evangelist, in recording this promise, adds that Christ "said this ... of the Spirit whom they who believed in Him were to receive; for the Spirit had not yet been given, seeing that Jesus had not yet been glorified."[27] Faith was therefore the source, as it were, of the coming of the Holy Spirit upon us. Well, so long as Christ was living on earth, the faith of the disciples was imperfect. It would only be entire, it would only be able to blossom out into its full plenitude, when the Ascension had removed the human presence of their Divine Master from their sight. "Because you have seen me, you have believed," said the Risen Jesus to Thomas; "blessed are they who

---

[26] St. Augustine, *Enarr. in Ps.,* CIX; *Sermones* CXLIII and CCLXIV; St. Leo, *Sermo* II on the Ascension.   [27] John 7:38-39.

have not seen, and yet have believed."[28] After the Ascension, the disciples' faith, more instructed, would seek Christ further away, on high, enthroned beside the Father and equal to the Father.[29]

It was because the apostles' faith became purer, more interior, livelier, more efficacious after the Ascension, that "streams of living water" flowed into them like an impetuous torrent.

We know, indeed, how magnificently Jesus fulfilled His divine promise; how, ten days after the Ascension, the Holy Spirit, sent by the Father and the Son, descended upon the apostles gathered together in the upper room; with what abundance of graces and charisms that Spirit of Truth and Love was infused into the apostles' souls.

3. The work of the Divine Paraclete in the souls of the apostles: He fills them with truth, love, strength and consolation.

What, indeed, was the work of the Holy Spirit in the souls of the apostles on the day of Pentecost?

For you to understand that properly, I must first recall to you the teaching of the Church on the character of divine works. You know that in the realm of super-natural life, of grace, as much as in the works of natural creation, everything that is produced outside of God, in time, is accomplished by the Father, the Son and the Holy Spirit, without distinction of Persons. The Three Persons act in the unity of their divine nature then. The distinction between the Persons exists only in the incomprehensible communications that constitute the inner life of the Trinity.

But in order to make us remember more easily these revelations about the Divine Persons, the Church, in her language, specially attributes this or that action to one of the three Divine Persons, by reason of the affinity that exists between the particular action

---

[28] John 20:29.   [29] St. Leo, *Sermo* II on the Ascension, c.4.

and the exclusive properties by which that Person is distinguished from the others.

Thus, the Father is the First Source, who proceeds from no other, but from whom proceed the Son and the Holy Spirit. That is why the work which indicates the first origin of everything, creation, is attributed to Him specially. Has the Father alone created? Certainly not; the Father and the Holy Spirit create at the same time as the Father and in union with Him. But there is between the property, special to the Father, of being the First Source in the divine communications, and the work of creation an affinity by virtue of which the Church can, without error of doctrine, attribute creation specially to the Father.

The Son, the Word, is the infinite expression of the thought of the Father, He is considered above all as Wisdom. The works in which this perfection shines forth especially, like that of the governing of the world, are attributed to Him in particular. He is, indeed, that Wisdom, the Word of God coming "from the mouth of the Most High,"[30] who "reaches ... from end to end mightily, and orders all things sweetly"[31]—in a perfect equilibrium.

The Church applies the same principle to the Holy Spirit. What is He in the adorable Trinity? He is the completion, the ending of path, the consummation of life in God; He closes the interior cycle of the wonderful operations of the divine life. And that is why, in order that we may remember this property that is personal to Himself, the Church attributes to Him specially everything which, in the work of grace, of sanctification, is in regard to completing, crowning, consummation. He is the Divine Artist who, by His finishing touches, brings the work to its sovereign perfection; He is the "Finger of God's right hand."[32] The work attributed to the Holy Spirit—in the Church, as in souls—is that

---

[30] "O" Antiphon of December 17: "O Wisdom, coming forth from the mouth of the Most High, reaching from one end to the other, mightily and sweetly disposing all things: come and teach us the way of wisdom."   [31] Wisdom 8:1; Ecclesiasticus (Sirach) 24:5; Isaiah 11:2.   [32] Hymn, *Veni Creator Spiritus.*

of leading to its end, to its completion, to its ultimate perfection, the unceasing labor of holiness.

Let us now, for a few moments, contemplate the divine workings of this Spirit in the souls of the apostles.

He fills them with *truth*. You will say to me straight away: had not Christ Jesus done that? Oh, certainly! Did not He Himself declare this?—"I am ...the truth."[33] He had come into this world "to bear witness to the truth,"[34] and we know, also from Himself, that He accomplished His mission entirely: "I have finished the work."[35]

Yes, but now that He has left His apostles, it is the Holy Spirit who is going to become the Teacher inside souls. "He will not speak on His own authority," said Jesus,[36] referring to the Holy Spirit—proceeding from the Father and the Son, receiving from them divine life; He will give us the infinite truth which He receives through His ineffable "proceeding." "He will utter the message that has been given to Him"[37]—that is to say, all truth. He "will recall to your minds everything I have said to you";[38] He "will bring honor to me, because it is from me that He will derive what He makes plain to you."[39]

What else? The apostles did not need to go to the trouble of working out what they should reply when the Jews brought them before the tribunals and forebade them to preach the name of Jesus: it was the Holy Spirit who inspired their replies. "Do not," Christ had said, "be anxious how or what you are to answer ...for the Holy Spirit will teach you in that very hour what you are to say."[40] And thus, "you shall receive power when the Holy Spirit comes upon you, and you shall be witnesses for me," in Judea and Samaria and to the ends of the earth.[41]

---

[33] John 14:6. [34] John 18:37. [35] John 17:4 (Rheims).
[36] John 16:13. [37] Ibid. (Knox).
[38] John 14:26 (Knox). [39] John 16:14 (Knox).
[40] Luke 12:11 (RSV, Cath.); Matt. 10:19-20; Mark 13:11. [41] Acts 1:8.

And as it is by the tongue, the organ of speech, that witness is given and preaching of the name of Jesus is spread throughout the world, this Spirit on the day of Pentecost descended visibly in the form of tongues.

But these are tongues of fire. And why? Because the Holy Spirit comes to fill *with love* the hearts of the disciples. He is Love in person, subsistent Love, in the life of God. He is also like the breath, the breathing-forth of the Infinite Love from which we draw life. It is recounted in Genesis that God "breathed the breath of life"[42] into matter formed from the mud of the ground. This vital breath, was the symbol of the Spirit to whom we owe super-natural life. On the day of Pentecost, the Divine Spirit brought such an abundance of life to the whole Church that, to signify it, "there came a sound from heaven, as of a mighty wind coming, and it filled the whole house where the apostles were assembled."[43] By descending upon them, the Holy Spirit infused into them that Love which is Himself. It was necessary that the apostles be filled with love, so that in preaching the name of Jesus they might make love of their Master arise in the souls of their hearers. It was necessary that their testimony, dictated by the Holy Spirit, be so full of life as to attach the world to Jesus Christ.

This love, ardent like a flame, powerful as a tempestuous wind, was also necessary for the apostles so that when they would have to preach His name they would be able to confront the dangers foretold by Christ. The Holy Spirit filled them with *strength*.

Look at St. Peter, prince of the apostles. On the eve of the Passion of Jesus, he promises to follow Him, even unto death; but that very night, at the voice of a servant-girl, he denies His Divine Master: he swears: "I do not know this man you are talking about."[44] But see him now on the day of Pentecost. He proclaims Christ to thousands of the Jews; he reproaches them, in unre-

---

[42] Gen. 2:7.   [43] See Acts 2:2.   [44] Mark 14:7; Matt. 26:74.

strained language, for having crucified Him. He bears witness to His resurrection, and he briskly exhorts them to do penance and receive baptism.[45] He is no longer the timid disciple who fears danger and keeps his distance;[46] he is the witness who declares before all, in firm and bold words, that Christ is the Son of God.

What strength there is in St. Peter's words! The apostle is no longer recognizable. The power of the Holy Spirit has changed him, the love he bears for his Master is henceforth strong and generous. Our Lord Himself had foretold this transformation, when He said to His disciples before ascending into heaven: "Wait here in the city"—in Jerusalem—"until you are clothed with power from on high."[47]

See also this same Peter and the other apostles a few days after that event. Look at how the Jews were moved by their words, at the miracles they worked, at the conversions they brought about in the name of Jesus. The chief priests and the Sadducees, who had caused Christ's death, called His disciples before them and forebade them to preach the Savior. You know how they replied: "Whether it is right in the sight of God to listen to you rather than to God, decide for yourselves. For *we*"—we on our part—"cannot but speak of what we have seen and heard."[48] In other words: "We must bear witness; we cannot obey your orders."

What was it that made them speak with such courage?—they who, on the night of the Passion foresook Jesus; they who, during the days that followed the Resurrection, kept themselves hidden behind closed doors because of the fear the Jews inspired in them: "the doors ... closed for fear of the Jews."[49] It was the Spirit of truth, the Spirit of love, the Spirit of strength.

It is because their love of Christ is strong that, for Him, they deliver themselves up to torments. For the Jews, seeing that the apostles took no heed of their prohibition, called them before the

[45] Acts 2, vv. 23, 38.　　[46] Mark 14:54.　　[47] Luke 24:49.
[48] Acts 4:18-20.　　　　　　　　　　　　　　　　[49] John 20:19.

tribunal. But Peter declared in the name of all: "We must obey God rather than men."[50]

You know what the Sanhedrin then did. To get the better of this constancy, they had the apostles scourged before releasing them. But note what the sacred writer adds: that the apostles departed from the tribunal "rejoicing that they had been counted worthy to suffer disgrace for the name of Jesus."[51] And where did it come from, this joy in suffering and humiliation? From the Holy Spirit. For He is not only the Spirit of strength, He is also the Spirit of *consolation*. "I will ask the Father, and He will give you another Consoler to dwell with you ... the Spirit of truth."[52]

Is not Christ Jesus Himself already a Consoler? Certainly He is. Has He not said to us: "Come to me, all you who labor and are burdened, and I will give you rest"?[53] Is He not, as St. Paul reveals to us, a High Priest who has "compassion on our infirmities" because He has Himself experienced sorrow?[54] But this Divine Consoler was to disappear from the bodily eyes of the disciples; that is why He prayed His Father to send them *another* Consoler, equal to Himself, God as He is God.

Because He is the Spirit of truth, this Consoler contents the needs of our intellect. Because He is the Spirit of love, He satisfies the desires of our heart to the full. Because He is the Spirit of strength, He sustains us in toil and trials and tears. The Holy Spirit is the Consoler par excellence.

> Thou of Comforters the best,
> Thou the soul's delightful guest,
> Sweet refreshment here below.[55]

Oh, come within us, "Father of the Poor," "Giver of heavenly gifts," "Comforter full of goodness," "Soul's delightful guest," "Sweet refreshment here below."

---

[50] Acts 5:29.   [51] Acts 5:41.   [52] See John 14:16-17.   [53] Matt. 11:28.
[54] Hebr. 4:15; 5:2-3.   [55] Sequence, *Veni Creator Spiritus*.

4. **The assembly of disciples in the upper room represents the whole Church. The marvelous and incessant action of the Holy Spirit in the Church. Pentecost lasts for ever.**

It is for us that the Holy Spirit came: the assembly in the upper room represents the whole Church. It is *"for ever,"* and not otherwise, that the Spirit has come. This is the very promise of Jesus: "to dwell with you for ever"[56]

At Pentecost, He came down visibly upon the apostles. Starting from that day, Holy Church has spread over all the earth. The Church is Jesus's kingdom; and the Holy Spirit, with the Father and the Son, governs this kingdom. He completes in souls the work of holiness begun by the Redemption. He is, in the Church, what the soul is to the body: the Spirit that animates and vivifies; that safeguards unity (even though His action may produce many and various effects); that brings to her all her vigor and beauty.

See, indeed, what a deluge of graces and charisms comes down upon the Church on the morrow of Pentecost. We read in the Acts of the Apostles—the story of the Church in her beginnings—that the Holy Spirit descended visibly upon those who were baptized, filling them with marvelous graces. With what pleasure St. Paul enumerates those graces! "There are varieties of gifts, but the same Spirit" who is their source. "The manifestation of the Spirit" is given to each, for the good of the whole. "To one, through the Spirit, is given the utterance of wisdom; and to another, the imparting of knowledge ... to another, faith"—an extraordinary faith—"to another, the gift of healing." Here is given the power to work miracles; there, the gift of prophecy. Elsewhere, the discernment of spirits; or a diversity of languages, or the interpretation of language. And the Apostle adds: "But all these things are the work of one and the same Spirit," who produces all these gifts, distributing them to each in particular as He pleases.[57]

[56] John 14:16.   [57] See 1 Cor. vv. 4, 7-11.

It was the Holy Spirit, promised and sent by the Father and by Jesus, who gave this fullness and intensity of super-natural life to the first Christians. They, all different as they were, were nevertheless, because of the love the Spirit poured into them, "of one heart and one soul."[58]

Since then, the Holy Spirit dwells in the Church in a permanent and unfailing way, exercising there a ceaseless activity of life and sanctification: "He will dwell with you for ever."[59] He renders the Church infallible in the truth: "When He, the Spirit of truth, has come," said Jesus, "He will guide you into all truth,"[60] guarding you from all error. He makes a wonderful super-natural fruitfulness be a splendor of the Church; He makes arise and blossom in virgins, martyrs, confessors those heroic virtues which are one of the marks of holiness. In a word, He is the Spirit who, by His inspirations, works in the depths of souls to make the Church— which Jesus purchased by His precious blood once and for all— be "without spot or wrinkle or any such thing, but holy and unblemished,"[61] worthy of being presented by Christ to His Father on the day of final triumph.

This interior activity of the Spirit is ceaseless. For Pentecost has not ended. Under its historic form, as a visible mission, there is no doubt it has ended. But it lasts for ever in its power; the grace of Pentecost remains. Henceforth the mission of the Holy Spirit in souls is invisible, but is no less fruitful.

Look at the Church, on that same day when she celebrates the Ascension. What is her prayer, after having sung of the glorification of her Divine Spouse and having rejoiced at it with gladness? She addresses herself to Christ Jesus: "O King of Glory"—whose works show forth your power—"you who have this day ascended in triumph above all the heavens, do not leave us orphans, but send us the Spirit of Truth, the Promised of the Father."[62] O Almighty

---

[58] Acts 4:32. [59] See John 14:17. [60] See John 16:13.
[61] See Eph. 5:27. [62] Antiphon of the Second Vespers of the Ascension.

High Priest, now that you are seated at the right hand of your Father and rejoice in the fullness of your triumph and of your priestly standing, pray to your Father, as you have promised us, that He will send us another Consoler. Through the sufferings of your humanity, you have merited this grace for us; the Father will hear you, because He loves you. Because you are His Beloved Son, He will send with you the Spirit He Himself promised when He said: "I will pour out ... upon the inhabitants of Jerusalem the Spirit of grace and of prayers."[63] Send Him *within us,* into our souls, that He may dwell there for evermore.

The Church prays as if Pentecost were to be renewed for us. She repeats this prayer every day of the Octave of the Ascension; and then, on the day of the Solemnity of Pentecost, she multiplies her praises in addressing the Spirit in a language full of poetry and richness: she invokes Him with unequalled insistence and in the most moving of accents: "Come, O Holy Spirit, fill the hearts of thy faithful, and enkindle in them the fire of thy love!"[64] Then, in the Sequence *Veni, Sancte Spiritus:*

> Come, thou Holy Spirit, come,
> And from thy celestial home
> Shed a ray of light divine...
>
> Thou of Comforters the best,
> Thou the soul's delightful guest,
> Sweet refreshment here below...
>
> O most blessed Light divine,
> Shine within these hearts of thine,
> And our inmost being fill...

And, in the Hymn, *Veni, Creator Spiritus:*

> O Fount of life, O Fire, O Love,
> And sweet anointing from above...

[63] Zacharias 12:10.   [64] Versicle of the Alleluia of the Mass.

Kindle our senses from above,
And make our hearts o'erflow with love;
With patience firm, and virtue high,
The weakness of our flesh supply.

If our Holy Mother the Church puts these desires in our souls and these prayers on our lips, it is not solely to bring to our minds a remembrance of the Spirit's visible mission that took place in the upper room, but also in order that this mystery be renewed in us all in an interior manner.

Let us repeat with the Church those ardent aspirations. Let us especially ask the Heavenly Father to send us this Spirit. Through sanctifying grace, we are His children. Well now, it is the fact of our being His children that impels the Father to shower His gifts upon us. It is because He loves us as His children that He gives us His Son: Holy Communion is "the children's Bread," *Panis filiorum.*[65] It is also because we are His children that He sends us His Spirit, who is one of His most perfect gifts: "highest Gift of God most high."[66] What, indeed, does St. Paul tell us? "Because you are sons, God has sent the Spirit of His Son into your hearts."[67] He is the Spirit of the Son, because He proceeds from the Son, as from the Father; and the Son sends Him at the same time as the Father does. That is why in the Preface of Pentecost we sing: "It is truly right and just ... that we should at all times, and in all places, give thanks unto thee, O holy Lord, Father almighty, everlasting God; through Christ our Lord, who, ascending above all the heavens, and sitting at thy right hand, poured out on this day the promised Holy Spirit upon the children of adoption."

So then, it is to all the children of adoption, to all those who are the brethren of Jesus through sanctifying grace, that the Spirit is given. And because this gift is divine and contains all the most precious gifts of life and of holiness, its being poured into us—an

---

[65] Sequence, *Lauda Sion.*   [66] Hymn, *Veni Creator Spiritus.*
[67] Gal. 4:6 (Rheims).

effusion so copiously manifested on the day of Pentecost—is a source of joy that fills the whole world with gladness: "Wherefore the whole world rejoices with overflowing joy."[68]

5. Workings of the Holy Spirit in our souls. Our duties towards Him.

You will perhaps say to me: "Have we not already received the Holy Spirit at baptism, and more specially still in the Sacrament of Confirmation?"

Assuredly; but we can always receive Him more abundantly; we can always receive from Him lights more intense, strengths more powerful; He can always make deeper wells of consolation rise up in our hearts, set those hearts afire with more ardent love.

And these fruitful workings of the Spirit within us can be renewed not only during the holy days of Pentecost, but also each time we receive a sacrament, an increase of grace, for He is but one with the Father and the Son, and "if anyone loves me," Jesus said, "my Father will love him, and we will come to him and make our abode with him."[69]

The Holy Spirit comes within us to dwell there. He dwells there in order to sanctify us, to guide the whole of our supernatural activity; He makes us sharers in His gifts of wisdom and understanding, of counsel and fortitude, of knowledge and piety, of fear of the Lord, which are so many super-natural aptitudes deposited within us to make us act as children of God ought to act: "Whoever are led by the Spirit of God, they are sons of God."[70]

He dwells within us, this divine guest, full of love and kindness. His sojourn in our hearts is simply for the purpose of helping us, enlightening us, strengthening us. He only leaves us if we have the misfortune to drive Him out from our soul through a mortal sin. It is this that St. Paul describes as extinguishing the

[68] Preface of Pentecost.   [69] John 14:23.   [70] Rom. 8:14.

390 BOOK TWO: THE MYSTERIES OF CHRIST

Spirit[71]—banishing this Spirit of Love by preferring to Him, in an absolute way, that which is created. Let us therefore follow the counsel of the apostle and not "grieve" the Spirit,[72] not resist His inspirations through a sin (whatever it may be, even a light one) that is fully deliberate, coldly accomplished, through a "No" that is a response of our will to everything He suggests to us that is good and right.

For His action is extremely delicate; and when a soul resists Him deliberately, frequently, that soul give offense to the Spirit, forces Him, little by little, to be silent. Then that soul comes to a halt on the path of holiness, and even runs a great risk of departing from the way that leads to salvation. What can such a soul do, without instructor to guide it, without light to illuminate it, without strength to sustain it, without joy to transport it?

Rather, be faithful to this Spirit who comes within us, with the Father and the Son, to take up His abode there. "Do you not know that you are"—through grace—"the temple of God," says St. Paul, "and that the Spirit of God dwells in you?"[73] Every increase of grace is like a new reception of this divine guest, a new taking of possession of our soul by Him, a new embrace of love.

And how beneficial these workings are in a faithful soul! He makes the soul know the Father: "Through thee may we the Father know,"[74] and, making Him known, He produces in the soul, through the gift of piety, the attitude of adoration and love that it ought to preserve towards our Heavenly Father. Listen to what St. Paul so explicitly says: "The Spirit helps us in our weakness; for we do not know how to pray as we ought, but the Spirit Himself intercedes for us with sighs too deep for words."[75] And what is this

---

[71] 1 Thess. 5:19.   [72] Eph. 4:30.
[73] 1 Cor. 3:16.   [74] Hymn, *Veni, Creator Spiritus*.
[75] Rom. 8:26 (RSV, Cath.) [*Translator's note:* Marmion's French has, not "we do not know *how* to pray," but "do not know *what* to ask for in our prayers." This is in accord with the Rheims.]

prayer? "You have received," St. Paul says, "a spirit of adoption ... by virtue of which we cry, 'Abba! Father!' The Spirit Himself gives testimony to our spirit that we are sons of God."[76]

He makes us know the Son also: "May we know also the Son."[77] He manifests Christ Jesus to us; He is that interior Teacher who makes us know Jesus, who makes us enter into comprehension of His words and His mysteries; because, says Jesus, He proceeds from me as from the Father; He glorifies me in you (the Apostles): "He will glorify me, because He will receive of what is mine and declare it to you."[78] By spreading within us the divine knowledge, by taking us through love into the presence of Jesus, by inspiring us to do always what is pleasing to Him, He makes Christ reign in us. Through His infinitely delicate and sovereignly efficacious action, He forms Jesus in us. And does not the substance of all holiness consist of simply that?

Let us, then, ask Him to come within us, to dwell there, to increase there the abundance of His gifts. Fervent prayer is one condition of His coming into our souls.

Humility is another condition. Let us present ourselves to Him with a deep-seated conviction of our interior poverty; that disposition of soul is excellent for receiving Him of whom the Church sings:

> Where thou art not, man hath naught,
> Nothing good in deed or thought,
> Nothing free from taint of ill.[79]

Let us, in consequence, make our own these fervent aspirations of the Church: "Come, O Holy Spirit, fill the hearts of thy faithful; and kindle in them the fire of thy love."[80]

---

[76] Rom. 8:15-16.

[77] Hymn, *Veni Creator Spiritus.*

[78] John 16:14.

[79] Sequence, *Veni, Sancte Spiritus.*

[80] Alleluia versicle of Pentecost Day.

In our labor rest most sweet,
Pleasant coolness in the heat,
Solace in the midst of woe...

Heal our wounds, our strength renew,
On our dryness pour thy dew,
Wash the stains of guilt away.[81]

Despite our wretchedness, let us invoke the Holy Spirit. Because of that very wretchedness, He will grant our prayers.

And since He is but one with the Father and the Son, let us address ourselves to the Father also: Father, send within us, in the name of your Son Jesus, the Spirit of Love so that He may fill us with a deep inward feeling of our being God's children. And you, O Jesus, our High Priest, now seated at the right hand of your Father, call on Him for our sakes so that this mission of the Spirit, which you promised and merited, may be an abundant one. May it be an impetuous river making glad the city of souls; or rather, in your own words O Jesus, "fountains of living water,"[82] springing up into life eternal.

Jesus "was speaking of the Spirit which those who believed in Him were to receive."[83]

---

[81] Sequence, *Veni, Sancte Spiritus.*   [82] John 7:38 (Jerus.)
[83] Ibid., v. 39.

CHAPTER EIGHTEEN

"In Remembrance of Me"
(*Corpus Christi*)

Introduction: The Eucharist is a mystery of faith.

All the mysteries of Jesus are essentially mysteries of faith; without faith we can neither accept nor contemplate any of them.

However, the degree of light that illuminates our faith in each of them is different. Look at Bethlehem: we glimpse in the manger only a little child. Without faith we would not recognize in that child the Son of God, the Sovereign Master of all creatures; but we hear the voice of angels from heaven celebrating the coming of this Savior of the world; and we see a marvelous star guide the kings of the Orient to His feet. At the baptism of Jesus our eyes see only a man who submits, like the other Jews, to a rite of penitence; but the heavens half-open, and the voice of the Eternal Father makes itself heard and proclaims that this man is His Beloved Son in whom He is infinitely well-pleased. It is the same on Tabor: in this mystery of the Transfiguration, faith is powerfully aided. The glory of the divinity with which the humanity of Jesus is penetrated shines out visibly to illumine it, and the disciples, dazzled, hide their faces upon the ground. On the other hand, the divinity is veiled when Christ dies on the cross, like the lowest of men, in the midst of torments; and yet the centurion declares that He is the Son of God; and nature herself, through the convulsions she suffers at that unique moment, renders solemn homage to her Creator. At the Resurrection, what do we see? Jesus is wholly resplendent with glory; but at the same time He proves to His apostles that He is always Himself, is man as well as God. He makes them touch Him, He eats with them, He shows them the scars of His wounds, so as to make it clear to them that He is not merely a spirit but is the same Jesus in whose company they have lived for three years.

You therefore see my point. Though in each mystery of Christ there is enough "shade" to make our faith meritorious, there is also enough light shining to aid our faith. In all of them we see manifested the ineffable union of the divinity with the humanity.

But there is one mystery where both the divinity and the humanity, far from revealing themselves, disappear to our senses. It is the mystery of the Eucharist.

What is there upon the altar before the Consecration? A bit of bread, a little wine. And after the Consecration? For the senses— for touch, sight, taste—bread and wine still. Faith, only faith, penetrates beneath those veils, to reach the divine reality that is totally hidden there. Without faith, we shall never see anything but bread and wine; we shall not see God; He does not reveal Himself there as He does in the Gospel. We do not see even the *man*:

> On the cross was hid thy Godhead's splendor;
> Here thy manhood lieth hidden too.[1]

When, during His life on earth, Christ declared Himself to be the Son of God, He gave proof of what He said. One could certainly see that He was a man; but a man whose teaching could only come from God: "He whom God has sent speaks the words of God,"[2] a man who performed miracles that only God could

---

[1] Hymn, *Adoro te devote*.   [2] John 3:34.

work: "Not from the beginning of the world has it been heard that anyone opened the eyes of a man born blind. If this man were not from God, he could do nothing."[3] Along with the man born blind, Nicodemus the pharisee likewise acknowledged this: "Rabbi ... we know that you are a teacher who comes from God; for no-one could perform the signs that you do unless God were with him."[4] Faith was necessary, but the miracles of Jesus and the sublimity of His doctrine aided the faith of the Jews—the faith of simple men as well as that of the learned.

In the case of the Eucharist, there is room only for pure faith; faith founded solely on the words of Jesus: "This is my body, this is my blood."[5] The Eucharist is, above all, a "mystery of faith": *Mysterium fidei.*[6]

That is why in this mystery, more than all those we have considered up to now, we ought to listen solely to Jesus. Reason is so confounded that those who, in this, do not listen to Christ must say, like the Jews to whom Our Lord promised the Eucharist: "This saying is hard, and who can hear it?"[7] And they went away from Christ's presence. Let us, on the other hand, go to Jesus as did the faithful apostles whom Christ asked on that occasion, "Will you also go away?" and let us say to Him, with Peter: "Lord, to whom shall we go? You have the words of eternal life. And we have believed and have known that you are the Christ, the Son of God."[8]

Therefore, let us consult Christ on the subject of this mystery. Christ Jesus is Infallible Truth, Eternal Wisdom, Omnipotence. That which He promised—why should He not have carried it out?

---

[3] John 9:32-33.   [4] John 3:2 (Jerus.)   [5] Matt. 26:26-28; Mark 14:22-24.
[6] Canon of the Mass.   [7] John 6:61 (Rheims).   [8] Ibid., vv. 69-70.

1. The Sacrifice of the Altar perpetuates the memory of Jesus.

When our Divine Savior instituted this mystery with the object of perpetuating the fruits of His Sacrifice, He said to His apostles: "Do this in remembrance of me."[9] So, beyond its primordial purpose of renewing His immolation and of allowing us to participate in it by holy communion, Christ added to it the character of memorial. And how does this mystery preserve the memory of Christ? How does it recall Him to our hearts?

The Mass preserves the memory of Jesus, first of all as a Sacrifice.

Of course, as you know, there is only one Sacrifice, one which is full, total, perfect, which has paid off everything, merited everything, and from which every grace flows. And that is the Sacrifice of Calvary; there is no other. "By virtue of that one single offering, He has achieved the perfection of all whom He is sanctifying," says St. Paul.[10]

But in order that the merits of this Sacrifice be applied to all the souls of all times, Christ has willed that it be renewed on the altar. The altar is another Calvary, where the immolation of the cross is remembered, re-presented and reproduced. Thus, wherever there is a priest to consecrate the bread and the wine, we preserve the memory of Christ's Passion. That which is offered and given on the altar is the body which was delivered up for us, the blood which was shed for our salvation.[11] It is the same High Priest, Christ Jesus, who offers them again, through the ministry of His priests. How, therefore, can we fail to think of the Passion when we are present at the Sacrifice of the Mass, where everything is identical, save for the manner in which the oblation is carried out?[12]

[9] Luke 22:19; 1 Cor. 11:24. [10] Hebr. 10:14 (Jerus.)
[11] Matt. 26:28; Mark 14:24; Luke 22:19-20. [12] "In this divine sacrifice which is celebrated in the Mass, that same Christ is contained and immolated in an unbloody manner, who once offered Himself in a bloody manner on the altar of the cross": Council of Trent, Sess. XXII, cap. II.

No Mass is said, no Holy Communion received, without our being reminded that Jesus was delivered up to death for the world's ransom. For, says St. Paul, "*as often as* you shall eat this bread and drink this cup, you proclaim"—you announce, you make known, you bring to mind—"the death of the Lord, until He comes."[13] That is the way of it until He comes again on the Last Day.

Remembrance of Christ by those He came to redeem by His immolation is in this manner perpetuated, living and fruitful, till the end of time.

The Mass is therefore truly the memorial Christ has left us of His Passion and death. It is the testament of His love. Wherever the bread and wine are offered, wherever there is then a Consecrated Host, there quite evidently the immolation made by Christ is commemorated: "Do this in memory of me."

What above all the Mass recalls to us is the memory of the Passion of Jesus. It was on the eve of His death that Jesus instituted it. It was as a testament of His love that He left it to us.

But it does not exclude the other mysteries. Look at what the Church does. She is the spouse of Christ; no-one knows better than she the intentions of her divine head. In oganizing the public worship she renders to Him, she is guided by the Holy Spirit. Well then, what does she say? As soon as the Consecration is completed, she first recalls the words of Jesus by saying: "Do this in memory of me." And immediately afterwards she adds:[14] "Wherefore, O Lord, we thy servants, as also thy holy people, calling to mind the blessed Passion of the same Christ, thy Son, our Lord, and also His Resurrection from the dead and His glorious Ascension into heaven, do offer unto thy most excellent Majesty ... a pure Host, a holy Host, an unspotted Host, the holy Bread of eternal life, and the Chalice of everlasting salvation."[15]

---

[13] 1 Cor. 11:26.   [14] [*Translator's note*: Marmion is, of course, quoting from the prescribed liturgy of his time.]   [15] A similar prayer is said after the Offertory: "Receive, O holy Trinity, this oblation which we make to Thee, in memory of the Passion, Resurrection and Ascension of our Lord Jesus Christ..."

The Greeks, after mention of "the Ascension to the right hand of the Father" also refer to "the second and glorious coming" of Christ.[16]

So then, although the Mass recalls, directly and in first place, the Passion of Jesus, it does not exclude remembrance of the *glorious* mysteries which are linked so closely to the Passion, of which they are, in a sense, its crowning.

Since it is the Body and Blood of Christ that we receive, the Mass presupposes the Incarnation and the mysteries that rest on or follow from it. Christ is upon the altar with His divine life that never ends, with His mortal life (of which doubtless the historical form has ended, but of which the substance and the merits remain), with His glorious life, which will have no end at all.[17]

All this, you know, is really a part of what the Sacred Host gives our souls in holy communion. In giving Himself to us, Christ delivers Himself up in the substantial totality of His works and His mysteries, as in the oneness of His Person. Yes, let us say, with the psalmist, who sang in advance of the glory of the Eucharist:[18] "He has made a remembrance of His wonderful works, being a merciful and gracious Lord: He has given food to those that fear Him."[19]

The Eucharist is like a synthesis of the marvels of the Incarnate Word's love for us.

---

[16] See D.E. Vandeur, *La Sainte Messe, Notes sur la liturgie,* 35th thousand, pp. 164 and 223-226.   [17] See Msgr. Gay, *De la triple vie de Jésus que la Sainte Eucharistie contient et communique,* in *Élévations sur la vie et la doctrine de Notre Seigneur Jésus-Christ,* 114th elevation.

[18] The Church applies these words to the Holy Eucharist in her Office for Corpus Christi.   [19] Ps. 110 (111):4-5.

2. Manna, figure or symbol of the Eucharistic Sacrament.

If we now consider the Eucharist, the Blessed Sacrament, we shall discover in it wonderful properties that no-one but God could have devised.

I have told you often, following St. Paul to whom this idea is dear, that the principal events in the history of the Jewish people under the Old Testament were symbols—sometimes hidden, obscure; sometimes apparent, luminous—of realities that would throw light on the New Covenant established by Christ. Well, according to the very words of Our Lord, one of the most characteristic figures or symbols of the Blessed Sacrament had been *manna*. With particular insistence, our Divine Savior showed points of comparison between this food that fell from the heavens to feed the Hebrews in the desert, and the Eucharistic Bread that He was to give to the world. Therefore, it is entering into the sentiments of Christ if we study the figure or symbol so as better to grasp the reality.

Now, see in what terms the sacred writer (through whom the voice of the Holy Spirit is heard) speaks to us of manna. "You nourished your people with food of angels and gave them bread from heaven, ready to hand, untoiled-for, having in it all that is delicious, satisfying every taste. For your sustenance showed your sweetness to your children, and serving every man's will, it was accommodated to what each liked."[20]

In her office for Corpus Christi, the Church has taken up these magnificent words in order to apply them to the Eucharist.[21] We are about to see how truly and fully they express the properties of the Eucharistic Food; to see how much greater reason we have to sing about the Sacred Host what the inspired author sang of manna.

[20] See Wisdom 16:20-21.   [21] Canticles of the third nocturn of Matins (Monastic Breviary); cf. second antiphon of Lauds.

Like manna, the Eucharist is nourishment—but spiritual nourishment. It was in the midst of a meal—the Last Supper—under the form, the appearance, of food, that Our Lord willed to institute it. Christ Jesus gives *Himself* to us as nourishment for our souls: "My flesh is food indeed, and my blood is drink indeed."[22]

Again like manna, the Eucharist is bread come down from heaven. But manna was only an imperfect figure or symbol; that is why Our Lord said to the Jews who were recalling to Him the miracle in the desert: "Moses did not give you bread from heaven," it is my Father who gives the *true* bread from heaven: "For the bread of God is that which comes down from heaven and gives life to the world"[23]—"to the world," not simply a particular people, but all mankind.

And as the Jews murmured on hearing Him call *Himself* "the bread come down from heaven," Jesus added: "I am the bread of life. Your Fathers ate the manna in the desert, and have died ... I am the *living* bread that comes down from heaven. If anyone eat of this bread he shall live forever"—for He plants within our very *bodies* the seed-germ of resurrection—"and the bread that I will give is my flesh for the life of the world."[24]

You see how clearly Our Lord's own words show us that the divine reality of the Eucharist surpasses in fullness, in substance and in its fruits, the nourishment given of old to the Jewish people.

This Bread from heaven gives us life by its nourishment of grace within us. It has in it all that is sweet and delicious: *Omne delectamentum in se habentum.*[25]

There is nothing so joyous as a marriage-feast. Holy communion is the soul's marriage-feast: which is to say, a source of profound joys. How could Christ, the Truth and the Life, Well-spring of all good and all beatitude, *not* fill our hearts with joy? In letting us drink of the wine-cup of His divine blood, how could

[22] John 6:56.   [23] See John 6:32-33.   [24] John 6, vv. 48-49, 51-52.
[25] [*Translator's note:* These words have a special resonance through their being sung at Benediction when the Blessed Sacrament is adored.]

He fail to fill our souls with a spiritual joyousness that enlivens our charity and sustains our fervor? Look at Him in the upper room after He had instituted this divine sacrament. To His apostles He speaks of His joy—His own joy, an altogether divine joy—saying: "These things I have spoken to you that *my* joy may be in you, and that your joy may be made full."[26] This is one of the effects of the Eucharist, when it is received with devotion; it fills the soul with a super-natural sweetness that makes the soul prompt and dedicated to the service of God.

Let us not forget, however, that this joy is above all spiritual. The Eucharist being par excellence the "mystery of faith," *mysterium fidei,* it may happen that God permits this wholly interior joy to have no reaction upon the part of our being where the feelings are. It may happen that very fervent souls are weighed down still by aridity and lack of emotional feeling after having received the Bread of Life. Let them in no way be surprised at this; and above all, let them not be discouraged. If they have brought to the receiving of Christ all the proper dispositions possible, if they suffer in their powerlessness, let them be reassured and remain in peace. Christ, ever living, acts in silence but sovereignly, in the inner depths of the soul, to transform it into Himself. That is the most precious effect of this heavenly food: "He who eats my flesh, and drinks my blood, abides in me and I in him."[27]

What is next to say? This living Bread which gives life, this delicious food which brings joy, is "untoiled-for"; it is granted to us "without labor." That was one of the properties of manna. How much more is it true of the Eucharistic Food!

What, indeed, is asked of us so that we may sit down at the "marriage-feast of the King" and fruitfully eat the Bread of Heaven? Only that we come to it as a guest wearing a "wedding garment"[28]—that is, that we be in a state of grace, and have the right intention.

[26] John 15:11.   [27] John 6:57.   [28] Matt. 22:11.

Nothing else is required on our side. But for Jesus? Oh, indeed! It was not "without labor" that He prepared this feast for us. It needed the abasements of the Incarnation; it needed humility, and toil during the obscure years of His hidden life; it needed the fatigue of His apostolate, His struggles against the Pharisees, His combats against the prince of darkness; and finally—what sums up, contains and crowns all—the sorrows of the Passion. It was only at the cost of immolation by the shedding of His blood, and sufferings without name, that Christ Jesus merited for us this truly unheard-of grace of uniting us closely with Him by giving us as food His sacred body, and as drink His precious blood.

That is why He willed to institute this Sacrament on the eve of His Passion, as though to give us the most touching of proofs of His excess of love for us: "Jesus ... having loved His own who were in the world, loved them to the end."[29] It is because it was conferred at such a cost that this gift is replete with the "sweetness" of the infinite love of Christ Jesus for us: "Your sustenance showed your sweetness..."[30]

Those are some of the marvels prefigured by manna, and fulfilled, for the life and joy of our souls, by the wisdom and kindness of our God.

How can we not be in wonderment, as the Church is? How can we fail to surround these sacred mysteries with all our reverence and adoration? "Grant us, we beseech thee, so to venerate the sacred mysteries of thy body and blood, that we may ever feel within us the fruit of thy redemption."[31]

---

[29] John 13:1.   [30] Wisdom 16:21.
[31] Collect for the Feast of Corpus Christi.

3. **We find in this Sacrament the power of the mysteries of Jesus.**

Of all the properties that Holy Scripture attributes to manna, there is one that is particularly remarkable. Manna was a food that accommodated itself to the tastes and wishes of the one who took it: "serving every man's will, it was accommodated to what each liked."[32]

In the Bread of Heaven which is the Eucharist, we can also find (if I can put it this way) a *taste* of all the mysteries of Christ, and the power of all His states. We are here considering the Mass, not as a memorial but as a source of graces. This is a fruitful aspect of the Eucharistic mystery, and I want to dwell on it for a few moments. If we let it sink deep into our souls, we shall feel an increase within us of love and desire for this divine food.

As you know, Our Lord gives Himself as food in order to maintain within us the life of grace; and, further—through the union this Sacrament establishes between our souls and the person of Jesus (one "who eats my flesh, and drinks my blood, *abides in me, and I in Him*"),[33] through the charity this union nourishes— Christ brings about such a transformation as that which made St. Paul say: "I live, or rather, it is not I who live; it is Christ who lives in me."[34] That is the distinctive power of this ineffable Sacrament.

But for us this transformation admits of many degrees and comprises many stages. We cannot bring it about all at once; it happens little by little, in the measure that we enter further into an understanding of Christ Jesus and His states, since His life is our model, and His perfection the example for ours.

Devotional contemplation of the mysteries of Jesus constitutes one of the elements of this transfiguration. I have already said to you that when, through a lively faith, we put ourselves in contact with Him, Christ produces in us, through the never-failing

[32] See Wisdom 16:21.   [33] John 6:57.   [34] See Gal. 2:20.

power of His sacred humanity united to the Word, that resemblance which is a sign of our planned destiny.[35]

If that is true of the simple contemplation of the mysteries, how much deeper and more extensive in this domain will the action of Jesus be when He dwells in our souls by sacramental communion! That union with Christ is the greatest and most intimate that in the present life we could possibly have: the union that takes place between the Bread and the one who takes it. Christ gives Himself to be our food; but—the exact opposite of what happens with bodily nourishment—it is we who are assimilated to Him. Christ becomes our life.

The first benefit of manna was that it nourished. The distinctive grace of the Eucharist is likewise to maintain the divine life in our soul, by making us participate in the life of Christ.

But just as the manna was "accommodated to the taste" of the one who took it, so also with the life that Christ gives us. It is *all* His life that passes into our souls to be the example and the shape of our life; to produce in us the various feelings of the

---

[35] [*Translator's note:* That is, the destiny ("*prédestination*") planned and desired by God for everyone, here considered in relation to hypothetical individuals on the highway to that destiny. "Predestination," as used by Marmion and the Church, really means "planned destiny" and emphatically does not imply that God has a salvific plan for some and not all. See *Gaudium et Spes,* 22: "Since Christ died for all, and since all men are in fact called to one and the same destiny, which is divine, we must hold that the Holy Spirit offers all the possibility of being made partners, in a way known to God, in the paschal mystery." God's plan and desire for each individual is that he or she be "conformed to the image of Christ" in an individual way. Whether that plan and desire is fulfilled by eternal salvation in the individual case depends upon the individual, aided by grace (and the same paragraph of *Gaudium et Spes* has a reference to non-Christian "men of goodwill in whose hearts grace is active invisibly"). In his poem *As Kingfishers Catch Fire,* Gerard Manley Hopkins highlighted in striking words the apposite concept of the "just man" being one whose actions conform to the divine plans and desires for him individually; to the way the Father *sees him as He desires him to be,* that is to say, as conformed to the image of His Son: "The just man justices;/Keeps grace: that keeps all his goings graces;/*Acts in God's eye what in God's eye He is* —/*Christ.*" This is exactly what Marmion is saying.]

heart of Jesus; to make us imitate all the virtues He practiced in His various states; and to pour into us the special graces He merited for us in living His mysteries for us.

Doubtless, and we should never forget it, there is under the Eucharistic appearances the substance simply of the *glorified* body of Jesus, such as it is at present in heaven, and not such as it was, for example, in the manger at Bethlehem.

But when the Father looks on His Son Jesus in the heavenly splendors, what does He see? He sees Him who, for our sakes, lived on earth for thirty-three years; He sees all that this mortal life contained of mysteries, satisfactions and the merits of which these mysteries were the source; He sees the glory His Son gave Him in living each of them. In each of them also, He sees always the same Beloved Son, albeit that it is simply in His glorified state that Christ is enthroned at His right hand.

In the same way, the one whom we receive is Jesus who was born of Mary, who lived at Nazareth, who preached to the Jews of Palestine. This is the Good Samaritan; this is He who healed the sick, delivered Mary Magdalene from the devil, raised Lazarus from the dead. This is He who, wearied, slept in the boat; this is He who, in His agony in the garden, was crushed by anguish; this is He who was crucified on Calvary, who rose, glorious, from the tomb; this is the mysterious pilgrim on the road to Emmaus who made Himself recognized "in the breaking of the bread";[36] this is He who ascended to heaven, to the right hand of the Father; this is the Eternal High Priest, ever living, who never ceases to pray for us.

All these states of the life of Jesus, the Eucharist gives us in substance, with their special properties, their spirit, their merits and their power. Under the diversity of states, under the variety of the mysteries, is perpetuated the identity of the Person who lived them, and who now lives eternally in heaven.

When, therefore, we receive Christ at the Holy Table, we can

---

[36] Luke 24:35.

look at Him and converse with Him in any of His mysteries, even though He is now in His life in glory, for we find in Him the one who lived for us and merited for us the grace which those mysteries contain. Christ, dwelling within us, communicates that grace to us, in order to bring about, little by little, that transformation of our life into His—which is the distinctive effect of the Sacrament. To understand this, it is enough to run through the prayers in the Masses of the different feasts of the Savior—the prayers the priest says in a low voice (the *secreta*); and the postcommunions. The object of these prayers, which hold a special rank among those of the Eucharistic Sacrifice, varies according to the nature of the particular mysteries then being celebrated.[37]

We can, for example, unite ourselves to Jesus as living in the "heart's-embrace of the Father,"[38] equal to His Father, God as His Father is. He whom we adore within us after holy communion, we adore as the Word, co-eternal with the Father, God's own Son, in whom the Father delights. "Yes, I adore you within me, O Divine Word. Through the intimate union I have with you at this moment, grant me to be also, with you, in the heart's-embrace of the Father, now by faith, later in the eternal reality, in order that I may live with the very life of God, which is your life."

We can adore Him, as the Virgin Mary adored Him when He, the Word Incarnate, was living within her before He appeared to the world's sight. Only in heaven shall we know with what feelings of reverence and love the Virgin bowed down interiorly before the Son of God who in her womb was taking our flesh.

Again, we can adore Him, present within us, as we would have adored Him twenty centuries ago in the stable at Bethlehem, with the shepherds and the wise men. He will then communicate to us the grace to imitate the special virtues of humility, poverty, detachment, that we contemplate in Him in that state of His hidden life.

---

[37] See pp. 105-106 above.   [38] See John 1:18.

If we wish, He will be within us as the one in agony who obtains for us, through His wonderful submission to the will of His Father, grace to bear our daily crosses. He will be the divine risen one, who gives us the grace to detach ourselves from everything earthly, to "live for God"[39] more generously and fully. He will be within us the Triumpher who, in the fullness of His glory, ascends to heaven and bears us along after Him so that already we may live there by faith, hope and holy desires.

The Christ thus contemplated and received is the Christ reliving within us all His mysteries. It is Christ's life entering into our life and, with all its own beauty, its particular merits and its special graces, substituting itself for our own life: "Serving every man's will."

4. How to participate in this mystery: by the Sacrifice of the Mass, by holy communion, by visiting the Blessed Sacrament. The profound reverence that ought to surround this mystery.

In the account I have just given you, I have implied that the most perfect participation in this divine mystery is sacramental communion.

But, as you know, communion itself presupposes sacrifice. That is why we are already associating ourselves with the mystery of the altar by being present at the Sacrifice of the Mass.

We would give anything to have been at the foot of the cross with the Virgin, St. John and Mary Magdalene. Well, the oblation of the altar reproduces and renews the immolation of Calvary so as to perpetuate its memory and apply its fruits.

During Holy Mass we should unite ourselves to Christ, but to Christ immolated. He is, on the altar, "the Lamb as though slain,"[40] the Lamb offered as victim, and it is with His Sacrifice that Jesus wills to associate us. Look at what happens after the

---

[39] See Rom. 6:11.   [40] See Apoc. 5:6.

Consecration. The priest, his joined hands resting on the altar—a gesture that signifies the union of the priest and all the people with the Sacrifice of Christ—says this prayer: "We most humbly beseech thee, Almighty God, command these offerings to be borne ... to thine altar on high, in the sight of thy Divine Majesty..."[41]

The Church speaks here of two altars, relating them to each other in thought: the altar on earth, and an altar in heaven. Not that in the sanctuary of heaven there would be a material altar; but the Church wishes to indicate that there is only one Sacrifice. The immolation carried out mystically on earth is one with the offering that Christ, our High Priest, makes of Himself in the heart's-embrace of the Father, to whom He offers, for us, the satisfactions of His Passion.

"These offerings" (the phrase in that prayer) are, says Bossuet, in truth the body and blood of Jesus, but they are that body and blood *with all of us,* and with all our wishes and prayers, and the whole together make up one and the same oblation.[42]

Thus, at that solemn moment, we are admitted "behind the veil,"[43] into the sanctuary of Divinity; but we are so because of and with Jesus; and there, before Divine Majesty, in the presence of all the heavenly court, we are presented with Christ to the Father, for the Father to lavish upon us (as the same prayer says) "every heavenly grace and blessing."

Oh, if our faith were a lively faith, how reverent would be our presence at this Holy Sacrifice of the Mass! what care we would take in seeking to purify ourselves from all that soils us, so as to be less unworthy to enter, in train of Christ, into the Holy of holies; there to be, along with Christ our divine head, a living "host"! As St. Gregory so well says: "Christ will indeed be a Host," a Victim, "for us, when we make ourselves a host with Him"[44]—when we offer *ourselves* in order to share, through our generosity and our sacrifices, His life of immolation.

---

[41] Canon of the Mass.   [42] Bossuet, *Explications de quelques difficultés sur les prières de la messe,* ed. Lachat, XVII, p. 60.

[43] Hebr. 6:19.   [44] *Dialogue,* IV, cap. 59.

The Eucharistic Sacrifice gives us the Sacrament. We only participate fully in the Sacrifice by being united to the Victim. In the prayer that I have just been explaining to you, the Church asks that we "be filled with every heavenly grace and blessing"— but on condition that we associate ourselves with this Sacrifice by receiving the body and blood[45] of Jesus: "...that as many as shall partake of the most holy body and blood of thy Son at this altar" may receive every grace and blessing.

It is therefore only through holy communion that we enter fully into the mind of Jesus, that we fully carry out what His heart desired on the day when He instituted the Eucharist. "Take and eat."[46] "If you do not eat the flesh of the Son of Man ... you will not have life in you."[47] Holy communion is the foremost of the Eucharistic duties.

But let us bring to this Eucharistic feast the best of dispositions. As you know, this divine sacrament produces its fruits in the soul who receives it in a state of grace and with the right intention; there is no doubt about that. But how abundant these fruits are is in measure of the degree of fervor of each person.

I have explained to you at length elsewhere[48] how these dispositions come down to faith, confidence, surrender of the whole of ourselves to Christ and the members of His mystical body. I cannot return to that subject here.

There is, however, one disposition I do want to touch on here, because this is the one the Church herself indicates in a prayer of the Mass of Corpus Christi. It is reverence. "Grant ... that we so reverence the sacred mysteries of thy Body and Blood that we continually feel the fruit of thy redemption within us."

---

[45] [*Translator's note*: It is not necessary to receive under both species, for the Church teaches that by receiving under one species alone we receive the body, blood, soul and divinity of Christ.]   [46] Matt. 26:26.

[47] John 6:54 (Jerus.)   [48] In *Christ, the Life of the Soul*, Book II, Ch. 8 (*The Bread of Life*, Panis Vitae), sections 5 and 6.

The Church asks that we "reverence" Christ in the Eucharist. And what is the reason for that? It is twofold.

In the first place, because Christ is God.

The Church speaks to us of "sacred mysteries." The word "mysteries" indicates that under the Eucharistic species—the *appearances* of bread and wine—is hidden a reality. By adding the word "sacred" she implies that this reality is holy and divine. He who is indeed hidden in the Eucharist is He who, with the Father and the Holy Spirit, is Infinite Being, Omnipotence, Source of all things. If Our Lord had appeared to us in the brightness of His glory, the sight of such splendor would be more than we could bear. In order to give Himself to us, He hides Himself, no longer beneath the frailty of a flesh capable of suffering, as in the mystery of the Incarnation, but under the appearances of bread and wine. Let us say to Him: "Lord Jesus, for love of us, to draw us to you, to become our food, you veil your majesty. But you shall lose nothing of our homage by doing so. The more you hide your divinity from our eyes, the more also do we wish to adore you, the more also to bow down before you with reverence and love."

> Hidden God, devoutly I adore thee,
> Truly hidden underneath these veils...[49]

The second reason is that Christ Jesus humbled Himself and delivered Himself up for us.

The Church reminds us of this in that same prayer of the Mass of Corpus Christi: "O God, who in a wonderful Sacrament has left us a memorial of thy Passion..." Now, during His Sacred Passion—of which this Sacrament is the memorial par excellence—Christ suffered humiliations without precedent, ignominies untold.

But, says St. Paul, because "He humbled Himself," because He suffered such abasements, the Father "has exalted Him and has bestowed upon Him the name that is above all names, so that

---

[49] Hymn, *Adoro te devote*.

at the name of Jesus every knee should bend ... and every tongue confess that Christ, the Son of God, reigns for ever in the glory of His Father."[50]

Let us enter into the mind of the Eternal Father, revealed to us by St. Paul. The more Christ has lowered and humbled Himself, the more should we, after the example of the Father, exalt Him in this Sacrament which recalls to us His Passion, and the more profuse should our homage to Him be. Justice requires this, as much as does love.

And then, it was *"for us,"* was it not, that He delivered Himself up in that way?—"for us and for our salvation."[51] He suffered, and it was for me. His soul, completely holy though it was, sunk in the depths of sadness, worry and fear—and that was for me. He bore numerous insults on the part of the coarse soldiery, and He bore them for me. He was scourged and crowned with thorns, and for me. He died in torments indescribable, and He died for me, to draw me to Him. He "loved me and gave Himself up for me."[52] Let us never forget that each of the sorrowful episodes of the Passion was pre-ordained by Wisdom and accepted by Love for our salvation.

O Christ Jesus, really present on the altar, I prostrate myself at your feet. May all adoration be rendered to you in the Sacrament you willed to leave to us, in witness of the excess of your love, on the eve of your Passion!

Again, we can express that reverence, that veneration, by going to visit Christ in the tabernacle. Is it not, indeed, a failure of respect if we neglect this Divine Guest who awaits us? There in the tabernacle He remains, really present, this one who was present in the manger of Bethlehem, at Nazareth, on the hills of Judea, in the upper room, on the cross. It is this same Jesus who said to the Samaritan woman: "If you knew the gift of God!"—you who

---

[50] See Phil. 2:8-11.   [51] See Nicene Creed.   [52] Gal. 2:20.

thirst for light, for peace, for joy, for happiness; if you knew who I am, you would have asked of me, and I "would have given you living water," the water of divine grace which becomes a fount "springing up unto life eternal."[53]

He is there, really present, this one who said: "I am the Way, and the Truth, and the Life";[54] and "he who follows me does not walk in the darkness";[55] and "no-one comes to the Father but through me";[56] and "I am the Vine, you are the branches: he who abides in me, and I in Him, he bears much fruit; for without me you can do nothing";[57] and "him who comes to me I shall not cast out";[58] and "come unto me, all you who labor and are burdened, and I will give you rest ... you will find rest for your souls."[59]

He is there, the same Christ who cured the lepers, calmed the angry waves and promised the good thief a place in His kingdom. There in the tabernacle we find our Savior, our friend, our elder brother, in the fullness of His divine omnipotence, and the ever-fruitful power of His mysteries, with the infinite superabundance of His merits and the ineffable mercy of His love.

He awaits us in the tabernacle, not only to receive our homage there, but to communicate His graces to us there also. If our faith in His words is not just vain sentiment, we shall go close to Him and put our soul into contact, through faith, with His sacred humanity. Be assured that "power will go forth from Him,"[60] as of old, to fill us with light, peace and joy.

It is only if this attitude of respect and reverence enters deeply into our souls, that we can hope "continually to feel the fruit of Jesus's redemption within us." This reverence ought to be such as to make us attain to the divine gift in its fullness: "that we *so* reverence the sacred mysteries of thy Body and Blood, *that* we continually feel the fruit of thy redemption within us."

---

[53] John 4, vv. 10, 14.   [54] John 14:6 (Jerus.)   [55] John 8:12.
[56] John 14:6.   [57] John 15:5.   [58] John 6:37.
[59] Matt. 11:28-29.   [60] See Luke 6:19; 8:46.

5. How, through faith, we are united to Christ in this
   Sacrament, and, through Him, to the Father and the
   Holy Spirit.

But why then, you may ask me, does the Church seem to make all our dispositions towards this divine sacrament come down to "reverence"? what reason has she for doing so?

It is because this reverence is a homage of faith. The man who lacks faith does not bend the knee before the Sacred Host. This reverence has its source and its nourishment only in faith.

Now, as I have told you often, faith—root of our justification and fundamental condition of all progress in the super-natural life—is the first disposition for receiving the fruit of Christ's Redemption.

What, indeed, *is* this fruit for our souls? In a word, it is being reborn to the divine life of grace, to participate anew in the divine adoption. We only arrive there by faith. Faith is the primordial condition for becoming a child of God and for gathering, in its substance, this fruit of the divine tree of the cross: "To as many as received Him, He gave the power of becoming sons of God; *to those who believe in His name*: who were born ... of God."[61]

The reception of the Eucharist unites us first of all to the sacred humanity of Christ, and that union is brought about by faith. When you believe that the humanity of Jesus is the humanity of the Son of God, the Word's own humanity, and that in Jesus there is but one single Person, a Divine Person; when with all the strength and all the fullness of your faith you adore this sacred humanity, then through that humanity you enter into contact with the Word; for the humanity is the way that takes you to the divinity.

When Christ Jesus gives Himself to us in holy communion, He asks us the question He put to the apostles: "Who do you say that I am?" And we should reply with Peter: "You are the Christ,

---

[61] John 1:12-13.

414 BOOK TWO: THE MYSTERIES OF CHRIST

the Son of the living God."[62] I see only a fragment of bread, a little wine; but you, who are the Word, who are Eternal Wisdom and Infinite Truth, have said: "This is my body, this is my blood"; and because you have said it, I believe you are present under these humble and lowly appearances. Our senses say nothing to us; it is faith that makes us enter in and reach that divine reality behind the Eucharistic veils: *"Praestet fides supplementum sensuum defectui"*:

> Faith for all defects supplying
> Where the feeble senses fail.[63]

And Our Lord says to us, as to the centurion: "Let it be done to you according to your faith."[64] As you believe that I am God, I give myself to you with all the treasures of my divinity, to fill you with them and to transform you into myself; I give myself to you with all that is ineffably involved in my divine life within the Trinity.

For we do not unite ourselves solely to Christ. Christ is but one with His Father—"I and the Father are one,"[65] one in the unity of the Holy Spirit. Holy communion unites us at the same time to the Father and to the Holy Spirit. Christ, the Word Incarnate, is wholly the Father's; and when we go to communion, He takes us and unites us to His Father, as He Himself is united to Him. "I pray," O Father, said Jesus at the Last Supper after having instituted the Holy Eucharist—I pray not only for these, my apostles, "but for those also who through their word are to believe in me, that all may be one, even as you, Father, in me and I in you; that they also may be one in us ... that they may be one, even as we are one: I in them and you in me."[66] *"I in them and you in me."*

The Word unites us also to the Holy Spirit. In the adorable Trinity, the Holy Spirit is the substantial Love of the Father and the Son. Christ gives us the Spirit, as He gave Him to the apostles,

---

[62] Matt. 16:15-16.   [63] Hymn, *Pange lingua.*   [64] See Matt. 8:13.
[65] John 10:30.   [66] John 17:20-22.

so as to direct us through Him. He communicates to us this Spirit of adoption who, first giving us testimony that we are children of God,[67] helps us by His lights and inspirations to live as God's "very dear children."[68]

What a sanctuary is the soul that has just been to holy communion! In the first place, the Eucharist gives this soul the body and the blood of Christ, and the divinity of the Word united in Jesus indissolubly to the human nature. Through the Word, the soul is united to the Father and the Spirit, in the indivisibility of their uncreated nature. The Trinity dwells in us: our soul becomes heaven where the mysterious workings of divine life take place. We can then offer to the Father His beloved Son, for Him anew to place His delight in Him. We can offer this delight to Jesus, in order that the ineffable joys He experienced at the moment of the Incarnation be renewed in His sacred soul. We can pray to the Holy Spirit, asking Him to be the bond of love that unites us to the Father and the Son.

For comprehending these marvels and plunging into these deep abysses, there is only *faith*. The Eucharist is the mystery of faith: *Mysterium fidei*.

---

[67] Rom. 8:16.

[68] Eph. 5:1.

CHAPTER NINETEEN

THE HEART OF CHRIST
(*Feast of the Sacred Heart*)

Introduction: Love is the explanation of all the mysteries of Jesus. How we ought to have faith in the fullness of that love. The Church presents it to us as an object of worship in the Feast of the Sacred Heart.

Everything we possess in the realm of grace comes to us from Christ Jesus: "Of His fullness we have all received."[1] He has destroyed the wall of separation that prevented us from going to God, and in infinite abundance has merited for us all graces. Divine head of the mystical body, He is able to communicate to us the spirit of His states and the power of His mysteries, so as to transform us into Himself.

When we consider these mysteries, which of His perfections is it that we see shining forth particularly? It is love.

Love brought about the Incarnation: "*For us* ... He came down from heaven,"[2] became incarnate. It was love that made Christ be born into a flesh which was weak and susceptible of suffering, that inspired the obscurity of the hidden life, that nourished the zeal of the public life. Jesus delivered Himself up to death for us, and this was because He succumbed to an excess of love without measure.[3] That he rose again was "for our justification";[4] He ascended to heaven as a forerunner "to prepare a place" for us in

---

[1] John 1:16.   [2] Nicene Creed.   [3] John 13:1.   [4] Rom. 4:25.

that abode of beatitude.[5] He sent the Holy Spirit, the Consoler, so that He would not "leave us as orphans";[6] He instituted the Sacrament of the Eucharist as a memorial of His love. All these mysteries have their source in love.

It is necessary that our faith in this love of Christ Jesus be deep-rooted and constant. And why? Because it is one of the most powerful supports of our fidelity.

Look at St. Paul: never a man so worked or spent himself for Christ as he did. One day, in order to defend himself when his enemies attacked the legitimacy of his mission, he was driven to sketch out his own picture of his works, his labors and his sufferings. That vivid picture I am sure you know, but it is always a joy to re-read those pages, which are unique in the annals of the apostolate. "Often," says the great apostle, "I have been exposed to death; five times I received the punishment of forty lashes less one; thrice I was scourged with rods; once I suffered stoning; thrice I was shipwrecked; a night and a day I was adrift on the sea. And my numberless journeys, full of perils—perils from floods, from brigands, from my own nation, from unbelievers; perils in towns and in deserts, perils at sea. And my labors and hardships, my many sleepless nights; the tortures of hunger and thirst, my numerous fastings; and cold and nakedness. And besides these outward things, may I recall my anxious care for all the churches I founded?"[7] Elsewhere he applies to himself the words of the psalmist: "For your sake, says the scripture, we face death at every moment, reckoned no better than sheep marked down for slaughter."[8] And yet, what does he immediately add? "But in all these encounters we are more than conquerors."[9] And where do we find the secret of this victory? Ask him why he bears everything, even his being "weary of life itself";[10] why, in all his trials, he remains united to Christ with a firmness so unshakeable that not

[5] John 14:2; Hebr. 6:20.   [6] John 14:18.
[7] See 2 Cor. 11:23-28.   [8] Rom. 8:36 (Knox), Ps. 43 (44):22.
[9] See Rom. 8:37.   [10] See 2 Cor. 1:8.

"tribulation or distress, or persecution, or hunger, or nakedness, or danger, or the sword"—none of these can separate him from Jesus? He will reply to you: "Because of Him who has loved us."[11] What sustains, strengthens, animates, stimulates him is the love Christ bears for him: He "loved me and gave Himself up for me."[12]

And, indeed, the feeling that makes this ardent conviction arise in him is that he "wishes to live no longer for himself"[13]—he who had blasphemed the name of God and persecuted the Christians[14] —but for Him who loved him to the extent of giving His life for him.[15] *Caritas Christi urget nos,* "Christ's love compels us," he cries.[16] That is why he was willing—without reserve, without counting the cost—to deliver himself up for Him, for the souls who were His conquest: "I will most gladly spend and be spent myself."[17]

This conviction that Christ loves him gives us the true key to all the work of the great apostle.

Nothing so urges us to love as knowing and feeling oneself to *be* loved. "Every time we think of Jesus Christ," said St. Teresa of Avila, "let us remember the love with which He has showered benefits on us ... love calls forth love."[18]

But how are we to know about this love which is the basis of all the states of Jesus, which explains them, which sums up all the motives for them? how are we to obtain this knowledge, so salutary and fruitful that St. Paul made it the object of his prayer for his Christians? By contemplating the mysteries of Jesus. If we study them with faith, the Holy Spirit, who is Infinite Love, reveals deep things about them, and leads us to the love that is their source.

There is one feast which by its very object recalls to us in a general way the love the Word Incarnate has shown us. It is the

---

[11] Rom. 8, vv. 35, 37.   [12] Gal. 2:20.   [13] See 2 Cor. 5:15.
[14] Acts 26:9-10.   [15] 2 Cor. 5:15.   [16] See 2 Cor. 5:14.
[17] 2 Cor. 12:15.   [18] *Life, written by herself,* Ch. XXII.

Feast of the Sacred Heart. By this feast which accords with the revelations of Our Lord to St. Margaret Mary, the Church closes, so to speak, the annual cycle of the solemnities of the Savior; as if, having arrived at completion of the contemplation of the mysteries of her Spouse, it only remained to her to celebrate the very love that inspired them all.

Following the example of the Church, and now that we have gone through the review of the principal mysteries of our divine head, I will say to you a word or two on devotion to the sacred heart of Christ, on its object and its practice. We shall grasp once more this truth that is so important—that for us everything comes down to a knowledge, having effect in practice, of the mystery of Jesus.

1. **What, in a general way, devotion to the Sacred Heart of Jesus is. How deeply this devotion has its roots in the tenets of Christianity.**

"Devotion" comes from the Latin word *devovere*, to consecrate, to devote oneself, to a person one loves. Devotion to God is the total consecration of our life to God; it is the highest expression of our love. "You shall love the Lord your God with your *whole* heart, and with your *whole* soul, and with your *whole* mind, and with your *whole* strength."[19] This "whole" is what marks devotion: loving God with the *whole* of yourself, unreservedly, never ceasing to do so; loving Him to the extent that you devote yourself to His service with promptitude and ease—that is devotion in general; and, thus understood, devotion constitutes perfection: for it is the very flower of charity.[20]

Devotion to Jesus Christ is the devotedness of our whole being, our whole activity, to the person of the Incarnate Word (abstracting from any particular state of His person or any particular mystery of His life). By this devotion to Jesus Christ we strive to

[19] Mark 12:30. [20] Cf. St. Thomas, II-II, q. 82, a. 1.

know, honor and serve the Son of God manifesting Himself to us through His sacred humanity.

A particular devotion might be "devotedness" to God considered in relation to one of God's attributes or perfections in particular, like holiness or mercy, or again to one of the three Divine Persons; or it might be Christ contemplated in one of His mysteries, under one or other of His states. As we have seen in the course of these talks, it is always the same Christ Jesus whom we honor, it is always to His adorable person that we address our homage; but we consider His person under some particular aspect or manifesting Himself to us in some special mystery. Thus, devotion to the Holy Infancy is devotion to the same person, Christ, in the mystery of the Nativity as is devotion to Him as an adolescent at Nazareth. Devotion to the five wounds is devotion to the Word Incarnate considered in His sufferings—sufferings themselves symbolized by the five wounds of which He willed to keep the glorious scars after His resurrection. The devotion can have a special, immediate, object of its own, but it always terminates in the person Himself.[21]

Hence, you understand what is meant by devotion to the Sacred Heart. It is, in a general way, devotion to the person of Christ Himself manifesting His love for us and showing us His heart as a symbol of that love. Whom do we honor, therefore, in this devotion? Christ Jesus Himself, in person. But what is the immediate object of the devotion, its own special object? Jesus's heart of flesh, the heart that beat for us in the breast of the God-man; yet we do not honor it separated either from His human nature or from the Person of the Eternal Word to which this nature was united at the Incarnation. Is that all? No, the following is to be added: we honor this heart as a symbol of Jesus's love for us.

Devotion to the Sacred Heart comes down, then, to worship of the Word Incarnate, manifesting His love to us, and showing us His heart as a symbol of that love.

. . .

[21] St. Thomas, III, q. 25, a. 1.

I have no need to justify before yourselves this devotion that is so familiar to you. Nevertheless, it will not be without use for me to say a word on the subject.

You know that according to certain Protestants the Church is like a lifeless body; it would have received at the outset all it was going to have, and would stay like that, its features set. All that has arisen since then, whether in the matter of dogma or in the realm of devotion, is to their eyes no more than superfluity and corruption.

For us, the Church is a living organism, which, like every living organism, has to develop and be perfected. The deposit of revelation was sealed at the death of the last apostle; since then, no writing has been accepted as inspired, and in no case do the revelations of particular saints enter into the official deposit of the truths of the faith. But many of the truths contained in the official revelation are there only in germ; and it was only little by little that occasion was given, under pressure of events and the guidance of the Holy Spirit, to come to explicit definitions of them which establish in precise and definite formulas what before then had been known only in an implicit way.

From the first moment of His incarnation, Christ Jesus possessed in His sacred soul all the treasures of divine knowledge and divine wisdom. But it was only little by little that one saw them being revealed. In measure as Christ increased in age, that knowledge and that wisdom showed themselves; the powers of which He contained in Himself the seed-germ were seen appearing and flowering.

Something analogous happens for the Church, the mystical body of Christ. For example, we find in the deposit of faith this magnificent revelation: "The Word was God ... and the Word was made flesh."[22] This revelation contains treasures which have only come to light bit by bit. It is like a seed that has come to blossom forth in fruits of truth, to increase our knowledge of Christ Jesus. On the occasion of heresies arising, the Church,

[22] John 1, vv. 1, 14.

guided by the Holy Spirit, has defined that there is in Jesus Christ only one single Divine Person, yet two natures, distinct and perfect, two wills, two sources of activity; that the Virgin Mary is the Mother of God; that all parts of the sacred humanity of Jesus are adorable by reason of their union with the Divine Person of the Word. Are those new dogmas? No. It is the deposit of faith, explained, made explicit, developed.

What we say about doctrines applies fully to devotions also. In the course of the centuries, devotions have arisen which the Church, under the guidance of the Holy Spirit, has accepted and made her own. These are in no way innovations, properly so called. They are effects flowing from established dogmas of the Church and from activities organically part of her.

As soon as the teaching Church approves a devotion and confirms it with her sovereign authority, it ought to be our joy to accept it. To act otherwise would be no longer to share the sentiments of the Church, *sentire cum Ecclesia*; it would no longer be entering into the mind of Christ Jesus. For He said to His apostles and their successors: "He who hears you, hears me; and he who rejects you, rejects me."[23] Now, how can we go to the Father if we do not listen to Christ?

Relatively modern in the form it takes nowadays, devotion to the Sacred Heart has its dogmatic roots in the deposit of faith. It was contained in germ in St. John's words: "The Word was made flesh and dwelt among us"; and "Jesus ... loved His own who were in the world, loved them to the end."[24] What, indeed, is the Incarnation? It is the manifestation of God, it is God revealing Himself to us through the humanity, the human nature, of Jesus: "The new light of thy glory has shone upon the eyes of our mind";[25] it is the revelation of divine love to the world: "God so loved the world that He gave His only-begotten Son."[26] And this

---

[23] Luke 10:16.
[25] Preface of the Mass of Christmas.
[24] John 1:14; 13:1.
[26] John 3:16.

Son Himself has so loved mankind that He delivered Himself up for us: "Greater love than this no man has, that a man lay down his life for his friends."[27] The whole of devotion to the Sacred Heart is in germ in these words of Jesus. And to show us that this love had attained the highest degree, Christ Jesus willed that immediately after He had drawn His last breath upon the cross, His heart be pierced by a soldier's lance.[28]

As we are about to see, the love which is symbolized by the heart in this devotion is first of all the created heart of Jesus; but, as Christ is the Word Incarnate, the treasures of this created love show to us the marvels of *divine* love, the Eternal Word's love.

You can see how deeply into the deposit of faith this devotion goes. Far from its being an alteration or a corruption, it is an adaptation—at once simple and magnificent—of what St. John said about the Word who was made flesh and immolated Himself for love of us.

2. The various elements of devotion to the heart of Jesus.

If we now, in a few words, return to the various elements of this worship, we shall see how justified they are.

The proper and direct object of it is the physical heart of Christ. This heart is indeed worthy of adoration. Why is that? Because it is part of Christ's human nature, and because the Word united Himself to a perfect nature: *Perfectus homo*, "completely man."[29] The same adoration we give to the Divine Person of the Word extends to all that to which He is personally united, all that subsists in and through the Person of the Word. This is true of Jesus's human nature as a whole; it is true of each of the parts of which it is composed. The heart of Jesus is the heart of one who is God.

But this heart which we honor, which we adore in this humanity

---

[27] John 15:13 (Rheims).   [28] John 19:34.
[29] Creed attributed to St. Athanasius.

united to the Person of the Word, serves here as a symbol. A symbol of what? Of love. In ordinary language, the heart is an accepted symbol of love. When God says to us in Scripture: "My son, give me your heart,"[30] we understand that the heart here signifies love. Someone may say about someone else: "I esteem him, I respect him, but I can't give him my heart." One means by these words that friendship, intimacy, union, are not possible.

Thus, in devotion to the Sacred Heart of Jesus we are honoring the love the Incarnate Word bears for us.

Created love, first of all. Christ Jesus is both God and man— completely God and completely man: that is the very mystery of the Incarnation. As "Son of Man," Christ has a heart like ours, a heart of flesh, which beats for us with the tenderest and truest, the noblest and most faithful love there could ever be.

In his letter to the Ephesians, St. Paul said to them that he was praying earnestly to God that they be able to comprehend "the breadth and the length, the height and the depth" of the mystery of Jesus, so much was he dazzled by the incomparable riches it contained. He could have said exactly the same of the love of the heart of Jesus *for us*. He did say this, moreover, when he declared that Christ's love "is beyond all knowledge."[31]

And, indeed, we shall never exhaust the treasures of tenderness, kindness, benevolence, charity, of which the heart of the God-man is the burning hearth-fire. We have but to open the Gospels; on each page we shall see shining forth the goodness, the mercy, the stooping-down in love, of Jesus towards mankind. I endeavored, when speaking to you of some aspects of the public life,[32] to show you how deeply human, how infinitely delicate, this love is.

Christ's love is not a chimera, it is very real, for it is founded on the Incarnation itself. The Virgin Mary, St. John, Mary Magdalene, Lazarus, know this well. It was not exclusively a love of the will; it was one of the feelings too. When Christ Jesus said, "I have

---

[30] Prov. 23:26.   [31] Eph. 3:14-19 (Jerus.)   [32] See above, p. 238 ff.

compassion on the crowd,"[33] He truly felt compassion move the fibers of His human heart. When He saw Martha and Mary weeping at the loss of their brother, He wept with them: real human tears, springing from the emotion with which His heart was gripped. That is why the Jews who witnessed this spectacle said to themselves: "See how he loved him!"[34]

Christ Jesus does not change. He was yesterday, He is today, in heaven He remains the most loving of hearts, and the most lovable, we could ever meet with. St. Paul puts it in his own way when he tells us we should have full confidence in Jesus because He is a compassionate High Priest who knows our sufferings, our miseries, having Himself espoused our weaknessnes, sin excepted.[35] Christ can no longer suffer, of that there is no doubt—"death shall no longer have dominion over Him";[36] but He is still the one who was moved with pity, who suffered, who redeemed mankind through love: He "loved me and gave Himself up for me."[37]

This human love of Jesus, this created love—from what source is it drawn? from where is it derived? From uncreated, divine, love; from the Eternal Word's love, the Word to whom the human nature is indissolubly united. In Christ, although there are two perfect and distinct natures, keeping their specific energies and their own operations, there is but one Divine Person. As I have told you, the created love of Jesus is simply a revelation of His uncreated love. Everything the created love accomplishes is accomplished only in union with the uncreated love and because of it. The heart of Christ went to draw His human kindness from the Divine Ocean.[38]

On Calvary, we see a man like us, dying; one who has been a

---

[33] Matt. 15:32; Mark 8:2.   [34] John 11:36.   [35] Hebr. 4:15.   [36] Rom. 6:9.
[37] Gal. 2:20.   [38] "In the Sacred Heart you will find a symbol, and an image perceptible to the senses, of the infinite love of Jesus Christ, of that love which moves us to love Him in return": Leo XIII, Bull *Annum sacrum*, May 25, 1899, l.c.

prey to anguish, who has suffered, who has been ground down by torments, more than any other man will ever be; and we understand the love this man shows us. But this love, which by its very excess goes beyond our knowledge, is a concrete and tangible expression of divine love. The heart of Jesus, pierced upon the cross, reveals to us the human love of Christ; but behind the veil of Jesus's humanity is shown the Word's ineffable and incomprehensible love.

What wide perspectives this devotion opens up for us! How the nature of it attracts the faithful soul! For it gives us a means of honoring what is greatest, highest, most efficacious, in Christ Jesus the Word Incarnate: the love He bears for the world, the love of which His heart is the furnace.

3. **Contemplation of the benefits Jesus's love, symbolized by His heart, has earned for us is the source of the love we should give Him in return. Twofold character of our love for Christ: it should be affective and effective; in this Our Lord is our model.**

Love is active: of its nature it overflows. In Jesus, it could only be for us a never-failing source of gifts.

In a collect for the Feast of the Sacred Heart, the Church invites us to recall the sovereign benefits we owe to Christ Jesus's love, "to celebrate the singular benefits of His love for us." This contemplation is one of the elements of devotion to the Sacred Heart. How can we honor a love the manifestations of which we do not know?

This love, as we have said, is the human love of Jesus—a revelation of His uncreated love. To this uncreated love, which is common to the Father and the Holy Spirit, we owe everything. There is no gift which does not have its deepest source in that love. What has drawn beings out of nothing? Love. In a hymn for the Feast,[39] we sing that the earth, sea and stars are the work of love:

> That wondrous love which made the stars,
> And formed the earth and far-flung sea...

Even more than is creation, the Incarnation is due to love. It is love which made the Word come down from the splendors of heaven to unite Himself to a nature weak and mortal:

> O Savior, you were urged by love
> To make your own our mortal flesh.

But the benefits we should bring to mind above all are the Redemption, through the Passion; and the institution of the sacraments, especially the Eucharist. It is to the human love of Jesus as much as to the uncreated love that we owe them.

In contemplating these mysteries, we have seen what deep and ardent love they express. Our Lord Himself said: "Greater love than this no man has, that a man lay down his life for his friends."[40] It was to those lengths that He Himself went. Many virtues shine out in His Blessed Passion, but none attain the height that love did. It needed nothing less than an excess of love for Him to have—of His own will, in each phase of the Passion—gone down to the depths of humiliation, opprobrium, suffering and sorrow.

And in the same way that love brought about our redemption, it was love also that established the sacraments by which the fruits of Jesus's Sacrifice would be applied to each soul of good will.

St. Augustine[41] is pleased to take up the expression designedly chosen by the Evangelist in telling us of the wound made by the soldier's lance in the side of the dead Jesus on the cross. The sacred writer does not say that the lance "struck" His side or "wounded" His side; he says that it *"opened"* the side of the Savior: "One of the soldiers opened His side with a lance."[42] "That was the gate of

---

[39] Hymn of Vespers.
[41] *Tract. in Johann.*, CXX, 2.
[40] John 15:13 (Rheims).
[42] John 19:34.

life that opened," says the great Doctor of the Church. "Torrents of graces that would sanctify the Church were about to pour out on the world from the pierced heart of Jesus."

This contemplation of the benefits given to us by Jesus should become the source of our practical devotion to the Sacred Heart. Love alone can respond to love. Of what did Our Lord complain to St. Margaret Mary? Of not seeing His love repaid: "Behold this heart which has so loved mankind, but which receives from them nothing but ingratitude." It is, then, through love, through the gift of our heart, that we should respond to Christ Jesus. "Who will not love one who loves him? Will one redeemed not attach himself to his Redeemer?"

> Who, when loved, will not love back? —
> Love could our Redeemer lack?[43]

To be perfect, this love of ours should bear a twofold character.

There is *aff*ective love; it consists of the different *feelings* that make the soul vibrate regarding a loved person: admiration, pleasure in the person's company, joy, thankfulness. This love makes praise spring to our lips. We rejoice in the perfections of the heart of Jesus, we celebrate its beauty and greatness; we delight in the magnificence of its benefits: "My lips will greatly rejoice when I shall sing to you."[44]

This affective love is necessary. In contemplating Christ and His love, the soul should not hold back from admiration, pleasure, jubilation. Why is that? Because we should love God with all our being; it is God's desire that our love for Him shall correspond to our nature. Well, we do not have an angelic nature, but a human one in which feelings have their place. Christ Jesus accepts this form of love, because it is based upon our nature, which He Himself created. Look at Him at the time of His triumphal entry to Jerusalem, a few days before His Passion. "When

---

[43] Hymn of Lauds for the Feast of the Sacred Heart.   [44] Ps. 70 (71):23.

He was already near the descent from the Mount of Olives, the whole crowd of disciples, transported with joy, began to praise God with a loud voice for all the miracles they had seen: 'Blessed the King, who comes in the name of the Lord! Peace in heaven, and glory in the highest!' Then some of the Pharisees, from the midst of the crowd, said to Him: 'Master, rebuke your disciples.'" And what does Our Lord reply? Does He make them stop acclaiming Him? Quite the contrary. "He said to the Pharisees: 'I tell you that if these keep silent, the very stones will cry out.'"[45]

Christ Jesus is pleased with praises that burst out from the heart to the lips. Our love ought to break forth into affection. Look at the saints. Francis, the *poverello* of Assisi, was so carried away by love that he sang God's praises as he went along the roads.[46] Mary Magdalen of Pazzi ran through the cloisters of her convent crying: "O love, O love!"[47] St. Teresa of Avila thrilled all over each time she sang these words of the *Credo*: "His kingdom will have no end."[48] Read her *Exclamations*, and you will see how, when people are in love, the feelings of human nature blossom forth into ardent praises.

Never be afraid, therefore, of multiplying our praises addressed to the heart of Jesus. Litanies, acts of reparation, of consecration, are so many expressions of this *felt* love, without which the human soul does not attain the perfection of its nature.

On its own, however, this affective love is insufficient. For it to have its full value, its must be expressed in works: "The proof of love is that works can be shown."[49] "If you love me, keep my commandments."[50] That is the only touchstone. You will encounter souls who abound in affection, who have the gift of tears—and who do not take the least trouble in the world to repress their wrong inclinations, to destroy their bad habits, to

[45] See Luke 19:37-40.   [46] *Life of St. Francis* by Joergensen, Book 2, Ch. I.
[47] Her *Life* by Father Cepari, Book 2, Ch. XVI.   [48] *The Way of Perfection*, Ch. XXIII.   [49] St. Gregory, *Homil. in Evang.* XXIII, 1.   [50] John 14:15.

avoid the occasions of sin; who give way to temptation the moment it arises, or grumble as soon as disappointment or opposition comes along. With them, affective love is full of illusion; it is a fire of straw, unlasting, quickly burning to ashes.

If we truly love Christ Jesus, not only will we rejoice in His glory, sing of His perfections with all the fervor of our soul, be sad at the insults offered to His heart and seek to make amends to Him—but above all we shall strive to obey Him in all things; we shall accept with alacrity all the dispositions of His Providence in our regard, we shall employ ourselves to extend His reign in souls, to procure His glory. We shall, in the beautiful words of St. Paul, "gladly spend" ourselves and, if necessary, go to the lengths of "being spent"![51] The Apostle said this about charity towards our neighbor; but applied to our love for Jesus, this formula sums up wonderfully the practice of devotion to the Sacred Heart.

Look at our Divine Savior; in this, as in all our virtues, He is our best model. We find in Him two forms of love.

Consider the love He bears for His Father. Christ Jesus feels in His heart the truest sentiments of affective love with which a human heart could ever beat. The Gospel shows us how one day His heart, overflowing with a feeling of rapturous enthusiasm for the limitless perfections of the Father, broke forth into praises in the presence of His disciples. He "rejoiced in the Holy Spirit"— thrilled with joy under the action of the Spirit—and said: "I praise you, Father, Lord of Heaven and earth, that you have hidden these things from the wise and prudent, and have revealed them to little ones. Yes, Father, for such was your good pleasure."[52]

Again, you see at the Last Supper how His Sacred Heart is filled with affection for His Father, and how His feelings are expressed in an ineffable prayer.

And to show the whole world the sincerity of that love, and its

---

[51] 2 Cor. 12:15.　　[52] Luke 10:21.

vitality—"that the world may know that I love the Father"[53]—
Jesus immediately betook Himself to the Garden of Olives,
where He was to begin the long series of humiliations and sorrows of His Passion.

This twofold character is likewise found in His love for mankind. See how for three days a multitude of people follow Him,
attracted by the power of His divine words and the splendor of
His miracles. But weariness overcomes this crowd, who have no
food with which to replenish themselves. Jesus knows this. "I have
compassion for these people," He says—I pity them; "for they
have now been with me for three days, and have nothing to eat;
and if I send them back to their homes fasting, they will faint on
the way, for some of them have come from afar." *I have pity for
them.* What a deep feeling of compassion wrings His human heart!
And you know how Jesus put His pity into action. Seven loaves
multiplied themselves in His sacred hands to satisfy the hunger of
the four thousand living beings who had followed Him around.[54]

Above all, look at what happens at the tomb of Lazarus. Jesus
weeps; He weeps tears, real human tears. Could there be a more
touching, a more authentic, manifestation of the feelings of His
heart? And straight away He puts His power at the service of His
love: "Lazarus, come forth!"[55]

It is love that is revealed in the gift of Himself, a love which,
flooding forth from His heart, takes possession of His whole being, all His activity, to dedicate them to the interests and the glory
of the object of His love.

What should be the extent of the love we ought to show Christ
Jesus in return for the love He has for us?

It should include first of all the essential and sovereign love
that makes us regard Christ and His will as the Supreme Good
we prefer to all things. In practice, this love comes down to the

---

[53] John 14:31.   [54] See Mark 8:2-9.   [55] John 11:43.

state of sanctifying grace. Devotion, as we have said, is devotedness; but where is the devotedness of a soul that does not seek, at
all costs, to safeguard within itself, by a vigilant fidelity, the treasure of the Savior's grace? Who when tempted hesitates between
the will of Christ Jesus and the suggestions of His eternal enemy?

It is this love—you know it is so—which gives to our life all
its value, and which makes that life a perpetual homage, pleasing
to the heart of Christ. Without this essential love, nothing is of
value in the sight of God. Listen to the expressive terms in which
St. Paul puts this truth in high relief: "If I should speak with the
tongues of men and angels, but do not have charity,[56] I have become as sounding brass or a tinkling cymbal. And if I have
prophecy and know all mysteries and possess all knowledge, and
if I have all faith so as to remove mountains, yet do not have
charity, I am nothing. And if I distribute all my goods to feed the
poor, and if I deliver my body to be burned, yet do not have
charity, it profits me nothing."[57] In other words: I cannot be
pleasing to God if I do not have within me that essential charity
by which I attach myself to Him as Supreme Good. It is all too
evident that one cannot have true devotion where this love does
not exist.

In the next place, let us accustom ourselves to do all things,
even the smallest, from love, so as to please Christ Jesus. To
work, to accept our sufferings and afflictions, to fulfill from love
the duties of our state of life, in order to be pleasing to Our Lord,
in union with the feelings of His heart when He lived here below
like us—this constitutes an excellent practice of devotion to the
Sacred Heart. The whole of our life is thus directed to Him by an
orientation full of love.

---

[56] [*Translator's note*: "Charity": "here is meant the supernatural virtue
comprising love of God above all things and love of neighbor for God. The
Greek word implies, not a mere sentimental feeling, but a sense of appreciation
of the worth of God in Himself and in one's neighbor": note in Confraternity
version.]   [57] See 1 Cor. 13:1-3.

It is this, moreover, that gives to our lives an increase of fruitfulness. As you know, every act of virtue, of humility, of obedience, of religious devotion, done in a state of grace, possesses its own merit, its special perfection, its particular splendor; but when the act is dictated by love, this adds to it a new efficacy and a new beauty. Without its losing any of its own value, the merit of an act of love is joined to it. "At your right hand stands the queen, in Ophir gold arrayed."[58] The queen is the faithful soul in whom Christ reigns through His grace; she takes her place at the right hand of the King, clad in vesture woven of gold, which signifies love. The varied colors[59] symbolize the different virtues, each of which keeps its glints of light: but love, which is the deepest source of them, enhances their brightness.

Love reigns thus as sovereign in our heart so as to direct all its movements to the glory of the Father and of Jesus His Son.

4. **Precious advantage of devotion to the Sacred Heart: it makes us, little by little, have the true attitude which ought to characterize our relations with God. Our spiritual life depends, in large part, on the idea of God we habitually form for ourselves. Diversity of the aspects under which souls can consider God.**

Just as the Holy Spirit does not call every soul to shine in an equal way through the same virtues, so also in the matter of private devotion He leaves them a holy liberty, which we ourselves ought carefully to respect. There are some souls who feel especially urged to honor the mysteries of the childhood of Jesus; others are attracted to the wholly interior charms of the hidden life; others again cannot disengage themselves from meditation on the Passion.

[58] Ps. 44 (45):10 (Knox).   [59] [*Translator's note:* Marmion alludes to the version as in the Rheims: "in gilded clothing; surrounded with variety."]

However, devotion to the Sacred Heart of Jesus is one of those that should be most dear to us. And why? Because it honors Christ Jesus, not in a particular state of life or in one of His mysteries, as the ones previously considered do, but in the generality and the totality of His love—that love in which all the mysteries find their deepest explanation. Though characterized specially and clearly, this devotion takes on something of the universal. When we honor the heart of Christ, it is no longer upon Christ as child, adolescent or victim that our homage rests, but upon the person of Jesus in the fullness of His love.

Further, the general practice of this devotion aims, in the last analysis, at rendering Our Lord love for love: "He moves us to love Him in return."[60] It aims at seizing upon all our activity in order to penetrate it with love, so as to please Christ Jesus. The particular exercises are only means of expressing to our Divine Master this reciprocity of love.

That is a very precious effect of our devotion. For the whole of the Christian religion comes down to this point for us: that we deliver ourselves up, from love, to the service of Christ and, through Him, to the Father and the Spirit common to them both. This point is of capital importance and I wish, in order to end this talk, to consider it with you for a few moments.

It is a truth, confirmed by the experience of souls, that our spiritual life depends, in large part, on the idea of God we *habitually* form for ourselves.

Between ourselves and God there are fundamental relations based on our nature as creatures. There exist moral relations resulting from our attitude to Him; and this attitude is, for most of the time, conditioned by the idea we have of God.

If we form a false idea of God, our efforts to advance will often be sterile and in vain, because they will be off the track. If we have

[60] Leo XIII, Bull *Annum sacrum*, l.c.

an incomplete idea of God, our spiritual life will be full of gaps and imperfections. If our idea of God is true—as true as is possible here below for a creature living by faith—our soul, being in the light, will blossom forth in all sureness.

This habitual idea that we form of God is, therefore, the key to our spiritual life, not only because it rules our conduct towards Him but also because, often, it determines the attitude of God Himself to us: in many cases, God treats us as we treat Him.

But, you may say to me, what about sanctifying grace—does that not make us children of God? Certainly. However, in practice, there are souls who do not *act* as adopted children of the Eternal Father. One might say that their position of being children of God has only a nominal value for them; they do not understand that it is a fundamental state demanding to be ceaselessly manifested by acts corresponding to it, and that the whole of the spiritual life should be a development of the spirit of divine adoption, the spirit we received at baptism through the power of Christ Jesus.

Thus, you will encounter souls who habitually consider God in the way the Israelites regarded Him. God revealed Himself to them amid thunder and lightning on Sinai.[61] God, for this "stubborn"[62] people prone to unfaithfulness and idolatry, was only a Lord who must be worshipped, a Master who must be served, a judge who must be feared. The Israelites had received, as St. Paul put it, "a spirit of bondage ... in fear."[63] God only appeared to them in the majesty of His grandeur and the sovereignty of His power. As you know, He treated them with rigorous justice: the earth opened to swallow up the guilty Hebrews;[64] those who touched the Ark of the Covenant without their duties giving them the right to do so were struck dead;[65] venomous serpents made the murmurers perish;[66] people scarcely dared utter the name of Jehovah; the high priest, trembling, entered into the

---

[61] Exod. 19:16 ff.   [62] Deut. 31:27 (Jerus.)   [63] Rom. 8:15.
[64] Num. 16:32.   [65] 2 Kings 6:6-7.   [66] Num. 21:5-6.

Holy of holies once a year, armed with the blood of animal-victims immolated in sacrifice for sin.[67] That was "the spirit of bondage."

There are souls who spend their lives having, habitually, these feelings of purely servile fear. If they did not fear the punishments of God, they would see no harm in offending Him. They habitually regard God only as a master, and they do not seek to please Him. They resemble that servant of whom Christ speaks in the parable. A king, before setting out for a distant country, calls his servants together and entrusts a valuable piece of money to each of them, saying "Trade with this while I am away." One of the servants keeps the money in safe custody, without using it to make more. "Here is your coin," he says on the king's return; "I hid it in a napkin because I feared you, since you are a stern man: you take up what you did not lay down, you reap what you did not sow." And what does the king reply? He takes the negligent servant at his word: "Out of your own mouth I judge you, you wicked servant. You regarded me as a stern man ... Why, then, did you not put my money in the bank, where it would gain interest?" And the king commands that the money which had been given to that servant be taken away from him.[68]

It is only at a distance that such souls act in relation to God. They treat Him solely as a great lord; and God treats them in the same way, He does not give Himself fully to them. Between them and God, personal intimacy cannot exist. In them, interior expansion is impossible.

Other souls, more numerous perhaps, habitually regard God as a great benefactor; they act as a rule only "for the reward."[69] This idea is by no means false. We see Christ Jesus compare His Father to a master who rewards—and with what magnificent liberality!—the faithful servant: "Come and share the joy of your Lord."[70] Christ Himself tells us that He ascends into heaven to "prepare a place" for us there.[71]

---

[67] Levit. 16:11 ff.   [68] See Luke 19, vv. 12-13, 20-24.
[69] Ps. 118 (119):112.   [70] Matt. 25:21 (Knox).   [71] John 14:2.

But when, as happens with certain souls, this attitude is habitual to the point of becoming exclusive, then, apart from its lacking nobility, it does not correspond fully to the spirit of the Gospel. Hope is a Christian virtue, it powerfully sustains the soul in the midst of adversity, trials, temptations; but it is neither the only nor the most perfect of the theological virtues—virtues specific to our state as children of God. What, then, is the most perfect virtue? Which among them is it that wins the palm? It is, replies St. Paul, charity, *love.* "So there abide faith, hope and charity, these three; but the greatest of these is charity."[72]

5. Christ alone reveals to us the true attitude of the soul towards God. Devotion to the heart of Jesus helps us to acquire it.

That is why—without losing sight of fear (not, however, the servile fear of a slave who dreads punishment, but fear of insulting God who created us); without putting aside thoughts of the reward that awaits us if we are faithful—we should seek to have habitually towards God the attitude, composed of filial confidence and love, which Christ Jesus revealed to us as being that of the New Covenant.

Christ, indeed, knows better than anyone what our relations with God should be; He knows the divine secrets. In hearing Him we run no risk of being led astray: He is Truth itself. Now what attitude to God does He wish us to have? Under what aspect does He wish us to contemplate and adore God? Certainly He teaches us that God is the Supreme Master, whom we must adore: "It is written, 'The Lord God shalt thou worship, and Him only shalt thou serve.'"[73] But this God, whom we must adore, is a Father: "True worshippers will worship the Father in spirit and in truth, for such the Father seeks to worship Him."[74]

Is adoration the *only* sentiment with which our hearts are to

[72] 1 Cor. 13:13.   [73] Luke 4:8; Deut. 6:13.   [74] John 4:23 (RSV, Cath.)

beat? Does it constitute the only attitude we should have to-wards this Father who is God? No. Christ Jesus added to it *love*, a full and perfect love—one without reserve or restriction. When Jesus was asked what the greatest commandment of all was, what did He reply? "You shall love the Lord your God with your whole heart, and with your whole soul, and with your whole mind, and with your whole strength."[75] *You shall love...* A love that delights in this Lord of such great majesty, this God of such high perfec-tion; a love that benevolently seeks the glory of the Beloved; a reciprocal love towards this God who "first loved us."[76]

Thus, God wishes our relations with Him to be imbued at the same time with filial reverence and with deep love. Without rever-ence, love risks degenerating into a counterfeit liberty, supremely dangerous. Without a love that in all its fervor soars up to our Father, the soul lives in error and does injury to the divine gift.

And to safeguard within us these two sentiments which seem contradictory, God communicates to us the Spirit of His Son Jesus, the Spirit who, through His gifts of fear and piety, harmo-nizes within us the deepest adoration and the tenderest love in due proportion: "Because you are sons, God has sent the Spirit of His Son into your hearts."[77]

This, as Jesus taught us, is the Spirit who ought to rule and govern the whole of our life. This is "the Spirit of adoption" of the New Covenant, contrasted by St. Paul with the "spirit of bondage" of the Old Law.

You will perhaps ask me the reason for this difference. It is that, since the Incarnation, God looks on the humanity of His Son Jesus and, because of Him, He envelops the whole of humanity in the same gaze of delight of which His Son, our elder brother, is the object. That is why He also wills that, like His Son and with Him and through Him, we may live as His "very dear children."[78]

· · ·

[75] Mark 12:28-30; Deut. 6:5.   [76] 1 John 4:10.
[77] Gal. 4:6 (Rheims).   [78] Eph. 5:1.

Again, you may say to me: How are we to love God when we do not see Him?—"No-one has ever seen God,"[79] He "dwells in light inaccessible,"[80] inaccessible to us here below. That is true; but God has revealed Himself to us in His Son Jesus: He "has shone in our hearts ... the glory of God in the face of Christ."[81] The Word Incarnate is the authentic revelation of the Father and His perfections, and the love that Christ shows us simply manifests the love the Father bears for us.

In itself, indeed, God's love is incomprehensible, is completely beyond our understanding. It has not entered into the mind of man to conceive what God is. God's perfections are not distinct from His nature, God's love is God Himself. *"God is love."*[82]

How, then, can one have a true idea of the love of God? By looking at God who manifested Himself to us in tangible form. And what is this tangible form? The humanity of Jesus. Christ is God, but God revealing Himself to us. Contemplating the sacred humanity of Jesus is the surest way to arrive at a true knowledge of God. He who sees Christ "sees also the Father";[83] the love that the Word Incarnate shows us reveals the *Father's* love for us: for "I (the Word) and the Father are one."[84]

Once established in our minds, this ordered reality does not change. Christianity is God's love manifesting itself to the world through Christ; and all of our religion ought to come down to contemplating this love in Christ, and to responding to Christ's love in order to attain to the Father.

Such is the divine plan; such is the mind of God concerning us. If we do not adapt ourselves to this, there will be for us no light or truth; there will be for us no security or safety.

Now, the essential attitude this plan of God demands of us is that of adopted children. We remain beings drawn out of nothing, and before this "Father of infinite majesty"[85] we should prostrate ourselves in feelings of the most humble reverence. But upon this

---

[79] John 1:18 (Jerus.)   [80] 1 Tim. 6:16.   [81] 2 Cor. 4:6 (RSV, Cath.)
[82] 1 John 4:8.   [83] John 14:9.   [84] John 10:30.   [85] Hymn, *Te Deum.*

fundamental relationship to which our position as created beings gives rise is superimposed—not in order to destroy that relationship, but to crown it—a relationship infinitely higher, more extensive, more intimate; one which results from our divine adoption, and which all comes down to serving God through love.

This fundamental attitude which ought to be our response to the reality of our heavenly adoption is particularly assisted by devotion to the heart of Jesus. In making us contemplate the human love of Christ for us, this devotion admits us into the secret of the divine love. In disposing our souls to give it recognition by a life of which love is the driving-force, it maintains in us those feelings of filial piety that we ought to have towards the Father.

When we receive Our Lord in holy communion, we possess within us that Divine Heart which is a furnace of love. Let us earnestly ask that He Himself will make us understand this love, for in this a ray of light from on high is more efficacious than all human reasonings. Let us ask Him to set alight in us a love of His Person. St. Teresa of Avila says that "if, through one grace from the Lord, His love is imprinted in our heart one day, all will become easy to us: very rapidly and without the least trouble we shall go on to works of love."[86]

If this love for the person of Jesus is in our heart, our activity will spring forth from it. We may encounter difficulties, be subject to great trials, undergo strong temptations; but if we love Christ Jesus those difficulties, those trials, those temptations, will find us steadfast: "No waters in flood can quench love."[87] For when "the love of Christ impels us," we "live no longer for ourselves," but for Him who loved us and died for us.[88]

---

[86] *Life, written by herself,* Ch. XXII. Bossuet wrote: "Start by loving the person; love of the person will make you love the doctrine, and love of the doctrine will lead you, gently and strongly, both together, to practice it. Do not fail to know Jesus Christ and to meditate on His mysteries; it is this that will inspire your love of Him. A desire to please Him will follow from that, and this desire will bear fruit in good works": *Meditations on the Gospel,* The Last Supper, Part I, 89th day.   [87] See Song of Songs, 8:7.   [88] 2 Cor. 5:14-15.

CHAPTER TWENTY

CHRIST, CROWN OF ALL THE SAINTS
(*Feast of All Saints*)

Introduction: Christ is inseparable from His mystical body.

The Father made all things subject under Christ's feet; He constituted Him "head over all the Church, which is indeed His body and the fullness of Him."[1]

These lines of St. Paul indicate to us the mystery of Christ Jesus considered in His mystical body which is the Church.

In all the preceding talks, we have had the joy of contemplating the person of Jesus Himself, His states, His abasements, His struggles, His greatness, His triumphs; we have not been able to detach our eyes from that adorable humanity which is for us the example of every virtue, the one and only source of all grace.

But all the mysteries of the God-man result in the establishment and sanctification of the Church: "For us men and for our salvation..."[2] Christ came in order to constitute for Himself a body of persons, a "spouse," that would appear before Him "in all her glory," having no "spot or wrinkle or any such thing, but ... holy and without blemish."[3]

So close and intimate is the union contracted with her that He is the Vine and she the branches; He is the head and the Church constitutes the body; He is the Spouse and she His spouse. United, they compose what St. Augustine so well calls "the whole Christ."[4]

---

[1] Eph. 1:22-23.   [2] Nicene Creed.   [3] Eph. 5:27.   [4] *De unitate Ecclesiae*, 4.

Christ and the Church are inseparable; you cannot imagine one without the other. That is why, at the end of these talks on the person of Jesus and His mysteries, we must now speak of this united society which St. Paul calls "the fullness of Christ,"[5] and without which the mystery of Christ does not attain its completion.

On this earth, as you know, that ineffable union is brought about in faith, by grace and charity; it reaches its consummation in the splendors of heaven and the beatific vision. And thus, having reached the end of her annual liturgical cycle, the Church celebrates the glory of the kingdom of Jesus in one solemn feast, All Saints. It joins together as the object of its praise the whole multitudinous company of the elect, in order to extol their triumph and their joy and at the same time urge us to follow their example, so that we may share their felicity.

For that society is one, as Christ is one. Time will be followed by eternity; souls here below are formed to perfection, but the end of the journey is found only in that glorious society. Moreover, our degree of beatitude is in line with the degree of charity we have reached at the hour when we leave this earth.

I will first set forth the reasons we have for aiming at this heavenly beatitude. After that, we shall see what the means are for attaining it.

1. **Motives we have for aiming at holiness: the will of God, and the infinite price that was paid by Jesus for our perfection.**

The first reason we have for aiming at perfection is that it is God's will: "This is the will of God, your sanctification."[6] God wishes us, not only to be saved but to become holy. And why is God decided on this? Because He Himself is holy: "I am the Lord your God: be holy because I am holy."[7] God is holiness itself; we are His creatures; He desires that the creature shall reflect His

---

[5] Eph. 4:13.   [6] 1 Thess. 4:3.   [7] Levit. 11:44; 19:2.

image. Indeed, He wishes us as His children to be perfect: "You ... are to be perfect, even as your Heavenly Father is perfect."[8] That is a precept, a command, of Jesus.

God finds His glory in our holiness. Never forget this truth: that each degree of holiness to which we shall have come, each sacrifice we have made in order to acquire it, each gleam of virtue that adorns our soul, will be a glory for our Father for ever.

We sing every day, and, it seems to me, daily with more happiness: "You alone are holy, Jesus Christ"[9]—and that is why you are the great glory of the Father. For all eternity Christ will give great glory to His Father, showing Him His five wounds that are a magnificent expression of the sovereign fidelity and perfect love with which He has always done what His Father asked of Him: "I do always the things that are pleasing to Him."[10]

It is the same with the saints. They take their place "before the throne" of God[11] and render Him ceaseless glory. The ardent zeal of apostles; the witness of martyrs purpled with their own blood; the deep knowledge of doctors of the Church; the dazzling purity of virgins—these, each and all of them, constitute homage that is pleasing to God.

In this "great multitude which no man could number,"[12] each saint will shine with a distinctive splendor; and God will take delight for ever in the efforts, the struggles, the victories, of that saint (which are like so many trophies at the feet of God, to honor His infinite perfections and recognize His rights).

It is, therefore, a legitimate ambition for us to aim with all our strength at obtaining for God this glory He derives from our holiness; we ought greatly to aspire to be part of that blessed company in which God Himself delights—a motive, this, for not contenting ourselves with a mediocre perfection, but rather for seeking, unceasingly, to respond in fullest measure to the desire of God, "Be holy because I am holy."

· · ·

[8] Matt. 5:48.   [9] *Gloria* of the Mass.   [10] John 8:29.   [11] Apoc. 7:9.   [12] Ibid.

Another reason is that the higher our holiness is, the more do we exalt the blood of Jesus, the price at which that holiness was bought.

St. Paul tells us that Christ "delivered Himself up for" the Church, even to death on a cross, "that He might sanctify her" by making her a glorious body, "not having spot or wrinkle or any such thing, but ... holy and without blemish."[13] That was the whole object of His Sacrifice.

Now, one of the sources of most wounding affliction for Jesus in His agony in the Garden was foreseeing that His blood would be unavailing for so many souls who would refuse the divine gift: "What profit is there in my blood?"[14] Christ knew that a single drop of this blood would be enough to purify whole worlds and sanctify multitudes of souls. So as to obey His Father, He had, with a love beyond our expression, consented to shed to the last drop this blood that contained the infinite power of the divinity. And yet, He had reason to say, "What profit is there in this blood?"

Christ's great ambition, with every beat of His heart, was to glorify His Father; that is why He desired with so much vehemence—"how distressed I am until it is accomplished!"[15]—to give His life so as to bring to His Father innumerable souls who would bear much fruit of life and holiness: "By this is my Father glorified, that you bear *much* fruit."[16]

But how many understand the ardor of Jesus's love? how many respond to the desires of His heart? How numerous the souls are who do not observe the divine laws! Others keep the commandments, but very few deliver themselves up to Jesus and to the action of His Spirit with that fullness which leads to holiness.

Blessed are those souls who abandon themselves without reserve to the divine good pleasure! United entirely to Christ, who is the Vine, they bear much fruit and glorify their Heavenly Father; they proclaim especially the power of the blood of Jesus.

---

[13] Eph. 5:25-27.   [14] Ps. 29 (30):10(9).
[15] Luke 12:50.   [16] John 15:8 (RSV, Cath.)

Look at this indeed: what song is sung by the elect whom St. John shows in his Apocalypse casting themselves down before the Lamb? "You were slain, and have redeemed us for God with your blood, out of every tribe and tongue and people and nation ... To you blessing and honor and glory and dominion, forever and ever."[17] The saints acknowledge that they are trophies of the blood of the Lamb—trophies that are more glorious the higher their holiness is.

Let us, then, seek with all the ardor of our souls to purify ourselves more and more in the blood of Jesus, seek to produce those fruits of life and holiness that Christ Jesus merited for us by His Passion and death. If we become saints, our souls will, for all eternity, thrill at the joy we shall give Christ by singing the triumphs of His divine blood and the almighty power of His grace.

2. Fundamental character of our holiness: it is the supernatural bringing into effect of what God has planned as our free destiny in Jesus Christ.

You will ask me: how do we arrive at that holiness which is so pleasing to God and so glorious for Jesus and is for our souls a never-failing source of an eternal joy, the depths of which we cannot conjecture? For, says St. Paul, "it has not entered into the heart of man to know what things God has prepared for those that love Him."[18] What road do we follow to come to that blissful state where the soul will contemplate all truth and rejoice in the fulness of all being?

That is a question of high importance; but before replying to it, I first wish to indicate the inherent nature of our holiness. Indeed, we cannot safely choose our way unless we have first identified the destination to be reached. If we have well understood the character with which under God's plan our holiness should be invested, the route to follow in order to get there will no longer be a secret to us.

[17] See Apoc. 5, vv. 9, 13.   [18] See 1 Cor. 2:9.

What, then, is that character? What is the essential quality that God requires of our perfection?

It is to be super-natural.

You know that truth, which I have explained at length elsewhere; but so vital is it, that it will not be without interest to return to it for a short while.

As I have said to you often, the dawn of divine mercy towards us dates from the eternal choice God has made of us, freely, through love: "He chose us in Him," Christ, "before the foundation of the world, that we should be holy."[19]

Let us consider this "choosing" for a moment.

We know that the Eternal Father has always contemplated, contemplates without ceasing, His Word, His Son: in Him He sees the whole of Himself with His infinite perfections; for this unique Word expresses in a divine language all that God is. *Our* thoughts are finite, limited, paltry, and yet, in order to express them we must have recourse to a great variety of words. By one single word God at once expresses His thought which is infinite. He comprehends Himself in His Word.

To grasp one thing fully, says St. Thomas somewhere,[20] it is necessary to know also the multifarious limitations to which that thing is susceptible. God, who comprehends Himself perfectly, sees in His Word all the diverse modes in which creatures can reflect or reproduce His perfections. God did not throw things at random into space; He did not create with blind force. Infinite Knowledge, He has done all things according to designs conceived in His Eternal Wisdom. In contemplating His Word, God sees, in one unique glance, the limitless multitude of possible beings; and from all eternity He decided to choose,[21] from within

---

[19] Eph. 1:4.   [20] I, q. XIV, a. 5 and 6; q. XV, a. 2.

[21] [*Translator's note*: It is perhaps not entirely clear what Marmion means by this. Is he distinguishing between "all possible beings" and beings that God will, as it were, actually actualize? Is he distinguishing between the whole of

this multitude, creatures who would in themselves be the realization of, and would manifest outwardly, albeit in limited measure, the infinite perfections of His Word.

In the ever-existent order of the divine disposing, God foresaw that man, whom He had made king of the earthly creation, would not stay at the height of his election and would turn aside from the plan traced by his Creator for uniting him to Himself: Divine Wisdom was not taken unawares.[22] To bring back fallen man, His thought rested especially on Him whom St. Paul calls "the firstborn of every creature,"[23] and who is the Word Incarnate.

The Father contemplated His Word *incarnate*, made flesh. In this humanity united hypostatically to His Word, He saw the epitome, the complete synthesis, of all created perfection; He revealed to us on Tabor that this God-man was the masterpiece of His thought and the object of all His delight: "This is my beloved Son, in whom I am well-pleased."[24]

---

creation and humanity (with the implication that the latter, as created "after the image and likeness of God" are able to reflect, in a special way, the Word, since they alone of created beings, with the angels, possess free will)? In so far as human beings are concerned, he is certainly not implying that some, and not all, are given the opportunity to be chosen for eternal salvation. Other parts of the book are instructive as to Marmion's meaning.

First, "From the sole fact of our creation, we correspond to a divine idea, we are the fruit of an eternal thought contained in the Word ... our individual holiness consts in bringing into effect this thought which God has conceived of us before our creation" (p. 59). Next: "It is a firm tenet of our faith that God wishes to save everyone," wishes all to be saved (p. 160). And finally Marmion's insistence, throughout the book, that what ultimately determines whether an individual is "chosen" is *the reponse of the individual's free will* to the divine call, to such divine light as the individual has received, to divine grace. Saul "listens to the call, he follows the star" (p. 166). All this against the backgound that although God, being outside time, has eternal foreknowledge of how the individual's free choice will be exercised, the individual's free will is truly free. God's grace will never be lacking.]

[22] [*Translator's note*: God, being outside time, foresaw the Fall, and the Redemption, eternally. This is very remarkable and shows that the Eternal God's ways are by no means our ways.]   [23] Col. 1:15.   [24] Matt. 17:5.

This humanity of Christ expresses outwardly the Divine Word in earthly form; it was chosen freely, through love.

That is not all. God willed to give to His Christ a retinue. This is "the great multitude that no man could number."[25] The saints are so many reproductions of the Word, in less perfect form. The ideal for each one of us is the Word. Each of us ought to be for God a special interpretation of one of the infinite aspects of His Word. That is why we sing, about each saint: "There is not found one like him" (or her).[26] There are not two saints who interpret and manifest Christ with the same perfection.

When we are in heaven, we shall, amid joy beyond description, contemplate the Blessed Trinity. We shall see the Word, the Son, who proceeds from the Father as an Archetype of all possible perfection; we shall see that the sacred humanity of Jesus interpreted in a universal way the perfections of the Word with which it was united; we shall see that God has associated with His Christ so many brethren who reproduce in themselves the divine perfections, manifested and rendered tangible here below in Christ Jesus. In this way is Christ "the firstborn among many brethren"[27] who are to be like Him.

Let us never forget St. Paul's words, that God chose us in His Son Jesus: "He chose us *in Him*."[28] In this eternal decree we find the source of our true greatness. When, through our holiness, we fulfill the idea of God about us, we become for Him like a part of the glory His Son Jesus is for Him: "the brightness of His glory";[29] we are like prolongments—rays—of that glory when, each one in his own place and situation, we strive to interpret and make real in us the divine ideal, of which the Word Incarnate is the unique Examplar.

Such is God's plan; such is our planned destiny—that we be conformed to the Word Incarnate, the Son of God by nature and

---

[25] Apoc. 7:9.   [26] Office for Confessor Pontiff, second antiphon of Lauds; cf. Ecclesiasticus 44:10: "There was not found the like to him in glory" (of Abraham).   [27] Rom. 8:29.   [28] Eph. 1:4.   [29] Hebr. 1:3.

our model of holiness: He "predestined us to be conformed to the image of His Son."[30]

It is from this eternal decree, this planned destiny, full of love, that the whole series of mercies dates for each one of us. To turn this plan into reality, to make His designs converge upon us, God gives us *grace*, a mysterious participation in His nature. Through it, we become, in His Son Jesus who has merited it, true adoptive children of God.

We shall therefore no longer have only the simple relationship of creatures with God; we are not only to unite ourselves with Him through homage and the duties of a natural religion founded on our position as created beings. With nothing of that relationship being destroyed, and no part of those duties being diminished, we shall enter into a more intimate relationship with God, that of children, one that will create in us special duties towards a Father whom we love: "Be ... imitators of God, as very dear children."[31] A relationship and duties wholly super-natural, these, because they go beyond what is required of our nature, beyond our nature's rights; and because it is only the grace of Jesus that makes them possible.

You understand now what is the fundamental character of our holiness.

We can only be saints if we are so according to the divine plan: that is to say, through the grace we owe to Christ Jesus; that is the primordial condition. Which is why this grace is called "sanctifying" grace. So true is this, that outside of that grace not even salvation is possible. There are in the kingdom of the elect only souls who resemble Jesus: well now, the fundamental resemblance we are to have with Him is only brought about through grace.

As you see, God has Himself has determined the character of our holiness. To wish to give it another character is, as St. Paul

[30] See Rom. 8:29.   [31] Eph. 5:1-2.

says, "beating the air."[32] God has Himself established the way that we must follow: not to take it is to lose one's way and finally to be lost: "I am the way ... no-one comes to the Father but through me."[33] God has Himself laid down the foundation of all perfection; outside of it one is only building on sand: "For the foundation, nobody can lay any other than the one which has already been laid, that is Jesus Christ."[34]

That is true of salvation, that is true of holiness. Holiness only draws on its source, only finds its support, in the grace of Christ Jesus.

3. How Christ is for us the source of all holiness, by being the Way, the Truth and the Life.

It is *in God's own way* that we must go to God; we shall only be saints in the measure that we adapt ourselves to the divine plan. I have indicated to you the broad outline of this magnificent plan; let us see in more detail how Christ Jesus is for us the source of all holiness.

Suppose a soul who in a burst of generosity, under the inspiration of the Holy Spirit, goes down on his knees before the Heavenly Father, and says to Him: "O Father, I love you, I desire nothing as much as your glory; I want for the whole of eternity to glorify you by my holiness; what ought I to do? Show me what you expect of me." What would the Father reply to him? He would show him His Son Jesus, and would say to him: "This is my beloved Son, in whom I am well-pleased; hear Him." Then He would withdraw, leaving this soul at the feet of Jesus.

And what does Jesus say to us? "I am the Way, and the Truth, and the Life."[35] Three words, of very profound meaning, on which I would like to meditate with you. They should always be engraved in the depths of our hearts.

[32] 1 Cor. 9:26.   [33] John 14:6.   [34] 1 Cor. 3:11 (Jerus.)   [35] John 14:6.

You desire to go to my Father? says Jesus; you wish to unite yourself to Him who is the source of all good and the fount of all perfection? You do well; it is I who made this desire arise in your heart; but you can only bring it about through me: "No-one comes to the Father but through me."

As you know, there is an infinite distance between creature and Creator; between one who has being only through participation and one who is Subsistent Being itself. Take the highest angel in the heavenly hierarchy of angels: between him and God there is an abyss which no created strength can cross.

But God has thrown a bridge across that abyss. Christ, God-Man, connects man to God. The Word became flesh; in Him a human nature was united to the divinity: the two natures, divine and human, are united in an embrace so intimate, so indissoluble, that there is but one single Person, that of the Word, in whom the human nature subsists. The abyss of separation is filled up.

Christ, being God, being one with His Father, is the Way that leads us to God. If, therefore, we wish to go to God, let us strive to have unlimited faith in the power that Jesus has to unite us to His Father. What, indeed, did Our Lord say? He said He willed that where He is, His disciples should be also: "Father, I will that where I am, they also whom you have given me may be with me."[36] And where is Christ? *In sinu Patris*, in the heart's-embrace of the Father.[37]

When our faith is a lively one, and we give ourselves wholly to Jesus, He draws us in train of Him, takes us with Him, so that we enter into the heart's-embrace of the Father. For Jesus is both the way and the end of the journey. He is, through His humanity, the way—"the road by which we go"; and He is, through His divinity, the journey's-end—"the homeland to which we go."[38] That is what constitutes the great sureness of this way: it is perfect, and it contains in it the road's very destination.

[36] John 17:24.   [37] John 1:18.
[38] St. Augustine, *Sermo* XCII, c. 3; *Sermo* CXXIII, c. 3.

It is an excellent thing in prayer to make acts of faith in the almighty power Jesus has to lead us to His Father.

O Christ Jesus, I believe that you are true God and true man, that you are a divine way, of an infinite efficacy for making me cross over the chasm that separates me from God. I believe that your sacred humanity is perfect, is so powerful that, in spite of my miseries, my shortcomings, my weaknesses, it can draw me to where you are, in the heart's-embrace of the Father. May I listen to your words, may I follow your example, and may I never be separated from you!

It is a precious grace to have found the way that leads to the end we wish to reach. But it is also necessary to walk there in the light. The end is a super-natural one, above our created powers. That is why the light needed to bathe our route in brightness must likewise come from on high.

God is so magnificent that He will Himself be our light. In heaven, our holiness will be to contemplate Infinite Light, and in its splendor to draw from the source of all life and all joy: "In thy light we shall see light."[39]

Here below, this light is inaccessible to us because of its brightness; our sight is too weak to bear it. And yet it is necessary for us, if we are to reach our goal. Who will be our light? Christ Jesus. "I am *the Truth*." He alone can reveal to us the infinite splendors. He is "God from God, Light from Light."[40] Being true God, He is Light itself, without darkness or shadow: "God is light, and in Him is no darkness at all."[41] This light came down into our valleys, tempering the infinite splendor of its rays beneath the veil of the sacred humanity. Our eyes, feeble as they were, could see this divine light which was hidden and revealed at the same time beneath the infirmity of a flesh capable of suffering: He "shone in our hearts ... the glory of God, shining on the face of

[39] Ps. 35 (36):10.   [40] Nicene Creed.   [41] 1 John 1:5 (RSV, Cath.)

Christ Jesus";[42] "the true light that enlightens every man who comes into the world."[43]

Christ Jesus, the Eternal Word, teaches us to look at God, He reveals Him to us. He says to us: "I am the Truth"; if you believe in me, not only will you learn to know the truth of all things, but you will be in the Truth: "He who follows me does not walk in the darkness, but will have the light of life."[44]

What, therefore, do we have to do to walk in the light? To let ourselves be guided by the words of Jesus, by the maxims of His Gospel, to consider all things in the light of the words of the Incarnate Word. Jesus tells us, for example, that the blessed who possess His kingdom are "the poor in spirit, the meek, those who mourn, those who hunger and thirst after righteousness, the merciful, the pure of heart, the peacemakers, those who are persecuted for righteousness' sake."[45] We ought to believe Him, to unite ourselves to Him by an act of faith, to lay in homage at His feet the assent of our intellect to His words; to strive to live in humility, meekness, mercy, purity; to keep peace with all, to bear persecution with patience and trust.

If we live thus, in faith, the Spirit of Christ will take possession of our soul little by little, to guide it in all things, to direct its activity so that it accords with the Gospel. Excluding from its own judgments merely natural lights, the soul sees all things through the eyes of the Word—"The Lord will be your everlasting light"[46]—and living in the Truth, advances ceaselessly along the Way; united to Truth, lives by His Spirit. The thoughts, the feelings, the desires of Jesus become the soul's thoughts, feelings, desires; the soul does nothing that is not fully in accord with the will of Christ. Is not that the very basis of all holiness?

It is not sufficient for us to have found the Way and to walk on it in the Light; we also need food to sustain us on our pilgrimage.

[42] 2 Cor. 4:6.   [43] John 1:9.   [44] John 8:12.
[45] See Matt. 5:3-11.   [46] Isa. 60:19 (RSV, Cath.)

This food of super-natural life—it is again Christ who gives it us: "*...and the Life.*"

In God is infinite Life: "With thee is the fountain of life."[47] The torrent of this ineffable and subsistent life has filled the soul of Christ with the fullness of its power: "As the Father has life in Himself, even so He has given to the Son also to have life in Himself."[48]

And the Son—what does He do? He comes to grant us part in this divine life: "I came that they may have life, and have it more abundantly."[49] He says to us: As I live by the life that the Father communicates to me, similarly one who eats me will live by me: "As I live because of the Father, so he who eats me will live because of me."[50]

To live by this divine life is holiness. Indeed, to exclude from this life everything that can destroy or diminish it—sin, infidelities, attachment to the merely created, views that are purely natural; to make this life flower through the virtues of faith, hope and love which unite us to God—putting these together, we have (as I have told you)[51] the twofold element of our holiness.

In being Himself Life, Christ Jesus becomes our holiness, because He is its very source: He "has become for us ... sanctification."[52] In giving Himself to us in the Holy Eucharist, He gives us His humanity, His divinity; He stirs up the fire of love; He transforms us, little by little, into Himself, in such a way that we live no longer of ourselves, but through Him and for Him. He establishes between our desires and His, between our will and His, such a similitude, such an accord, that (as St. Paul said) "I live now not with my own life but with the life of Christ who lives in me."[53] No formula is more expressive than these words of the apostle for summing up the whole work of holiness.

---

[47] Ps. 35 (36):10(9).   [48] John 5:26. [*Translator's note*: This is applied on pp. 135 and 374 and elsewhere to the eternal proceeding of the Son from the Father.]   [49] John 10:10.   [50] John 6:58 (RSV, Cath.)   [51] See p. 330 ff.   [52] 1 Cor. 1:30.   [53] Gal. 2:20 (Jerus.)

4. Feelings that ought to animate our seeking to be holy: a deep humility and an absolute confidence.

From this teaching are born the feelings that ought to animate us in seeking to be holy: a deep humility because of our feebleness, and an absolute confidence in Christ Jesus. Our super-natural life swings backwards and forwards between two poles: on the one hand, we should have an inner conviction of our powerlessness to attain perfection without the help of God; on the other hand, we should be filled with an unshakeable hope of finding everything in the grace of Christ Jesus.

Because it is super-natural, because God—sovereignly Master of His designs and of His gifts—has placed it above what the whole of our created nature requires, above the rights of that created nature, the holiness to which we are called is inaccessible without divine grace. Our Lord said to us: "Without me you can do *nothing*."[54] St. Augustine[55] remarks that Christ Jesus did not say, "Without me you cannot do great things"; He said: "Without me you can do *nothing* that will lead you to life eternal." St. Paul has explained in detail this teaching of our Divine Master. Paul has assurance through Christ, but he adds: "Not that we are sufficient of ourselves to think anything, *as from ourselves*, but our sufficiency is from God."[56] "Our sufficiency is from God": it is He who gives us the power of willing and bringing all things to that super-natural end: "It is God who of His good pleasure works in you both the will and the performance."[57] And so, we cannot, for our holiness, do anything without divine grace.

Should we, therefore, be disheartened? Quite the contrary! The inner conviction of our powerlessness should neither drive us to discouragement nor serve as an excuse for sitting back and not making an effort ourselves. Though we can do nothing *without* Christ, with Him we can do everything: "I can do all things in Him who strengthens me."[58] I can do all things (it is Paul again

---

[54] John 15:5.   [55] *Tract. in Johann.*, LXXXL, 3.   [56] 2 Cor. 3:5.
[57] Phil. 2:13.   [58] Phil. 4:13.

who tells us), not by myself but "in Him who strengthens me." Whatever be our trials, our difficulties, our weaknesses, we can, through Christ, reach the highest sanctity.

Why is that? Because in Him are amassed "all the treasures of wisdom and knowledge";[59] because "in Him dwells the fullness of the Godhead bodily";[60] and because, being our head, He has the power to make us sharers in all this. It is "of His fullness"— fullness of life and holiness—"that we draw,"[61] so much so that we "lack no grace"![62]

What great assurance is engendered in us by faith in these truths! Christ Jesus is ours, and in Him we find everything: "How can He (the Father) fail to grant us ... all things with Him."[63] What, then, can prevent us from becoming saints? If, on the day of the Last Judgment God asks us: "Why have you not reached the height of your vocation? Why have you not attained the holiness to which I was calling you?" we shall not be able to reply: "Lord, my weakness was too great, the difficulties were insurmountable, the trials beyond my strength." God would reply to us: "On your own, it is but too true that you could do nothing. But I have given you my Son; in Him you lacked nothing of what was necessary for you. His grace is all-powerful, and through Him you could have united yourself to the very source of life."

That is so true! A great genius, the greatest the world has known perhaps, a man whose youth was spent in licentiousness, who drank the cup of pleasure to its dregs, whose mind was enamored of all the errors of his time, Augustine, was converted and attained sublime sanctity. One day (this is his own account), urged by grace but held back by his dissolute inclinations, he saw some children, young girls, virgins shining with purity, and some widows, made venerable by their virtue; and he seemed to hear a voice putting this gentle invitation to him: "What these here do, and those there, cannot you do also? What they are, cannot you

---

[59] Col. 2:3.   [60] Col. 2:9.   [61] John 1:16.
[62] 1 Cor. 1:7.   [63] Rom. 8:32.

become?"[64] And despite the heat of the blood that boiled in his veins, despite the turbulence of his passions and his long-standing habits of vice, Augustine delivered himself up to grace; and grace made of him—made of him for all eternity—one of the most magnificent of its trophies.

When we celebrate the Feast of All Saints, we ought to repeat to ourselves the words St. Augustine heard: "Why cannot you do what those did?" What motives have you for not aiming at holiness? Oh, I know very well what each of you is tempted to say: "I have such and such a difficulty, there is such and such an obstacle standing in my way; *I* would never be able to become a saint." But be assured that all the saints have met with "such a difficulty" or found "such an obstacle standing in their way"—and much bigger ones still than yours!

So therefore, no-one can say, "Holiness is not for me." What is it that can make it impossible? God *desires* it for us; He wants us to be holy for His glory and for our joy: "This is the will of God, your sanctification."[65] God isn't making fun of us. When Our Lord says to us, "Be perfect,"[66] He knows what He is asking of us, and He does not demand anything that is beyond our powers when we lean upon His grace.

One who claimed to arrive at perfection through His own strength would be committing the sin of Lucifer, who said: "I will raise myself up, I will place my throne in heaven ...I will be like the Most High."[67] Satan was struck down and hurled into the abyss.

As for us, what shall we say? what shall we do? We nourish the same ambition as this prideful angel; we wish to reach the objective aimed at by this proud one. But whereas he claimed to attain it of himself, we shall declare that without Christ Jesus we can do nothing. We shall say that it is with Him and through Him that we can enter into heaven. O Christ Jesus, I have such faith in you

---

[64] *The Confessions of St. Augustine*, Book VIII, Ch. 11.   [65] 1 Thess. 4:3.
[66] See Matt. 5:48.   [67] See Isa. 14:13-14.

that I believe you are powerful enough to effect this marvel of raising a lowly creature like me, not simply up to the hierarchies of angels but up to God Himself; it is only through you that we can arrive at this divine summit. With all the powers of my soul, I aspire to that celestial height which your Heavenly Father has planned as our destiny; I desire, ardently, as you have asked on our behalf, to share your glory itself, to participate in your own joy as Son of God; I aspire to that supreme felicity, but through you alone; I desire that my eternity be one of singing your praises and ceaselessly repeating with the elect: "You have redeemed us for God with your blood."[68] Yes, Lord, it is you who have saved us; it is your Precious Blood shed upon us that has opened the gates of your kingdom and prepared a place in the incomparable company of your saints. To you, praise, honor and glory, for ever!

A soul who lives always in these feelings of humility and confidence gives great glory to Christ Jesus, because the whole life of that soul is an echo of the Savior's own words, "Without me you can do nothing"; and because that soul proclaims that He is the source of all salvation and all holiness, and directs all glory to Him.

Let us say with the Church in one of her most wonderful prayers,[69] "O God, I believe that you are almighty, that your grace is efficacious enough to raise me up, miserable creature that I am, to a high degree of sanctity. I believe that you are likewise Infinite Mercy and that, if I have left you often, your love, which is full of kindness, never abandons me. It is from you, O my God, Heavenly Father, that every perfect gift descends; it is your grace that makes us faithful servants, pleasing to you by reason of works that are worthy of your majesty and your praise. Grant that, detached from myself and from all that is merely created, I may unimpededly run the course of holiness on which, like a giant, your Son has gone

---

[68] Apoc. 5:9.   [69] "Almighty and merciful God, from whom the gift comes for your faithful people to do unto you worthy and laudable service, graciously grant that we may run without stumbling towards the attainment of your promises": Collect of the Mass for the Twelfth Sunday after Pentecost.

before; so that through Him and with Him I may arrive at the bliss you have promised us!"

The saints lived by these truths; that is why they have reached the heights where we contemplate them today. The difference that exists between them and us does not arise from a greater number of difficulties that we have to overcome, but from the ardor of their faith in the words of Jesus Christ and in the power of His grace, as also from their more ardent generosity. We can, if we wish, act in the same way ourselves: Christ remains always the same, as powerful, as open-handed in the distribution of His grace as ever; it is only in ourselves that we find obstacles to the pouring-forth of His gifts.

Souls of little faith, why do we doubt God—our God?

5. **Practical conclusions: to honor the saints and ask them for their help; to seek to imitate them, whilst remaining united to Jesus Christ. Not to let oneself be disheartened by miseries and trials.**

What practical conclusions shall we draw from these beneficent truths of our faith? The first thing is that we ought to celebrate the feast days of the saints with all our hearts. To honor the saints is to proclaim that they are the fulfillment of a thought in the divine mind, that they are masterpieces of the grace of Jesus. God places His delight in them, because they are the already-glorious members of His beloved Son; they already form part of that resplendent kingdom won by Jesus for the glory of His Father: "You ... have made them for our God a kingdom."[70]

Next, we ought to invoke them. There is no doubt that Christ Jesus is our only mediator: "One God, and one Mediator between God and men," as St. Paul says;[71] we have access to the Father only through Christ. Nevertheless Christ, not in order to diminish His mediation but to extend it, wishes the courtiers of His

---

[70] Apoc. 5:10.   [71] 1 Tim. 2:5.

heavenly kingdom to offer Him our prayers, which He Himself will present to His Father.

Moreover, the saints have the most lively desire for our good. In heaven, they contemplate God; their will is ineffably united to that of God. That is why they desire our sanctification, as God does. Then too, they form with us one single mystical body, by right of which, in Paul's expression, "we are members of one another."[72] They have for us an immense charity which they derive from their union with Jesus, the one head of that body of which they are the chosen élite, and in which God has places ready for us.

To this relationship of homage and prayer that unites us to the saints, we should add our efforts to resemble them. Our hearts should be animated, not by flaccid semi-intentions[73] which never come to anything, but by a firm and sincere desire for perfection, by an efficacious will to respond fully to the merciful designs of the divine destiny planned for us in Jesus: "according to the measure of Christ's bestowal."[74]

And what is needed for that? What means are to be employed for perfecting so considerable a work, one so glorious for Christ and so fruitful for us?

The answer is: "*Remain united to Jesus Christ.*" He Himself has told us this. "You wish to bear much fruit? to arrive at great holiness? Then remain united to me, as the branches remain united to the vine."[75] And how do we remain united to Him? First of all, by sanctifying grace, which makes us living members of His mystical body. And then, by that right intention, frequently renewed, which makes us seek to please our Heavenly Father—in all things and wherever Divine Providence has called us to be. Such an intention orientates all our activity towards the glory of God, in union with the thoughts, the feelings, the will of the heart of Jesus

---

[72] Eph. 4:25; 1 Cor. 12:12 ff; Eph. 5:30.   [73] [*Translator's note*: Marmion's word is "velleities." A "velleity" is a slight degree of volition. A "velleity," or wish, to do something is contrasted with a firm will to set about doing it.]

[74] Eph. 4:7.   [75] See John 15:4-5.

our model and our head: "I do always the things that are pleasing to Him."[76] That formula, by which Jesus summed up His whole relationship to His Father, excellently expresses the whole work of human holiness.

"And what of our miseries?" you may say to me. In no way at all should they discourage us. Our miseries are very real: our weaknesses, our slavery to sin—we know these well enough; but God knows them better than we do. And, when it is recognized and avowed, our feeling of being weak honors God. And why? Because there is in God one perfection for which He wills to be glorified eternally, a perfection which is perhaps the key to all that happens to us here below: it is *mercy*. Mercy is love in its meeting with another's misery; if there were no misery there would be no mercy. The angels declare the holiness of God; but we—well, we shall in heaven be living witnesses to Divine Mercy. In crowning our works it is the gift of His mercy that God crowns: He "crowns you with mercy and compassion,"[77] and it is this that, in the heart of our beatitude, we shall extol throughout eternity: "For His mercy endures for ever."[78]

Let us no longer be disheartened by trials, by things that stand in our way. They will be greater and deeper as God calls us higher. Why this law?

Because that is the road along which Jesus passed; and because the more we wish to remain united to Him, the more we must resemble Him in the deepest and innermost of His mysteries. St. Paul, as you know, made the whole of the interior life come down to a knowledge, put into practice, of "Jesus Christ and Him crucified."[79] And Our Lord Himself tells us that His Father, the Vinedresser, "prunes the branch to make it bear even more fruit."[80] God has a powerful hand and His purifying activity reaches depths that only the saints know. By the temptations He

[76] John 8:29.   [77] Ps. 102 (103):4.   [78] Ps. 135 (136):1 ff.
[79] 1 Cor, 2:2.   [80] See John 15:2.

permits, by the adversities He sends, by the feelings of being deserted and the frightful loneliness He sometimes produces in the soul, He tries that soul in order to detach it from what is merely created. He digs deep into it, in order to empty it of itself; He "pursues" it, He "persecutes it, in order to possess it";[81] He delves to its very marrow; He "breaks its bones," as Bossuet says somewhere, "in order to reign in it alone."

Blessed the soul that abandons itself into the hands of this Divine Worker! Through His Spirit—that Spirit, all fire and love, who is "the Finger of God's right hand,"[82] God the Eternal Artist will engrave on it the features of Christ, so as to make it resemble His Beloved Son according to the ineffable design of His wisdom and mercy.

For God places His glory in making us supremely blest. All the sufferings He permits or sends are so may titles to glory and heavenly beatitude. St. Paul declares himself powerless to describe the splendor of the glory, and the depths of happiness, which will crown the slightest of our sorrows that are endured through divine grace: "The sufferings of the present time are not worthy to be compared with the glory to come that will be revealed in us";[83] "For our present light affliction, which is for the moment, prepares for us an eternal weight of glory that is beyond all measure."[84]

That is why he encouraged his dear faithful so much. Look, he said to them, at those who take part in the games and in the races in the arena. How many precautions they take! what privations they impose on themselves! what effort they put into it! And all that, for what? To receive the applause of one hour, to enjoy the glory—ephemeral and always disputed—of winning "a perishable crown": whereas if we struggle, it is for a crown that will never perish, a glory without end, a joy that will never be lost.[85]

---

[81] Words of Dom Pie de Hemptinne. See *Une âme bénédictine*, 4th ed., p. 95.

[82] Hymn, *Veni, Creator Spiritus.*   [83] Rom. 8:18.

[84] 2 Cor. 4:17.   [85] 1 Cor. 9:25.

Undoubtedly, in these moments that are rich in graces, the soul is plunged into sorrow and suffering, into aridity and dryness. Let it remain firm beneath the blows of the Supreme High Priest! For God puts the unction of His grace even into the bitterness of the cross. Look at St. Paul. No-one lived in a more intimate union with God in Christ than Paul did: who could separate him from Jesus?[86] And see how, by God's permission, the devil insulted him, and overwhelmed with his arrow-shafts the soul and the body of the apostle. No less than three times St. Paul cried out in his anguish to Jesus. And what was Christ's answer to him? "My grace is sufficient for you, for strength is made perfect in weakness."[87] Christ's strength is never shown so strikingly as in the difficulties over which it will triumph.

> 6. The objective of the eternal plan for our holiness is to laud the power of the grace of Jesus: "Unto the praise of the glory of His grace."

Here—and I could not end this talk in a better way—we touch on the deep reason for this astonishing disposition of Providence, who wills that the work of our holiness be finely wrought in weakness and trials.

"For," said St. Paul, "by grace you have been saved through faith; and that not from yourselves, for it is the gift of God; not as the outcome of works, lest anyone may boast."[88]

Who, then, merits all praise? To whom does the glory of our holiness return? To Christ Jesus.

When the Apostle expounds the divine plan to his dear faithful of Ephesus, he indicates its supreme objective to them in the following words: "unto the praise of the glory of His grace"[89]— so that the munificence of His grace may be exalted.

---

[86] Rom. 8:35.   [87] 2 Cor. 12:9.   [88] Eph. 2:8-9.   [89] Eph. 1:6.

It is so as to "show ... the overflowing riches of His grace in kindness towards us in Christ Jesus"[90] that God has planned our destiny of being co-heirs of His Son.

Here below, we owe all to Jesus. He has merited for us by His mysteries all the graces of justification, pardon and sanctification of which we have need: Christ is the very source of our perfection. Like the vine that spreads the nourishing sap into the branches to make them bear fruit, so Christ ceaselessly spreads His grace into all those who stay united to Him. It is this grace that animates apostles, illuminates doctors of the Church, sustains martyrs, makes those who confess the faith steadfast, and adorns virgins with their incomparable purity.

On high also, all the glory of the saints derives from this same grace: all the splendor of their triumph is fed by that one and only source; it is because they are tinctured with the blood of the Lamb that the robes of those chosen are so resplendent. And the degree of their holiness is measured by the degree of their resemblance to the Christ, the divine model.

That is why, at the start of this magnificent solemnity of All Saints, in which the Church brings together all the heavenly elect for one and the same praise, she invites us to "adore the Lord, the King of kings" who at the same time is "the crown of all the saints"[91]—*He Himself* is their crown.

In heaven, we shall understand that all the mercies of God have Calvary as their starting-point; that the price of the unending happiness in which we shall then rejoice for ever was the blood of Jesus. Let us not forget this: In the heavenly Jerusalem we shall be inebriated with divine bliss; but this bliss—all of it, every instant—will have been paid for by the merits of the blood of Christ Jesus. "The stream of the river" that, eternally, "makes the city of God joyful"[92] will have its source in the Sacrifice of our Divine High Priest. It will be an immense joy for us to acknowl-

---

[90] Eph. 2:7.   [91] Invitatory of Matins.   [92] Ps. 45 (46):5.

edge this, and to sing to Jesus: "Oh, it is to you that we owe everything; all praise, honor, thanksgiving be rendered to you!"

Like all the elect we shall "cast our crowns at his feet,"[93] to declare that we have them from Him.

The whole mystery of Christ, the Incarnate Word, leads to this final goal. God wills that His Son Jesus should be for ever exalted, because He is His own and only Son, the object of His delight; because this Son, though wholly God, brought Himself down to nothing so as to sanctify His mystical body: "Therefore God ... has exalted Him."[94]

Let us, therefore, enter with deep faith into these divine thoughts. When we sing our praises of the saints, we extol the power of the grace that lifted them up to those summits; and nothing is more pleasing to God because, by that praise, we unite ourselves to the innermost of His designs, which is to glorify His Son: "I have both glorified it, and I will glorify it again."[95] Let us ourselves seek to bring into effect, with the help of that same grace, the thought of God about each one of us: again, it is to this perfect conformity that all holiness comes down.

I have, in all these talks, tried to show you to what a degree the Father has united us to His Son Jesus; I have sought to place beneath your eyes our divine model, at once so incomparable and so accessible. You have seen that Christ has lived each of His mysteries for us; that He unites each of them to us in the closest way, so that little by little we may reproduce in ourselves, under the action of His Spirit, His ineffable features and, in accord with the destiny planned for us, become like Him.

Let us never cease contemplating this model. Christ Jesus is God, appeared among us, living among us, in order to show us the way and to lead us to life. For He has Himself said that eternal life consists in proclaiming, with our lips as by our deeds, that

---

[93] See Apoc. 4:10.   [94] Phil. 2:9.   [95] John 12:28.

His Father is the true God, and that He is true God with Him but come into this world in our flesh to bring back humanity to God.

If during our life we have faithfully followed Jesus; if, each year, with faith and with love, we have contemplated Him in the cycle of His mysteries, seeking thus to imitate Him and to remain united to Him, then we may be assured that the unceasing prayer He, as the one Mediator, addresses to the Father for us will be granted. Through His Spirit, He will imprint His living image in our souls, and the Father on the Last Day will recognize us as members of His beloved Son and will make us His Son's co-heirs.

We shall enter into that community which Christ, our divine head, has willed to constitute wholly pure and resplendent. On that day of final triumph, He will, in the very words of St. Paul,[96] "deliver the kingdom to God the Father" as the marvelous trophy of His all-powerful grace. May we all meet Him there, for the greatest joy of our souls and for the glory of our Heavenly Father! "Unto the praise of the glory of His grace."

"The Word Remaining with the Father

is Truth and Life. Taking Upon Him

Our Flesh, He Became The Way."

St. Augustine, *Tract. in Johann.*, XXXIV, 9.

---

[96] 1 Cor. 15:24.

FR. BENEDICT GROESCHEL, C.F.R., is Director for the Office for Spiritual Development for the Archdiocese of New York. In 1987 he founded, with eight other friars, the community of the Franciscan Friars of the Renewal. He is the author of many books, including *Stumbling Blocks or Stepping Stones: Spiritual Answers to Psychological Questions* and *Arise From Darkness: What to Do When Life Doesn't Make Sense.*

AIDAN NICHOLS, O.P., a Dominican priest, is currently the John Paul II Memorial Visiting Lecturer, University of Oxford. He has also served as the Prior of the Dominicans at St. Michael's Priory, Cambridge. He has written over thirty books, including *Lovely Like Jerusalem: The Fulfillment of the Old Testament in Christ and the Church* and *The Holy Eucharist: From the New Testament to Pope John Paul II.*

Zaccheus Press

Zaccheus Press is a small Catholic press devoted to publishing fine books for all readers seeking a deeper understanding of the Catholic faith.

To learn more about Zaccheus Press, please visit our webpage. We welcome your comments, questions, and suggestions.

www.zaccheuspress.com

A nd behold, there was a rich man named Zaccheus, who was the chief among the tax collectors. And he sought to see Jesus, but could not because of the crowd, for he was short of stature. So he ran ahead and climbed up into a sycamore tree to see Him, for He was going to pass that way.

—Luke 19:2-4